Red Creative

Red Creative

Culture and Modernity in China

Justin O'Connor and Xin Gu

Bristol, UK / Chicago, USA

First published in the UK in 2020 by
Intellect, The Mill, Parnall Road, Fishponds, Bristol, BS16 3JG, UK

First published in the USA in 2020 by
Intellect, The University of Chicago Press, 1427 E. 60th Street,
Chicago, IL 60637, USA

A catalogue record for this book is available from
the British Library.

Copy editor: Newgen
Cover designer: Aleksandra Szumlas
Production editor: Tim Mitchell
Typesetting: Newgen

Paperback ISBN 9781789382303
Hardback ISBN 9781789383218
ePDF ISBN 9781789382327
ePUB ISBN 9781789382310

Printed and bound by TJ Books Limited, UK.

To find out about all our publications, please visit
www.intellectbooks.com
There you can subscribe to our e-newsletter,
browse or download our current catalogue,
and buy any titles that are in print.

This is a peer-reviewed publication.

To our fathers, Dennis O'Connor and Gu Genfa 顾根法

Contents

Contents

Acknowledgements

We would like to thank all those who have seen parts of this book and have given us their comments. We are grateful to Kate Oakley, who read a version when its coherence was slightly more than slime mould, and to Seb Olma and David Hesmondhalgh, whose early enthusiastic comments have kept us going. Laikwan Pang's generous comments on *Shanghai Modern* were very much appreciated too. Heartfelt thanks to Elena Trubina, who managed to read some of the most convoluted and turgid drafts, even commenting on them. We would also like to thank Julian Meyrick, for his keen editorial insights, and Declan Martin, who did the grunt work on the footnotes.

We are indebted to the Shanghai Jiaotong University, which has hosted our *Shanghai City Lab* for six years, and especially to Professor Shan Shilian and Associate Professor Wen Yuan. Not forgetting Professor Wang Jie, now at Zhejiang University, who made first contact. Thanks to Li Yan, at Sichuan Normal University, for many statistical insights, and to Ma Da at Creative 100, who allowed us an inside view. Conor Roche in Shanghai kept us up to date with insight and conversation.

Thanks to the Universities of Monash and South Australia, for giving us the space and time to develop and write this book, and to the Australian Research Council, for their patience in getting outputs from two grants: DP150101477: *Working the Field: Creative Graduates in China and Australia*, and LP0991136: *Soft Infrastructure, New Media and Creative Clusters: Developing Capacity in China and Australia*.

Introduction

Unknown Knowns

The creativity moment

This book emerged from an encounter between China and 'the West' around three interlinked concepts – culture, creativity and modernity. More specifically, the book's point of departure was the arrival in China, in 2005, of a Western discourse of 'creativity', primarily framed as 'creative industries' or 'creative economy'. This new term was coined by the UK New Labour government in 1998, towards the end of a decade in which the West had won the Cold War, and had extended the global market, along with its regulatory and ideological apparatuses, to all but a few obdurate backwaters. Though taking flight from a context specific to the United Kingdom, the 'creative industries' soon gained global traction (though with important exceptions). It identified a new economic sector, rooted in culture and utilizing the 'human capital' of talent and creativity – things all countries possessed as abundant natural resources. But the creative industries were part of a broader imaginary, of a different future in which social, cultural, economic and perhaps political change would be driven by creative and innovative individuals working outside the existing cultural and socio-economic hierarchies. The creative industries became intertwined in the popular imaginary with the new dot-com digital revolution, where ideas, technology and entrepreneurship had 'disrupted' the incumbency of the corporate dinosaurs. It seemed that 'creativity', confined to the world of art and culture during the Fordist age of planning, corporations and mass consumption, was now to be made available across the social landscape. After a period since the mid-1970s in which industrial modernity seemed to have migrated to the East, creativity opened up a new modernity in which the West would again take the lead and set the standards.

The creative imaginary was rooted in a powerful economic rationale. Building on the idea of the information and knowledge economy, which had been variously formulated in the 1960s and 1970s as the next stage of capitalism, creativity represented a widening of this economy to include the kinds of knowledge and skills which had traditionally been associated with 'culture' and 'the arts'. Creative production and consumption, turbo-charged through new communications

1

and information technologies, and through expanding spending power, education and leisure time, became a growth sector in its own right. It provided new skilled jobs and generated wealth distributed as wages, profits and taxes. Yet its economic benefits extended beyond this growth into multiple 'spill overs' across the economy. In the form of the 'creative economy', creativity would act as a new kind of innovation system with complex catalytic effects across all sectors. Indeed, highly visible spaces of creative intensity in cities – the various official and unofficial 'creative quarters', or even one or two trendy café zones – could act as synecdoche for the wider creativity of the city. In the imaginary that surrounds the creative economy, a new kind of society, a new kind of modernity can be glimpsed.

In this way, a new phase of economic growth was to call on forms of subjectivity which had previously been outside of, or even oppositional to, the economy. Aspects of subjectivity linked to the emotions, spirituality or the specific qualities of the senses that were traditionally associated with art and culture, were now to be called upon. Since the eighteenth century, these had been excluded from what we might call the techno-rational-administrative systems of modernity. This involved the separation of the 'economic' from ethical, customary and cultural systems of society within which it had been encased, a process noted by Karl Marx, Max Weber, Karl Polanyi and Fernand Braudel amongst others.[1] Indeed, it was the ability to isolate the economy from these wider social systems, at the level of the polity as well as the individual subject, that had been the very mark of the modern person and modern administration. The system of industrial Fordism, and the sociopolitical settlement with which it was associated, further removed these emotional, spiritual and aesthetic elements to a place separate from its rational-bureaucratic structures. Now, it was claimed, a new round of economic development would put creativity at its core, folding these excluded forms of experience into its post-industrial imaginary.

The creativity discourse was an attempt to annex the energies and qualities of the cultural to a new round of capitalist expansion. Because it appealed to these once-oppositional forms of knowledge and subjectivity, the creativity discourse could present itself as radical and emancipatory, framing a moment of historical creativity in which the world was to be transformed in the image of the new creative subjects. This creative economy would also require a transformed polity. The forms of political and economic regulation of an older Fordist economy needed to go, as did the forms of public administration – especially around education and culture – that had underpinned them. These older forms of regulation and administration were characterized, in this view, by a state form based on top-down administration and cultural hierarchy. If once these were historically progressive, they were so no longer.

Central to this transformation would be markets and networks. The first would not now be restricted to transactional relations between corporations and consumers. Consumers now were much more discerning and, with the rise of the Internet, able to provide feedback and increasingly shape and 'co-create' – especially with cultural consumption – the kinds of products being made (prosumers). At the same time, the type of value at stake was no longer that of marginal utility; it was the relationship between consumer and firm that formed the basis of mutually created value.[2] These were the kinds of relationships traditionally associated with cultural consumption, especially that of fans, in which emotional and signifying investment in the product ran high. In order to respond to these new consumers, increasingly uncoupled from taste orders centred on class, nationality and gender, and outside formal cultural hierarchies, the producers would have to be nimble, deeply immersed in these networks of value and able to respond rapidly to their fluctuations. The barrier between firm and market became fluid and permeable, as small and micro-enterprises worked between the two, moving from project to project, reconfiguring each time. It was in clusters and creative milieus where these entrepreneurial subject-networks could best emerge and sustain themselves, in turn demanding the transformation of urban spaces into creative cities capable of encouraging and supporting these milieus.

The new creative subjects – working in flattened, project-oriented networks outside of the large bureaucracies and corporations – were highly fluid agents. The new creative polity would have to step back from planning and regulation, and abandon the fixed cultural hierarchies established in the process of 'nation-building'. It needed to be responsive to emergent patterns of behaviour and demand, and to provide the space and capacities required by a new set of autonomous subjects who would be mobilizing creativity in a rapidly evolving socio-economic landscape.

Culture – as a distinct area of public policy linked to traditions of nation-building, to a hierarchical system of value judgement, and to long-standing notions of artistic autonomy – needed to be radically transformed. Cultural value, in this discourse, was not something that could be determined by governments, elites or experts, nor sanctified by tradition; it could emerge only from expressed preferences in the market. Cultural citizenship after 1945 had been positioned as an entry of 'ordinary people' into a shared patrimony.[3] Social citizenship, following legal and political rights, always implied access to culture. T. H. Marshall had suggested in 1950 that a state should grant to its citizens 'the right to a modicum of economic welfare and security [...] the right to share to the full in the social heritage and to live the life of a civilized being according to the standards prevailing in the society'.[4] (This had already been granted by the United Nations Universal Declaration of Human Rights in 1948.[5]) In the 1970s, as this aspiration to make and consume culture rapidly extended through society, there were disputes about how transformative this expansion of cultural participation might be on existing forms of cultural value, as seen in the debates about 'democratizing culture' versus 'cultural democracy'.[6] The creativity discourse suggested that with the expansion of the market in culture and the possibilities opened by the Internet, the 'citizen-consumer' would now provide the motor force for democratic cultural transformation. As consumer sovereignty theorists had it, 'every dollar is a ballot'.[7]

This equation of entrepreneurship and emancipation, markets and freedom, frequently combined with Schumpeter's notion of 'creative destruction', have come to stand, in the creativity discourse, as the fundamental force of social evolution. John Howkins renders it at its most simplistic: 'Everyone is creative. Creativity needs freedom. Freedom needs markets.'[8] The creativity at stake in this new economy was derived from a Western avant-garde and modernist tradition, itself reaching back to the notion of the autonomous artist rooted in the eighteenth century and, before that, the Renaissance. The creativity discourse would combine this artistic creativity, suitably stripped of its links to cultural value, with the notion of an 'open society' modelled on liberal democracy that alone could allow this creativity to flourish. Though now placed centre stage in the neo-liberal imaginary, this Faustian-Promethean view of historical creativity goes back to the moment of Europe's 'take-off' in the fifteenth century. The creativity discourse in fact is deeply Eurocentric, demanding that non-Western countries engage in a process of radical change in order to benefit from creativity and, at the same time, setting them up to fail.

Red creative?

It is this creativity discourse that arrived in China in the early 2000s, promising two payoffs. First, a new sector of the service economy was now available both for a 'middle class' consumer with leisure, education and money, and for the cities in which they lived. For China this would be a modernization, an 'upgrading' of the culture made available to the modern Chinese citizen, and it was a growing industry – profit, tax, wages, exports – in its own right. Second, the kinds of creative subjects required for this would also be made available for other areas of the service economy, especially around those which sought innovation in close contact with the consumer. However, it seemed that in order to obtain these payoffs China would need to significantly reconfigure its polity. It needed to further liberate the market system away from state (local and national) tutelage as well as from the dominance of large state-linked enterprises with their *guanxi* connections. In short, China would need to develop flat networks of small-scale creative enterprises and entrepreneurs, and the urban milieus in which they could thrive. For some this seemed to require democracy; for others, if not an elected democracy then the rule of law, providing clear rights to capital and allowing markets to function. Importantly, for a creative economy, China would need to break with its officially sanctioned hierarchy of cultural value. A combination of Chinese classical tradition and socialism, this value system was in direct opposition to the self-organization of subjects, networks and markets in a creative economy. There was a great hope therefore that the strong appeal of a creative economy – not only as a 'pillar industry' but also as a transition to a new kind of post-manufacturing advanced service economy – would provide the leverage for the wider transformation of the polity. Michael Keane framed this in the terms used by US Secretary of State John Foster Dulles in 1953: 'peaceful evolution' would bring a gradual transition from communism to democracy.[9] The 'conservatives' defending 'culture' would thus fight creative industries, in their view a dangerous Trojan horse, with everything they had.[10]

At stake was a China returning to the fold of global modernity. This had been central to the aspirations of the Chinese government since 1978 when, seeking to 'catch-up and surpass' – *ganchao* – it had rejected the Maoist path and sought reform of the system, opening up to the world and adopting a socialist market economy that, most expected, would gradually transition to a 'mature' capitalist economy. The stumbling block was always the leading role of the Communist Party whose rule was incompatible with liberal democracy, deemed to be the *sine qua non* of economic modernization. However much the 'cultural creative' agenda was framed as belonging to a primarily economic arena, it inevitably raised questions about the wider governance of individuals and communities. These questions went right to the heart of existing cultural policy settings in China. For the exemplary creative subjects required for this new economy were inevitably Western subjects, possessed of a creativity that was coterminous with the kinds of democratic freedoms exemplified by Western liberal democracies.

In the 1990s, many East Asian governments and elites – the 'tiger economies' of South Korea, Taiwan, Hong Kong and Singapore especially – were confident in their claim to a 'post-development' status. The association of modernization with Westernization, where development meant playing 'catch-up' with Euro-American political institutions and sociocultural values and lifestyles, no longer stood. East Asian economic development had been state-led and without a widespread adoption of Western democratic forms. This was no longer seen as a deviant or incomplete modernization but a valid alternative. East Asian political elites frequently linked state-led development with Confucian cultures or 'civilization', where the values of deference and collective solidarity took precedence over Western 'individualism' and social fragmentation.[11] Indeed, by the 1990s this view did not just entail the rejection of Western modernity but also the suggestion that it was in trouble, noting the economic and social malaise contrasted with high levels of economic growth and social peace in East Asia.

The 1997 Asian Financial Crisis shook this confidence at the same time as a new wave of innovation discourse was flowing through the circuits of global business, management and policy literature. It is nicely symbolic that the crisis rolled across Asia in the same year as the United Kingdom's 'New Labour' government launched the 'creative industries'. In a process we will describe in detail in Chapter 2, culture-derived creativity was now positioned as a driver of post-industrial economies. Indeed, it was intended to provide for the competitive advantage of 'creative' – read Euro-American – economies over the state and manufacturing-heavy competitor economies of East Asia and elsewhere.

In the flurry of 'policy transfer' that followed, it could appear that, despite all the claims of post-development and alternative Asian modernities, another round of 'catch-up' was in the offing. In China, the arrival of 'creative industries' was particularly ambiguous. Clearly China – with a revitalized Shanghai at its head – sought to move up the value chain into advanced business services, and the creativity discourse articulated a major new dimension of this trajectory. But was such creativity not predicated on a particular version of Western individualism, 'open' societies and the free circulation of ideas? That is, the creative industries spoke directly to the nature (and potential shortcomings) of Asian modernity and to China's expanding role within this, raising serious questions about prevailing sociocultural values and forms of governance. It seemed – again – that China's development would be indexed against its ability to be like the West although, because it could not cease to be China, it was always going to fail. In this scenario, Red Creative was an impossible conjunction. It is this encounter with which this book is concerned.

Unknown knowns

One of the authors of this book arrived in China at the same time as the creative industries, alighting in Shanghai with a couple of textbooks but no knowledge of the country or its languages. The other was born in Shanghai but had left in 2003, following her completion of a civil engineering degree at Tongji University to study culture-led urban regeneration in Northern Europe. What was clear to both of us, each with our different histories and perspectives, was that whatever was happening to cities in the West seemed to be happening in China too, and at an astonishing speed and scale. It was also clear that the languages, aspirations and imaginaries at play in this moment of arrival had long and complex histories, especially in a city such as Shanghai, which, we were routinely told when in other parts of the country, 'was not really China'. What follows is an attempt to make sense of this moment, to follow how it played out over the next decade and a half, and to trace what led up to it.

Both of us had been, and remained, involved in research and policy debates about creative industries and creative cities in the United Kingdom, Europe and Russia. To arrive in China in 2005 was an opportunity to see such an agenda unfold at close quarters, in a very different, and – for one of us – unknown context. For the other, both Shanghai and China were unknown in the way places you grow up in are unknown – just there around us, like the air. Birthplaces occupy that category so tellingly overlooked by Donald Rumsfeld in his epistemology of warfare: the unknown known. We know them, but they remain largely hidden, or unacknowledged, until we are obliged, often under compulsion, to bring them to consciousness.

To see your country of birth anew, via a foreign narrative of an alternative future, of what is useful and what should be jettisoned in order to get there, is to make that unknown known visible. To do this demands you learn to 're-know' your own country, in an internal struggle made familiar by much postcolonial writing. At the same time, for the non-Chinese author, the process involved making the known unknown – or at least strange. For what was this discourse demanding that a country of one billion, with historical roots reaching back into the Axial Age, must now *be creative?* Simply to walk down the Bund – with its grandiose waterfront buildings arranged like an encyclopaedia of Western architectural eclecticism – was to recognize that this kind of discursive tutelage was not new. The desperate attempt by the Chinese, under the impact of Western imperialism, to rethink the Middle Kingdom (in the strange conceptual language of a new world order) and then to radically transform the country through this new language – this had been the animating force of modern Chinese history. It was disconcerting, for one of us, to gradually realize that the language of creativity – which as autonomous culture had been a vital part of emancipatory modernity since the late eighteenth century, and had exploded since the Western 1960s – was now implicated in a discursive relationship between the West and China redolent of an older colonialism.

To give a full account of this new encounter, and one that would escape the deficit model so often used to describe China (and not only China), we felt that we had to give some historical account of the country's specific configuration of culture and modernity. In 2011, Claudia Pozzana wrote that in today's China there is greater familiarity with 'Western' cultural references than there is of Chinese cultural references in the 'West'. Entering a bookstore in China one is immediately aware of such a lack of proportionality. Even a cursory glance brings into view a sea of translations from any number of Western languages. Such is not even minimally the case in relation to what one finds on Chinese culture in European and American bookstores. China is viewed from abroad as through a dense fog that doesn't allow one to discern contours and reference points. From China, on the other hand, the gaze directed at Europe and the entire world can be very sharp, able to focus on a wide array of themes and issues. To 'Western' cultural eyes the image of 'China' produces an exotic fascination derived from the colonial tradition, joined with the no less colonial phantoms of a cultural 'otherness' considered mysterious and even menacing. This imbalance between a 'Western eye', deformed by a superstitious view of 'China', and a 'Chinese eye' trained by at least a century and a half of critical knowledge of the 'West', is even more pronounced today now that the Chinese economy and State are playing a leading role in world geopolitics.[12]

This was even more true in 2004, and truer still in terms of the field of cultural industries, creative industries, creative cities, creative clusters, culture-led regeneration and a whole slew of new concepts that were tumbling into a China keen to take the next step on its path to socialist modernization. In the following fifteen years, the literature on China certainly began to occupy more space on the commercial bookshelves, but catch-up has been slow. There are books explaining why, or why not, China will become democratic, and why, or why not, its economy is set to implode. There are fewer that try to understand China in its own terms, at least as a first step.

In our field, the literature began as consultancy reports given to, or commissioned by, various Chinese bodies, along with some pretty dense statistical publications by the Chinese and Shanghai Academies of Social Science. There were a few creative industry China watchers, some of whom appear in this book, and an increasing number writing on film, TV, new media and communications. In what was mostly a separate space were the Chinese history and literature specialists, who continue to provide an invaluable source of detailed research and understanding of modern and contemporary China. Many of these too will appear in this book. But we found that only a few were directly working on that knot of issues around culture, creativity and modernity that had been tied together by the new creativity discourse. So, we have had to use what has been at hand and improvise.

Neither of us is a Chinese historian, or a political scientist, or an international relations specialist – people who are routinely asked to comment on issues of China. Nor do we swim in the world of commercial consultancy and media industry journalism through which Chinese culture is absorbed into that global flow of growth figures, blockbusters stats, lifestyle analyses, industry prognostications and so forth. We would locate ourselves in that broad field which spans the political economy of culture (and communications) and cultural studies. What such a field might entail is discussed in detail over the course of the book, but in essence it concerns, first, an understanding of the structure and dynamics of the system of culture and communications, and its changing social, economic and political functions. Second, it suggests that the expansion of participation in culture is a crucial democratic gain and part of the wider emancipatory potential of modernity. We prefer to use the term 'cultural economy' to suggest that overlap of concerns between the political economy of culture and cultural studies. Our field is both analytical and normative, and this, in our view, is how it should be.

Both the analytical and normative aspects of this cultural field are rooted in the historical trajectory of Western modernity, and both have had great impact globally. The creativity agenda emerges out of this field, launching both an expanded economy of culture – the creative industries – and an expanded field for human creative emancipation. However, for us, this genda has been folded into a determinist economic and technological argument, which is fundamentally depoliticizing. It presents itself as highly analytical when in fact it is highly normative. It outlines a process of industrial-economic transformation which will determine, base superstructure-like, huge social, cultural and political changes. At the same time, what is simply presented as the next stage in the development of the productive forces – the information or knowledge economy, for example – is deeply embedded in existing patterns of global inequality and different historical trajectories, legacies of both colonialism and anti-colonialism. Unacknowledged by those extolling the economic transformation to be wrought by creativity is a highly normative account of 'creativity', both as a capacity possessed (or not) by individual subjects and by particular states. This creativity discourse, we suggest, offers a universal application but in practice privileges 'the West' as exemplary, and as such is a classic example of Western developmentalism. In this developmentalist discourse, following the Western path is always destined to fall short – a game of endless catch-up – while departing from that path is to become illegitimate, an aberrant modernity. The creativity discourse reproduced much of this, with China's own take-up constantly positioned as both in deficit and distorted.

But the creativity discourse does not by any means represent all of cultural-political economy or cultural studies. These are rooted in long-standing discourses of emancipation and human flourishing. The expansion and extension of participation in culture, of a shared system of meaning and value, have been vital to our sense of enlightenment, in the fullest and spiritual sense of that word. We suggest that the aspirations to emancipation and enlightenment, which we see as articulated in modernity, are not just Euro-American but have universal appeal.

Modernity might have been 'staged' in the West, as Timothy Mitchell has argued, but the West cannot be exemplary or normative for this modernity.[13] Modernity is now global, whether we like it or not. In this book, we want to emphasize the potential for dialogue, exchanges and circulation of ideas and concepts, signs and sounds, beliefs and aspirations, as well as the technologies and institutions involved in modernity. We also want to emphasize the possibility of different and distinct historical trajectories, specific articulations of modernity which must also be part of that ongoing dialogue. In this book, we try to do this for China.

This is important because, as we will argue, much of what is presented as Western modernity has been hollowed out by neo-liberal capitalism, a process of which the creative industries discourse forms a part. The recent transformation of Western capitalism has had significant and disturbing global impact. It has contributed to widening inequalities between and within nations; to an increase in geopolitical turbulence; to catastrophic threats to many of the species on this planet, including humans; and (cause and consequence) a widespread sense of nihilism and despair. In our attempts to understand this scenario, China – with the world's largest population and the second largest economy – plays a central role. It has been the beneficiary of the globalization and neo-liberalization of capitalism launched in the late 1970s. At the same time, it is not quite of that global order, which remains 'owned' by the West. In 2005, it seemed to many that it was only a matter of time before China would become part of that global order (though of course, like a migrant, it would never quite fit in). A decade later, it was by no means clear that China would join that global order on conditions set by the West – liberal democracy and/or the primacy of the rights of capital ('free markets'). In 2020, it looks like we are on the verge of a new Cold War.

The speed of these developments, during the too-long gestation of this book, has threatened to overtake the object we were trying to frame. This is a sketch on the run, with no clear sense of where that run will end. All we can say is that we do not paint China as saint or victim; we treat it as an equal in a dialogue that has become evermore pressing. We will discuss the contested and ambiguous idea of cosmopolitanism throughout the book, but for us its primary value lies in the possibility of a global dialogue of fundamental values, concerned not with a 'rules-based international order' but with how its transformation might enable us to become modern *differently*.

Outline argument and structure

The argument we try to set out in this book was developed backwards from the current conjuncture, but it is presented as a forward-oriented historical narrative.

We could not do full justice to the issues around creative industries without some account of the past. This account is schematic and partial and does not represent a history of twentieth-century China, merely some threads we have tried to pull out from the knot of the present. The context we try to establish consists of three broad propositions, acting like concentric circles around the question at hand.

The first and widest concerns the distinct historical trajectory of China, its civilizational momentum and weight and its traumatic encounter with the Western colonizing modern. China's socialism was, and remains, a crucial aspect of that encounter, animating its ongoing commitment to a modernizing project in a form the West seems to have abandoned. Viewed neither as deficit nor as catch-up, we have tried to keep both the distinctiveness and validity of the Chinese modern in play, if only to keep open the possibility of a different modern, of being differently modern. This does not imply that contemporary China *is* that different modern, nor that it is the only source of a different modern.

The second proposition relates to China's renewed encounter with Western modernity post-1978, and the multiple, contradictory emancipations this promised. On the one hand was the radical promise of the market, and the images of the modern this entailed – wealthy consumers in efficiently organized, glass-and-steel cities, a globalized economy humming in the background. On the other were newly emancipated subjects, loosened from the intensive supervision of the collective, setting out to explore a democratized modern culture and negotiate a new place within it. The internal conflicts of this Faustian-Promethean modernity – between the world-shattering energies of the economic-rational and the aspirations to personal emancipation and social justice – are coterminous with modernity itself. Our proposition is that the modern which China sought again from the West in 1978 was one that itself was undergoing radical transformation under the twin, conflicting-complementary impulses of a post-1960s cultural, and a post-1970s neo-liberal, revolution. How China negotiated this renewed and contradictory modern, from within its own civilizational and socialist resources, is central to the book.

Our third proposition is that the transition from a Fordist-Industrial system to an as yet loosely defined 'post-Fordism', in combination with a working through of the Cultural Revolution of the 1960s, presented something of a utopian moment. The world of economy and work, of top-down planning and instrumental reason, was to give way to one in which culture would be central. In bald outline, our proposition is that this moment of transition, which seemed to make real the utopian promise of culture, was captured by the discourse of the creative industries. The creative industries both mobilized and disavowed this utopian promise; it took the transformative energies of democratic culture but reduced them to an economic input. In this it formed a part of neo-liberalism's wider hollowing out of the public sphere, in which the aggregated preferences of the sovereign consumer took precedence over the deliberations of the political. Our proposition here is that China held on to that notion of the political and to the cultural-symbolic dimension this entailed, both of which had been crucial to the establishment of the modern nation state. At the same time, China made the creative industries agenda work for them in the face of a Western discourse that saw its 'despotic' polity as incompatible with the power of creativity. What China's success reveals about the creative industries agenda in general is discussed at length in this book.

One final, cross-cutting proposition is less of a framing device than a privileged case study by which some of our more abstract propositions may be grounded. Our account in *Red Creative* returns to Shanghai three times. This city, especially during the period from the 1911 Republican to the 1949 Communist Revolutions that we call *Shanghai Modern*, has always stood out as an alternative modern China. Rather than present *Shanghai Modern* as the path to a Western modernity China never took, we read it as an articulation of alternative modernities in which Chinese, and other forms of non-Western or minor Western knowledge, are in play. The actual course of the Communist Revolution as articulated in increasingly rigid terms by the current party leadership does not exhaust the possibilities of the Chinese modern, but nor can these possibilities be restricted to the adoption, to a greater or lesser degree, of capitalist modernity. Our particular focus is on how Shanghai's historical encounter with these modernities played out in the cultural sphere – consisting of intellectual, popular-urban and 'folk' culture parts – and fed into a burgeoning 'cultural industries' which emerged as an independent ally of the Chinese Communist Party (CCP) in its revolutionary modern project. Shanghai's leading role post-1992 in China's project of a cosmopolitan creative modernity draws heavily on this past but does so in highly selective fashion, reducing this partially recovered 'structure of feeling' to a consumer brand image. The last chapter shows how the city used the creative cluster model to integrate creative labour into the Chinese cultural industries system, using, and then curtailing, the transformative moment of the post-industrial city.

The chapters that follow try to make these arguments sequentially through a historical narrative, but there are also jump cuts between them as we seek to make the argument from different angles. There are no doubt gaping lacunae, the result not just of restrictions of space but also our own blind spots, but we hope that the argument manages to shine through.

Chapter 1 gives a fuller account of the creative industries discourse, including the 'cultural industries' that preceded this new term, and outlines in more detail the historical roots of the challenges this discourse presented to China.

Chapter 2 goes back to the origins of Chinese modernity in the traumatic encounter with the West. It shows how the Chinese state and intellectuals chose the radical path of breaking with their dynastic past and its deep-rooted thought structures in order to engage in a life or death process of modernization. We argue that at the same time as disavowing this 'Confucian' past it also retained and deployed it in ways that gave China a distinct trajectory towards the modern. This trajectory cannot be seen as a deficit in terms of a Western 'original', and we show how it works at the level of culture, contrasting the accounts given by Habermas (public sphere), Bourdieu (artistic autonomy) and Foucault (liberal governmentality) with the specific reality of China. In so doing we suggest how the formation of the 'intellectuals' and their relationship to the political project of Chinese modernity gave rise to a very different historical configuration. Their involvement in the political struggles of the Republican era (1911–49) should be read as a deliberate rejection of Western liberal democracy, not some historical failure.

Chapter 3 deals with the image of *Shanghai Modern* – the period in that foreign-controlled city between 1911 and 1949 – as a harbinger of a Chinese modernity quashed by Mao's peasant revolution. This is important for us, as the return of Shanghai to the forefront of China's reform programme in 1992 was taken to herald the country's return to global modernity. Shanghai's exemplary modernity stems in large part from its role as the centre of China's encounter with cultural modernity, driven by a commercial and cosmopolitan culture unencumbered by dynastic tradition. We take issue with this account of Shanghai, reading its 'cultural industries' – publishing, advertising, film, radio, recorded music – as sites where China's intellectuals attempted to forge a national-popular revolutionary subject. That is, they can be related to the revolutionary avant-gardes of Weimar Germany and the USSR rather than the commercial public sphere of a liberal imagination. Instead of contrasting a commercial and cosmopolitan city with the closed and primitive cultural propaganda being developed by Mao in Yan'an, we suggest that Shanghai's cultural industries represented a distinct model of an engaged radical intelligentsia that holds out possibilities for an alternative version of China's encounter with the cultural industries.

With Chapter 4 we move to the 1978 reforms, giving an account of these from the conceptual perspective of neo-liberalism. In particular we see Chinese modernization after Tiananmen as framed by depoliticization and a restriction of individual expression to consumer choices. However, though the primacy of market economics sets up similar dynamics in China as elsewhere, very definite limits are set by China's distinct civilizational past and its identification as socialist. It remains committed to the 'people's prosperity' and draws on historic forms of statecraft in ways which override the absolute rights of capital. We try to show how the withdrawal of the state from direct interference in everyday life allowed new forms of individual subjectivity to emerge, but that these new forms of 'self-sovereignty' are imbricated with the state in complex ways. We argue this individual-state relation is not zero-sum, as the state necessarily helps frame the ethical and political-legal context of everyday life. However, we argue that the ideological work of the party-state has become more strident as neo-liberal forms of social fragmentation continue apace.

In Chapter 5 we try to outline some countervailing tendencies to neo-liberalism, rooted in China's civilizational and socialist past. We show how this past continues to structure everyday economic and social activity, giving China a configuration distinct from the West. We also look at how these two sources are being used by the Chinese state to develop a new narrative of legitimacy and modernity outside of the framework of the liberal democratic West. We end by suggesting that the rise of new forms of digital governance represent a step away from the ideological and mark a new kind of convergence with the West.

Chapter 6 takes us back to Shanghai as a creative city. We begin with the new forms of Chinese urbanism pioneered in Shenzhen, and how these were then applied in Shanghai. The key difference was the mobilization of Shanghai's historical cachet in its bid to become a global city, and it attempted to do so through the imaginary of the 'creative city'. We argue that the creative city goes back before the work of Charles Landry and Richard Florida and needs to be seen in terms of a mobilization of new post-Fordist subjectivities. However, the deployment of *Shanghai Modern*, and its commercial and cosmopolitan past, reduces the power of this imaginary to new forms of urban consumption. As such, the cultural resources of historic Shanghai return as recoupable nostalgia, not an active remembering.

In Chapter 7 we look at China's cultural policy reforms since 1978. We return to the contrast between the cultural and the creative industries agendas. The use of 'cultural industries' was part of an attempt to extend the reach of a democratic culture in an age of mass reproduction and reach back to many of the concerns explored in Chapter 3. The 'creative industries' reduce the notion of culture to an economic input even as they draw on its transformative imaginary. We suggest that China retains the notion of cultural industries because it still relies on the space of ideological or symbolic governance that creative industries – as with neo-liberalism in general – wants to subsume under the market economy. However, retaining the notion of 'cultural industries' did not prevent reforms from subjecting it to remorseless commercialization. We look at the role of Chinese intellectuals and 'cultural workers' and their varied responses to the marketization of culture, and their cultural and economic marginalization. Then we present the new popular culture in China as, in part, a contestation of the historic role of intellectuals, though in a less violent way that in the Cultural Revolution. We argue that the Chinese state has attempted to both benefit economically from the market in culture and retain control over the 'commanding heights' as essential to its legitimation project. The Chinese state's concern with controlling the symbolic realm contrasts with the creative industries' emphasis on free markets and the sovereign consumer as inherently emancipatory. We cast doubt on this latter account and suggest that it is at the political-symbolic level – a site crucial to the Chinese state's legitimation – that we can locate the transformative effects of culture. We end the chapter by suggesting that the recent shift to forms of digital control is a significant and disturbing development.

Finally, in Chapter 8 we return to Shanghai. We look at the idea of the 'creative city' at the level of cultural production, tracing the 'epistemic community' behind the idea of 'creative clusters' and the 'creative milieu'. After showing how these increasingly became part of the city's real estate machine, we look at the social and subjective spaces available for the city's artists and cultural workers. Building on arguments of the previous chapter, we suggest that it is not primarily the issue of 'censorship' that matters (though it does matter) but the squeezing of the space of development and experimentation between the state and the market. On the one hand, a state-sanctioned space of production; on the other, a highly commercialized system of the rapid exploitation of ideas 'at scale'. This squeeze applies both to the ability to earn a living but also to that sense of subjectivity associated with creative workers, threading a career across the multiple projects of a precarious field. The *habitus* of the artist and cultural work in Shanghai is extremely constrained. On the one hand, from a pragmatic policy point of view, this lack of space hampers a really dynamic cultural ecology; on the other, it restricts the space of historical imagination available to Chinese society.

NOTES

1. F. Braudel, *Civilization and Capitalism, 15th–18th Century*, Vols. I–III (Berkeley: University of California Press, 1992); K. Polanyi, *The Great Transformation: The Political and Economic Origins of Our Time* (Boston, MA: Beacon, 1957); M. Weber, *Economy and Society* (Berkeley: University of California Press, 2013).

2. S. Zuboff and J. Maxmin, *The Support Economy: Why Corporations Are Failing Individuals and the Next Episode of Capitalism* (New York: Viking Penguin, 2002). Cf. E. Morozov, 'Capitalism's New Clothes', *The Baffler*, 4 February 2019, https://thebaffler.com/latest/capitalisms-new-clothes-morozov. Accessed 26 September 2019.

3. For discussion on cultural citizenship, cf. J. O'Connor, 'After the Creative Industries: Cultural Policy in Crisis', *Journal of Law, Social Justice and Global Development* 1 (2016): 1–18.

4. T. H. Marshall, *Citizenship and Social Class and Other Essays* (Cambridge: Cambridge University Press, 1950), 46.

5. Article 27, 1: 'Everyone has the right freely to participate in the cultural life of the community, to enjoy the arts and to share in scientific advancement and its benefits'.

6. For a good discussion of this see D. Looseley, 'Democratising the Popular: The Case of Pop Music in France and Britain', *International Journal of Cultural Policy* 18, no. 5 (2012): 579–92; G. Born, 'The Social and the Aesthetic: For a Post-Bordieuan Theory of Cultural Production', *Cultural Sociology* 4, no. 2 (2010): 171–208.

7. A crucial part of neo-liberalism was the theory of the sovereignty of the consumer in which every act of purchase was an exercise of everyday democracy, or as Von Mises had it 'every dollar was a ballot'. Cf. Q. Slobodian, *Globalists: The End of Empire and the Birth of Neoliberalism* (Cambridge, MA: Harvard University Press, 2018), 176.

8. J. Howkins, *Creative Ecologies: Where Thinking Is a Proper Job* (Beijing: Joint Publishing, 2011), 126.

9. M. Keane, *Creative Industries in China: Art, Media, Design* (Cambridge: Polity, 2012), 45.

10. Ibid.

11. Cf. A. Ong, *Flexible Citizenship: The Cultural Logics of Transnationality* (Durham NC: Duke University Press, 1999).

12. C. Pozzana and A. Russo, 'Continuity/Discontinuity', *Critical Asian Studies* 43, no. 2 (2011): 261–84, 262.

13. T. Mitchell, 'The Stage of Modernity', in *Questions of Modernity*, ed. T. Mitchell (Minneapolis: University of Minnesota Press, 2000), 1–34. See also A. Mbembe, *Necro-Politics* (Durham: Duke University Press, 2019).

1

The Creative Industries and the China Challenge

The cultural industries

In the late 1970s, the 'culture industry', Adorno and Horkheimer's polemical term for the mass commercial culture being produced in the United States after the war, began to shift to the more open, contested terrain of the 'cultural industries'. This was not some 'recognition' of the economic importance of these industries, but rather an opening up of a new kind of cultural-political space with regard to the commercial production of culture, especially the expanding media sector. Perhaps the first systematic account of the cultural industries as a site of political struggle was Oscar Negt and Alexander Kluge's 1972 *Öffentlichkeit und Erfahrung* (Public Sphere and Experience), where the rapid expansion of the cultural industries in the 1960s represented a challenge to the bourgeois public sphere, but also a chance to think about an expanded proletarian public sphere.[1] This new cultural-political space can be seen clearly in Augustin Girard's influential 1980 paper for UNESCO, written as head of research at the French Ministry of Culture.[2] Girard points to the huge commercial cultural sector and as a matter of urgency calls on the cultural policy establishment to take note. It was the same call as that made within the Greater London Council's (GLC) new left-wing Labour leadership, elected in May 1981, and by French President Mitterrand's new Minister for Culture Jack Lang in the same year.[3] Their contentions were that the vast majority of cultural consumption now took place outside the subsidized arts sector and the state media system; that the consumption of commercial culture was growing at extraordinary rates across all social levels; and that traditional, subsidized 'live' cultural forms were (following Baumol and Bowen) economically incapable of satisfying this demand.[4] In this context, a refusal to engage with the commercial sector was elitist and irresponsible, and cultural policy must engage with this sector to be democratic and to challenge some of the more 'negative tendencies' within it.

In the United States, an academic 'production of culture' school had begun to investigate how 'popular' and 'high culture' was produced within complex socio-economic 'art worlds' in which the position of the 'artist' was a constructed and contingent one.[5] Bourdieu's work on cultural production and consumption had begun to open up similar ground in France.[6] In the United Kingdom, Raymond Williams had also become interested in the material 'industrial' conditions of cultural production and their historical trajectories.[7] Indeed, a new kind of art history rejected transcendental notions of artists and placed ideas of individual genius squarely back within her or his social and historical context.[8] This recognition of the collective social basis of cultural production gave a new democratic valency to the concept of 'industry'.

The early 1980s saw left-leaning cultural policy-makers embrace markets and technology, both of which had previously seemed to mark the boundary between art and commercial culture. There was a more positive view of the new technologies of production, reproduction and distribution, a growing sense of seizing hold of a democratic modernity – breaking with Heideggerian anti-technological 'culture critique' as well as the formalist aesthetics of post-war modernist orthodoxy. The 1980s saw a rediscovery of inter-war 'left modernism', which had been much more sanguine about the political potential of the forms and technologies of mass culture. This was encouraged by the new forms of popular culture that had burgeoned since the 1960s, in which the lines between popular culture and 'high modernism' were constantly breached.[9]

The embrace of industry and technology within cultural production was necessarily accompanied by a selective revalourization of the market. Contemporary culture was not just about 'collective' production and technological reproduction/distribution but also involved its organization outside the state system, via the market. Social democratic politics were now much more open to the idea of markets and much more wary of the state, something that would accelerate as the USSR and its satellites began to crumble. How else, except through the market, could the production of and demand for culture be regulated?[10]

This positive valency can be understood only in terms of a social democratic policy context, in which capitalist enterprises – in this case the cultural industries – were subject to democratic forms of oversight and regulation. These issues were outlined clearly in the mid-1980s by Bernard Miege and Nicholas Garnham, both academics who had been close to the policy worlds of Jack Lang and the GLC.[11] Taking issue with Adorno and Horkheimer's account, they wanted to give a much more specific reading of the cultural industries, not so much as capitalist *ideology* but as capitalist *industries* engaged in the production of cultural commodities at a profit. The logic of cultural commodity production was very specific, giving rise to an industry built on volatile markets, highly fragmented creative labour and a commodity whose use value was never known in advance. This was a contradictory cultural space, in which autonomous cultural labour and multiplying user demands were mediated by a highly differentiated cultural industries that combined artisanal production at one end with globally financed corporations at the other.[12] Hence Girard's 'negative tendencies': concentration, monopoly, cross-ownership, vertical integration, ever-increasing levels of capitalization and so on. (Girard had also pointed to 'imbalances' at the international level, anticipating later accounts of unequal globalization of cultural industries.)

Those writing in the 'political economy' tradition – Garnham, Miege but also communications scholars such as Vincent Mosco – were very conscious of the crucial role of media and culture in the self-understanding (or systemic masking of this understanding) of contemporary societies.[13] The 'public sphere' in modern industrial societies was intensely mediated, and thus comprehending how the commodified production system impacted the nature of the cultural content was absolutely crucial – not only from a cultural but also a political perspective. Less concerned with expanded participation in cultural production (Garnham and Miege were wary of this, as for them it simply expanded the 'reserve army' of cultural labour) they were intensely focused on democratic participation in its regulation and management.[14] By using the term 'political economy' they rejected neo-classical economics' ahistorical *homo economicus* and saw the production and consumption of (cultural) commodities as a system built on a whole range of historically specific social and political foundations. Cultural production in a modern mixed economy and social democracy was thus fully open to the interventions of the state in pursuit of public policy goals, such as an open and accessible public media sphere. This stood in contrast to the 'de-regulation' current that began in earnest in the 1980s, pitting 'state control' against 'free markets' as the central choice in media and – gradually – in other forms of cultural policy.[15]

The cultural industries agenda intersected with work in economic and industrial geography across the 1990s, its 'cultural turn' forging close links with related agenda of the 'creative city'. These disciplines also challenged neo-classical economics in a way that had direct implications for urban and regional planning and economic development policy. Emerging in part out of Karl Polanyi's economic anthropology, writers such as Mark Granovetter identified how economic transactions were embedded in a whole range of social networks, ones that could materially affect the structure and dynamics of that economy.[16] Industrial geographers could not ignore the embeddedness of industrial activity in particular spaces and places. Cities and regions, indeed whole economic sectors, were 'path dependent' – that is, part of a complex, specific historical trajectory that could be altered but not evaded. It was out of this context that many of the first accounts of place-based cultural production systems emerged.[17]

This approach stressed 'agglomeration economies' – reminiscent of Alfred Marshall's 'industrial districts' with their distinct 'atmosphere' – and were later codified and globalized in the form of 'clusters' through the work of Michael Porter.[18] These social conditions enable cultural production by bringing together complementary firms and people to provide opportunities for information and resource exchange, collaboration, skills development and exposure to alternative ideas and practices, which propel both product innovations and the use of novel production processes and materials.[19] This work directly informed research and policy thinking in the field of cultural, and later creative, industries. In their analysis of agglomeration, of traded and untraded interdependencies, of tacit skills and embodied knowledge, of the importance of small- and medium-sized enterprises (SMEs), of socially embedded networks and norms, they provided important language for those concerned with the cultural economy. They also opened up links to other kinds of industrial districts based similarly on dense, socially embedded SME networks.[20] However, what was emerging here was not just a way of describing how cultural production worked and its reliance on urban agglomeration but also an account of how these ways of working were indicative of a much wider set of transformations.

Having described these new approaches, we need to situate them in the wider context of the rapid deindustrialization of many cities and regions of Europe and North America in the 1970s and 1980s. Up to this time, the cultural industries had been a concern of national and international agencies, linked to issues of social democracy, nation-building and the public sphere. However, starting with the GLC between 1979 and 1986, and continuing across UK cities and other 'deindustrializing' areas of Europe and North America, the cultural industries came to be seen as potential replacements, in part at least, for lost manufacturing industries at the local level. Less dependent on classic locational advantages such as proximity to raw materials or transport routes, reliant on human rather than expensive fixed capital, the cultural industries – along with other 'service' sectors – presented an attractive option to local authorities.

The arguments for the growing economic dimension of cultural production – pioneered by the GLC's economic development committee (including Nicholas Garnham), as well as Jack Lang's almost concurrent Culture Ministry under France's Mitterrand government – were frequently used by the cultural sector in making a case for higher, or justifying existing, levels of public funding.[21] But there was more to it than that. The cultural industries emerged at a moment when the 'sense of an ending' of an industrial civilization giving way to something else, was particularly intense across Europe and North America.[22] By the time the GLC had been abolished in 1986, this transition was being framed as a shift from Fordism to post-Fordism. If Adorno's Culture Industry represented mass production and consumption in an era of Fordist capitalism, the cultural industries were increasingly linked to post-Fordism.[23] The 'cultural industries' were not then just convenient replacement industries but exemplary of a new kind of economic future.

There were some key elements that marked the 'cultural industries' as very different from the 'creative industries' moment of the late 1990s. First, though the economic elements were to be embraced as a crucial dimension of cultural policy, the overall intention was that they would contribute to a more democratic culture rather than to 'the economy' per se. The introduction of economic concepts such as the 'value chain' as well as the serious investigation of employment statistics and industry trends in this period were to be used primarily to secure cultural ends. Second, these economic concepts and tools were there to correct 'negative tendencies' – issues of monopoly, exploitation, international domination and so on. They were also there to protect against 'market failure' – not the failure to achieve market success, as this term came to denote, but the failures intrinsic to the market mechanism per se. Third, though markets were embraced they were also redefined to reflect embedded sociocultural practices rather than the abstract neo-classical rational choice model. They were part of a mixed economy, not so much the Keynesian 'commanding heights' model of the 1950s, but one that had emerged from a decade of grassroots democracy and urban social movements, from the rapid decline of the political prestige of the state to the incipient energies of post-Fordism. These new local economies, and the new kinds of subjects they fostered, involved a 'culturalization of the economy' and were interwoven with notions of the creative city.[24]

UK New Labour: 1998

The creative industries agenda gradually replaced that of the cultural industries. If at first this seemed a matter of nomenclature only, it gradually emerged as a fundamental reframing of what was at stake.

The creative industries agenda, as launched initially by New Labour's Department of Culture, Media and Sport (DCMS), was an attempt to hitch funding for arts and culture to the wagon of the knowledge economy, where 'ideas' and those who generated them were to be the driving force of innovation.[25] It drew on long-standing notions of culture and artistic practice but increasingly sought to extract a 'creativity' from these which had a diminished relation to the wider set of values in which these practices had been traditionally set. The agenda's emphasis on creativity was explicitly linked to a remaking of economic and social subjects in a society of volatility and risk, where Ezra Pound's notion that 'artists are the antennae of the race' becomes a distributed search for innovation.[26] The reduction of creativity to economic input is at the root of the creative industries' close association with neo-liberalism, and we will discuss this more below. But the creative industries also inspired a socio-economic imaginary of an emancipatory self and wider social transformation through actively seeking out the 'new', reconfigured as 'innovation', in a combination of creative expression, entrepreneurialism and new technology. At a broader level, we might see the affective charge of the creative industries' imaginary as the reinvention of the modern beyond the bureaucracy, rigid rationality and self-repression of Fordist modernity. The 1960s' counterculture, which Daniel Bell saw as threatening to undermine capitalism through an excess of the pleasure principle, now seemed to have saved it. The bourgeois bohemians, financed by angel investors and fused with Silicon Valley technologies, were now at the bleeding edge.[27]

In distinguishing between the cultural and creative industries, we are not setting up some Manichean opposition. There are many areas of overlap. The DCMS coined the term as a way of getting more money for publicly funded arts and culture, in many ways merely continuing the post-Thatcherite strategy of justifying the continued public funding for art and culture through its purported economic benefits.[28] By the 1990s, the economic contribution of arts and culture was a well-established trope of argumentation to government. Many of those in the cultural sector went along with this new terminology, using 'cultural' and 'creative' interchangeably, as pragmatism demanded. And with good reason, because the notion of creativity in play here, even when hitched to the new force of digital technologies, was directly derived from the artistic or cultural sense of this term. This remained the case even as it migrated beyond the West, to East Asia and China.

In its first iteration in 1998, the change of terminology from cultural to creative industries was never intended to designate a radically new 'industrial' sector, let alone a new kind of economy. It was, on the surface, a pragmatic linkage of a plea for an increased arts and culture budget to the buzzwords of the new 'knowledge economy'. But in so doing, it inadvertently tapped the energy of a much more powerful zeitgeist. What started as partly a clever funding ploy ended in the radical de-coupling of the creative industries agenda from wider cultural policy values. But even as it reduced culture to its economic or 'instrumental' value, it remained tied to the discourses of culture, something reflected in its persistent definitional and taxonomic incoherencies. For, paradoxically given its birth in a statistically informed policy document, it remains unclear – twenty years after its initial iteration – exactly what is designated by the term 'creative industries'. We have critiqued the definition of the creative industries on a number of occasions and need only run through a basic summary here.

Creativity

First, although the words 'culture' and 'creativity' are often seen as equivalents, they are not. Creativity is a capacity of thought or action latent in a wide range of activities. Culture is a set of meanings and beliefs, knowledge and values embodied in patterns of social organization and behaviour. This 'anthropological' culture is frequently expressed in practices and objects – texts, performances, sounds, images and designs – which are specifically designated (or privileged) as 'art and culture'. These last are seen to reflect an exemplary form of creativity, which, until recently, were mostly associated with the figure of the artist. In the 1990s, this kind of creativity became more generally sought after as a model of 'creative thinking' valuable outside just arts and culture. But culture as a set of meanings, beliefs and patterns of behaviour also encompasses other quite different things such as tradition, ritual, celebration, social cohesion and national identity – outcomes which are not necessarily about 'creative capacity' per se. And many areas that are undoubtedly creative – in that they produce new knowledge or value (including intellectual property) or forms of practice – are not 'cultural' in this sense. Financial services and neuroscience are, for example, highly creative but we do not seek to include them in the creative industries sector.

All definitions have their ambiguities and arbitrary boundaries, but the term 'creative' has proved particularly problematic. 'Creative industries' was pulled out of the policy ether by think-tank 'wonks' before an important meeting between the new DCMS and the Treasury.[29] Following the hasty commissioning of a consultancy firm to do some head-counting, the notion made sense only in the context of the already existing 'arts and cultural sector', the main constituency for the DCMS. This was reflected in the taxonomy – a list of thirteen (now consolidated to nine) sub-sectors drawn from industrial and occupational classification codes in a way that had been established by researchers over the previous decade of 'arts and cultural industries' advocacy.[30] The now famous definition – 'those industries which have their origin in individual creativity, skill and talent and which have a potential for wealth and job creation through the generation and exploitation of intellectual property'[31] – could apply to a vast range of sectors (financial services, science and technology, engineering, pharmaceuticals etc.) but was clearly meant to denote the arts and cultural sector (making no distinction between public and private, reproduced or live).[32] This ambiguity allowed for the adding in of sectors like software, toys and games, and R&D in science and technology. All of which moves us well beyond the cultural or creative industries into an arbitrary identification of sectors reliant on 'ideas', 'creativity' and 'intellectual property'. This statistical bleed mirrors the more general inflation of the term 'creativity' to meaningless proportions, as it applies to almost any kind of human activity.[33]

Creativity relies on a cultural definition for its coherence, but it promotes its usefulness way beyond the cultural or cultural industries sector proper. It can do this because creativity is now defined as an 'input' rather than a quality of a product or practice, and is thereby uncoupled from its relationship to the wider set of values we designate as 'culture'. This was taken to its furthest length by the United Kingdom's National Endowment for Science, Technology and the Arts (NESTA), which moved away from a sector (cultural or creative) designated in terms of the kinds of products it generates and towards the idea of the 'creative economy' – a statistical and conceptual agglomeration of a range of activities based on the predominance of creativity deployed as input right across the economy.

NESTA defines creativity as 'the application of creative talent to commercial ends', which is standard for the Schumpeterian innovation literature.[34] What is telling, however, is that their definition of creativity does not refer to any cultural values produced but simply the quality of its input. For NESTA, creativity plays 'a role within the creative process that brings cognitive skills to bear about differentiation to yield either novel or significantly enhanced products whose final form is not fully specified in advance'.[35] This is operationalized by specifying the formal character of 'creative labour' in terms of five distinguishing characteristics: the labour must involve a 'novel process'; 'interpretation not mere transformation'; 'non-repetitiveness'; being 'mechanization resistant'; and making a 'creative contribution to the value-chain'.[36]

Outside of a notion of cultural value, these characteristics of creative labour can be applied to any form of skilled labour (surgeons, financial planners, engineers, scientists, teachers and so on). Equally, the identification of concentrations of graphic designers, software planners or advertising personnel – or indeed actors, musicians or video directors – in mining, financial services or construction does not make these industries more 'creative', even in the Schumpeterian sense of innovation for market. As the old design adage has it, they might just be employed to put 'lipstick on the pig'. Nevertheless, the golden word 'creativity' has now been wrested from any cultural value and been firmly nailed in place as mobile human capital for the knowledge economy.

The digital imaginary

The DCMS' rebranding of 'arts and cultural industries' included computer games (as had the cultural industries' taxonomies), but it also added a new category, 'IT, Software and Computing'. At a stroke, this added around 40 per cent to all employment and related metrics. The claims associated with the creative industries in terms of employment growth and contribution to GDP have been disputed ever since, as has its specific boundaries and conceptual unity.[37]

To the definitional confusions were added terminological ones, 'tech', 'creative', 'creative tech' and 'creative and digital' strewn like yesterday's confetti across a thousand consultancy reports. There is no doubting the transformative impact of computing and telecommunications on the sector but this does not mean that computer software and systems design should be counted as *part* of the cultural/creative sector any more than telecommunications infrastructure, consumer hardware, or the logistics and extraction industries with which the creative industries also work. The connections between child copper miners in Indonesia and the streaming services reliant on a whole global telecommunications and mobile device infrastructure are crucial for certain kinds of 'depth' cultural economy analysis.[38] However, the cultural economy proper, to quote Pratt, 'is indicative of a particular sub-section of economic activity that is concerned with cultural products and activities (such as music, film and fine art) as opposed to, say, transportation and mining'.[39] Software might be 'symbolic manipulation' but it is not 'cultural' in the sense that we would use it in 'cultural industries'. Yet despite endless critiques of the incoherence of the conceptual and statistical framework it provides, the term 'creative' – either inclusive of the cultural sector or a fuzzy supplement to it – is constantly used, even by agencies that are mostly sceptical of it.[40] As a rhetoric of evidence more or less impervious to critique, the idea of creative industries or creative economy draws on what Alan Badiou has called 'the power of the false'.[41]

There was a more positive explanation for this extension to 'IT, Software and Computing', for example Nicholas Garnham's suggestion in 2005 that

> the shift to the terminology 'creative industries' has taken place, and can only be understood and assessed, in the context of a wider debate about the impact of information and communication technologies (ICTs) and digitalisation and the relationship between the deployment of new communication networks and the products and services carried over them. In short, policy towards the 'creative industries' can no longer be separated from ICT policy in its various forms and the wider information society perspective within which that policy is formulated.[42]

This allowed the DCMS to connect to the new 'digital' economy, including both the technologies of communication and computing, which were beginning to transform the cultural industries (along with many other sectors), and the kind of 'start-up' companies exemplified by Silicon Valley, and whose maverick 'out-of-the-box' entrepreneurialism was seen – by a department trying to put itself at the cutting edge of economic innovation – as very similar to that of cultural businesses and their milieu. The policy narrative around the creative industries was rooted firmly in the evolutionary transition from an industrial to a post-industrial economy, framed now in a world of globalization and 'competitive advantage'.[43] The DCMS' definition directly evoked the buzzwords of the knowledge and innovation economy literature. The creative industries were positioned as part of the advanced service sector set to stave off competition from 'emerging' and/or manufacturing-based economies. Writing in the introduction to the 1998 *Cultural Industries Mapping Document*, the then Chancellor of the Exchequer Gordon Brown suggested the United Kingdom could become the 'creative workshop of the world' in anticipation of the country regaining the pre-eminent economic role it had once had, only this time in a post-industrial world. 'Creativity' and 'the digital' were combined into a new economic imaginary in which a post-industrial future might be glimpsed.

Creative economy, creative subjects

The homologies between the creative industries and the new digital economy were related to the obvious connections between 'creativity' and knowledge work.[44] Crucial here is the kind of subjects required for these industries. Both 'creative' and 'digital' entrepreneurs share similar roots in 1960s' countercultures and the political contestations of 1968. The ways in which the US countercultures fed into the early home computer development are well documented; indeed, these 'rebel' or 'bohemian' origins have been crucial to the 'Californian ideology' in which the computing revolution has been driven by libertarian mavericks from the margins of mainstream society.[45] In Europe, Boltanski and Chiapello have charted how much of the political gains of 1968 accrued to young managerial workers, especially in the new media and entertainment sectors.[46] Their pioneering of a new 'creative capitalism' has strong resonances with the turn of the millennium dot-com and start-up world that emerged alongside the creative industries agenda. Culture was crucial to both. The counterculture grew out of a cultural critique of industrial society pioneered by Herbert Marcuse and others, as noted in doom-laden terms by Daniel Bell – who pointed both to the rise of the information society and the pleasure principle that would fatally wound the capitalist work ethic.[47] Boltanski and Chiapello's creative capitalism drew on what they called the artistic critique of capitalism, which protested against capitalism, and especially the Fordist post-war order, in the name of 'life'. The countercultural and 'bohemian' roots of the creative and digital economies are clear; they allow for new kinds of subjects, working in new kinds of ways, in new kinds of milieux. The creativity that was to remake the subjectivities required for the creative economy was essentially derived from the idea of the creative artist.

Just as the creative industries rebranded the cultural industries, 'creative labour' is a direct transposition of artistic practice. NESTA's five characteristics in many ways adapt the classic eighteenth-century distinction between artistic work and manual labour, the former exemplifying freedom, the latter brute necessity. As we shall see, this was also part of a distinction between developing countries reliant on manufacture and 'advanced' economies which were able to mobilize creativity for the new innovation economy. Creative labour seeks to adapt 'artistic' sensibility and practice (breaking the rules, 'thinking outside the box', 'coming from left field') as well as the 'the shock of the new', the 'revaluation of all values' and the agonistic struggle with the existing order found in the modernist and avant-garde traditions. These qualities are exactly what are needed in the age of 'creative destruction' that had replaced the systems planning of Fordism. As the authors have observed:

> Managers and companies needed to look to the practices of those at home in a world of constant flux and who had developed the art of intuitive, iconoclastic and risk-laden innovation – the artists! [who are C]onstantly innovative, anticipating and responding to the market through an intuitive immersion into the field, willing to break the rules, going beyond the 9–5, thriving on risk and failure, mixing work and life, meaning and money.[48]

The creativity rhetoric, by now a powerful global trope, is intended to put the capacities associated with cultural creativity to productive work. What is ultimately at stake is not just the promotion of a particular growth sector – creative industries – but also a recreation of the new subjectivities required for an innovation-driven creative economy.

The critique of creative labour is now well established. The ubiquitous injunction to *be creative* has resulted in high levels of exploitation, including self-exploitation in the form of what Andrew Ross called 'sacrificial labour'.[49] The centrality of networking in the creative economy has tended to change the composition of social and cultural capital (fluid and multiple connections are more valuable than longer-term associations, for example), and has made workers more individualized and their use of networks more instrumentalized. The emancipation from the '9 to 5', the erosion of that fixed line between work and play essential to the 'artistic critique', was turned against creative labour, as 'always on' forms of work, and the inability to 'turn off' from networking and create personal space, spread. The creative artist has been thoroughly remade as *homo economicus*, in which calculations of utility and profit are applied to social and personal life in new ways.[50] The 'cultural' nature of creative work – the reliance on 'work' done in the lifeworld in the form of personal and social development – has resulted in what one tradition has called the 'social factory'.[51] That is, much of the production process in the creative industries relies on forms of valorization developed in the social world, especially the urban milieu, with the larger cultural industry firms, as well as real estate and digital media companies, using this social space as a site of accumulation.

Yet the 'creative industries' always had an excess beyond the instrumentalism with which it was freighted. John Hartley, one of the early proselytizers for the term, celebrated its success in getting 'creativity' taken seriously by 'the wealth-creating portfolios, the emergent industry departments, and the enterprise support programmes'.[52] It was 'win-win'. But if government was getting growth and innovation, what was culture getting? The unblocking of creativity, its ability to flow more freely through individuals and society, was to be transformative in ways that went beyond a prosaic 'innovation agenda'. For Hartley, creativity had spilled out of the confines of elitist high culture, and he had no problem with the commercial transactions which were its lifeblood. Popular, everyday culture was now democratically transformed by 'Web 2.0', wrong-footing the cultural industry behemoths just as it had the elitist defenders of the state subsidized canon. New computing and communications technologies enabled consumers to actively enter the cultural economy as more than the passive endpoint of the production process. Cultural studies had empowered the audience with their ability de- and re-code cultural texts; with Internet 2.0 and cheap digital production they could now become, as Henry Jenkins and others claimed, active co-creators of cultural products.[53]

In his radical neo-liberal vision of a society of creative individuals coordinated by the blind watchmaker of the market, not only were the historical claims of cultural citizenship to be redeemed but humanity itself be set again on the evolutionary path to a reinvented creative future.[54] As Sebastian Olma has pointed out, at a time when the art world had abandoned any pretence to creative autonomy, the creative industries had rediscovered the world-shaping power of Schiller's *spieltrieb*.[55]

In these ways, and in others that we will detail below, the creative industries agenda was more than an economic imaginary; or rather, this economic imaginary carried a strong affective charge derived from a series of personal and collective transformations that drew extensively on the repertoire developed within that of art, culture and the 'cultural economy'. The creative industries agenda was a reframing of these cultural values and affective energies in the form of an economic development programme, dissolving the opposition of culture and economy so that the former can be integrated productively into a market-led innovation agenda. This accounts for its continuing ideological effectiveness. Though now somewhat jaded, the discourse of creativity retains its energies in many places. Despite its overwhelmingly economic rhetoric, the creative industries agenda, through its call for a diffusion of creativity across the whole social space, seemed to articulate a new way of being modern. It has, buried deep within itself, a transformative charge, an image of a creative society and the unredeemed image of the future that we should take seriously.

A new modernity

Gordon Brown saw in the creative industries an *aufhebung* of Britain's pioneering industrial past into the new creative future. The question of how to deal with a deindustrialization caused by the rapid shift of manufacturing overseas had driven both cultural industries and creative cities since at least the early 1980s.[56] This was more than make do and mend; it was to be a systematic economic and cultural reinvention, beyond industrial Fordist capitalism. This forging of a new creative modernity was to be the work of the West.

For Daniel H. Pink, writing in a pre-Global Financial Crisis (GFC) age, right-brain creativity is the new force of innovation and is something the West (or at least in this account, the United States) does best:

> As the forces of Asia, automation, and abundance strengthen and accelerate, the curtain is rising on a new era, the Conceptual Age. If the Industrial Age was built on people's backs, and the Information Age on people's left hemispheres, the Conceptual Age is being built on people's right hemispheres. We've progressed from a society of farmers to a society of factory workers to a society of knowledge workers. And now we're progressing yet again – to a society of creators and empathizers, pattern recognizers, and meaning makers.[57]

More recently, Niall Ferguson has suggested, in a rather gloomy conclusion to his book arguing the normative superiority and ideal-typical status of Western modernity, that perhaps only innovation and creativity remain as key indicators of the superiority of the Western liberal democratic 'package'.[58] As recently as 2014, *Harvard Business Review* could run a headline: 'Why China Can't Innovate'.[59] The innovation agenda was not just a response to domestic deindustrialization but also to the rise of the 'Asian Tigers'. These had, by the 1990s, achieved a level of advanced industrialization through state-managed programmes of development running directly counter to the International Monetary Fund (IMF) script. In response, the comparative advantage of the West was held to be its ability to create ideas and innovate rather than simply manufacture things. If the West was being outstripped by state-directed industrial development, then perhaps the free circulation of ideas and commercial returns to knowledge-led innovation associated with Euro-American capitalism would continue to stand it in good stead against a more state-heavy East. For, as it became clear, much of the debate around creativity, innovation and the knowledge economy was predicated on older tropes about the West and the East, going back to Hegel's Lectures on the Philosophy of World History in the late 1820s in which he contrasted the dynamic freedom of the West with the despotic juggernaut of Asia, hobbled by its archaic traditions.[60]

What is interesting is why this creativity programme so quickly migrated from the post-industrial West to those countries over whom it sought to gain competitive advantage. Equally interesting is that this policy migration was facilitated by Western government-led agencies and Western-dominated international bodies such as the British Council and UNESCO, as well as myriad public and private educational and arts agencies.

The manner in which the creative industries agenda captured the zeitgeist and moved quite rapidly through circuits of what Jamie Peck called 'fast policy' has been well noted.[61] Underlying 'fast policy' agents – which included the British Council, various Northern European government and educational entities, and new global 'epistemic' communities[62] – have been slower-moving initiatives stemming from the UNESCO 2005 Convention, and related global development agencies.[63] These increasingly promoted the cultural and creative industries, terms that were often used interchangeably, but with 'creative' making a bridge between the cultural industries and a wider, usually undefined 'creative economy'.[64] It is as if the competitive advantage to be gained from creativity was secondary to the normative prescription of a benign modernization that creativity could lay out for the 'Asian Tigers', the BRIC economies (Brazil, Russia, India and China), and the Global South writ large. Creative modernity was too good not to share.

It is often argued that this creativity agenda, though originating in the West, is entirely capable of local adaptation. Policy mobility, once viewed as an ordered centre-periphery transformation, is now more disordered. 'Once released into the wild, policies will often mutate and hybridize in surprising ways', write Jamie Peck and Nick Theodore, noting the 'open ended and politicized processes of networking and mutation across shifting social landscapes'.[65] Indeed, global 'policyscapes' (not just in culture) have witnessed a proliferation of actors – national and local governments, consultants, intermediaries, gurus, academics, travel writers, 'creative tourists' as well as associated media (such as city guides, tourism-rating platforms and in-flight magazines) – who constitute the penumbra of an international 'epistemic community'.[66] These mobile 'fast' policy ideas not only mutate but also assemble a range of actors who create the specific (and provisional) territory to which the policy idea may be applied. Any core 'essence' of the policy is thus cast into doubt. From this perspective, any project to identify the origins of the 'creative industries' in the West may be of historical interest but it is not determinant of its development in a new context nor grounds for judgement as to its adequacy vis-à-vis this origin.

Arjun Appadurai famously presented a series of global cultural flows or 'scapes', which combined to create a 'complex, overlapping, disjunctive order', as an indication of a 'global cultural economy'.[67] These 'scapes' are increasingly 'deterritorialized', creating and dissolving new identities and communities, straying across borders and undermining the fixed boundaries of the nation state. The paths through which they flow are 'non-isomorphic' and unpredictable, undermining the colonial scenarios of centre and periphery, homogenization, Americanization and commoditization.[68] These non-isomorphic global flows produce highly local-ized communal identities, erratic and disjunctive configurations productive of a rich global difference.

However, from the perspective of the creativity agenda, we suggest that these discrete policy 'technologies' come with a high degree of ideational or imaginary power. Appadurai's 'ideoscapes', which 'frequently have to do with the ideolo-gies of states', are composed of 'elements of the Enlightenment world-view [...] a concatenation of ideas, terms and images, including 'freedom', 'welfare', 'rights', 'sovereignty', 'representation' and the master-term 'democracy'.[69] If the 'master-narrative of the Enlightenment' had a certain internal logic in the West, he argues, its diasporic spread across the world since the nineteenth century has relaxed this internal logic and 'provided instead a loosely structured synopticon of politics, in which different nation-states [...] have organized their political cultures around different "keywords"'.[70] Appadurai presents a kaleidoscopic semiotic mix, driven by local and pragmatic adaptions, where a word like 'democracy' can mean very different things in very different contexts.

We would suggest that this is to underplay the continuing powerful effect of this Enlightenment 'master-narrative'. What is startlingly absent from Appadurai's account of non-isomorphic cultural flows is any sense of the non-cultural under-pinnings of these flows in an era marked by the end of the Cold War and the sub-sequent dominance of the 'Washington consensus'. Flows of technologies and finance, people and things, media and their industries, were organized around ideas that were more than floating keyword signifiers.

Thus this Enlightenment 'ideoscape', which helped organize the flows of cultural goods and services of the 'creative economy', came on the heels of the failure of a concerted attempt by the Third World actors within UNESCO's MacBride Com-mission to challenge the dominance of the Global North in media and communica-tions.[71] The defeat of the New World Information and Communication Order, and the rapid marginalization of UNESCO in the 1980s – primarily via the withdrawal of funding by the United States and the United Kingdom – was part of a reassertion of the US-led global hegemony that reached an apex with the collapse of the Soviet bloc and the USSR in 1991. This period also saw a massive expansion of telecom-munications and a global pushback against national broadcasting systems, primarily by US-based corporations backed by their government and global governance agen-cies.[72] Which is all to say that underpinning Appadurai's non-isomorphic cultural flows was a series of geopolitical shifts in the global communications system.

In particular, Appadurai ignored the strong ideational connection between lib-eral democracy and an expanding global capitalism, one that became extremely powerful in the 1990s as socialist and communist alternatives disappeared beneath the horizon. This connection had a very clear and explicit internal logic, though it had been rebooted, so to speak, through the emergent framework of neo-liberalism. It had a high degree of ideational cohesion that led to very real policy initiatives with very real consequences, whether this be the World Bank/IMF's austerity-driven reforms of indebted developing countries, the expansion of the General Agreement on Tariffs and Trade (GATT)/World Trade Organization (WTO), or the Washington Consensus writ large, that soft power flesh around the hard kernel of enforceable compliance. We might also point to the growing influence of the doctrine of democratic regime change that led to the Iraq war, and which could be seen as an act of 'tough love' built on the incontrovertible principle that liberal democracy was the sole guarantee of historical progress.

The 'ideoscape' is central to the kinds of global policy conjuncture in which 'creativity' brought new kinds of industries, new kinds of cities and new kinds of subjects together in a strongly affective formation. Creative industries arrived in 1998, seven years after the collapse of the USSR, and following a decade of debt-restructuring, austerity and neo-liberal reforms, which positioned the BRIC economies as new global growth engines entirely within the ambit of the Washington Consensus. At the same time, the 1997 Asian Financial Crisis was a blow to the self-confidence of the 'Asian Tigers' whose authoritarian development model now seemed outdated and ill-adapted to the new wave of innovation coming out of a US-led decade of growth.[73] It was widely assumed that China – along with the 'Asian Tigers' and BRIC countries – would inevitably head towards some kind of accommodation with liberal democratic forms. All of these primed important sections of Western governments and elites, who had already bought into discourses of innovation and the knowledge economy, to accept that such an economy required new kinds of creative subjects – subjects that might thrive best in those 'open' economies that had seen off the challenge of state-directed socialism in the USSR and, indeed, within their own domestic political arenas. It is here that we must take Appadurai's 'enlightenment world-view' seriously. More than a set of convenient keywords, it was also an affective imaginary which had been set around a neo-liberal, globalized capitalism in which 'open economies' and 'transparent' governance would provide the best guarantee of economic growth. Creativity was part of a strong reassertion, after a period of anti- and postcolonial contestation, that Western modernity was exemplary.

The China challenge

Thus, from a Western perspective, China seemed particularly ill-suited to the creativity agenda. Chinese culture has frequently been portrayed as being historically inward-looking, closed off behind its physical and mental Great Walls, refusing engagement with the diversity of a wider world. This has been a common trope not only among Western writers but also within China itself. To engage with this new creative modernization seemed to demand that, yet again, China had to move out of its traditional mindset and embrace the wind of change from the West. The association of modernization with a radical break with China's past has been, as we shall see, central to China's self-understanding. It reappeared in the soul-searching of the 1980s, represented best by the 1988 documentary *River Elegy*, which evoked the inertia of the Chinese past and the need for a new engagement with the 'ocean' of global history.[74] The image of Shanghai, as China's most Western city, has been crucial in this respect. Its historic association with the West would position it as spearhead in this next drive for modernization – a watchword of the CCP since 1978.

For Western observers, the problem has also been the 'balance' between state and market, and between state and citizen. China's authoritarian capitalism (if that is what it was) may be good for some things – like promoting manufacture and 'hard' infrastructure – but is unable to produce real creativity and wider innovation without some form of democratic and/or entrepreneurial 'bottom-up' involvement. These two sets of questions – China's closed inwardness and its authoritarian state – tend to run closely together.

On first sight, these questions appear as a function of China's transition from a statist command economy to a capitalist market economy. To what extent can the ruling Communist Party promote capitalism without a 'free' market economy and/or democracy? However, these questions have long been directed at other East Asian countries, which have pursued authoritarian statist routes to capitalism. Although China's state socialist past presented particular challenges, other East Asian countries also had state-directed economies and highly restricted (or non-existent) democratic structures. Many of these East Asian countries – Singapore perhaps pre-eminent among them – had successfully modernized, following a path different to that of the West (or at least different to that which the West presented as its past). They did so via heavy state investment, the promotion of national champions, protective tariffs and by gaining the assent of the middle classes to an authoritarian system in return for strong economic growth and strict labour discipline.[75]

By the end of the 1980s, these economically successful countries were able to present their path to modernization not as a deviation from a Western norm, a detour from which they were inevitably bound to rejoin the main route, but as a distinct East Asian path to development. Rejecting both Samuel Huntington's and Francis Fukuyama's universalizing claims for Western civilization and liberal market democracies, East Asian governments presented themselves as having achieved modernization without the dysfunctions that plagued the West – alienation, social fragmentation, grid-locked political systems and so on.[76] Using Huntington against himself, Confucian values – previously deemed to inhibit modernization – now provided a narrative of hard-working entrepreneurialism and acceptance of social hierarchy as the basis of economic success and social cohesion.[77]

These debates in turn take us back beyond contemporary state socialism and authoritarian capitalism to the long-standing coupling of tradition and authoritarianism in the figure of an 'Asiatic despotism' versus a future-oriented European modernity. This Eurocentric model had been challenged by economic historians, post-development and postcolonial theorists since the 1970s, as well as by the obvious success of East Asian economies.[78] However, the Asian Financial Crisis, new forms of technological innovation coming out of the United States and the growth of new economy discourses gave some Western countries a renewed sense of their capacity to lead global modernization. The belief that culture and creativity could not be adequately promoted by an authoritarian political system lay at the heart of liberal democratic self-understanding. Although the question of cultural and creative industries in China is usually presented as some archetypal conflict between state and market, we might better see it as part of an ongoing reframing of the nature of capitalist modernity.

Creativity and enlightenment

For many Western observers, a wholesale transformation of the Chinese polity would be necessary for the potential of the creative economy to be actualized. The creative industries – harbingers of the wider creative economy – require new kinds of subjects who can operate effectively only in a new kind of polity.

Will Hutton, a long-time supporter of the New Labour project in the United Kingdom, suggested that China's economic modernization was only half achieved. State-led capitalism has spurred rapid economic growth, but this was about to come apart because the polity has not been reformed on Western lines.[79] Hutton suggests a crisis is about to hit China; instead, his book came out just before the West was hit by one of its own. Hutton's historical argument is straightforward. Western capitalism became globally dominant because it grew up in conjunction with 'Enlightenment values' and the Westphalian state system that underpinned these. Enlightenment values emerged out of a new public sphere mediating between the state and the individual, and this had been made possible because of a fragmentation of state authority and the intense rivalry between these states within a relatively stable state system. This allowed a free circulation of knowledge and the contestation of tradition; the rule of law facilitating new forms of property, trade and finance; and increasing restraints on the action of states by 'opinion', demanding that its actions be rationally justified. The emergence and global success of European capitalism is absolutely inseparable from these Enlightenment values, and it is they that made the difference when the European system encountered the powerful Qing Empire in the early nineteenth century.

> These four elements – the pluralism developed by nearly continual war and state competition; profitable long-distance trade and the companies it created; a robust soft institutional infrastructure; and the universalisation of technology – kindled Europe's miracle and allowed it to overtake China [...] Uniting, underpinning, and embodying all four elements was the Enlightenment, and the public institutions it underwrote.[80]

The separation of state and society and the accountability of the former to the 'reasoned collective judgement' of the latter is the essence of Enlightenment, and this public sphere also underpins 'good economy and society'.[81] These non-market institutions allow the market to be successful because they link its operations to the aspirations of individuals to 'substantive freedom and the capacity 'to choose a life that one has reason to value'.[82] Crucially, China is lacking not just Enlightenment values but 'Enlightenment attitudes'.[83]

> So here is the mechanism, plural public institutions; and here is a consequence, human happiness. Enlightenment institutions need Enlightenment people to breathe life into them; modernity has to be won by real people who are prepared to imagine a life that they themselves want to make and are prepared to act on that concept, leaving behind the universe in which preferences are inherited and fixed [...] [T]his involves a mental shift from the traditional to the modern.[84]

Hutton repeats here the kind of discourse directed at China in the nineteenth century, not just by outsiders but by radical reformers within China itself. However, the modernity evoked here is now one associated with a knowledge economy that will continue to represent the West's great advantage. This is not just the 'hard knowledge' of science and technology skills (which is now more easily acquired by countries such as China) but also 'soft knowledge':

> the bundle of less tangible production inputs involving leadership, communication, emotional intelligence, the disposition to innovate, and the creation of social capital that harnesses hard knowledge and permits its effective

embodiment in goods and services and – crucially – its customisation. Their interaction and combination are at the heart of the knowledge economy.[85]

Soft knowledge and soft skills – what he calls 'tacit interactions' – are central to the knowledge economy; it is these which will continue to give the West its edge. These skills in turn rest, for Hutton, on a shift to Ronald Ingleharts's 'post-materialist' values, a sociological account of the impact of countercultural values on mainstream American society.[86] Creative industries then, like the knowledge economy as a whole, demand a cultural as well as a political transformation in China. One is not possible without the other. and both are related to a wider set of 'Enlightenment values', now inflected by post-1968 'cultural' values, within which economic growth has to be framed. No amount of exhortation to *be creative* will work unless the Chinese political system and the culture that it sustains are changed. This change will represent a transition to a complete modernity, a final break from the Chinese past and a full embrace of those universal values derived from the European Enlightenment that alone can underpin the global community.

This discourse directly echoes those of Adam Smith and Georg Hegel, in which the European 'rational' state and market economy index a universal historical progress.[87] Hutton does not consider the links between these kinds of universalizing discourses and European imperialism, nor the obvious contradictions between Enlightenment values and the actual experiences of that imperialism.[88] However, what is of most interest here is the new role of the knowledge economy in binding these values and capitalism together again. In an earlier epoch, it was the achievement of nation-statehood and the mobilization of the capacities of free citizens that was to drive modernization; now it is the circulation of useful knowledge enabled by the Enlightenment public sphere, joined to post-1960s' cultural capacity to handle this knowledge in a new service economy.

Hutton draws heavily on Joel Mokyr, who makes the case for capitalism as a Schumpeterian knowledge economy, driven by entrepreneurs operating in a social and political system which facilitates and rewards innovation.[89] Against this are the forces of vested interest and inertia – state bureaucracies, rent-seeking corporations, trade guilds, religious institutions and so on – which continually seek to impede their progress. In his evocation, not of knowledge per se but of 'useful knowledge' – practical and commercial – Mokyr (and Hutton follows him on this) sees the knowledge produced by the Enlightenment, and that required for the expansion of capitalism, as one and the same thing. What Hutton adds to this free circulation of useful knowledge is the emphasis on social networks, shared values and interpersonal skills (including emotional intelligence) that mark one of the key homologies between the creative industries and this knowledge economy.

It is this capacity to mobilize the 'soft infrastructure' that gives liberal democracy its innovative edge.

Both Hutton and Mokyr want to expand the narrow focus on markets in neo-classical economics – Frederick Hayek's 'extended order' of the market – by emphasizing the role of institutions and value systems in the emergence and operation of these markets.[90] Neither sees any contradiction between capitalism and the Enlightenment values embedded in the democratic public sphere. Indeed, the latter appear to find their justification in the facilitation of the former rather than any value they might have in their own right. Hutton's evocation of the creative economy insists on civil and political rights but, unlike Amartya Sen, puts them right back in the economic driving seat.[91] In this way, as in much of the creative industries literature, the new creative capacities (or 'capabilities' as Sen would have it) of the individual subject are justified primarily by their contribution to innovation-driven competitiveness.[92]

Hutton's concern is with Enlightenment values and the soul of capitalism, inflected through an account of the post-Fordist economy and 'post-materialist values'. What is interesting is his folding of the classic 'bourgeois revolution' thesis – that capitalism at some point demands political democracy to secure its interests, usually led by the bourgeoisie but latterly pushed along by workers and peasants[93] – into a demand for open markets and the free exchange of information. Hutton fails to recognize that innovation – 'useful' knowledge linked to commercialization – is perfectly possible in a non-democratic capitalism. He suggests that the kinds of cultural capacity required for innovation are incompatible with non-democratic capitalism, and yet divested as such cultural capacities are from any source of value outside economic innovation, it is hard to be as sanguine as he is. As Hayek and later neo-liberals argued, open markets and the free exchange of 'useful' information are not necessarily dependent on political democracy.[94] Ronald Coase, one of the key theorists of Chicago neo-liberalism, writes about China having successfully introduced a 'market for goods' and that now is the time for it to develop a 'market for ideas', making its economy 'knowledge-driven and innovative'.[95] There is no mention here of political democracy or civil rights; the only freedom required is that of the market.

There is in these knowledge economy accounts a too-easy association between the useful and the commercial, and an assumption that what is commercial is fully compatible with the open public sphere of 'opinion'. This ignores not just the increasing privatization of research and the mass extraction of private data for commercial use, but also the deliberate funding of commercial research to obfuscate the public sphere – as in tobacco and climate change. The evolution of knowledge capitalism and the creative economy has shown that there is no necessary connection between the commercialization of knowledge, the 'emotional' and tacit skills required for its production and monetization, and some wider process of democratization.[96] The autonomy of the 'creative worker' is increasingly monitored and subject to performance metrics,[97] just as the utopian world of creative work has to be set against the increased routinization and work-discipline among the low skilled,[98] as well as a context in which the highly skilled are increasingly forced into low-skilled jobs.[99] The required number of those with soft, creative skills is being rapidly reduced by computerization and robotics.[100] As much literature around cultural work has emphasized, the notion that the creative industries are intrinsically equitable and autonomous, or that they are necessarily coupled with an extension of social democracy, is simply not born out by the evidence.[101]

Hutton's classic New Labour attempt to link an updated social democracy with knowledge capitalism and the creative economy is deeply problematic – particularly when he suggests not only that they are necessarily co-dependent but also that the forms and values of European modernity represent their only possible configuration. Hutton presents as a deepening of 'enlightenment values' what is perhaps better seen as a new form of biopolitics, or of governmentality.[102] In Chapter 4, we will explore its links with neo-liberalism in more detail. But the social democratic promotion of 'creativity' has been a crucial part of the shift from a welfare to a 'workfare' society.[103] We are encouraged to become 'entrepreneurs of the self', to develop our capacity as individuals to navigate the 'risk society'. Hutton ignores the ways in which the soft skills and emotional intelligence he sees as rooted in a deepening of enlightenment can also be figured as new forms of the exploitation, commodification and privatization of our everyday life, our social connections, our affects; where the lifeworld as such has been annexed by new forms of distributed production, and the 'general intellect'[104] and 'immaterial labour'[105] are part of the 'social factory'.[106]

As we shall see, looked at from this perspective of developing new capacities in its population and new forms of governmentality to manage these, China certainly faces many significant challenges, but how to transition to enlightened liberal democracy is not necessarily chief among them.

Conclusion

For many in the West, Deng Xiaoping's 'reform and opening' was a natural resumption of a modernization process interrupted or distorted by Mao's Communist regime. Frank Dikotter suggests we reject the standard framing of Chinese history around the inevitable arrival of 1949, and that 'globalisation, rather than revolution' should be the organizing framework for understanding Chinese history in the twentieth century.[107] This framing around the ability, or otherwise, of

China to be 'open' to new ideas and move outside the stifling weight of its own history is now a new orthodoxy, but it is one that has long historical roots in the encounter between China and the West. This particular injunction to openness also comes at a time when the 'revolutionary' modernity represented by the ('short') twentieth-century Communist movement had been deemed simply a deferral or derailment of full or 'normal' modernity. However, if the development of creative forms of production and consumption in the contemporary economy requires new kinds of creative subjects operating in an open market economy, both facilitated by the basic forms of the liberal democratic state, then this marks much more than a break with Communism – it also implicates the whole of the Chinese past. The 'cultural creative industries' as policy construct is inevitably implicated in a much longer history of the interconnections between culture and modernization that goes back to the encounter between China and the West from the middle of the nineteenth century.

At stake in the post-1978 reforms, and in the specific role played by the creative and cultural industries, are questions around the configuration of state, market and subjectivity that go to the heart of debates around the trajectory of contemporary capitalism. The historical coupling of creativity and liberal democracy in the figure of an exemplary Western modernity is indeed a source of concern for the Chinese government. The discourse of creativity touches on the relationship between capitalism and modernity, and the privileged status of 'Euro-Modernity' as a universal model of this modernity.[108] Therefore, rather than follow any standard account of China's post-1978 reforms in terms of 'catch-up', 'one-sidedness', 'unevenness', 'lateness', or any of the other deficit models used to identify divergence from the ideal-typical and Eurocentric model of modernity, we suggest that the status of 'culture' in the post-1978 reforms needs to be understood as part of a longer historical process in which states, markets and subjectivities were configured very differently to that of 'the West'. It is to this we turn in the next chapters.

NOTES

1. O. Negt and A. Alexander Kluge, *Public Sphere and Experience: Towards an Analysis of the Bourgeois and Proletarian Public Sphere* (Minneapolis: University of Minnesota Press, 1993).

2. A. Girard, 'Cultural Industries: A Handicap or a New Opportunity for Cultural Development?', in *Cultural Industries: A Challenge for the Future of Culture*, ed. UNESCO (Paris: UNESCO, 1982).

3. F. Bianchini, 'GLC R.I.P. 1981–1986', *New Formations* 1 (1987): 103–17; N. Garnham, 'Public Policy in the Cultural Industries', in *Capitalism and Communication: Global Culture and the Economics of Information* (London: Sage, 1990); B. Rigby, *Popular Culture*

in Modern France: A Study of Cultural Discourse (London: Routledge, 1992); D. Looseley, *The Politics of Fun: Cultural Policy and Debate in Contemporary France* (Oxford and Washington, DC: Berg, 1995).

4. W. Baumol and W. Bowen, *Performing Arts: The Economic Dilemma* (New York: Twentieth Century Fund, 1966).

5. Cf. H. Becker, *Art Worlds* (Berkeley: University of California Press, 1982); R. A. Peterson, ed., *The Production of Culture* (Beverly Hills, CA: Sage, 1976); P. DiMaggio, 'Market Structures, the Creative Process, and Popular Culture', *Journal of Popular Culture* 11 (1977): 436–52.

6. P. Bourdieu, *Distinction: A Social Critique of the Judgement of Taste* (London: Routledge, 1986).

7. R. Williams, *Culture* (London: Fontana, 1981).

8. See discussion in J. O'Connor, *The Arts and Creative Industries* (Sydney: Australian Council for the Arts, 2011), 42–51, https://www.academia.edu/7072840/Arts_and_Creative_Industries. Accessed 26 January 2020.

9. Mark Fisher called this 'popular modernism'. See M. Fisher, *Ghosts of My Life: Writings on Depression, Hauntology and Lost Futures* (Winchester: Zero Books, 2014); and also O'Connor, The *Arts and Creative Industries*, 57–72.

10. Nicholas Garnham, who worked with the GLC, was explicit in his claim that the market was crucial to a modern democratic cultural policy. See: Garnham, 'Public Policy in the Cultural Industries', in *Capitalism and Communication*.

11. B. Miege, 'The Cultural Commodity', *Media, Culture & Society*, 1 (1979): 297–311; B. Miege, 'The Logics at Work in the New Cultural Industries', *Media, Culture & Society* 9 (1987): 273–89; B. Miege, *The Capitalisation of Cultural Production* (New York: International General, 1989); Garnham, *Capitalism and Communication*. For his take on the creative industries: N. Garnham, 'From Cultural to Creative Industries, an Analysis of the Implications of the "Creative Industries" Approach to Arts and Media Policy Making in the United Kingdom', *International Journal of Cultural Policy* 11, no.1 (2005): 15–29.

12. The most comprehensive overview of this field is D. Hesmondhalgh, *The Cultural Industries*, 4th ed. (London: Sage, 2019). Cf. 27–38 for the distinctiveness of the cultural industries.

13. V. Mosco, *The Political Economy of Communication* (London: Sage, 2009); for an overview see Hesmondhalgh, *Cultural Industries*, 47–80.

14. N. Garnham, 'The Media and the Public Sphere', in *Habermas and the Public Sphere*, ed. C. Calhoun (Cambridge, MA: MIT Press, 1992), 359–76; N. Garnham, *Emancipation, The Media, And Modernity: Arguments about the Media and Social Theory* (Oxford: Oxford University Press, 2000); Miege, 'The Cultural Commodity'.

15. Cf. Hesmondhalgh, *Cultural Industries*, 135–75

16. K. Polanyi, *The Great Transformation: The Political and Economic Origins of Our Time* (New York: Beacon, [1944] 1957); M. Granovetter, 'Economic Action and Social

Structure: The Problems of Embeddedness', in *The Sociology of Economic Life*, ed. M. Granovetter and R. Swedberg (Oxford: Westview Press, 1992).

17. The work of Storper and Christopherson on film production, and later Alan Scott on a number of different product systems, stand out as crucial in identifying the various factors involved localized systems of cultural commodity production. See: S. Christopherson and M. Storper, 'The City as Studio; the World as Back Lot: The Impact of Vertical Disintegration on the Location of the Motion Picture Industry', *Environment and Planning D: Society and Space* 4 (1986): 305–20; S. Christopherson and M. Storper, 'The Effects of Flexible Specialization on Industrial Politics and the Labour Market: The Motion Picture Industry', *Industrial and Labour Relations Review* 42, no. 3 (1989): 331–47; A. J. Scott, *The Cultural Economy of Cities* (London: Routledge, 2000).

18. A. Marshall, *Principles of Economics* (London: Macmillan,1920); M. Porter, 'Location, Competition and Economic Development: Local Clusters in a Global Economy', *Economic Development Quarterly* 14 (2000): 15–34.

19. M. Storper, *The Regional World* (New York: Guildford Press, 1997); Christopherson and Storper, 'The City as Studio' and 'Effects of Flexible Specialization on Industrial Politics and the Labour Market'; M. Storper and A. J. Venables, 'Buzz: Face-to-Face Contact and the Urban Economy' (London: Centre for Economic Performance, London School of Economics and Political Science, 2003), http://eprints.lse.ac.uk/20008/1/Buzz_Face-to-Face_Contact_and_the_Urban_Economy.pdf. Accessed 26 January 2020.

20. See, for example, M. Piore and C. Sabel, *The Second Industrial Divide: Possibilities for Prosperity* (New York: Basic Books, 1986).

21. R. Hewison, *Cultural Capital: The Rise and Fall of Creative Britain* (London: Verso Books, 2014).

22. F. Kermode, *The Sense of an Ending: Studies in the Theory of Fiction* (Oxford: Oxford University Press, 1967).

23. The classic statement of this was S. Lash and J. Urry, *The End of Organised Capitalism* (London: Polity, 1987) followed by a work in which they more explicitly linked these transformations to the cultural industries: S. Lash and J. Urry, *Economies of Signs and Space* (London: Sage, 1994).

24. For a fuller discussion see J. O'Connor, 'Creative Industries: A New Direction?', *International Journal of Cultural Policy* 15, no. 4 (2009): 387–404; J. O'Connor, 'The Cultural and Creative Industries', in *The Ashgate Companion to Cultural Policy and Planning*, ed. D. Stevenson and G. Young (Abingdon: Routledge, 2013), 171–84; K. Oakley and J. O'Connor, 'Cultural Industries: An Introduction', in *The Routledge Companion to the Cultural Industries*, ed. K. Oakley and J. O'Connor (London: Routledge, 2015), 1–32; M. Banks and J. O'Connor, 'Inside the Whale (and How to Get Out of There): Moving on from Two Decades of Creative Industries Research', *European Journal of Cultural Studies* (2017): 1–18; J. O'Connor and M. Gibson, *Culture, Creativity, Cultural Economy: A*

Review, 2015, http://acola.org.au/PDF/SAF01/6.%20Culture%20creativity%20cultural%20economy.pdf. Accessed 6 October 2014.

25. Hewison, *Cultural Capital*; Garnham, 'From Cultural to Creative Industries'.

26. E. Pound and E. Fenollosa, *Instigations of Ezra Pound* (Whitefish, MT: Kessinger Publishing, 2008).

27. D. Bell, *The Cultural Contradictions of Capitalism* (New York: Basic Books, 1976); D. Brook, *BOBOs in Paradise: The New Upper Class and How They Got There* (New York: Simon and Schuster, 2000).

28. Cf. Hewison, *Cultural Capital* and Hesmondhalgh, *Cultural Industries*.

29. Hewison, *Cultural Capital*.

30. DCMS, *Creative Industries Mapping Document* (London: Department of Culture, Media and Sport, 1998); Cf. J. O'Connor, *Cultural Production in Manchester*, 1998, https://www.academia.edu/8697375/Cultural_Production_in_Manchester_1998_. Accessed 16 September 2019. As of 2015 these became: *Advertising and Marketing: Architecture; Crafts; Design: Product, Graphic and Fashion Design; Film, TV, Video, Radio and Photography; IT, Software and Computer Services; Publishing; Museums, Galleries and Libraries; Music, Performing and Visual Arts.*

31. Ibid.

32. John Howkin's book *The Creative Economy*, with which this definition is often associated, pointed to industries that dealt in intellectual property, monetized ('making money from ideas') via patents, copyright, trademarks and proprietary designs. However, only copyright could be said to predominantly pertain to the cultural sector (though it should be noted that IP does not cover all the different kinds of transactions within the sector either) and the vast majority of IP-generating economic activity has little to do with the cultural/creative industries. For further discussion, see: J. Howkins, *The Creative Economy: How People Make Money from Ideas* (London: Allen Lane, 2001).

33. Cf. O. Mould, *Against Creativity. Everything You Have Been Told About Creativity Is Wrong* (London: Verso, 2018).

34. NESTA, *A Dynamic Mapping of the UK's Creative Industries* (London: NESTA, 2012), http://www.nesta.org.uk/publications/dynamic-mapping-uks-creative-industries. Accessed 9 October 2014.

35. Ibid., 24.

36. Ibid.

37. G. Tremblay, 'Creative Statistics to Support Creative Economy Politics', *Media, Culture & Society* 33, no. 2 (2011): 289–98; J. O'Connor and M. Gibson, *Culture, Creativity, Cultural Economy: A Review*, Report for Australian College of Learned Academies, 2014, https://www.academia.edu/8368925/Culture_Creativity_Cultural_Economy_A_Review. Accessed 6 October 2014; Garnham, 'From Cultural to Creative Industries'.

38. A. Pratt, 'The Cultural Economy: A Call for Spatialised "Production of Culture" Perspectives', *International Journal of Cultural Studies* 7 (2004): 117–28.

39. A. Pratt, 'Locating the Cultural Economy', in *Cultures and Globalization: The Cultural Economy*, ed. H. Anheier and Y. R. Isar (London: Sage, 2008), 42–51, 44.

40. Y. R. Isar, *The Cultural Industries and the Economy of Culture* (Brussels: Culture Action Europe, 2015), https://cultureactioneurope.org. Accessed 19 September 2019.

41. A. Badiou, *Deleuze: The Clamor of Being* (Minneapolis: University of Minnesota Press, 2000), 55.

42. Garnham, 'From Cultural to Creative Industries', 20

43. M. Porter, 'The Competitive Advantage of the Inner City', *Harvard Business Review*, May–June (2005).

44. Allen Scott calls cultural commodity production the 'cultural-cognitive industries'. See: A. J. Scott, 'Beyond the Creative City: Cognitive–Cultural Capitalism and the New Urbanism', *Regional Studies* 48 no. 4 (2014): 565–78

45. R. Barbrook and A. Cameron, 'The Californian Ideology', *Science as Culture* 6, no. 1 (1996): 44–72; on the myth of tech-mavericks, see S. Olma, *In Defence of Serendipity. For a Radical Politics of Innovation* (London: Repeater Books, 2016).

46. L. Boltanski and E. Chiapello, *The New Spirit of Capitalism* (London: Verso Books, 2005).

47. H. Marcuse, *One-Dimensional Man* (New York: Beacon, 1964); Bell, *Cultural Contradictions of Capitalism*.

48. J. O'Connor and X. Gu, 'A New Modernity? The Arrival of "Creative Industries" in China', *International Journal of Cultural Studies*, Special China Issue, 9, no. 3 (2006): 271–83, 274.

49. A. Ross, *No Collar: The Humane Workforce and its Hidden Costs* (Chicago: Temple University Press, 2004); A. McRobbie, *Be Creative: Making a Living in the New Culture Industries* (Cambridge: Polity, 2016).

50. Cf. P. Fleming, *The Death of Homo Economicus: Work, Debt and the Myth of Endless Accumulation* (London: Pluto Press, 2017).

51. For an overview in respect to cultural labour, cf. R. Gill and A. Pratt, 'In the Social Factory. Immaterial Labour, Precariousness and Creative Work', *Theory, Culture & Society* 25, no. 7–8 (2008): 1–30.

52. J. Hartley, 'Introduction', in *Creative Industries*, ed. J. Hartley (Oxford: Blackwell, 2005), 5.

53. H. Jenkins, *Convergence Culture. Where Old and New Media Collide* (New York: New York University Press, 2008).

54. J. Hartley and J. Potts, *Cultural Science: A Natural History of Stories, Demes, Knowledge and Innovation* (London: Bloomsbury Press, 2014).

55. S. Olma, *Autonomy and Weltbezug: Towards an Aesthetic of Performative Defiance* (Breda: Avans Hogeschool, 2016).

56. Cf. D. Hesmondhalgh, K. Oakley, D. Lee and M. Nesbett, *Culture, Economy and Politics. The Case of New Labour* (London: Palgrave Macmillan, 2015).

57. D. H. Pink, 'Revenge of the Right Brain'. *Wired*, 2 February 2005, http://www.wired.com/2005/02/brain/. Accessed 9 August 2016.

58. N. Ferguson, *Civilization: The Six Killer Apps of Western Power* (London: Penguin, 2011), 324.

59. J. B. Gewirtz, 'China's Long March to Technological Supremacy: The Roots of Xi Jinping's Ambition to "Catch Up and Surpass"', *Foreign Affairs*, 27 August 2019.

60. Cf. H. Wang, *The Politics of Imagining Asia* (Cambridge, MA: Harvard University Press, 2011); M. E. Indelicato and I. Pražić, 'Legacies of Empire: From the "Religions of China" to the "Confucian Heritage" Learner', *Paedagogica Historica* 55, no. 2 (2018): 277–94.

61. J. Peck, 'Struggling with the Creative Class', *International Journal of Urban and Regional Research* 29, no. 4 (2005): 740–70; L. Kong, C. Gibson, L.-M. Khoo and A.-L. Semple, 'Knowledges of the Creative Economy: Towards a Relational Geography of Diffusion and Adaptation in Asia', *Asia Pacific Viewpoint* 47, no. 2 (2006): 173–94; L. Kong, 'Transnational Mobilities and the Making of Creative Cities', *Theory, Culture & Society* 31, no. 7/8 (2014): 273–89.

62. P. M. Haas, 'Epistemic Communities and International Policy Coordination', *International Organization* 46, no. 1 (1992): 1–35; Cf. P. Alasuutari, *The Synchronization of National Policies. Ethnography of the Global Tribe of Moderns* (London: Routledge, 2016).

63. Cf. J. O'Connor, *Resources of Hope. Creative Economy and Development in the Global South* (Koln: Institut für Auslandsbeziehungen 'Input', 2019), https://www.ifa.de/wp-content/uploads/2019/06/ifa_input_OConnor_Creative-Economy-and-Development.pdf. Accessed 20 September 2019.

64. B. Garner, *The Politics of Cultural Development: Trade, Cultural Policy and the UNESCO Convention on Cultural Diversity* (London: Routledge, 2016); B. Garner and J. O'Connor, 'Rip It Up and Start Again? The Contemporary Relevance of the 2005 UNESCO Convention on Cultural Diversity', *Journal of Law, Social Justice and Global Development* (forthcoming); C. de Beukelaer and J. O'Connor, 'The Creative Economy and the Development Agenda: The Use and Abuse of "Fast Policy"', in *Art and International Development*, ed. P. Stupples and K. Teaiwa (London: Routledge, 2016), 27–47.

65. J. Peck and N. Theodore, 'Mobilizing Policy: Models, Methods and Mutations', *Geoforum* 41 (2012): 169–74, 173; Cf. J. Peck and N. Theodore, 'Follow the Policy: A Distended Case Approach', *Environment and Planning* 44, no. 1 (2012): 21–30

66. J. O'Connor and X. Gu, 'Creative Clusters in Shanghai: Transnational Intermediaries and the Creative Economy', in *Making Cultural Cities in Asia: Mobility, Assemblage and the Politics of Aspirational Urbanism*, ed. J. Wang, T. Oakes and Y. Yang (London: Routledge, 2016), 21–35.

67. A. Appadurai, 'Disjuncture and Difference in the Global Cultural Economy', *Theory, Culture & Society* 7, no. 2–3 (1990): 295–310, 296.

68. Appadurai uses Stuart Hall's account of encoding/decoding, in which those who receive semiotic content have a high degree of latitude in how they read and use ('decode') that which the sender had 'encoded'. See: S. Hall, 'Encoding, Decoding', in *Culture, Media,*

Language. Working Papers in Cultural Studies, 1972–1979, ed. Centre for Contemporary Cultural Studies (London: Routledge, 1980), 128–38.

69. Appadurai, 'Disjuncture and Difference', 229.

70. Ibid., 300.

71. Cf. C. Sparks and C. Roach, 'Editorial: Farewell to NWICO?', *Media, Culture & Society* 12, no. 3 (1990): 275–81; U. Carlsson, 'The Rise and Fall of NWICO', *Nordicom Review* 24, no. 2 (2017): 31–67.

72. Cf. Hesmondhalgh, *Cultural Industries*, 135–75.

73. Cf. A. Bolesta, *China and Post-Socialist Development* (Bristol: Policy Press, 2015).

74. *River Elegy* is a CCTV documentary directed by Jun Xia in 1988.

75. A. Ong, *Flexible Citizenship: The Cultural Logics of Transnationality* (Durham, NC: Duke University Press, 1999); H. -J. Chang, *Kicking Away the Ladder: Development Strategy in Historical Perspective* (London: Anthem Press, 2003).

76. S. Huntington, 'The Clash of Civilisations', *Foreign Affairs* 72, no. 3 (1993): 22–49; F. Fukuyama, *The End of History and the Last Man* (New York: Free Press, 1992).

77. Ong, *Flexible Citizenship*.

78. The literature is now extensive. From an economic history perspective cf. R. B. Wong, *China Transformed: Historical Change and the Limits of European Experience* (Ithaca: Cornell University Press, 1997); K. Pomeranz, *The Great Divergence: Europe, China and the Making of the Modern World Economy* (Princeton, NJ: Princeton University Press, 2000). From a postcolonial perspective, cf. D. Chakrabarty, *Provincializing Europe: Postcolonial Thought and Historical Difference* (Princeton, NJ: Princeton University Press, 2000). See also H. Wang, *China from Empire to Nation State* (Cambridge: Harvard University Press, 2014).

79. W. Hutton, *The Writing on the Wall: China and the West in the 21st Century* (London: Little, Brown, 2007).

80. Ibid., 58.

81. Ibid., 170.

82. Ibid., 171. Hutton is quoting A. Sen, *Development as Freedom* (Oxford: Oxford University Press, 1999), 285.

83. Ibid., 1.

84. Ibid., 171.

85. Ibid., 311.

86. R. Inglehart, *The Silent Revolution: Changing Values and Political Styles Among Western Publics* (Princeton: Princeton University Press, 1977); R. Indergaard and C. Weizel, *Modernization, Cultural Change, and Democracy: The Human Development Sequence* (Cambridge: Cambridge University Press, 2005).

87. Cf. Wang Hui's discussion of this with regards to China: Wang, *China from Empire to Nation State*, Ch. 3.

88. Extensively analysed by P. Mishra, *From the Ruins of Empire: The Revolt against the West and the Remaking of Asia* (London: Penguin Books, 2012).

89. J. Mokyr, *The Gifts of Athena: Historical Origins of the Knowledge Economy* (Princeton: Princeton University Press, 2002).

90. F. Hayek, *The Fatal Conceit: The Errors of Socialism* (Chicago: University of Chicago Press, 1988).

91. Hutton quotes Amartya Sen in support but, though Sen sees political and civil rights as contributing to growth, for him they are also valuable in themselves. This point he directed at Singapore's President Lee Kuan Yew who, in turn, argued that these rights could be denied if economic development required it. For further discussion, see: Sen, *Development as Freedom*, 15.

92. Cf. NESTA, *A Manifesto for the Creative Economy* (London: NESTA, 2013), http://www.nesta.org.uk/sites/default/files/a-manifesto-for-the-creative-economy-april13.pdf. Accessed 9 October 2014.

93. B. Moore, *Social Origins of Dictatorship and Democracy: Lord and Peasant in the Making of the Modern World* (Boston: Beacon, 1966).

94. W. Davies, *The Limits of Neoliberalism. Authority, Sovereignty and the Logic of Competition* (London: Sage, 2014); W. Streeck, *Buying Time: The Delayed Crisis of Democratic Capitalism* (London: Verso, 2014); C. Crouch, *Post-Democracy* (Chichester: John Wiley, 2004).

95. R. Coase and N. Wang, *How China Became Capitalist* (London: Palgrave Macmillan, 2012), 203.

96. The literature is growing. Cf. N. Ettlinger, 'The Openness Paradigm', *New Left Review* 89 (2014): 89–100; E. Morozov, *The Net Delusion: The Dark Side of the Web* (Philadelphia: Public Affairs, 2011); A. Taylor, *The People's Platform: Taking Back Power and Culture in the Digital Age* (London: Fourth Estate, 2014); S. Zuboff, *Surveillance Capitalism: The Fight for a Human Future at the New Frontier of Power* (London: Profile Books, 2019).

97. D. Hesmondhalgh and S. Baker, *Creative Labour: Media Work in Three Cultural Industries* (London and New York: Routledge, 2011).

98. T. Miller, 'Hollywood Cognitarians', in *The Routledge Companion to the Cultural Industries*, ed. K. Oakley and J. O'Connor (London and New York: Routledge, 2018), 319–29.

99. B. Lessard and S. Baldwin, *Net Slaves: True Tales of Working the Web* (New York: McGraw-Hill, 2000).

100. Cf. the review of recent literature on this by J. Lanchester, 'The Robots Are Coming', *London Review of Books* 37, no. 5 (2015): 1–8.

101. M. Banks, *The Politics of Cultural Work* (London: Palgrave, 2009); K. Oakley and D. O'Brien, *Cultural Value and Inequality. A Critical Literature Review* (London: Arts and Humanities Research Council [AHRC], 2015).

102. M. Foucault, *Society Must Be Defended: Lectures at the Collège de France, 1975–1976* (London: Penguin, 2003); P. Miller and T. Rose, *Governing the Present* (London: Polity, 2008)

103. Foucault, *Society Must Be Defended*, 226; U. Beck, *Risk Society: Towards a New Modernity* (London: Sage, 1992); B. Jessop, 'Towards a Schumpeterian Workfare State: Preliminary Remarks on Post-Fordist Political Economy', *Studies in Political Economy* 40, no. 1 (1993): 7–39.

104. C. Vercellone, 'From Formal Subsumption to General Intellect: Elements for a Marxist Reading to the Thesis of Cognitive Capitalism', *Historical Materialism* 15, no. 1 (2007): 13–36.

105. M. Lazzarato, 'Immaterial Labour', in *Radical Thought in Italy*, ed. P. Virno and M. Hardt (Minneapolis: University of Minnesota Press, 1996), 132–46.

106. Gill and Pratt, 'In the Social Factory'. See also A. McRobbie, 'Is Passionate Work Neoliberal Delusion?', *Open Democracy*, 22 April 2015, https://www.opendemocracy.net/transformation/angela-mcrobbie/is-passionate-work-neoliberal-delusion. Accessed 22 October 2015.

107. F. Dikotter, *The Age of Openness: China before Mao* (Berkeley: University of California Press, 2008), 3.

108. 'Euro-Modernity' is a term used by Lawrence Grossberg. See L. Grossberg, *Cultural Studies in the Future Tense* (Durham, NC: Duke University Press, 2010). As we will have occasion to note below, just as 'Confucianism' is an immense simplification of a complex historical formation, so too is 'Euro-Modernity'. Benjamin Schwartz warns of the simplification of both, and like many others, he wants to identify different, perhaps contradictory, strands within modernity – in his case ideals of democracy, equality and justice, sitting alongside the Faustian and Promethean search for 'wealth and power'. This will be discussed below. Cf. B. Schwartz, *In Search of Wealth and Power: Yen Fu and the West* (Cambridge, MA: Cambridge University Press, 1964), 237–47.

2

Culture, Modernity and the Nation State

A traumatic modernity

Culture and modernization have been inextricably linked in China. The two notions emerged at the same time and under the same emergency: the threat of defeat and dismemberment by imperialist powers unless the country could modernize itself. This encounter resulted in a jolt of self-awareness, where a world centred on the Middle Kingdom – *tianxia* – became one nation among others. It was a shock registered initially in the field of diplomacy and new forms of international law, but it gradually deepened into a self-awareness of a distinct and ancient 'civilization' now under threat.[1]

As Raymond Williams's well-known etymology of the word in European languages illustrates, 'culture' as it emerged over the course of the eighteenth and nineteenth centuries acquired the meaning of a general social progress from primitive to civilized, as well as designating a range of particular 'civilizations'.[2] These were classified either in terms of a teleological progress leading up to the modern European nation state – as in the Hegelian formulation – or, later in the nineteenth century, as an evolutionary competition for survival under the rubric of 'Social Darwinism'. The deepening of Chinese self-recognition, in its encounter with the West, resulted, towards the turn of the century, in a group of new terms: 'civilization' (*wenming*), 'national essence' (*guocui*), 'culture' (*wenhua*) and a term for 'literature' (*wenxue*) as a privileged form of that culture. The shock of self-recognition demanded new concepts and terms, and many of these were borrowed from a Japan which had taken the lead in transforming its polity.[3] The new words did not just designate a newly conscious national essence; their novelty and provenance suggested culture was a site demanding active, urgent intervention. Not only that, but these terms emerged already inserted within a powerful binary of Eastern (*dongfang*) and Western (*xifang*) that could only cause a sense of foreboding about the survival of one in the face of the other. Social Darwinism, introduced into China by Yan Fu in the mid-1890s,[4] represented a call to arms – evolve or go extinct – that was part of a general context in which a reformed 'culture' would be essential to survival.[5] 'Culture' was thus a source of identity and of deep anxiety, with many scholar-officials (*shi*) coming to feel that there were no resources in Chinese culture capable of effecting this renewal.[6] The price of national renewal was felt to be that of consigning China's cultural project to a traditional, and redundant, past.

Modernization was initially associated with the obvious technological – especially military – superiority of the Western powers. As Confucian scholar and administrator Feng Guifen wrote: 'What we have to learn from the barbarians is only one thing: solid ships and effective guns.'[7] From the 1860s, the 'self-strengthening movement', led by a concerned gentry and elements of the imperial administration, set itself the task of acquiring Western technological knowledge while keeping its essential Chinese values intact. Captured by the famous adage 'Chinese learning for essence and Western learning for means', this attempt to separate substantive value and instrumental means was already being challenged by the 1880s.[8] It could not simply be a question of adopting Western military and other technology, nor just learning the techniques and protocols of speaking to the powers that wielded these technologies in the new diplomatic language of formally equal sovereign states. Qing scholar-officials, inside and outside the administration, increasingly recognized that the acquisition and productive use of such knowledge would demand wider and deeper internal transformations in the Qing Empire.

The self-strengthening movement had begun to focus on large-scale agricultural, commercial and industrial reforms in order to provide the economic foundations of a strong military and state. In the decades following the often-violent encounter with the Western powers, it became apparent that the Qing Empire was not dealing with science and technology alone but with a new kind of polity – that of the nation state. Although coming (as Qing scholars quickly discovered) with a bewildering variety of institutional forms, there were some core identifiable characteristics of these nation states. They all claimed in some way to rule over a particular people or 'nation', and their rootedness in this nation was the basis of their legitimacy. More importantly, these states had acquired the ability to harness the capacities of their people-nation and project it across the globe with unprecedented effectiveness. Their military power was underpinned by new forms of administration that could mobilize a newly identified social body made up of new kinds of subject. After China's defeat by the Japanese in 1895 and the humiliating Treaty of Shimonoseki, the idea that foreign knowledge could be simply grafted onto a Chinese essence was increasingly rejected. Thus began a process of intellectual engagement with the Western powers in which not just the survival of the dynasty, but also the long-standing civilizational project it represented, depended on its ability to utilize Western knowledge to meet the threat posed by these powers.

This encounter with the Western powers raised complex issues for the Qing Dynasty, where scholars and reforming administrators were forced to look beyond traditional or inert forms of Confucianism.[9] The project to open up traditional categories to allow the emperor to be re-legitimated in terms of a new Chinese people-nation, one capable of acting as a historical subject as demanded by the exigencies of survival in the face of external threat, resulted in an accelerating engagement with Western ideas.[10] After 1895, and again following the failure of the '100 days reform' and the catastrophe of the Boxer Rebellion, both reformers and radicals alike agreed that responding to the imperialist threat – for that is how the elites saw this encounter[11] – would involve a restructuring of the polity in quite fundamental ways. These would be not just the standard 'modern reforms', such as those imposed on Egypt or the Ottoman Empire.[12] Rather, they would constitute a radical reframing of the very basis of state and society, from which an effective nation state (*minzuguojia*) could emerge, its legitimacy resting on the ability to identify, effectively represent and administratively mobilize a new kind of 'social body' made up of new citizens (*xinmin*). After 1900, the notion of 'national essence' and of Chinese civilization had been uncoupled from the specific dynastic form represented by the Qing, and had become an object of reform in its own right. This was to reach fruition in the New Culture and May Fourth movements of 1916 and 1919, which looked for a radical restructuring of 'culture' as a foundational aspect of a new political project.[13]

The word 'new' (*xin*) is crucial as it gained almost totemic value after the turn of the century. It signified not just reform but also a systemic rejection of the old as the precondition for that reform. The external threat of Imperialist exigency demanded a new, linear sense of history. As Chen Duxiu wrote: 'The evolution of human civilisation is replacing old with the new, like a river flowing on, an arrow flying away, constantly continuing and constantly changing.'[14] It was a history whose law was progress, and in which each nation-people must find a *raison d'etre* or perish. The recognition of 'national essence' came with a sense that it needed to be radically reconstructed in order to break with the past. But how could traditional forms of thought provide the basis for such a radical renewal when they were responsible for leaving China at the mercy of the imperialist powers? For an increasing number of radical reformers and revolutionaries, the 'new' necessarily had to be derived from the West, and their forms of knowledge and practice adopted, however painful this might be. The present (*jin*) becomes opposed to the past (*gu*), a past whose rejection is a precondition for arriving at the modern.[15] This radical break with the past is expressed by Chen Duxiu's iconoclastic essay of 1916:

> We shall regard everything from the founding of our nation until 1915 as ancient history; let all things from the past perish as of 1916, and everything hereafter begin with 1916. We should exert new energy (*xinxue*) in order to present a new character, a new country, and new society, and new family, and a new

nation (*minzu*). Once we have this new nation, then we will begin to live up to our vows as humans [...] , we will begin to have enough value to interact with the white race [...] , and we will begin to have the qualifications to inhabit this piece of land we live upon.[16]

This did not go uncontested, but it did become the dominant trope in China's project of modernization (including the Marxist), as it did, suitably adapted, for Western observers. In this way, the encounter between the Qing Empire and the new, powerful European nation states has been locked into a binary account of the 'traditional' (or 'feudal'[17]) and the 'modern', and in which the index of modernity is the ability to change from a traditional empire into a modern nation state. Very briefly here we want to loosen up this linear, even teleological account in order to think through the issues currently at play around culture and modernization.

Traditional and modern

In Benedict Anderson's seminal account of the rise of nationalism, pre-modern dynastic legitimations inevitably gave way to those in which the state rooted itself in a nation.[18] These new 'imagined communities' rested on forms of collective identity – identities which the state claimed to represent – made possible by new forms of print-based communication (newspapers and the novel especially) and the logo-centric, de-sacralized forms of reasoning (including the 'empty time' of the calendar and clock) these gave rise to. In this account, the new form of the nation state – a state form whose legitimacy derived from a claim to represent a distinct people-nation that it would lead into a linear, secular future[19] – could only appear to a pre-modern Qing Empire as a radically threatening alternative system destined to replace it. From this perspective, the period from 'self-strengthening' and the late Qing reforms, through the 1911 revolution and into the full nation-building projects of the 1920s – reforms in state administration, diplomacy, education, military technology and organization, agriculture, industry, transport and so on – need to be seen in terms of a new nation-state formation in embryo, gradually breaking out of the moribund forms of the feudal pre-modern. We suggest, however, that this is not necessarily so, and that we need to break from such 'methodological nationalism'.[20]

The standard narrative for modern China has been one in which a feudal Qing Dynasty (inevitably) failed the historical test of transforming itself into a modern state (Japan's Meiji Restoration being a stand-out example of successful self-reform). This failure ushered in a chaotic historical period in which various agents competed to establish a nation state, a form alone capable of embarking on a coherent modernization programme and pulling its population from an agrarian past into an industrialized future. Both liberal democratic and Marxist accounts posit the Qing Empire as 'feudal' and historically disqualified from the task of Chinese state-building and modernization. The late Qing might have begun to implement new military and administrative reforms, to promote infrastructure, markets and an indigenous industrial capitalism, and launch various educational and scientific initiatives, but these were to be seen as the beginnings of a modernization project in which – as Chen Duxiu, one of the leaders of the May Fourth movement was to write – Mr. Confucius would eventually be replaced by Mr. Science and Mr. Democracy.[21]

This narrative, constructed around the opposition of pre-modern empire and modern nation state, has been increasingly challenged. The firm equation of nation state and modernity – what Perry Anderson has called an *entelechy*[22] – has somewhat unravelled. However, we view the continued role of the nation state, its strict equation with the force of historical progress – methodological nationalism – has been seriously weakened. So too the strict opposition between 'tradition' and 'modern' which have been woven into its narrative.

The May Fourth movement of 1919 fixed an equation of the imperial dynasty with (Confucian, feudal) tradition and the nation state with modernity. Tradition referred to ingrained beliefs and practices, useless knowledge, empty forms and a deference to the past whose overcoming would be central to modernization. Getting rid of these things would involve the kind of 'cultural revolution' with which Lu Xun is often associated.[23] The call to break with tradition came out of a longer period of deep demoralization among Chinese intellectuals (*zhishifenzi*) faced with the historical 'impasse' of their encounter with the West. Therefore, the revolution announced by the May Fourth movement could only be a 'bitter' one.[24]

The exigencies of a forced modernization were thus experienced as a civilizational issue, demanding a transformation of fundamental values, meaning systems and social practices, rendering traditional systems both redundant and obstructive. As Perry Anderson wrote (apropos of Russia):

> Confronting the expansion of the industrialized powers of the West, every major extra-European society faced the dilemma of how best to avoid subjugation by them. Did the only hope of independent survival lie in swift emulation of them, or was that simply a road to self-destruction, from whose dangers rediscovery of the deepest sources of indigenous tradition, duly purified, could alone save the nation?[25]

The challenge of the West lay not just in its very real economic and military power but also in a normative, ontological threat that seemed set to shatter existing state and social structures (which it mostly did) along with the traditional meaning systems with which these were entwined. Theodore Huters, using Mao's notion of China as 'semi-colonial', suggests that China was in a unique situation,

> [w]herein a nation was obliged, under an indigenous government, to so extensively modify its culture to save it that questions inevitably rose as to whether the resulting entity was that which was intended to be saved in the first place.[26]

Following encounters with the West, reformers across the Ottoman lands, the subcontinent of India and elsewhere across Asia were often forced to radically rethink traditional legitimation and the foundational purpose of good government. Such experiences produced a profound shock whose effects continue to this day.[27] These ongoing conflicts and tensions touch on how states and citizens negotiate historically formed identities and meaning systems within a global system dominated for two centuries by norms taken from Western modernity.[28]

Confucianism beyond 'tradition'

In China, 'tradition' tends to mean 'Confucianism', and we need to discuss this in some detail before moving on to the notion of culture as reform.

Approaching 'Confucianism' as a form of 'traditional' knowledge is fraught with difficulties, not least being the very construction of that Confucianism by Western 'orientalist' knowledge production.[29] We are less concerned here with Confucianism as a structuring philosophical foundation and more as an active resource for specific historical actors thinking through fundamental ethical and political questions.[30] Confucianism is a complex evolving set of concepts and practices, intertwining with those other traditions of thought commonly named as Legalism and Daoism, which formed part of the available repertoire of concepts.[31] It is crucial that any such approach to this Confucian tradition be more than that of an encounter between the traditional pre-rational and the modern rational. It would need to be in a space in which Western and Chinese systems or traditions are allowed a dialogue, or at least a negotiated translation, around the terms and the knowledge and values they designate.

Mark Elvin has made a powerful argument that, uniquely among pre-modern systems of belief such as Christianity, Judaism, Islam, Hinduism and Buddhism,

> Confucianism is the only one that has to all intents and purposes disappeared. To put it more precisely, what has vanished is *scriptural* Confucianism, the system

of meanings, values and explanation of the place of human life in the universe
that was based on the Classics, and closely related sources such as Mencius, as
privileged repositories of the truth.[32]

What is left is 'a sort of psychological "momentum" or "hangover" [...] in the
present-day Chinese world'.[33] We suggest, however, that this Confucian tradition
continues to inform Chinese modernity. Confucianism may, according to Elvin,
have dissolved as a scriptural tradition, but this is in contrast to other 'pre-modern'
religions whose scriptures may persist with a body of believers, but whose own
relationship with modernity is not explored. In what ways does scriptural Christianity still inform the Western polity? Be that as it may, the collapse of a scriptural tradition does not necessarily equate to the disappearance of the long historical tradition which encompassed everyday practices, shared ethical and cultural
norms, institutional memories in statecraft and the civilizational narrative that
has remained central to Chinese society and politics since the nineteenth century.

We would suggest that despite its disappearance as a scriptural 'religion',
we can see the continuing presence of Confucian concepts and practices in the
encounter with the West, and the ways they (mis)interpreted, adopted, modified
and indeed rejected Western culture and politics. Elvin suggests that a key reason
for Confucianism's disappearance was its lack of other-worldliness, 'that it was
that very closeness to human affairs that made Confucianism so vulnerable, once it
seemed to have lost the mandate of history'.[34] For us, its very 'worldliness' under-
scores how it would necessarily inform the anxious adoption and adaption of
Western concepts to the Chinese world. The very lack of transcendent doctrinal
beliefs and its rootedness in human affairs have underpinned Confucianism's more
recent return as a philosophical tradition capable of articulating an approach to
the world very different from that of the West.[35]

An example is Peter Zarrow's *After Empire*, which tries to show in detail how
administrators and scholars in the late Qing attempted to confront the new political realities facing the dynasty – especially the new popular legitimation required
of the emperor – using a Confucian framework.[36] Rather than portray this as an
encounter of mutually incomprehensible thought structures, one of which – the
traditional – must give way before the other, Zarrow looks to processes of 'translation' between the two.[37] Thus, *After Empire* may be seen as an attempt to reconstruct how forms of Confucian knowledge and discourse engaged in intense dialogue with new Western concepts and techniques of government.

Wang Hui's *The Rise of Modern Chinese Thought* is likewise an ambitious
attempt to retrieve the Confucian tradition and show how it continued to frame
China's engagement with the West, even after the collapse of the Qing state and the
scriptural tradition with which it was so closely bound. The Confucian tradition

seemed to give way before the challenges of the West, but at the same time its conceptual and ethical frameworks were crucial in the agonistic struggle to articulate China's ethical-historical distinctiveness.[38] Wang Hui's retrieval of attempts by Qing scholars to think through and meet the Western challenge by reframing and reconstructing Confucian terms helps to refute the easy portrayal of traditional China as a feudal relic set to be swept aside by modernity. Indeed, such a negotiation/translation of terms between China and the West might persist even though the Chinese actors themselves explicitly reject traditional forms of knowledge. It is this critique of modernity from within the Confucian (and later socialist) traditions of China that Wang called 'anti-modern modernity'.[39]

Chinese modernity

The disappearance of the imperial system does not mean a definitive break with the past and the adoption of forms and language of the Western nation state. For what we see in the 40 or so years after 1911 is the continuation of a struggle by a series of proto-states, using various indigenous, foreign and hybrid forms of political thought and practice, to unify the territory of the Qing Empire under new forms of the national-popular.

Wang Hui's work strongly suggests the ways in which Confucian patterns of thought continued to inform Chinese politics long after the collapse of the Qing. Indeed, for Wang, in Confucianism's concerns with benevolence, rites, the heavenly order and so on, we can see ways of thinking about social bonds, the purpose of good government and the ethnical constraints on its actions ignored by those who dismiss it as 'feudal'. Confucian ways of thinking were first reworked to undermine the Qing state, followed by an explicit disavowal of the Confucian system in the face of the Qing's failure to engage in meaningful reform. But at the same time, Confucian thought also informed a growing critique of the West and became part of a search for a different kind of modernity.

It is not just forms of thought but also structures of practice that are at stake here. Wang Hui's retrieval of Confucian thought is of a part with his attempt to disrupt the narrative of the inevitable collapse of the 'traditional' Qing Empire and its replacement by a 'modern' nation state. Though many sought Western knowledge as the only way out of the impasse, they inevitably utilized this in the light of prior forms of knowledge and practice, but also, we would suggest, in terms of a civilizational project that was distinct from that of the West (even if articulated or translated via its language). This can be seen in the growing rejection of nineteenth-century liberal democratic forms after the bitter disappointments of the 1911 revolution. New forms of radical and revolutionary thinking emerged – the 'awakening of Asia' – which, especially after 1917, were to feed into revolutions and anti-colonial struggles for the next 50 years.

The accelerated rejection of Western liberal democracy after the First World War, and the weakness of Chinese liberalism more generally, has been portrayed as an instrumental choice. That is, other political technologies (the Leninist party for example, but also other state-led forms of political mobilization) seemed to provide a more direct route to the modern than constitutional democracy. Benjamin Schwartz suggested, apropos of Yan Fu (an earlier proponent of the benefits of Western liberal government), that liberalism was seen as a means to an end – to build a viable Chinese nation state – rather than as an end in itself. While Schwartz saw liberalism's 'spiritual core' as the 'worth of people within society', Yan Fu's instrumental 'concept of liberalism as a means to an end of state power is mortally vulnerable to the demonstration that there are shorter roads to that end'.[40]

Schwartz's 'state power' here sidesteps the fact that in the Chinese context this also meant civilizational survival, giving it added exigency. But there were other reasons for the rejection of liberalism: for example the inadequacies of representative democracy, the prevalence of market relations and its evasion of the 'social question' that grew out of the 'Confucian' state-society configuration (a point we will return to in the following chapter). Wang Hui illustrates how the 'Empire' and many of the Confucian ethical and political categories that were entwined with it persisted after the Qing Dynasty's demise in 1911. He also points to the very obvious, though frequently overlooked, fact that between 1911 and 1949 there were no attempts – other than that of the Japanese – to dismantle the territorial integrity of what had been the Qing Empire. On the contrary, the legitimacy sought by the internally contending powers – these being finally the Kuomintang and the Communist Party – revolved around their ability to restore a Chinese nation state co-extensive with the Qing Empire. This survival marks it out as unique among the great pre-modern empires.[41]

What this chaotic period represents is not, we would suggest, the story of a (attempted) replacement of an empire by a nation state – as with the Ottoman, Austro-Hungarian or Moghul Empires – but the radical reconstruction of an entity built up over millennia in very different ways than the West. The task of recreating and subsequently governing China was one forced upon it by its encounter with the imperialism of the Western nation states, but it was a task for which Western statecraft provided few models. In both Republican and Communist periods, Western and Soviet models of rapid industrialization and administrative technologies (including the Leninist party) sat alongside persistent administrative and ideological forms derived from the Qing Empire and before. This is not to talk about Mao (or Chiang Kai-Shek for that matter) 'becoming an emperor', or the Communist Party re-instigating the Empire as pre-modern throwback (as with Stalin and Ivan the Terrible, for example). Nor is it to essentialize some basic meme of Chinese history (again like Russia and 'autocracy'). Rather, it is to sug-gest that a rich and complex Confucian heritage, intertwined with the political and social technologies of the Qing and Ming Empires, continued to provide resources through which the empire-turned-nation state was to be governed.

There has been a long tradition of identifying characteristics of the modern nation state far back in Chinese history, the better to assert imperial China's 'advanced' nature.[42] Imperial China's massive infrastructure projects, its edu-cational system, its techniques of market intervention, its informational system (including a census), its famine and flood relief administration and so on are often taken as signs of a future modernity way in advance of what could be found in Europe. As Wang Hui argues, however, identifying aspects of imperial China with a 'proto-nation state' still assumes that the nation state is the singular form of mod-ernity. Others have pointed to the tautology of the claim that, as the modern Euro-pean nation state is the paradigm of modernity, then the fact that the Qing (and Ming) Empire did not display this or that European characteristic shows it was not modern. Bin Wong has highlighted both the ways in which certain 'modern' elem-ents were present in China before they were in the West, and that certain elements of the Western modern (like contracted rights, and a public sphere) were clearly absent from China. This, he argues, is not because these aspects of Chinese state and society remained 'pre-modern' but because the imperial state had solved its core challenges differently and with different consequences to the West.[43]

Imperial China had for centuries engaged in administrative practices that were later identified as 'modern' when developed by European states in the latter part of the eighteenth century. These emerged out of the specific ways in which the imperial state dealt with the 'challenges, capacities, claims and commitments' involved in the creation and securing of an empire on a scale unknown in Europe, surpassing those of Rome and Byzantine.[44] For example, concern with society's welfare and the requisite knowledge of the 'social body' that went with this were present in China long before they appeared in the eighteenth century in the form of what Michel Foucault was to call 'biopower'.[45] On the other hand, as we shall see below, the public sphere, for Habermas a core category of the modern, is absent.[46] All of which is to say that China's modernity, even though ushered in by a vehe-ment renunciation of the stupidity, oppressiveness and weakness of the Qing state and its Confucian armature, was demonstrably different from that of the West.

The culture complex

The word 'culture' grows out of a notion of 'cultivation', a process of transform-ation of the self and the social that has long roots in both Western and Chinese culture.[47] As Wang Hui notes, the Latin root for culture is *colere* – 'later expanded to refer to the nurturing of one's interests, spirit and intellect' – while,

> [t]he Chinese concept of 'culture' came together from the words *wen* and *hua*. *Wen* refers to natural patterns as well as the order of rites and music. *Hua* connotes the developmental stages of *wen* (birth, transformation, change).

Wang immediately adds that 'the modern concept of "culture" is intimately connected with the state'.[48] (We saw in the last chapter that it also connected with a process of transformation necessary to the creation of that state.) This intimate association of culture and state is of course a major trope in the characterization of modern Chinese culture as fundamentally different from the West, and is clearly at stake in discourses of creativity as we have seen. The (relative) 'autonomy' of the cultural sphere is crucial to Western self-understandings and informs much of the prescriptive policy around the cultural and creative industries (and innovation more generally). We will therefore start this discussion of modern Chinese culture with the work of Tony Bennett and others who have foregrounded the role of culture as a project and site of governmentality.

Bennett suggests that 'culture' should not be seen as a distinct ontological realm or space manifesting the 'general properties of the symbolic or logics of representation' but rather a term denoting a set of beliefs, practices and institutions – a 'complex' – involving:

> the public ordering of the relations between particular kinds of knowledges, texts, objects, techniques, technologies and humans arising from the deployment of the modern cultural disciplines (literature, aesthetics, art history, folk studies, drama, heritage studies, cultural and media studies) in a connected set of apparatuses (museums, libraries, cinema, broadcasting, heritage etc.). The historical and geographical distinctiveness of this complex consists in its organisation of specific forms of action whose exercise and development has been connected to those ways of intervening in the conduct of conduct that Foucault calls governmental.[49]

How are we to understand the Chinese 'culture complex'? One obvious approach would be to identify the extent of Chinese cultural modernization with the appearance of various elements of the list adumbrated by Bennett: art schools, modern publishing technologies, new museums, cultural journals, universities and modern cultural industries – modern forms perhaps coloured by a 'content' derived from 'classical' meaning systems and practices exemplified in calligraphy, ceramics, music, bronzes and literature. While this has its merits (and we shall look at some aspects of this 'complex' in relation to Shanghai), here we want to dig deeper into the socio-structural system within which such a culture complex might emerge. Rather than try to excavate a distinct lineage of modern Chinese aesthetics and culture[50] – a task for which we are unqualified – we pursue the 'historical and geographical distinctiveness of this complex' across the encounter between European modernity and China.

Habermas and the public sphere

The public sphere is a category fundamental to discourses of Euro-modernity. In Habermas's definitive account, the public sphere emerges – after long historical gestation – in the eighteenth century as a space between the state and the economy. European states from the end of the Middle Ages sought to extend their interests from particular dynastic concerns to those that encompassed society or the nation as a whole.[51] These states gradually established a 'public realm' in which they sought to present their own interests – *raison d'état* – as co-extensive with this general interest. At the same time, 'economy' emerges as a new space in which 'private' interests – as in the Aristotelian *oikos* or management of the household – become connected up across the intersecting network of markets developing in the wake of the emergent mercantile and capitalist system.[52] The perceived collective requirements (legislative, institutional, diplomatic etc.) of this economy brings together these interconnected private interests into 'a zone of continuous administrative contact' with a state that claims to be acting in the 'public' interest.[53]

Habermas's public sphere emerges from this zone of contact, in which a 'rational' process of contestation and dialogue takes place around the right to define the nature of this collective social interest. ('Rational' here refers to the Weberian sense of instrumental-rational (means) and value-rational (ends) as calculated by autonomous individuals.) Underpinned by institutions such as coffee- and teahouses, journals and newspapers, learned academies and universities, the rational interests of (bourgeois) individuals could be expressed vis-à-vis the state and demand that it act in a manner that would secure their and, they argued, society's own prosperity. Habermas (as with Weber before him) saw this as not just about conflicting interests or an opposition between state and society but also as evolving a practice of rational-critical discourse on political matters.[54] The public sphere was open equally to all individuals willing to submit to the forms of rational discourse that underpinned it, and it increasingly subjected the state itself to procedures of rational justification, eventually – in the form of the press and political parties – becoming a kind of functional adjunct of this state itself.[55]

This public sphere, whilst very much about rational discussion and critical scrutiny of the state, was also the site of new forms of aesthetic communication – exemplified by the novel – in which individual subjectivities were both formed and put into contact with each other in ways that established a new bond of 'humanity' based on empathy with those you were never likely to meet.[56] For Habermas, this sphere of 'art' or 'culture' is separate from the 'reproduction of social life' – it is no longer a direct product of particular and immediate forms of life – and, by being transformed into, and circulated as, a commodity, is subject to public dispute and criticism.[57]

The associative chain between the public sphere, enlightenment, liberal democracy and the modern nation state has provided an ideal-typical model against which to judge progress to modernity. Historians of modern China have sought to demarcate tradition and modernity precisely around the emergence of this public sphere. They have identified its gradual emergence under the impact of Western influence in the early modern (*jindai*) period, or even looked back to evidence of the public sphere as a sign of proto-modernity in earlier times. Nevertheless, for many it was the emergence of new political ideologies, agents and technologies in the late Qing and early Republican periods that decisively announced the arrival of a properly 'modern' politics. We suggest, on the contrary, that to seek out an emergent public sphere as a sign of an incipient modernity is to force Chinese history into a Western format.

The configuration of power within Chinese society was very different to that of Europe. By the end of the first millennium, the Chinese state had succeeded in eliminating all 'feudal' elements competing with itself for power, a feat the Byzantine state had never managed.[58] The imperial state did not face distinct castes or estates with clearly defined legal rights and spheres of jurisdiction, as was the case with the aristocracy, the clergy or the urban elites in late medieval and early modern Europe. The success of the Chinese imperial state in achieving a monopoly of power with strong legitimation resulted in a basic alignment of interests between state and societal groups. This established an organization of power and administration, which reproduced this alignment at multiple levels in a fashion Bin Wong calls 'fractal'.

> This fractal quality admits of no easy dividing line between state and society. The fractal quality of Chinese ideology allowed the principles of social order to be articulated by different levels of government. The institutions developed to implement local order could also be replicated on small or larger scales. The elites and officials who created social order were linked in networks that also possessed a fractal quality.[59]

We might see something of this 'fractal' quality in Lothar Ledderose's *Ten Thousand Things*, where a notion of 'modularity' is used to explain the Chinese mass production in script, bronzes, porcelain, architecture and printing. The ability to organize mass production around basic modules that could be combined and scaled-up to huge dimensions evokes something about the production of state and social order in China.[60]

State and elites shared a broad set of values – famously promulgated through the imperial examination system – whereby local elites acted in what they considered to be in tandem with the overarching goals of the state and for the benefit of society. Unlike in Europe, the imperial state was not involved in an expansive assertion of its interests against other power actors who sought to negotiate their own rights in response.

In the European case, this process of negotiation resulted in the elaboration of legal and contractual frameworks for the exercise and delimitation of power over persons and property, becoming known across the eighteenth century as civil society.[61] This did not happen in China.[62] The imperial state, local administration and elites sought the welfare of the population as a primary concern, as an ethical-political duty and precondition of ensuring social order over the largest population on earth. The foundation of this social order were benevolence (ren) and righteousness (yi), and a respect for the rituals and forms of life that were shared by all levels of society.[63]

Some historians have identified an emergent urban public sphere in the mid-nineteenth century, whereby urban elites benefiting from printing presses, Western learning, newspapers and new public spaces began to take matters into their own hands and initiate new forms of modernizing administration outside the structures of the Qing state.[64] However, as Bin Wong points out, such independent initiatives were not new.[65] As with the 'self-strengthening' movement, local elites were used to taking on administrative responsibilities, not in opposition to the state but because they shared its values and goals. Similarly, and in a way that recalls Bin Wong's notion of the 'fractal', Philip Huang also rejected a public sphere, positing instead a 'third realm' between state and society in which there was extensive collaboration and participation between formal and informal elements of the Qing state and various elites.[66]

Of course, by the end of the century many of these urban intellectual and economic elites began to oppose the Qing state. This was marked symbolically by Kang Youwei and Liang Qichao's 1895 petition to the emperor in the wake of the humiliating Treaty of Shimonoseki – the first time such scholars had attempted such a public address, opening up a new space which in Europe would become that of the 'intellectual'.[67] It led to the 1911 dismissal of the emperor and the ensuing pursuit of national 'revolution' during the Republican era. This opposition to the dynasty certainly grew out of a new sense of modern rational political dialogue rooted in the new public of the cities. In this, they frequently relied on

Western political concepts freshly translated. However, as Philip Huang shows, the reforms instigated by the late imperial and new Republican states involved less a new 'public sphere' than an expansion of the 'third realm' in which elites and the state collaborated.

> The twin processes of modern societal integration and modern statemaking in late Qing and Republican China, limited though they might have been in contrast to the West, led to greater interpenetration of the two and expanded third-realm activities.[68]

Building on these insights, we might characterize efforts at reform and revolution as attempts to repurpose or reconstruct the dynastic state as a fully public (gong) state in which the 'people' would be in power (minzu – democracy). We may see these efforts in the light of long-standing Confucian values and practices that were to be radically recast under the impact of new Western political concepts. However, these Western concepts were put to uses for which they were frequently unsuited. What had been at stake in the reform and revolutionary movements since the 1890s was the ability of the imperial dynasty to fully represent a new public (gong) conception of the state in which the interests of the people, not those of the dynasty, were represented. But the overwhelming concern of reformers and revolutionaries alike was not, as with the Habermasian account, to oppose raison d'état in order to carve out an autonomous civil society. Rather, it was to seek the effective grounds for a reformed nation state, one capable of ensuring collective protection and prosperity, recast in a new language of citizens and social contract, and that could effectively mobilize the nation-people. Such a task drew on long-standing tropes of thought and practice that cannot be fully understood outside Confucian forms.

One such trope was the state (and scholar-administrators) as a primary actor in this process of revolution – famously encapsulated in Sun Yat-Sen's notion of the Chinese people as 'just a heap of loose sand'. It contrasts strongly with the notion of people as an autochthonic motor of history in late-eighteenth- and early-nineteenth-century European revolutionary thought. Another is the way in which scholars and later 'intellectuals' sought not to carve out a space of self-legislating reason for themselves which the state must, to some extent, respect. Rather, reforming intellectuals sought to exhibit a self-disciplining commitment to finding a 'true-path' (wangdao) where their actions could be framed as part of a collective pursuit of an ethically founded polity.[69] Autonomy was not a primary concern, as we will discuss below.

The new discourse of citizenship that emerged in the late Qing and the Republican period was less about a space of autonomy from the state than the creation of citizens with the ethical and intellectual capacity to form a renewed nation state through which a Chinese civilization might survive.[70] Equally, their claim to a more open public dialogue was founded less in liberty *from* the state than in allowing modern scientific and rational thinking to flow more freely into the state administration, the better to reform it.

The public sphere and the 'social question'

We might extend this discussion by looking at the 'social question', which came to challenge the bourgeois public sphere in the nineteenth century.[71] The 'social question' began to perplex European liberalism from the late eighteenth century (especially post-1789), and forms a later, less-discussed part of Habermas's book.[72] We refer here to the tension between European liberalism's civic and political liberties and the 'substantive freedom' of the social realm, where formal equality and actual inequality generated accelerating frictions within the public sphere. Hegel and Marx were both concerned by this differentiation between *bourgeois* and *citoyen*, central to the transformation of the private realm of 'civil society' (*bürgerliche Gesellschaft*) into an 'economy' (or system of needs) operating as a quasi-natural system. The highly fissiparous nature of a society driven only by private competing interests, and workers attached to these by punitive and stultifying work regimes, undermined the very possibility and legitimacy of the social bond.[73] It was from this problematic that the socialist and social liberal reformist movements arose towards the end of the nineteenth century in Europe. This problematic did not exist in anything like the same form in late Qing or Republican China, and we will try to suggest why this was so.

Zygmund Bauman argued, in his *Legislators and Interpreters*, that eighteenth-century European states moved from a 'wild' to a 'garden' culture, in which a previously 'untended' social body was increasingly 'cultivated' in order to enhance the resources available to the state.[74] This transition, discussed below, forms part of that discovery of the social associated with Foucault's work. From our perspective, whatever new administrative technologies were invented by European states in response to this 'discovery', the basic proposition of a cultivated 'social garden' was at least a thousand years old in China. As we saw above, the way the imperial state had solved its historical challenges resulted in a very different state-society configuration. Thus, the persistent tension or contradiction within liberalism between the formally equal participation in the public sphere and the unequal or constrained 'social' sphere rooted in a private economic realm did not appear in China. The responsibilities of the state for 'the social' had been part of Confucian notions of 'benevolence' (*ren*) for many centuries. And, as we have seen, the lines between state and society were permeable and governed by norms of behaviours rather than explicit (and legally contestable) rules.[75]

If in China the notion of a 'public' (*gong*), and the way it articulated a non-antagonistic relationship between state and society, was very different from that in Europe, this also applied to the Chinese programme of economic reforms which are inevitably positioned by Westerners as a sign of the modern. The notion of a distinct and 'disembedded' economic order – market relations set free from traditional and communal constraints, their governance given over to 'natural' economic laws working though rational, instrumentalized individuals – was a key plank of Western-imposed modernizing reforms, such as in colonial Egypt.[76] (They continued as such until the 1960s.) This was entirely alien to the Chinese polity and, as with many other traditional societies, seen as a direct threat to the social order. In China, new kinds of commercial ventures, technologies and infrastructure were sought out and promoted by reforming elements in the Qing administration. These were, as in many late-coming industrializing nations, dependent on the state for their construction. They were also set within a national reform process that was explicitly about the development of the whole social order. Failure to secure the common welfare – *Minsheng*[77] – would undermine state legitimation. There was no question of the state 'taking sides' with capital against labour in the manner of the British state. Thus, at no point did the 'semi-colonial' Chinese state attempt to dispossess the peasantry and install a colonially dependent *latifundia* at the expense of this peasantry.[78]

In this sense, the reforming administrative and economic elites were never going to assert their interests against the state *per se*. Their agenda was about nation state (re-)building and societal integration rather than securing economic liberalism. The issue was not simply new, efficient economic and administrative institutions – such as we might see in Egypt and the Ottoman Empire[79] – but also the creation of modern citizens essential to a strong nation state. In this, the 'social' was already accepted as central both to public virtue and to state legitimation.[80]

Just this brief sketch should indicate that the culture complex would be structured very differently in China. We cannot take for granted the notion of a public sphere opposed to the state, or citizenship secured against it in the form of negotiated contracts or rights – nor, we might add, the definition of a rational civil society made up of individuals acting autonomously in pursuit of clearly outlined interests and values. Finally, we should add that the particular trajectory 'modern reforms' were to take in China would thus diverge very early on from forms of 'liberal democracy' and the introduction of capitalist class relations upon which this was predicated. How then did this inflect notions of culture and aesthetics?

Bourdieu and the bourgeois subject

As part of his critical account of the class-based nature of taste in *Distinction*, Bourdieu sketched the emergence of 'art' as a historically distinct category of experience in post-Renaissance Europe, linking it to the 'rise' of the bourgeoisie.[81] The Renaissance introduced the ideal of 'man' supplanting God as primary creator, associating the genius-artist with the very possibility of bringing the new into the world. Bourdieu outlined how a new kind of object – the work of art as exemplary act of creation – called for, and depended on, a new kind of 'gaze', one based on contemplation or delectation for its own sake rather than directly utilitarian judgement. This gaze, and the works of art that went with it, took a long time to be constructed across subjects and institutions. In *Distinction*, and in his later *The Rules of Art*, Bourdieu is concerned to show how the emergence of 'art' and the 'disinterested gaze' re-enforced the distinction between the activities of the leisured class and those subject to the hard necessity of manual labour. It was a division captured by the idea of the liberal (as in 'free') arts versus the mechanically constrained products of the artisan. The bourgeois subject is distinguished by an autonomy of taste, which testified to his or her broader competence to act as a free citizen – something impossible for those driven by necessity.[82]

Bourdieu's concern with art's historicity is part of his attempt to link it to forms of class domination. Indeed, much of his and others' work in this context has traced the relations between the public sphere of culture and forms of class solidarity and exclusion.[83] However, what Bourdieu mostly leaves implicit is how art's ability to act as a marker of social distinction is not simply due to the wealth required to consume it or an absence of manual labour (as indicated by signs such as corpulence or wearing fine clothes). It also formed part of a wider historical field in which the disinterested, free appreciation of art represented a self of 'worth', one able to fully participate in society as an autonomous citizen.[84] It was in the mid-eighteenth century that the Third Earl of Shaftesbury had linked older ideals of republican *virtu* – an individual's virile power and capability, the control over world and the self – to a new sense of aesthetic taste. It was this coupling of taste judgement with *virtu* that Bourdieu tried to excavate in *Distinction*.

Bourdieu also traces the ways in which, across the second half of the eighteenth and the first of the nineteenth century, the realm of the aesthetic disentangled itself from direct association with the bourgeoisie, emerging as a zone of autonomous creation. As we noted with Habermas, the public sphere within which literature and the fine arts circulated (often as commodities) saw these subjected to new forms of 'rational' criticism in such a way as to give their formal and thematic content more autonomy vis-à-vis established taste and indeed religious, political and even moral concerns.[85] As the fine arts became 'art', that term came to represent a space of free creative play, giving access to realms of experience sharply differentiated from those of economic, administrative, scientific and finally ethical reason. In *The Rules of Art*, Bourdieu charted a radicalization of this distinctive aesthetic sphere into autonomous art – *L'art pour l'art*. Its full emergence in mid-nineteenth-century Paris – linked to the work of Flaubert, Baudelaire and Manet – is coterminous with that of *modernité*.[86] Bourdieu suggests, via the figure of Flaubert, that modernist autonomy forsakes the bourgeoisie after the mid-nineteenth century, remaining nevertheless within the orbit of the 'dominated fraction of the dominant class'. The value of that autonomy remains a key stake in the artistic field but for Bourdieu it is also a historically emergent value that needs to be defended and extended.[87]

The association of art and autonomy runs deep within Western notions of art and is engrained within the artistic habitus. In their different ways, both Bourdieu and Rancière see this as a historical gain, where this autonomy is able to escape direct tutelage by the ruling classes.[88] Though artistic 'autonomy' has been seriously challenged since the end of modernism (something to which Bourdieu himself contributed), it remains a core value at stake in the contestations around cultural value. We would suggest that the value of this autonomy – its function, so to speak, or what Sebastian Olma calls *Weltbezug*[89] – rested not just on an absence of external tutelage ('artistic freedom') but also on its claims to have a unique access to the chthonic forces at work in the profound movement of historical transformation producing the modern world. This ability was linked to the figure of the genius as historical seer or visionary, a figure that went beyond the formula of *'L'art pour l'art'* as the genius communicated with the very depths of the world-historical process.[90]

However, we would suggest that this historical gain – as with Bourdieu's genealogy of the emergent bourgeois habitus, the privileging of artistic autonomy and *ex nihilo* creativity – was deeply intertwined with Europe's imperialist-capitalist expansion, and the world it was bringing into being. The virile control over self and world, central to an emerging bourgeois habitus, is unthinkable outside this world-historical moment. The historical creativity of an all-powerful Europe was surely mirrored in its enormously expanded capacity of fabula – the invention of new forms of art no longer tied to objective truths or subordinate to wider social functions.[91] In this unprecedented proliferation of artistic invention, the inherent nobility and hierarchy of the varied forms of 'fine art', based on Aristotelian models, gave way to a concept of art which, as Rancière has argued, primarily inhered in the senses.[92] The new sphere of 'the aesthetic' that appeared in the mid-eighteenth century thus linked the faculty of imagination or invention to a privileged, almost sacred, site of free creation.[93] It is this power of imaginative invention, with its roots in the definitive era of European world-historical power, that is recalled in the contemporary promotion of 'creativity', albeit now as purely economic innovation.

Western post-Renaissance art thus became associated with the 'modern' in non-Western society and acted as a powerful model for the development of those institutions – museums, art schools, conservatoires, concert halls, criticism, journals and so on – that Bennett has termed the culture complex.[94] But their deployment, in a place such as China, was necessarily restricted, not only by the material constraints of a pre-industrial society, but also by a very different local 'culture complex'.

Two crucial elements that animated a Western 'culture complex' – the association of the bourgeois subject with an aesthetic taste exemplifying their autonomous *virtu* and fitness for citizenship, and the emergence of art as a zone of free creation that could often stand for human creative possibility per se – had very limited resonance in the Chinese context. This relates to the obvious absence of a bourgeoisie in China – that is, a powerful mercantile class whose capital investments were intertwined with the state's own expansionist ambitions – let alone one with a habitus constructed around the figure of the citizen and man of property, asserting both autonomy and personal worthiness against the claims of the state.

China was structured around cultural beliefs and practices which, as we have suggested, were very different to those of the West. Of course, the power commanded by *virtu* and aesthetic taste, and the radical freedom wielded by the autonomous play of art, had genealogies rooted in a Christian and Greco-Roman tradition, reconfigured in the Renaissance, that had few precedents in China.[95] But these distinctive cultural lineages rested not simply on some essential meme of Confucianism or Greco-Roman Christianity but on the ways in which these two might combine with changing socio-historical processes to configure relations between individuals, social groups and the state, as well as relations to the self.[96]

Foucault and governmentality

Bourdieu, concerned as he was to highlight the place of art in strategies of class distinction, has less to say about how such strategies relate to the role of the state and the configuration of the 'social body'. Bourdieu frequently takes it for granted that the individual bourgeois habitus, in which taste performs a central constructive role, corresponds to a wider class-consciousness, solidarity and strategies of power. Yet central to eighteenth-century debates around taste were concerns that such myriad individual tastes might undermine the social bond itself and thus the viability and nature of the sovereign power. The fissiparous potential of purely individual taste cultures called into question the very possibility of society.

The Earl of Shaftesbury's civic humanism was an attempt to solve this question precisely through the aesthetic. Aesthetic taste opened up individuals to 'fellow feeling', allowing a sense of the common or public good to emerge at the level of affect rather than (merely) reason. At the same time, the spontaneous emergence of fellow feeling allowed a new conception of a social order – in which the multitude was held together not by force but by common feeling – and one that founds, rather than undermines, as in the case of absolute power, a free republic.[97] The power to make aesthetic judgements was now linked to the power of art to stimulate feelings of social sympathy and affection (as we also saw in relation to Habermas and Anderson above). Aesthetic taste had an educative function for the bourgeois subject, one not available for the necessity-driven lower classes; it enhanced and displayed the power of the autonomous self as well as strengthening the bonds of civic affection.[98] Of course, as became clear in the nineteenth century, such taste would eventually be viewed as having an educative, civilizing function for the lower classes domestically and in the colonies, its extending to them in some form as desirable.[99]

Immanuel Kant's *Critique of Pure Judgement*, which more or less framed the discourse of aesthetics for the following century and a half, attempted a more sophisticated philosophical justification for this *sensus commun*. As Howard Caygill has brilliantly shown, this idea of *sensus commun* was crucial in providing a rational basis for the liberal polity, though in this case with the more statist German (Prussian) context in mind.[100] Rather than myriad individuals whose individual desires would lead to social dissolution, we have a unified and unifying aesthetic taste, derived from a disinterested contemplation of beauty, which holds society together and founds the possibility of a state based on reason and affection. Art as an exemplary set of objects and practices essential to autonomous self-cultivation is taken up by the state as a site through which citizens might be both created and governed – not merely through laws and regulations but also via the disinterested pleasures of the beautiful, and the sympathies these make possible within society.

This brings us to Michel Foucault's concept of governmentality that, mainly through the work of Ian Hunter and Tony Bennett, has been a major influence on more recent writings on culture as policy.[101] This relates to two aspects of Foucault's work. First, the discovery of a social body as something to be mapped and harnessed as resource, which Foucault termed 'biopower'. Second, is the move away from sovereignty (power as emanating from the king or central power source) and also (to some degree) disciplinary power (the power over individual bodies and behaviour) towards governmentality. This move involved a recognition within government and elites, faced with the autonomous spheres of economy and civil society, that *raison d'état* might be secured by 'less government rather than more'.

Instead of through coercion, government might be better advised to influence behaviour by aiming to 'steer' free liberal subjects in ways amenable to the interests of state. That is, governments sought to influence 'the conduct of conduct'.[102]

Hunter and Bennett's work attempted to identify the specific working of art and culture within this governmentality complex. Hunter suggested that the aesthetic, as developed especially in late-eighteenth-century Germany, was not simply about taste but also a work of the self on the self, or what Foucault called a 'technology of the self'.[103] The aesthetic opened up a space of self-transformation in which subjects might constantly monitor their behaviour in the light of a freely chosen ethical ideal. Recalling Kant's universal imperative, but now reached through the realms of affect and imagination, this was linked to the idea of *bildung* central to the nineteenth-century Prussian and other Germanic states. Hunter's work focuses on the specific ways in which the British state adapted this aesthetic 'technology of the self' to its own purposes as it began to implement universal education (and political suffrage) in the later nineteenth century. Hunter has a complex political agenda in this book, which we will leave aside here. Important for us was the use of technologies of self, derived from aesthetic freedom, by government education policies to stimulate forms of autonomous 'self-transformation' along with the internalization of an 'authority' to monitor this process.

Bennett's work focuses more on the public institutions that accompanied this culture-based governmentality – those he lists in the quote above, such as museums, libraries and art galleries, and the kinds of knowledge that go with them.[104] These institutions are central to the creation and governance of liberal subjects who are to be aligned with the overall project of the state. They must be brought to want freely what the state wants. In this account we have a sphere of art and culture – the latter, as Williams notes, increasingly identified with the former[105] – that is less a public sphere distinct or autonomous from the state and more a 'surface' on which that state works, at a distance, on individuals and communities.[106]

China's culture complex

How then might the culture complex be conceived in China? We have already suggested the absence of a bourgeois habitus in Bourdieu's sense; moreover, the 'technologies of self' we might associate with the neo-Confucian tradition, and their imbrication with the skills of literature, calligraphy, line drawing, music and so on, bore little relation to the anthropocentric universe of the Renaissance and the claims for 'creativity' which grew out of this.[107] Chinese culture looked to forms of 'imitation' in order to understand a world, or *dao* ('way'), that already existed. It was part of a process of self-discipline that allowed one to act on the world by responding to, and channelling, the possibilities it presented.[108] This notion of finding a way, a 'true-path' (*wangdao*), was always linked to a wider ethical project of a social order (secured in an immanent-transcendental manner by *tian*, or heaven)[109]. It was not about that restless and perilous seeking of the freely created new – implicating both self and history – that the aesthetic imagination became in late-eighteenth-century Europe. Rather, it could lead to specific constructions of obedience and of mass replication that, to European eyes, looked entirely uncreative.[110]

In China, as we have seen, 'culture' as a set of linked concepts and terminologies was rapidly assembled at the end of the nineteenth century, a direct consequence of its encounter with the powerful states of the West. It did not involve anything like an 'aesthetic complex' but was always concerned with a way of designating China as a viable historical nation-subject in a world of competing nation states. 'Culture' was used to identify a distinct civilizational entity and a 'people' who could act as citizens of such a nation state rather than dynastic subjects hobbled by the past. Culture was thus a forward-oriented project, something to be acted on with urgency, written under the sign of the new, and through which a radically renewed state and society project could be pursued.

Benjamin Schwartz may accuse the May Fourth iconoclasts of instrumentalism or utilitarianism (as did many of their Chinese critics), latching on to the institutions of liberal government as a route to a modern powerful state rather than its intrinsic values.[111] But when Wang Hui argues that in China 'the modern concept of "culture" is intimately connected with the state', we cannot simply measure the project of Chinese state-building against that of European liberalism as ideal-typical. Founding a state was part of an ethico-political project that was configured differently in China, and what they sought through the modern political technologies of the West was written under different aspirations and exigencies. While the May Fourth radicals may reject the past and grasp the 'new' as identified with the modern West, the deeper sources of their project lay rooted in a different tradition.

Thus, Hunter questions the standard historiological distinction between 'nationalism' and 'culturalism' where, as he says, the latter refers to the 'whole civilisation' rather than the 'narrower political unit of the nation within that larger cultural whole'. Chinese revolutionary nationalism is associated with this narrower unit.

> The problem with this thesis, long accepted as the norm in Chinese studies in the West, is that there was never the theoretical possibility of a 'narrower political unit' within the 'larger cultural whole' of Chinese civilisation, for the two had always been, and continued to be, coterminous.[112]

That is, the project of a strong state was in its turn an instrument for the protection and renewal of a civilizational project. As Schwartz noted, the Qing reformers had all been committed to the preservation of the Chinese 'Way' (in the sense of ethical polity), a 'Way' closely identified with 'the existence of what we would now call the state'. He quotes Yen Fu from 1898: 'There can be no Way without a state and a people to sustain it.'[113] Such a renewal project cannot be reduced to the implementation of 'modern administrative reforms' but refers to the survival of a whole civilizational entity.

The attempt to mobilize a nation-people would certainly involve adapting Western liberal concepts, but there would be no aesthetic 'surface' on which the state would work to produce self-governing subjects. Not only was the aesthetic habitus absent, but the idea of 'surface' would not easily apply to a society in which power was 'fractal' and which worked at multiple levels through 'forms of life', rituals, and shared rules of practice, rather than rights and responsibilities contracted between state and 'civil society'. Clearly, in the late nineteenth century, these traditional forms of life, the accepted patterns of practice and shared values, were in deep crisis. Not only did the arrival of Western-led capitalism give rise to challengingly 'modern' social forms – especially in big cities like Shanghai – but the traditional forms seemed incapable of providing the basis for the project of a new state. To many, this perceived failure seemed to demand a complete rejection of those traditional forms and the language in which they were couched, even as this attempt sought to preserve that very civilizational project. And yet the distinct sociocultural structures through which the state and elites had sought to govern China were inevitably the means through which this project of survival and transformation must make place.

The Chinese imperial state had sought to acquire knowledge of its population and its practices, with a view to enhancing these, at least a thousand years before the European states. Foucault's identification of the modern state as one that had the power to 'make live and let die'[114] had many precedents in China. The imperial state, through its educational and administrative system, also had the tools to effect changes in behaviours that were simply not available to European states until the nineteenth century. In the light of this, the reforms that accelerated from the 1860s – the military, diplomatic, administrative, agricultural and industrial reform initiatives as well as those aimed at educational and scientific development – cannot be seen simply as imitations of Western reforms; they are also responses from deep within the resources of the Chinese state and society.[115]

The disappointments of the 1911 revolution and subsequent reform efforts; the political quagmire within parliamentary politics, fraught by intense rivalries around constitutional and legalistic minutiae; the sense of shock created by the First World War, in which Western civilization tore itself apart; and, eventually, the new 'awakening of Asia' announced by the Russian Revolution in 1917, echoing back to similar movements in Turkey, India and China's own 1911 Republican Revolution itself – all these changed the political landscape around the New Culture and May Fourth movements. Western political liberalism no longer appeared as the only political form of the modern and was certainly found severely wanting in the Chinese revolutionary project. Revolution – a radical renewal of the Chinese state and society – in the form of the restructured (1920) Nationalist Kuomintang (KMT) party and the small, new (1921) Chinese Communist Party (CCP), was no longer sought within the forms of European parliamentary democracy but through the possibilities of mass mobilization opened up through the Leninist party model.

Wang Hui suggests that the attempt of Kang Youwei and Liang Qichao to create a new constitutional state in the years following 1911 – one which would function as a new sovereign and act politically to integrate a new society of citizens – was a failure.[116] It did not succeed, Wang suggests, because it was purely top-down and could not connect with the people, or 'the masses' as they were becoming known. Rather, he sees a new kind of political party very different to nineteenth-century parliamentary ones. This new party

> focused much more on direct social mobilization, promoting political integration by means of confrontational politics. For this political organization, leadership or 'hegemony' (including 'cultural hegemony') was bound up and integrated with the formation of the popular will, and its legitimacy derived from 'revolution'.[117]

The state-building projects of both the KMT and CCP, using new political tools derived from the Leninist party, sought not just to establish a state administration (strong or otherwise) but to effect 'a complete restructuring of the state itself though social mobilisation'. From the Northern Expedition (1926–28) onwards, when the KMT led a national coalition of forces aimed at unifying China by defeating the northern warlords,

> the political party was the organizer, participant and political integrator of social mobilization, and it was through this function of political integration that the party gained control of state power.[118]

In these circumstances, the 'integration' of newly created subjects (generated via confrontational class politics), and the establishment of 'hegemony' by the political party as the 'modern prince', would not rely on the same 'culture complex' as the West. The drive to new forms of mass education and literacy took place within an older configuration of serving the social body and a newer one of nation-building, which did not need to be predicated on individual autonomy and self-transformation as in Hunter's account. Citizenship was about building the social as part of a nation-state project – societal integration and state-making – and 'cultural hegemony' would thus be configured very differently.

The revolutionary project did emerge, in terms that explicitly rejected a 'feudal' Confucian and imperial past. However, post-May Fourth modernization could be said to have taken place under the sign of the 'mass' – Taylorism, Le Corbusier and Lenin – rather than liberal democracy.[119] The 'disciplinary' institutions of school, factory, office, prison (and the city itself)[120] had appeared rapidly, especially after 1911.[121] Such disciplinary institutions, as much a part of nation-building as capitalist development, should be understood in relation to emergent notions of 'mass society', the mechanized social body and 'corporatism' rather than as simply late arrivals from a nineteenth century industrial revolution. The examples of the Soviet Union (and to some extent the United States), Japan, fascist Italy and Nazi Germany suggested new technologies to organize and mobilize the masses. In these countries, this involved mass production, housing, transport, energy distribution and, as we have seen, political organization. These went along with new forms of mass communications – advertising, signage, the printing press (using the new simplified language and growing literacy), radio, cinema, recorded music – directing minds and bodies around new urban spaces, through a growing array of consumer goods, and into new forms of political activism.[122]

The role of urban centres is important, as we shall explore more in terms of Shanghai. However, we should also note that these new forms of mass communication might have been initially produced within the urban centres but they were increasingly applied to the rural masses by the new political parties (KMT and CCP) as part of their efforts at peasant mobilization around, and integration into, a revolutionary state project. This focus on the rural was not, unlike in the Soviet Union, an index of 'backwardness'. The new Republic continued to be, like the Qing, an agrarian state with the bulk of its population living on the land. In this respect, the KMT, with its roots in urban and cosmopolitan finance, was always ill at ease and the Communists, once they had left Shanghai, in their element. There is little doubt that the prior structures of a Confucian polity provided a vast range of governmental affordances allowing Mao to rework a revolutionary urban ideology into an agrarian programme with great efficiency.

Conclusion: Literati and intellectuals

Those intellectuals who from 1895 broke away from the existing dynastic regime and sought to identify and create a new culture for a new citizenship did so as part of that true-path (*wangdao*) to an ethico-political community in which the state was central. The burning question for these intellectuals concerned the new forms of this culture and how this was going to create the new nation. As we shall see in relation to Shanghai, though many intellectuals in the 1890s sought to recreate a new literature (*wenxue*), new cultural forms – 'print capitalism', film, music and urban life itself – would emerge as crucial to the creation of a new 'mass' citizenship. This 'mass citizenship', and the mobilization of China's huge population it sought, very quickly stepped outside the orbit of 'liberal governmentality'.

Artists and intellectuals, increasingly now linked to an international circuit of ideas, texts and reputations,[123] did not operate in that paradigmatic cultural field which Bourdieu derived from mid-nineteenth-century France. His cultural field was split between commercial production aimed at the bourgeoisie (with some cheaper, 'low quality' popular culture underneath it) and 'restricted' production aimed at a peer-audience who lacked the purchasing power (individually or collectively) to make this commercially viable.[124] As we suggested above, many European artists claimed a link between their work (and 'genius') and the people – whether in the form of art with a 'social' content or the more visionary sense of access to the historical depths in which this people was rooted.[125] The social 'responsibility' of art had thus emerged at the same time as claims for its autonomy, and the former was especially marked in countries where the gap between modern progress and social reality was most marked. Russia is the classic example in the European context, but it also applies to non-European countries faced with the disruptive modernization that imperialism and capitalism brought with it.

Let us finish by discussing the acceleration of a 'circulatory history' consequent upon the expansion of European trade and empire at the end of the nineteenth century. Prasenjit Duara makes a distinction between capital 'C' Culture, concerned with 'transcendent', foundational values (often) dominated by elites, and small 'c' culture, 'everyday' popular and often far more open to 'circulatory history' – flows of ideas, people, things, trade beyond and across national boundaries.[126] These flows did not simply put Western models of modernity into play, but a whole flux of new and old ideas from the 'minor West' (especially minor nationalism, anti-imperialist and revolutionary traditions) as well as the responses from across Asia (and beyond) struggling with the devastating impact of European power. While much of this concerned the elites in various countries, other social strata were drawn in, from the workers and peasants, the traders and intermediaries, as well as those aspirant literati no longer able to see a route to social advancement and security. In this context, the lines between big 'C' and little 'c' cultures, both within and across national boundaries, became fluid, with many national liberation struggles being welcomed as cosmopolitan events – the precondition for a kind of internationalist citizenship.

In China, the traditional position and social responsibility of scholar-officials – having a responsibility for the masses but remaining aloofly distant from them – was reconfigured by radical nationalism and anti-imperialism. This was a complex drama in which many forms of self-worth and sources of income were shattered as the Qing state gave way to a period of conflict and confusion. As we shall see in the next chapter, the new post-Republican intellectuals, witnesses to new forms of mass industrialization and economic development, also experienced the rise of new cultural technologies and mass markets. If many saw these as irredeemably commercial, others saw their potential for creating revolutions and building new states.

The ensuing debates about popular literature, cinema and popular music involved arguments that went beyond Bourdieu's commercial and restricted production. They were about the relationship between aesthetics and the masses, about the mobilization of affect and energy, vision, perception and action, towards political goals. The autonomy at stake in regards to many of these artists and intellectuals was not that of *L'art pour l'art* but a kind of professional autonomy or sphere of action which allowed them to act as partners with the party or state in the production of culture. Such a partnership, of course, was to be site of great conflict, disappointment and, frequently, tragedy.

NOTES

1. J. Hevia, *English Lessons: The Pedagogy of Imperialism in Nineteenth-Century China* (Durham, NC: Duke University Press, 2003). However, Wang Hui points to long-established protocols of international diplomacy developed in the relations with the various powers – including Imperial Russia – active in central Asia. H. Wang, *China's Twentieth Century* (London: Verso, 2016).

2. R. Williams, *Keywords: A Vocabulary of Culture and Society* (London: Fontana, 1976).

3. Cf. L. H. Liu, *Translingual Practice: Literature, National Culture and Translated Modernity in China, 1900–1937* (Stanford, CA: Stanford University Press, 1995).

4. T. Huters, *Bringing the World Home: Appropriating the West in Late Qing and Early Republican China* (Honolulu: University of Hawai'i Press, 2005), Ch. 2.

5. Social Darwinism often intertwined 'race' and 'civilization'. The anti-Manchu sentiments associated with a growing Republicanism asserted a 'Han civilization' against a foreign dynasty. This tended to disappear after the 1911 revolution removed the Manchus and sought grounds to unite the 'five nations' covered by the Qing Empire. Cf. S. Zhao, *A Nation-State by Construction: Dynamics of Modern Chinese Nationalism* (Stanford, CA: Stanford University Press, 2004), especially Ch. 5; Wang, *China's Twentieth Century*, Ch. 1.

6. We use 'scholar-officials' (shi dafu: 士大夫) to designate those who had passed the Imperial examinations (Keju, 科举). They did not become 'intellectuals' (zhishifenzi: 知识分子) until

the 1920s. We discuss this below. Cf. T. Cheek, *The Intellectual in Modern Chinese History* (Cambridge: Cambridge University Press, 2015), 4–5.

7. Quoted in O. A. Westad, *Restless Empire: China and the World Since 1750* (London: Vintage, 2013), 91.

8. Cf. J. Spence, *The Search for Modern China*, 2nd ed. (New York: Norton, 1999), 224–26. Also, Huters, *Bringing the World Home*, Ch. 2.

9. Confucianism (and even that term is controversial) is of course a highly complex historical, and we will specify this term more as we proceed.

10. Hence, we see an explosion in translations of social theory in China from the 1870s onwards and an intense encounter between these and new forms of Confucian thought Cf. Z. Fu, 'The Sociology of Political Science in the People's Republic of China', in *The Development of Political Science: A Comparative Survey*, ed. D. Easton, L. Graziano and J. Gunnell (London: Routledge, 1991), 223–51. Also, P. Zarrow, *After Empire: The Conceptual Transformation of the Chinese State, 1885–1924* (Palo Alto, CA: Stanford University Press, 2012).

11. Writers such as Frank Dikotter suggest that the encounter with the West – parsed as globalization – was not seen by the middle classes, workers and peasants as coercion or existential threat – as witnessed by their enthusiastic or nonchalant adoption of new forms of material culture. We return to this in the next chapter. Cf. F. Dikotter, *The Age of Openness: China before Mao* (Berkeley: University of California Press, 2008) and F. Dikotter, *Exotic Objects: Modern Objects and Everyday Life in China* (New York: Columbia University Press, 2006).

12. See P. Mishra, *From the Ruins of Empire: The Revolt against the West and the Remaking of Asia* (London: Penguin Books, 2012).

13. Cf. P. Duara, *Rescuing History from the Nation: Questioning Narratives of Modern China* (Chicago: University of Chicago Press, 1995).

14. Quoted in M. Jacques, *When China Rules the World: The End of the Western World and the Birth of a New Global Order* (New York: Penguin Books, 2009), 20; cf. L. S. K. Kwong, 'The Rise of the Linear Perspective on History and Time in Late Qing China c.1860-1911', *Past & Present* 173, (2001): 157–90. On notions of time cf. P. Duara, *The Crisis of Global Modernity: Asian Traditions and a Sustainable Future* (Cambridge: Cambridge University Press, 2015), Ch. 2, 'Circulatory and Competitive Histories', 53–90.

15. Cf. L. O. Lee, *Shanghai Modern: The Flowering of a New Urban Culture in China, 1930–1945* (Cambridge, MA: Harvard University Press, 1999), Ch. 2; A. Greenspan, *Shanghai Future: Modernity Remade* (London: Hurst and Co., 2014), 71

16. Quote from Huters, *Bringing the World Home*, 220.

17. The old Chinese word for decentralization (*Fengjian*) was repurposed, via Japan as 'feudalism'. Cf. Duara, *Crisis of Global Modernity*, 84–85.

18. B. Anderson, *Imagined Communities: Reflections on the Origin and Spread of Nationalism* (London: Verso, 1983).

19. Cf. Duara, *Crisis of Global Modernity*, Ch. 2.

20. Huters, *Bringing the World Home* makes this point strongly, as we shall see. But also, Duara, *Rescuing History from the Nation*.

21. Cf. Westad, *Restless Empire*, 204.

22. P. Anderson, 'Imitation Democracy', *London Review of Books* 37, no. 16 (2015): 19–24, 20.

23. We discuss Lu Xun more below. But his highly ambiguous relation to tradition is well discussed in G. Davies, *Lu Xun's Revolution: Writing in a Time of Violence* (Cambridge, MA: Harvard University Press, 2013), especially Ch. 6.

24. R. Rana Mitter, *A Bitter Revolution: China's Struggle with the Modern World* (Oxford: Oxford University Press, 2004). Also, Mishra, *From the Ruins of Empire*.

25. P. Anderson, 'Incommensurate Russia', *New Left Review* 95 (2015): 5–43, 36. He adds that Russia had resources 'historically shallow' compared to China, India and Japan.

26. Huters, *Bringing the World Home*, 2.

27. For an expansive pan-Asian account see Mishra, *From the Ruins of Empire*.

28. Nationalism appeared as the essential means for a constructing a nation state capable of withstanding the colonial powers, as it did for implementing modernization programmes in various combinations of state, capital and market. For many, the economic rise of non-Western states in the last 40 years has suggested a post-imperialist era in which most nation states have now embraced capitalism and consumerism, and are manfully struggling to fully implement the liberal democratic package that makes these possible. But the very real tensions within 'emerging' economies as well as those, like China, finding themselves at the forefront of a global economic order fraught with long-term problems, cannot be wished away so easily. They have not been displaced by the substitution of 'the West' by 'Global North' set within a Washington Consensus enshrining a global legal-regulative order no longer so obviously tied to the normative model of 'Western democracy'.

29. Cf. A. Sun, *Confucianism as a World Religion: Contested Histories and Contemporary Realities* (Princeton and Oxford: Princeton University Press, 2013); P. van der Veer, *The Modern Spirit of Asia: The Spiritual and the Secular in China and India* (Princeton and Oxford: Princeton University Press, 2013). See also H. Wang, *The Politics of Imagining Asia* (Cambridge, MA: Harvard University Press, 2011).

30. The work of Francois Jullien is exemplary here. Cf. F. Jullien, *The Propensity of Things* (Cambridge, MA: Zone Books, 1999). Also D. Hall and R. Ames, *Anticipating China: Thinking Through the Narratives of Chinese and Western Culture* (Albany: State University of New York Press, 1995).

31. Cf. B. Schwartz, *In Search of Wealth and Power: Yen Fu and the West* (Cambridge, MA: Cambridge University Press, 1964) on Legalism. See the last footnote on Daoism.

32. M. Elvin, 'The Collapse of Structural Confucianism', in *Another History: Essays on China from a European Perspective* (Sydney: Wild Peony Press, 1996), 352–89, 352; emphasis added.

33. Ibid., 352.

34. Ibid., 389.

35. Cf. X. Yao, *Reconceptualising Confucian Philosophy in the 21st Century* (New York: Springer and Higher Education Press, 2017). For a strong statement of 'political Confucianism'; cf. J. Qing, *A Confucian Constitutional Order,* trans. E. Ryden (Princeton: Princeton University Press, 2013).

36. Zarrow, *After Empire.*

37. For example, Confucian administrators and scholars grappled with the concept of emperor as exemplifying 'benevolence', and thus his central role in securing the heavenly order established for the material and spiritual benefit of humanity. How this related to the new concept of the national-popular that infused the legitimation discourses – and very real power – of the western states was a central concern. On Liang Qichao's attempt to think the nature of a citizen-state through Confucian forms, Zarrow takes a different approach to Elvin, seeing not simply a paean to the western nation state but an attempt to refigure a Chinese response in the light of ethico-political concepts directly drawn from Confucian thought. Zarrow's chapter on Liang Qichao in *After Empire* has strong echoes in Mishra, *From the Ruins of Empire.*

38. H. Wang, *China from Empire to Nation State* (Cambridge: Harvard University Press, 2014). This is a translated introduction to his (现代中国思想的兴起, *The Rise of Modern Chinese Thought*). 4 Vols, (Beijing: Sanlian Shudian, 2004).

39. Cf. S. Anshu, F. Lachapelle and M. Galway, 'The Recasting of Chinese Socialism: The Chinese New Left since 2000', *China Information* 32, no.1 (2018): 139–59, 145–46.

40. Schwartz, *In Search of Wealth and Power,* 240. Quoted in Huters, *Bringing the World Home,* 66.

41. This is extensively discussed in Wang, *China from Empire to Nation State* and in Wang, *China's Twentieth Century.*

42. Takeuchi Yoshimi provides one such example. See: T. Yoshimi, *What is Modernity: Writings of Tekeuchi Yoshimi* (New York: Columbia University Press, 2005), 53–82.

43. R. Bin Wong, *China Transformed: Historical Change and the Limits of European Experience* (Ithaca, NY: Cornell University Press, 1997).

44. Bin Wong, *China Transformed,* Ch. 4, 73–104. See also M. Elvin, *The Pattern of the Chinese Past* (Stanford, CA: Stanford University Press, 1973), Ch. 1.

45. M. Foucault, *Security, Territory, Population: Lectures at the College de France 1977–78* (London: Palgrave Macmillan, 2007).

46. J. Habermas, *The Structural Transformation of the Public Sphere* (Cambridge, MA: MIT Press, 1989).

47. Williams, *Keywords.*

48. Wang, *China's Twentieth Century,* 48.

49. T. Bennett, *Making Culture, Changing Society* (London: Routledge, 2013), 4.

50. On this, see Z. Li, *The Chinese Aesthetic Tradition* (Honolulu: University of Hawai'i Press, 2010).

51. Habermas, *Structural Transformation of the Public Sphere.*

52. As described by Adam Smith. See, for example, A. Smith, *The Wealth of Nations* (London: Penguin, 1982).

53. Habermas, *Structural Transformation of the Public Sphere*, 24.

54. 'The medium of this political confrontation was peculiar and without historical precedent: people's use of their reason' (Habermas, *Structural Transformation of the Public Sphere*, 27).

55. Here was one of the roots of Kant's *sapere aude*. Cf. Immanuel Kant's 1784 essay 'An Answer to the Question: What Is Enlightenment?', in *Kant's Political Writings*, ed. H. S. Reiss (Cambridge: Cambridge University Press, 1970), 54–60

56. Here we find an anticipation of Anderson's 'imagined communities' in which strangers were bound by a sense of communality-in-simultaneity created by the proliferation of the printed word (Anderson emphasizes the novel as exemplary of modernity) made possible by the new market economy.

57. Habermas, *Structural Transformation of the Public Sphere*, 37.

58. Elvin, *Pattern of the Chinese Past*.

59. Bin Wong, *China Transformed*, 121.

60. L. Ledderose, *Ten Thousand Things: Module and Mass Production in Chinese Art* (Princeton, NJ: Princeton University Press, 2000).

61. Habermas restricts civil society to commodity exchange and social labour; it was the identification of areas of 'common concern' over and above civil society that produces the public sphere. Habermas, *Structural Transformation of the Public Sphere*, 30–36.

62. Bin Wong's idea of 'fractal' alignment might be seen as a form of Confucius' *li hai yue*, 'rites and music', where patterns or forms of life, repeated at different scales, provide the basis of the social order rather than contracted rights.

63. Cf. M. Keith, S. Lash, J. Arnoldi and T. Rooker, eds., *China Constructing Capitalism: Economic Life and Urban Change* (London: Routledge, 2013), 44–49; also, Wang, *China from Empire to Nation State*.

64. The most comprehensive and influential version of this was William Rowe's account of Hankow: W. Rowe, *Hankow: Commerce and Society in a Chinese City, 1796–1889* (Stanford, CA: Stanford University Press, 1984); W. Rowe, *Hankow: Conflict and Community in a Chinese City, 1796–1895* (Stanford, CA: Stanford University Press, 1989).

65. Bin Wong, *China Transformed*, 163–66.

66. P. Huang, '"Public Sphere"/ "Civil Society" in China?: The Third Realm Between State and Society', *Modern China* 19, no. 2 (1993): 216–40. Cf. the whole issue for an extensive debate, including a response from William Rowe.

67. Emile Zola's foundational *J'accuse* was published in January 1898.

68. Huang, '"Public Sphere"/ "Civil Society" in China?', 229.

69. Cf. Davies, *Lu Xun's Revolution*, 39–40; Schwartz, *In Search of Wealth and Power*, 10–21; Cheek, *Intellectual in Modern Chinese History*, 32–34.

70. Peter Zarrow links this to the foundational ideal of the CCP, where the need to 'serve the people' was an ideal for all citizens to attain. 'And under the party the citizen was first and foremost a member of the state, that is, a member of the national community devoted to its interests' (Zarrow, *After Empire*, 298).

71. The idea of 'the public sphere' and the 'social question' arrived in China at the same time. We might suggest that these two concepts came via different routes. The public realm was a crucial element of that qualification for statehood (and thus formal diplomacy), as discussed in the last chapter, and came through elite routes. The social question emerged more through circuits of ideas of the 'minor West' – through Irish and Polish revolutionaries, oppositional intellectuals and artists, and gradually coming out of the Asian revolutions of the twentieth century.

72. Habermas, *Structural Transformation of the Public Sphere*, Ch. 14 and Ch. 15 especially.

73. Hegel's reading of Adam Smith's *The Wealth of Nations* led to him both reframing 'civil society' as 'economy' and his identification of the increasingly destructive power of private interest and the division of labour. His solution was the integrating power of the state. Cf. S. Buck-Morss, *Hegel, Haiti and Universal History* (Pittsburgh: University of Pittsburgh Press, 2009), 3–10. Marx's critique of Hegel's statist solutions to the social question can be found in his 1843 'A Contribution to a Critique of Hegel's Philosophy of Right', in *Early Writings* (London: Penguin Classics, 1992).

74. Z. Bauman, *Legislators and Interpreters: On Modernity, Post-Modernity and Intellectuals* (Cambridge: Polity, 1989).

75. Cf. the claim by one of the founders of modern Chinese sociology Fei Xiaotong in, F. Xiaotong, 'A Society without Litigation', in *From the Soil: The Foundations of Chinese Society* (Berkeley: University of California Press, 1992), 101–8.

76. T. Mitchell, *Rule of Experts: Egypt, Techno-Politics, Modernity* (Berkeley: University of California Press, 2002).

77. This term was articulated in the *Discourses on Salt and Iron* in the first century BCE. See I. Weber, *China's Escape from the 'Big Bang': The 1980s Price Reform Debate in Historical Perspective* (London: Routledge, 2019).

78. Cf. H. -F. Hung, *The China Boom: Why China Will Not Rule the World* (New York: Columbia University Press, 2016), 38–41.

79. Cf. the discussion in Mishra, *From the Ruins of Empire*, 46–123. Also Mitchell, *Rule of Experts*.

80. The task outlined by Liang Qichao in his famous 1902 essay 'Renewing the People' (echoing a famous eleventh-century Chinese sage) was how best to forge new citizens, imbuing them through education with the new kind of civic virtue or public morality (*gong de*) necessary for a strong nation state. See Mishra, *From the Ruins of Empire*, 124–83; Zarrow, *After Empire*, 56–88; Cheek, *Intellectual in Modern Chinese History*, 43–48, who note that Liang's essay recalled that of Zhu Xi.

81. P. Bourdieu, *Distinction: A Social Critique of the Judgement of Taste* (London: Routledge, 1984).

82. P. Bourdieu, *The Rules of Art: Genesis and Structure of the Literary Field* (Cambridge: Polity, 1996).

83. See for example P. Paul Di Maggio, 'Cultural Entrepreneurship in 19th Century Boston: The Creation of an Organization Base for High Culture in America', *Media, Culture & Society* 4 (1982): 33–50.

84. On constructions of 'worth' see B. Skeggs, 'Imagining Personhood Differently: Person Value and Autonomist Working-Class Value Practices', *Sociological Review* 59, no. 3 (2011): 496–513.

85. J. Habermas, *The Structural Transformation of the Public Sphere* (Cambridge, MA: MIT Press, 1989), 36–43; J. Habermas, *The Theory of Communicative Action: Vol. 1* (Boston: Beacon, 1984). Also on aesthetic autonomy, cf. N. Luhmann, *Art as a Social System* (Stanford: Stanford University Press, 2000).

86. A term coined by Baudelaire in his 1864 essay 'The Painter of Modern Life'. Cf. J. Mayne, ed. and trans., *The Painter of Modern Life and Other Essays* (London: Phaidon Press, 2000).

87. See Postscript to Bourdieu's *The Rules of Art*: 'For a Corporatism of the Universal'.

88. Cf. J. Rancière, *Aisthesis: Scenes from the Aesthetic Regime of Art* (London; Verso Books, 2013). For Kant and Schiller this was couched as freedom from arbitrary rule by the Feudal elite.

89. Which can be translated as 'art's appropriate relation to the world'. S. Olma, *Autonomy and Weltbezug: Towards an Aesthetic of Performative Defiance* (Breda: Avans Hogeschool, 2016).

90. Ezra Pound's notion that 'artists are the antennae of the race' comes from this.

91. Speaking of the impact of classical mythology on European art, Malcolm Bull writes: 'whatever way you looked at it, the renaissance had fostered a third category between the true and the false, namely that of images which were acknowledged to be false but were nevertheless admissible [...] Culture could no longer operate on the assumption that its content was true'. The space of this third category was *fabula*, invention – the creative imagination that extended beyond the reach of reason. M. Bull, *The Mirror of the Gods: Classical Mythology in Renaissance Art* (London: Penguin, 2006), 394.

92. J. Rancière, *The Politics of Aesthetics: The Distribution of the Sensible* (New York: Continuum, 2004).

93. Bourdieu, *Rules of Art*, 293–97. Cf. also I. Singer, *Modes of Creativity* (Boston: MIT Press, 2010); L. Pang, *Creativity and Its Discontents: China's Creative Industries and Intellectual Property Rights Offences* (Durham, NC: Duke University Press, 2012).

94. A good example of this modernizing 'culture complex is Ataturk's importation of western cultural forms as part of his modernising project'. Cf. S. K. Birkiye, 'Changes in the Cultural Policies of Turkey and the AKP's Impact on Social Engineering and Theatre', *International Journal of Cultural Policy* 15, no. 3 (2009): 261–74.

95. Cf. Li, *Chinese Aesthetic Tradition*.

96. A similar point was made regarding the economic realm by Michel Callon in his introduction to M. Callon, *The Laws of the Markets* (London: John Wiley, 1998), 1–4. Callon questioned the kinds of cultural determinism (such as in R. F. Benedict, *Chrysanthemum and the Sword: Patterns of Japanese Culture* [Boston, MA: Mariner Books, 1989]) where essential memes were held to explain the specific development of Japanese society.

97. Cf. T. Dykstal, *The Luxury of Skepticism: Politics, Philosophy, and Dialogue in the English Public* (Charlottesville: University of Virginia Press, 2001), 77–104.

98. Cf. T. Eagleton, *The Ideology of the Aesthetic* (Oxford: Blackwell, 1990), Ch. 2.

99. Thomas Macaulay, in his famous 'Minute on Indian Education', argued for the introduction of English literature into the colonial Indian education system, claiming it would benefit 'the mind of a whole society [...] of knowledge diffused, – of taste purified, – and of arts and sciences planted in countries which had recently been ignorant and barbarous'. Cf. B. Ashcroft, G. Griffiths and H. Tiffin, *The Post-Colonial Studies Reader* (London: Routledge, 1995), 429.

100. H. Caygill, *The Art of Judgement* (Oxford: Blackwell, 1990).

101. Cf. J. Lewis and T. Miller, *Critical Cultural Policy Studies: A Reader* (Oxford: Blackwell, 2003); T. Miller and G. Yudice, *Cultural Policy* (London: Sage, 2002).

102. Cf. G. Burchell, C. Gordon and P. Miller, *The Foucault Effect: Studies in Governmentality* (Hemel Hempstead: Harvester Wheatsheaf, 1991); N. Nikolas Rose, *Powers of Freedom: Reframing Political Thought* (Cambridge: Cambridge University Press, 1999); P. Miller and T. Rose, *Governing the Present* (London: Polity, 2008).

103. I. Hunter, *Culture and Government: The Emergence of Literary Education* (Basingstoke: Palgrave Macmillan, 1988).

104. T. Bennett, *Culture: A Reformer's Science* (London: Sage, 1998); Bennett, *Making Culture, Changing Society*. For a version of this that takes place in the nineteenth-century city, cf. P. Joyce, *The Rule of Freedom: Liberalism and the Modern City* (London: Verso, 2003).

105. Williams, *Keywords*.

106. Bennett, *Making Culture, Changing Society*, 23–48.

107. Cf. Li, *Chinese Aesthetic Tradition*.

108. Cf. F. Jullien, *A Treatise on Efficacy* (Honolulu: University of Hawai'i Press, 2004).

109. Duara, *Crisis of Global Modernity*.

110. E. Evasdottir, *Obedient Autonomy: Chinese Intellectuals and the Achievement of Orderly Life* (Honolulu: University of Hawai'i Press, 2004); Ledderose, *Ten Thousand Things*.

111. Schwartz, *In Search of Wealth and Power*.

112. Huters, *Bringing the World Home*, 18.

113. Schwartz, *In Search of Wealth and Power*, 17. Schwarz identifies Legalism as a distinct and oppositional strand within Chinese thought, whose pragmatic focus on the state achieving 'wealth and power' he sees as akin to the 'Faustian-Promethean strain' of Western capitalist modernity (not his term, he largely avoids the word capitalism). Thus, he characterizes the growing reform movement at the end of the Qing (and by implication

post-May Fourth political movements) as the return of Legalism. Our approach has been to include Legalism within Confucianism, which is rather crude. However, we have been suggesting a more socio-structural approach to the question of culture and reform, rather than identifying strands of thought. That is, however we might identify certain roots of the Faustian-Promethean strain in Western thought, this cannot be identified with the 'rise of capitalism' in any easy way. So too Legalist thought may well have informed the response, but it can only be understood in the wider configuration of social and political practices we have described as Confucian.

114. M. Foucault, *Society Must Be Defended: Lectures at the Collège de France, 1975–1976* (London: Penguin, 2003).

115. Bin Wong, *China Transformed*.

116. Wang Hui's *China's Twentieth Century* engages in an illuminating discussion of German public administration, operating not in the Hegelian and Weberian form of bureaucracy as the incarnation of abstract reason and formal law, but as a social integrator. Drawing on theorists such as Wolfgang Seibel, German public administration could also be seen to act as social integrator of different social interests. Long before political parties and parliaments, German public administration interacted with various social interest groups in a way that generated a social cohesion around 'symbolic sense-making' and 'the creation of patterns of identity' (31). Here we see resonances between the Chinese social-political configuration and other, less visible configurations in the West.

117. Wang, *China's Twentieth Century*, 35.

118. Ibid., 36.

119. We use Le Corbusier here as cipher for modern mass housing and city planning.

120. Cf. Joyce, *Rule of Freedom*.

121. Cf. Dikotter, *Exotic Objects*, 109–32.

122. What Susan Buck-Morss called the dreamworld of 'industrial modernity'. See: S. Buck-Morss, *Dreamworld and Catastrophe: The Passing of Mass Utopia in East and West* (Cambridge, MA: MIT Press, 2002), especially Ch. 4 and Ch. 5, 152–208.

123. On the internationalization of intellectuals towards the end of the nineteenth century, cf. R. Williams, *The Politics of Modernism: Against the New Conformists* (London: Verso, 2007). For a Pan-Asian account of the same cf. Mishra, *From the Ruins of Empire*.

124. Bourdieu's focus on Flaubert's version of *L'art pour l'art* ignored crucial aspects of artistic autonomy at play in the European context. Bourdieu's virtuoso account of Flaubert's *Madam Bovary* is precisely about a new space between *L'art pour l'art* and the 'social novel'. Cf. Bourdieu, *Rules of Art*.

125. Bourdieu situates Flaubert as achieving artistic autonomy over and against the 'social' novel, subtly undermining its formal operations. However, Bourdieu ignores the extent to which Flaubert was held up as model of abandonment of social responsibility and indeed, in his rejection and ridicule of historical meaning (in *Salammbô* and *The Temptation of St Anthony*, for example). The classic confrontation between 'pure' and 'engaged' art is

that of Sartre's *L'Idiot de la Famille*. For accounts of the 'visionary' relation of art and history in the nineteenth century, one could look to Victor Hugo and the Russian novel. Cf. G. Steiner, *Tolstoy or Dostoevsky: An Essay in the Old Criticism* (New Haven, CT: Yale University Press, 1959).

126. Duara, *Crisis of Global Modernity*. We might also use the term 'porosity' as developed by Buck-Morss, *Hegel, Haiti and Universal History*, 112–14.

3

Shanghai Modern: Cultural Industries and Modernity

Introduction

In the last two chapters, we questioned the narratives around China's encounter with the West and its own pursuit of modernity – capitalist or otherwise. The European 'take off' into the modern was both contingent and specific; as such, it could be made universal only at the cost of great violence. We suggested that China had a distinct route to the modern, one no longer exemplified by a Western 'ideal type', and in which 'traditional' or 'pre-modern' practical ethics and political forms had a continuing role. We also suggested that the 'culture complex' in China was structured very differently to that in the West, and many of the fundamental tropes of modernity – the public sphere, the autonomous artist, liberal governmentality 'at a distance' – did not apply in China. This led to a very different configuration of artists, intellectuals and the state. In particular, the Western notion of *ex nihilo* creativity pursued by the autonomous artist can be seen as deeply connected to the moment of historical 'take-off' in which European capitalism presented itself as a Faustian-Promethean force capable of remoulding the world in its image. Here we focus on the role of Shanghai in this route to the modern.

This is not a straightforward task as Shanghai figures in complex ways in both Western and Chinese imaginaries of the modern. Shanghai represents the site where modernity made landfall in China. For many Western commentators, the wild capitalism culminating in Shanghai's 1920s and 1930s heyday allowed commerce and popular culture to break free of tradition, elites and the state, arriving at a new proto-capitalist, post-Confucian Chinese modernity at home in a globalized world.[1] We call this period Shanghai Modern, and it acts as a beacon to a contemporary Chinese modernity and a model for a new culture and economy in China – both, it is claimed, currently thwarted by the heavy hand of the party-state. Shanghai above all is seen to represent the country's return to the fold of contemporary modernity and – potentially, if the party-state would let it be – its pathway to the future. For the current Chinese regime, the issue has been more

85

about how best to deploy the historical figure of Shanghai Modern in the context of its 'reform and opening' since 1978 (or 1992, in Shanghai's case). As we shall see in Chapter 6, officially sanctioned academic discourses positioned historic Shanghai as confirming the strength of an indigenous Chinese entrepreneurialism able to adapt Western ideas, technologies and modern lifestyles for the greater good of the nation in a new global economy. Both accounts find in Shanghai Modern an anticipation of the contemporary convergence between culture and commerce, though they have different views about the role of the state in this convergence.

In this chapter, we look in detail at the historical role claimed for Shanghai in China's path to modernity. For Leo Ou-Fan Lee, Shanghai's contemporary return reopens different possibilities within Chinese modernity that were frozen by the harsh geopolitical conflicts of nation-building, world war and revolution, allowing a revisiting of an earlier, more open, cosmopolitan modernity.[2] The return of Shanghai, bringing back an 'urban cultural sensibility rooted in cosmopolitanism',[3] was directly contrasted with the rural, the backwards and the closed, as well as the brutal politics of nation-building and revolution.

We want to argue that this image misrepresents the structural position of Shanghai in Chinese modernity, and effects a separation of politics and culture in a way that sidelines much of the artistic and intellectual project of Shanghai Modern. It ends by associating urban cosmopolitan sensibilities with the freedoms of the market, setting these, if not against, then certainly in a distinct space from, politics and the Chinese state.

A brief history

The outlines of Shanghai's history are well known. Until 1850 it was a small city of around 350,000 on the edge of China's leading economic region, Jiangnan. It was transformed by the arrival of the maritime powers of Britain, France and, shortly thereafter, the United States and (more ominously) Japan. They used the powers confirmed by the 1842 Treaty of Nanking to assert their control of the north bank of the Huangpu River (tributary to the huge internal waterway of the Yangtze), carving out a new territory ('concessions') adjacent to the old Chinese walled city. Here they established their own legal and administrative systems, an enclave of 'modernization' on the edge of the Qing Empire. The city rapidly developed into one of Asia's biggest ports, using Chinese intermediaries to expand its trade up the Yangtze into the huge interior. Jerry-built mass housing provided accommodation for Chinese labour and great profits for the colonial owners of some of the most expensive real estate in the world. As Chinese landowners and merchants relocated to the city – especially after the mid-century ravages of the

Taiping Rebellion, discussed in more detail below – an entrepreneurial Chinese 'middle class' began to emerge.[4] By the end of the nineteenth century, this middle class was taking advantage of foreign technology, expertise and capital to partici-pate in the industrialization of the city and its hinterland.

The foreign municipal councils embarked on a thoroughgoing 'Haussmanization' of the city, giving it a water, sewerage, transport, electric lighting and gas-supply infrastructure to rival any city on earth.[5] By the 1920s, Chinese capital – still impenetrably organized outside the Western banking system – had begun to move beyond industry and trade and into the new consumer economy of leisure, enter-tainment and shopping, which gave Shanghai its distinct identity as capital of Chinese modernity.

Modernization seemed to create an embryonic Chinese capitalist, entrepre-neurial middle class – the classic development script in microcosm. This middle class was actively involved in the reform movements of the late nineteenth and early twentieth centuries, combining calls for rational and scientific administration with strong nationalist and anti-colonial sentiments. Given that the Chinese middle class comprised a small minority caught between the bulk of the Qing Empire and the might of the foreign powers, there was, however, no question of a 'bourgeois revolution'. They were also increasingly caught between their nationalist demo-cratic aspirations and the militancy of the trade unions and the Communist Party after the First World War. After dispatching the Communists from Shanghai and other cities in 1927, the Kuomintang increasingly took nationalist aspirations in an authoritarian direction, and by the time of the Japanese invasion of 1937 had more or less nationalized Chinese capital. The arrival of the Communists at the end of the Civil War in 1949 merely sealed the decline of that entrepreneurial Chinese capitalism that had seemed to be emerging in the wake of Western modernization.

But Shanghai did not just stand for economic, administrative and technological modernization. As Leo Ou-Fan Lee's book had it, the city also stood for mod-ernity.[6] Shanghai is where the word 'modern' first entered the Chinese lexicon. The creation of a Chinese enclave (over 80 per cent of the population in the foreign concessions) escaping the ravages of the Taiping Rebellion, the constraints of the Qing state, and an openness to the ideas and energies swirling around Shanghai produced a new kind of Chinese urban culture. Although immigrants were ini-tially brought under the tutelage of regional associations and their landowner/ merchant patrons, by the end of the nineteenth-century new customs, values and identities were emerging, along with an urban leisure and consumption economy.[7]

By the end of the 1920s, Shanghai's 'cultural industries' manifested similar pat-terns to those in New York, London and Berlin. Shanghai had the first cinemas in Asia, a popular press, bookshops (which soon also sold records), a commercial film and music industry, multiple radio stations, and it was China's publishing centre.

The era witnessed an explosion of teahouses and dancehalls, hotels and restaurants, bars and nightclubs, department stores and popular entertainments – many funded by Chinese capital. These provided opportunities for Chinese entrepreneurs and consumers, as well as the multinational population that thronged the concessions. They were serviced from an urban proletariat who mostly lived in abject poverty, creating a spectacle of squalor and riches few writers could resist. Prostitution, gambling, drinking, opium: Shanghai acquired a distinct image of glamorous, amoral, rank decadence. For the Chinese Communists – Mao building on the image of the peasant more than the urban working class – this urban decadence was an index of the destruction imperialism and capitalism had wrought on China. As such, though Shanghai remained vital economically after 1949, its history, along with its imaginary, was buried under opprobrium.

A revived urban modernity?

Marie-Claire Bergere's reading of Shanghai's contemporary significance is a common one: the city is 'the place where raw capitalism and political and cultural tradition meet and co-exist in harmony'.[8] Shanghai's mission, acting as gateway for the entry of 'regulated Westernisation', is to represent that 'modernity' to which '1 billion Chinese aspire and to which they are learning to adapt'.[9] 'Raw capitalism' is thus equated with 'modernity'; 'political and cultural tradition' refers not only to the Confucian or classical Chinese tradition but also includes the contemporary party-state, to which this raw capitalist modernity must adapt (at least temporarily). The collapse of modernity into capitalism, and both into Westernization, is, of course, the now classic narrative of normative Western modernity and Chinese backwardness.

Lee's *Shanghai Modern* was a far more complex and nuanced evocation of Shanghai's modernity, not just about 'raw capitalism' or a site of state 'regulated Westernization', but a particularly urban modernity which he associates with a globalization rendered as 'cosmopolitan'. Lee attempted to establish a connection between the re-emergence of Shanghai after 1992 and an older Chinese cosmopolitanism lost in 1949 (though partially preserved in its mirror-city of Hong Kong).[10] Lee evokes the cosmopolitan world of Shanghai in the 1920s and 1930s, building on and extending an international scholarship – much of it North American – which had tried to unearth this period from the demonology of imperialism and capitalism under which it had been buried by Communist historiography. In this revised image, instead of the decadent, alien semi-colony, we have a thriving metropolis providing space for growing Chinese financial and industrial capital and an emergent urban middle class enjoying material comforts and popular culture at a level similar to its counterparts in other great international cities.

Be that as it may, it is barely conceivable historically that the Shanghai model could ever have been extended to the rest of China. Holding up Shanghai as an embryonic cell out of which Chinese capitalism could have spread ignores the central organizing role of the state in all capitalist development. Shanghai's capitalism was not 'raw' – presumably meaning a pure bottom-up process of entrepreneurial self-organization – but a complex configuration of markets, workers, businesses, capital, laws and technology whose framework was established and sustained by extraterritorial military and financial power. It was clear to most Chinese capitalists, intellectuals and politicians that without the facilitating role of an autonomous nation state, capitalism in China could only ever be dependent on the legal-regulatory role of the imperialist powers, just as it would always be open to their depredations. The notion that capitalism could have organized itself in China, had the revolutionary nation-building projects not tried to annex or abolish it, is simply wishful thinking.

Moreover, as we suggested above, Shanghai's capitalism – raw or otherwise – did not just crash into 'tradition'; its success was predicated on, and strongly influenced by, a long process of indigenous commercial development and related sociocultural transformations from the sixteenth century onwards. The rapid acceleration of these indigenous developments under the impact of Western technology, capital and political organization certainly transformed what it was to be Chinese, as they did the aspirations to, and possibilities of, a Chinese modernity. But the dominating focus of both urban and rural populations was on a strong nation state that could ensure the survival of the historic territory of Ming and Qing China in the face of external threat and internal dissolution. The task of building such a state relied on all sorts of material and immaterial resources from Shanghai but ultimately the sociopolitical dynamics of this lay outside it, in the rural areas. Nation-building and effective societal integration were seen as the quintessential priorities for a Chinese modernity in the late Qing and Republican periods. From this perspective, much of Shanghai Modern – outside the resources it generated to create a nation-people – was a distraction or irrelevance.

Pre-1949 Shanghai, Akbar Abbas argues, was 'non-viable'. It had managed to become one of the most open cities in the world but its cosmopolitanism had come at the cost of its 'de-linkage' from the rest of China.[11] It was incapable, alone, of effecting that transition to a real national community ultimately achieved by the Communist mobilization of the peasantry.[12]

Problematizing Shanghai modern

Shanghai's central role in the emergent modern China of the Republican period rests for Lee on its hosting (thanks to its enclave status) of the cultural technologies and commercial infrastructure necessary to the creation of a nation state as an 'imagined community'. This new urban culture was dominated by a 'print capitalism' and Shanghai was its centre.[13] The city was also to become the centre of China's film and (though Lee does not mention this) music industries.[14] Shanghai's centrality relied on its insertion within a complex space of global flows – intellectual and artistic ideas certainly, but also new printing and reproduction technologies, new forms of commerce (such as joint stock companies and copyright laws) and, importantly, new sources of capital. Shanghai's post-1992 return as a driving force in a new modern China would surely – in Lee's view – suggest a role for both artistic autonomy and commercial cultural production in reimagining a new Chinese (urban) 'public sphere' and the kind of citizens who would emerge within it.

This commercial arena, for Lee, was one in which a search for new audiences, their unknown desires and pleasures, began to flesh out the forms of life of a new, modern China, going beyond the rational, conceptual world of political reason. But while this registers the 'newness' of Shanghai Modern, it does so by privileging the autonomy of artists and the new cultural industries over and above the competing nation-building efforts of the KMT and CCP, as it does the cosmopolitan metropolitan over the closed agrarian world that grounded these political projects.

Lee's book tried to excavate a distinct urban modernity, one in which the abstract proclamations associated with May Fourth intellectuals – that China was to be future-oriented and repudiate its past – would be fleshed out through the lived experiences of the urban and the new textual forms and technologies to which these had given rise. He looks to Anderson's thesis that 'a nation is first an "imagined community" before it becomes a political reality', with that imagined community being produced through 'print capitalism', especially 'novels and the newspaper'.[15] He wishes to combine this imagined community with Habermas's public sphere, where both are crucial for nation-building: 'In my view this was precisely what constituted the intellectual problematic for China at the turn of the century, when the intellectuals and writers sought to imagine a new community (*chun*) of the nation [...] as they tried to define a new reading public.'[16]

These intellectuals and writers sketched the broad contours of a new vision of China for this emergent public of 'newspaper and journal readers and students in the new schools and colleges'. This visionary imagination preceded the efforts of nation-building, with its 'rationalization' and 'disenchantment'. But, though it lacked a 'cogent intellectual discourse or political system', it popularized those 'concepts and values' which 'elite intellectuals such as Liang Qichao' simply proclaimed.[17]

Popularization involved the wide dissemination of these concepts and values in the form of journals, newspapers and textbooks, but also in illustrated magazines and advertising materials. These new forms of print (and film) represented a fleshing out of the experience of modernity and its affective lived reality. This popularization was thus a process of discovery, in which various commercial enterprises helped 'define a new reading public', attempting to ascertain and satisfy the unknown pleasures of the new urban dwellers.

The May Fourth movement had set the seal on a paradigmatic change in time consciousness in modern China.[18] Lee cites the ways in which calendars (advertising tobacco, make-up, medicines and so on) had already, since 1872, based themselves on the Western Gregorian system and, with the proliferation of clocks across the city, brought the experience of modernity – 'homogenous, empty time' – into the everyday lives of the new Chinese citizens.[19] Lee also discusses how the visions of the 'new woman', abstractly invoked by May Fourth intellectuals' attack on 'feudal' practices, became more ambiguous, complex and anxiety-filled as this figure revealed herself in new forms of commercial urban popular culture. For Lee, commerce lay at the heart of these new urban desires, as it did the forms of representation that both responded to, and further stimulated, these desires. Commerce is not opposed to art and culture but is the context in which it thrives, opening up in modern China new cosmopolitan horizons and (briefly) providing the space in which independent writers could thrive.

Shanghai then emerges as a space of autonomous culture, one framed by a radical break with the traditional past, founded on the freedoms of market-based cultural technologies and at a necessary distance from politics and the state. As such, Lee's account clearly chimes with the 'post-political' feel of the 1990s – and not just in China. State and nation recede as culture, markets and accelerated global exchange remake the world, and China's place within it. It is this moment to which the historical image of Shanghai Modern spoke. We now want to problematize the city's image as a commercially driven space of free cultural exploration carved out against both tradition and revolutionary nation-building.

Shanghai Modern represents neither the path to a capitalist modernity China never took, nor the commercial cultural capital now available for a new cosmopolitan post-Mao China. The opposition Lee establishes between a cultural 'imaginary' made possible by commerce, and the rationalizing political-institutional to which it eventually fell victim, is not sustainable. The political struggle in China over the imagined nation took place intensively on the site of the cultural, in which the affective world of the modern was very much in play, as were the new cultural technologies across which it was being reframed. This political struggle should not be seen as an alien intrusion by the party-state but as part of a wider ethico-political project widely shared by artists and intellectuals.

In what follows, we look first at 'print capitalism' and how it formed part of a new kind of intellectual-national project, working very much through a new mass market. We then look at the new cultural industries of film and music and how this intellectual-national project was reframed within these new commercial and technological dynamics, and the forms of collective experience which they helped articulate and shape.

Print capitalism

'Print capitalism' in Anderson's formulation is the *sine qua non* of the modern nation state, both real and imagined.[20] The Chinese scholar-administrators at the end of the nineteenth century set themselves the task of creating a new citizenry out of an unknown popular mass with cultural tools whose use was uncertain. The educational project was absolutely central to this, and one for which the task of production and dissemination of content was more or less 'subcontracted' to Shanghai's printing industry. Fully nationalized eventually by the Communists, 'print media' remains at the heart of the contemporary Chinese state cultural policy.[21]

Shanghai was the centre of 'print capitalism' in China because the foreign concessions provided a protected space in which to embark on politically radical journalism and book publishing. It was also where new printing technologies arrived in China along with new commercial forms (and their legal underpinnings, such as the joint stock company) and, most importantly, the capital required to undertake what became an industrial scale production.[22]

Lee evokes Robert Darnton's well-known work on 'the business of enlightenment' where he uncovered an extensive network of printers and publishers who were busy popularizing the work of the *philosophes* within an emergent European public sphere.[23] The Chinese literati-reformers faced a different political terrain, which was less about opening up a space of critical reason against the state and more about reforming or re-founding that state in a situation of existential threat. Lee's use of Darnton also fails to register the different nature of print capitalism in late-nineteenth- and early-twentieth-century Shanghai.[24]

Neither Chinese 'print culture' nor 'print commerce' (which were effectively what Anderson was referring to) can be seen as signs of the modern. Xylographic printing began in China nearly eight centuries before Gutenberg. 'Print commerce' was a later development but was a thriving sector by the time of the Ming dynasty and grew rapidly through the Qing. As we saw with respect to other forms of Western modernity (and something entirely ignored by Anderson) an extensive network of commercial print production and distribution had developed across imperial China well before its encounter with Western modernity. This seriously vitiates the opposition between empire and nation state that is at the centre of his account of modernity.[25] It also raises doubts as to the nature of the 'imagined community' in imperial China, which already bore many of the marks Anderson identifies with the societies infused by 'print capitalism' in the early modern period.

A different approach is taken by Meng Yue, who charts the rise of Shanghai as a centre of print culture and commerce, beginning in earnest after 1862, when two of the most important centres of Chinese learning – Hangzhou and Suzhou – were devastated by the Taiping army.[26] Many of the scholar-administrators from these cities came to Shanghai as a refuge, seeing it as a base from which the whole Jiangnan region might be recovered for the Qing state. This 'recovery' formed an essential part of that 'self-strengthening' associated with Zeng Guofan and Li Hongzhang, who set up a new militia system with associated administrative, taxation and military (arsenals, polytechnic) institutions as a precondition for the defeat of the Taipings. The 'self-strengthening' movement, and its unorthodox administrative innovations, set up a reform dynamic that gradually began to undermine the fixed forms of the Qing state. Meng Yue suggests the same for the publishing world that emerged as part of this self-strengthening in Shanghai. Chinese scholar-administrators, as we suggested in Chapter 2, began to interrogate Confucian texts as guide to their reform of the Qing, a process that rapidly began to point beyond what the imperial state could actually deliver.

> Shanghai was Suzhou reborn – in the sense that it liberated Suzhou from its unfulfilled, oppressed, and ruptured cultural dreams. Shanghai was also a Suzhou turned modern – modern in the sense that the practice of science and technology for order building was, self-contradictorily, dissolving that order.[27]

Print culture and commerce in Shanghai thus attracted newly displaced, mobile and entrepreneurial scholar-gentry of the late Qing, who inadvertently found a place in which unorthodox (unruly) ideas could be developed.[28] It put them together with a rising group of artisan-entrepreneurs who had moved into a publishing industry which was being transformed by new Western technologies. It was in this context that the production of newspapers, political essays, journals and books concerned with reform and revolution, and the translation and dissemination of the new learning that were necessary to this, occurred. Importantly, it was not until the late nineteenth century that the 'new' learning – that which previously circulated in the space of a new kind of Chinese cultural and scientific literati – began to be equated with being 'Western'.

The shift to 'print capitalism' proper came about not only through accelerated mechanization but also by the opening up of a massive new market for text books consequent on the belated, and mostly ineffectual, educational reforms of the

Qing in 1906. The abolition of the millennium-old imperial examination system, and the founding of schools and colleges intended to incorporate 'new' learning, opened up a huge new market which publishing firms in Shanghai were quick to fill. Most famous – and that discussed extensively by Lee – was Shanghai's pre-eminent publishing house, the Commercial Press, which saw its textbook business as part of its political ambition to create new citizens for a new nation to be. In this, they were more successful than the Qing's educational reforms and provided the central plank of that 'imagined community' of which Lee spoke.

This new 'print capitalism' involved large premises and workforces, extended distribution networks and high levels of capital with consequent pressure to secure returns. But at the same time, this 'print capitalism' was also a political-intellectual project. The traditional scholar-administrators – on their way to becoming 'intellectuals' – were never ousted by the artisan-entrepreneurs and they continued to set the overall project of creating a Chinese nation through educational publishing. Shanghai's 'print capitalism' thus involved a complex reconfiguration of relations between an intellectual elite, now in control of a powerful printing industry, and a series of states (Qing, Republican, KMT and Communist) that asserted ever-greater authority, but never absolute control, over it.[29]

In print capitalism, intellectuals had a dominant voice.[30] It was the textbook market, rather than newspapers or journals, that formed the heart of the Chinese printing industry. Just as the Qing state looked to commercial publishing to provide its textbooks, subsequent governments also worked in close collaboration with Shanghai's printing industry. This print industry in turn recognized its dependence on the state to provide secure markets – in the sense of a major and regular client and to provide the secure legal context in which business could be conducted. Shanghai's 'print capitalism' was not an industry 'like any other', not when nation-state building was at stake. It was a public service carried on through commercial means.[31] 'Print capitalism' was crucial to building those citizens whose outlines were yet unclear through an education system only beginning to be formed, by a state that was still in the making.

From literary revolution to revolutionary literature

Alongside educational reform came the reprogramming of the language itself into a national vernacular. The creation of a new simplified Chinese script would not only facilitate literacy but also promote the integration of local dialects into the coherent whole of a new nation state. Such a project – which at one point included Lu Xun's famous proposal to introduce Latinized script[32] – was familiar across the Asian world, most tellingly perhaps in the lands of the Ottoman Empire where a new Latin script drew an absolute line between the modern Turkish present and the archaic Ottoman past.

For the scholar-intellectuals, this process of renovation, as we saw in Chapter 3, involved what had recently come to be known through the neologism *wenhua*. Christopher Reed suggests this 'culture' could be more accurately translated as 'literary culture' and 'refers not only to the literary arts and methods associated within them, but also to broad education and learning, and to their acquisition'.[33] This, however, misses the aspect of transformation and 'influence' in *wenhua*, as identified by Laikwan Pang: 'As *wen* [writing/ culture] is always associated with *hua* [transformation], *wenhua* is political.'[34]

In 1902, Liang Qichao (himself a print entrepreneur) looked to the West where

> a newly published book could often influence and change the views and arguments of the whole nation. Indeed, political novels should be given the highest credit for being instrumental in the steady progress made in the political sphere in America, England, Germany, France, Austria, Italy and Japan.[35]

As such, 'if one intends to renovate the people of a nation one must first renovate its fiction'.[36] This call for 'literary revolution' was taken up by the New Culture movement (especially in the *New Youth* magazine, published in Beijing) and accelerated by that of May Fourth. They sought to promote a new vernacular language, *baihua*, against the classical dynastic formalism of *wenyan*.[37] They wanted a language that would instruct readers and gain market share for their particular brand of 'new-style' prose, poetry, criticism, social commentaries and treatises,[38] and that would give direct access to the masses – a language that only scholar-intellectuals themselves could supply. As with education, this direct access and reform would come through the adoption and promotion of *baihua* by the state working with the apparatuses of the printing industry.[39]

The co-creation of a new nation-people would not just be distributed between state forms and intellectuals but also necessarily had to work through the market. This is presented as ironic, even hypocritical, by some authors, as if any involvement in commercial culture somehow vitiated a left-wing project. However, the 'popular', as articulated/interpellated in new forms of commercial culture, was an intensive site of political struggle. This was a power struggle between an intellectual elite and the new commercial forms which challenged their traditional role and which these intellectuals sought initially to dismiss as debased. However, it became clear that the 'commercial', at the same time as threatening their traditional position, was also a site of struggle over the articulation of new forms of individual and collective experience, one which called for a new set of approaches from intellectuals and political parties alike if they were to prevail.

In the literary field, the advocates of *baihua* immediately began to denigrate an earlier form of popular fiction associated with the new reading public of Shanghai. The 'Mandarin Duck and Butterfly School' of romantic fiction, which had previously been linked to social progress and the promotion of modern values, as well as contributing to Shanghai's commercial publishing industry, was now positioned as 'low-brow' and morally dubious.[40] This dispute points to a persistent conflict within Shanghai's publishing world, where New Culture intellectuals seeking to sell books came into conflict with more popular, and lucrative, tastes – tastes that the printing industry continued to cater to and thereby finance its more 'elevated' publishing project.[41] This professional rivalry should also be seen as an aspect of the pressing question of what this 'popular' was, and how it could be appealed to – in what language and through what forms – in order to facilitate the people's effective mobilization.

This question emerged across a sharpening of the political situation as the 'national revolution' regained momentum through the growing power of Chiang Kai-shek's KMT in the south, followed by his successful Northern Expedition, which, in 1928, established a more or less viable national state. Both the KMT and the CCP (which the former violently purged in Shanghai and elsewhere in 1927) were Leninist party-machines, their political-organizational technology being the main element they took from the Bolshevik Revolution in 1917.[42] Here was a new way of recreating the relations between elites and masses for purposes of national revolutionary state-building. As such, the language of the masses – how to interpellate their interests and aspirations – was absolutely crucial to their political purpose. It was the active search for the appropriate form and content of that address that traversed the political and intellectual debates of the 1920s and 1930s.

This intensified political exigency, over which loomed civil war and Japanese invasion, was expressed by Cheng Fangwu (of the left-wing Creation Society and a leading Communist opponent of Lu Xun) in his famous 1928 statement. After the KMT's Shanghai purge, and in full accordance with the Comintern's 'ultra-left' turn – but expressing many of the deep aspirations of intellectuals to find the 'true-path' (*wangdao*) to the ethical polity – Cheng declared that the 'literary revolution' was now to give way to 'revolutionary literature'.[43] The preferred form was 'realism', with artists entreated to 'be a phonograph', objectively reproducing the objective world in order to mobilize the people.[44] Julia Lovell captures some of this complex debate in her portrait of those writers who chose literary realism as their route to the masses:

> Quite apart from the difficulties of developing sufficient familiarity with a labouring milieu to write convincingly about it, such writers had to ponder awkward issues of narrative distance: how to prevent realism's aura of objectivity morphing into contempt for the suffering masses for whom they felt instinctive

sympathy. A self-confidence in the writer's ability to doctor the nation (through a Europeanised literature incomprehensible to the Chinese masses) collided with an acute sense of intellectual guilt and a self-loathing urge to erase bourgeois authorship with a literature 'of the people'.[45]

This increased sense of urgency and inadequacy arising from the new mobilizing language of class positioned intellectuals and writers as outside the masses and, as we shall see, in its heavy reliance on Western literary models, separate from the Chinese nation itself. This at a time when Mao was developing his notion of the 'mass line' (*qunzhong luxian*), in which immersion in the people was the primary political task.[46] It was this separation from the people and its prioritization of foreign literary models that fuelled the important critiques of Qu Qiubai, as we discuss below.

> The self-deceptions and impossibilities of the position of left-wing Chinese intellectuals animate much of Lu Xun's fictional and polemical work. In his work, the ongoing negotiation of elite-state configuration in the 1920s and 30s is couched less in terms of intellectual 'autonomy' than the ability, or right, to speak to and/or for the people. Lu Xun registered this with agonising clarity. Mordantly sarcastic about the pretensions of revolutionary writers (even though he joined the communist-led Left Wing Writers League), he was deeply conscious of the yawning gulf between his new vernacular language and the lives of the masses.[47]

Estranged as it was from the general population, the new vernacular was equally so from China's classical literary tradition. Lu Xun's work – which in certain books such as *Wild Grass* is disturbingly 'modernist' – often stages the self-wounding, self-hobbling process of learning a new, alien language in order to kill that classical language with which you are most at home. In this way (as with many of the modernist writers Leo Ou-Fan Lee discusses in the central portion of his book), the conflict between modernity and tradition is much more convoluted and disturbed than might be imagined from the bold proclamations of the May Fourth generation, with their straight historical line to the progressive future. That generation had to confront the arrival of the masses as a real fact as well as the recasting of the traditional role of intellectuals. Their central question was how were they to articulate a collective experience at a time of urgent political demands for national defence and revolution?

From literati to intellectuals

That such a fundamental rethinking was necessary should not be seen as a crushing of artistic autonomy under the wheels of political exigency. Having some sort of relationship to the unfolding political project of nation-building, and the mobilization of the masses this clearly demanded, was something intellectuals could not avoid. There were few Byzantiums to which they could sail, other than the dwindling islands of the foreign concessions. This was not a 'betrayal' of the intellectual before brute power as evoked in European circles,[48] and it cannot be reduced to the fear of a mass culture undermining their professional self-identity.[49] We might see it instead as a deepening or re-figuration of the engagement of an artist-intellectual tradition in the face of historical danger and possibility.[50]

Lee's distinction between the imagined and the institutional refers in one sense to the inevitable gap between a broad-ranging intellectual-political project and the reality of its implementation. But the field of the cultural cannot be distinguished in this way from the ethical-political project of nation-building in which these intellectuals participated. We suggested above that Western structures of artistic autonomy, *bildung* and related forms of aesthetic education were very different from Confucian (or neo-Confucian) traditions of self-cultivation as part of an overarching ethical-political order. There was no autonomous bourgeoisie seeking to define its qualification for political dominance through its ability to deploy its facility of aesthetic distinction. The traditional Chinese scholar-artists, historically associated with learning, administration and (from at least the eighteenth century) commerce, came out of a 'Chinese tradition [...] [which] delineated the ideal path for the 'men of letters' as one of engagement beyond the cultivation of one's self, to entail 'rectifying the family, governing the state, and appeasing "all under heaven"'.[51]

As such, they faced a very different task in late Qing and Republican China from that of the rising 'public' bourgeoisie of eighteenth-century Europe. The task of creating a new Chinese nation came at a time in which the existential threat to Chinese civilization (one 'coterminous' with the nation)[52] demanded the creation of those educated, patriotic and hard-working citizens who would be essential to its survival. Artist-intellectuals were seeking the *wangdao*, or 'true-path', a role in a renewed ethico-political community but in a context in which their traditional social position and function had been radically destabilized. Their seeking out of a 'way', in a world in which they had to work hard to define their new function and sense of self, took place in constant negotiation with the new mass political parties, with their centralized bureaucratic machines, and the new commercial cultural industries with their global networks.[53]

Shanghai by the mid-1920s was becoming one of the great metropolitan nodes in a global network in which flows of people and ideas had produced an international intellectual and artistic avant-garde. Its 'cosmopolitanism' was not opposed to national liberation and anti-colonial (or, later, anti-fascist) movements, and its project to embrace and push forward a Chinese modernity was not restricted to the model of Western liberal democracy, already by 1918 seen by many as historically redundant.[54] In Shanghai, the new intellectuals no longer had fixed links to the state, as the new form of mass mobilization represented by the Leninist party had no immediate role for traditional scholar-administrators. The CCP, which from 1928 had become the main focus of the revolutionary, if not nationalist, struggle, had few links with the intellectuals in Shanghai, other than Qu Qiubai.[55] Shanghai allowed a certain distance from direct political control, thus opening a new space for intellectuals to define their role. It was, however, a role in which the political project of a renewed modern China remained central.

Liang Luo suggests a similarity between the social responsibility of 'traditional' Chinese intellectuals and the Saint-Simonian notion of the avant-garde with its utopian socialist vision, noting 'this utopian vision, with its futuristic, prophetic power, attempted to restructure the world, not only reshaping individual psyches but also by reorganising collective solidarity'.[56] This new project, Luo adds, was – in contrast to that of the older scholar-administrators – profoundly internationalist in outlook, open to the porosity and circulatory vectors of global cultures. At the same time, this project of 'reorganising collective solidarity' was one that had to face a new mass public, not just for the printed word or image, but also new technologies of culture – film, radio, recorded music. These presented challenges which in many ways were not fully engaged with until the early 1930s. As we suggested previously, both the imagining and institutionalization of the modern Chinese citizen would necessarily take place in the era of Taylorism, Le Corbusier and Lenin – technologies of the mass – rather than the heroic constitutionalism of the eighteenth-century European bourgeoisie (revolutionary or otherwise). At their disposal were cultural technologies which were exactly contemporaneous with those being deployed in Europe, North America and the Soviet Union by states also faced with the governance of a new 'mass society'.

The distinction between the imaginary and the institutional was not a structural distinction between the 'cultural' and the 'political'; we prefer to see it as an opening up of a historical space of the possible, the new. This space of the possible, of historical creativity, involved both an imaginary and a political project, an aspiration to individual and collective transformation that it shared with many other strands of the contemporary avant-garde *and* popular culture. In the context of 1920s and 1930s' Shanghai, the new intellectuals had a space in which they felt they could define a new role for themselves, shaping a new popular collective in association with the political party. This is a project they shared with other avant-garde movements of the period.[57] What was distinctive in this situation was that they increasingly felt that they could only make good such a claim by engaging with the new forms of commercial cultural industries, predominantly located in Shanghai.

Organizing the experience of modernity

To understand this more, we can use Oskar Negt and Alexander Kluge's 1972 *Public Sphere and Experience* as well as *Babel and Babylon*, an important work by Miriam Hansen from 1991, which used many of its terms.[58] We have argued Habermas's public sphere cannot work in a Chinese context, and that it has also been subject to extensive criticism in the West itself. Developing a critique similar to those in the Anglophone world after Habermas's book was published in 1989,[59] Negt and Kluge suggested that the public sphere rested on bourgeois forms of participation which excluded other alternative, non-bourgeois 'publics'. But, importantly for us, they also link this 'alternative' public sphere to a concept of 'experience' – *erfahrung* in German – in which the affective and the normative, a 'context of living', are in play along with the more formal and institutional rational-critical debates of the bourgeois public sphere.[60]

The 'general horizon of social experience' is, for Negt and Kluge, articulated primarily via the cultural industries which are – as commercial enterprises – rooted firmly in the private interest sphere. For them, the politics of culture concerned the ways in which the cultural industries might be organized, regulated, and made accessible to non-elites. In this way, Negt and Kluge were trying to retrieve a more open and progressive connection between this 'general horizon of social experience' and the cultural industries from the pessimist outlook of the Frankfurt School. They looked to the work of the avant-garde theorists of the 1920s and 1930s, in particular Brecht, Kracauer and Benjamin, who had tried to explore the forms and dynamics of the new mass culture these technologies of reproduction had made possible. It is this that makes a connection with the situation in 1930s' Shanghai.

Miriam Hansen glosses Negt and Kluge's concept of *erfahrung*:

> On the one hand it refers to the capacities of having and reflecting upon experience, of seeing connections and relations, of juggling reality and fantasy, of remembering the past and imagining a different future; on the other, it entails the historical disintegration and transformation of these very capacities with the onslaught of industrialisation, urbanisation and a modern culture of consumption.[61]

This precisely captures the kind of fractured and contradictory experience at stake in Shanghai and China in the 1920s and 1930s. There, the rapid 'modernization' of social, cultural and political forms took place in very different historical circumstances and involved a configuration of nation, state, intellectuals and markets that was very different from that in Weimar Germany. Nevertheless, this more agonistic and convoluted experience of the modern, even under the great modernist rallying cry of 'Heat-Light-Power',[62] suggests that mix of danger and opportunity evoked by Marshall Berman's *All That Is Solid Melts into Air*, rather than the narrative of an easy adoption of a modern urban lifestyle as a natural and unproblematic sign of 'modernity'.

Where we think China is also distinctive is that the challenge for left-wing artist-intellectuals was not just how to understand this new modern public but also to help shape and articulate that new individual and collective experience of modernity as part of a larger revolutionary political project.

What both Hansen as well as Negt and Kluge point to are the complex, shifting sites of mediated social experience made possible by the arrival of new technologies of production, outside – initially at least – the traditional forms of tutelage of the bourgeoisie and the state. As in the great cities of early-twentieth- century United States and Germany, so too in Shanghai the new modes of modern city living and technologies of print, film and recorded music represented an opening up and mediation of a new 'general horizon of social experience'. The exploration of this new social experience was part of the modernist literary project of the 1920s and 1930s, and it was a central role of Shanghai artist-intellectuals to identify and define, and eventually try to shape, the new experience of those urban publics assembled by the new cultural technologies and city life. They did so, not apart from but in loose collaboration with, the political project of revolutionary nation-building.[63]

As we saw with respect to print capitalism, intellectuals were drawn to the relatively free space of Shanghai, a city at an appropriate geopolitical distance from the KMT capital of Nanjing and far from the rural bases of the CCP. But the city also brought together cultural technologies, finance and commercial know-how. Left-wing intellectuals, strongly linked with international networks of avant-garde artists and intellectuals, sought to articulate their project to register and shape that collective experience in line with the task of national mobilization and revolution. They did so knowing fully well their ignorance of the lives, emotions and desires of the masses (at least those outside Shanghai), of the visual and aural forms opened up by new technologies, and the complex intertextuality through which these lives were accessed, represented and articulated. This was something they sought to learn, and they had to do so in association with the commercial structures that were also trying to identify and shape the new urban public.

The mediation of this new horizon of popular social experience, in popular print, film and music, was uncertain, contested and complex. One of the primary tensions to navigate was that between the new commercial cultural technologies and forms, and older 'traditional' forms of popular culture. This (fluid) distinction between an older 'folk' and newer 'popular' culture goes back at least to the mid-nineteenth-century in Europe and early-twentieth-century in China. It involves a contrast between new forms of 'entertainment' produced by professionals for consumption by new kinds of urban publics, and those older forms involving low-paid, low-status 'professionals' (such as itinerant musicians or actors) but with higher levels of popular participation in their production (performing local opera, for example, was always a communal affair). If intellectuals in the West for a long time saw new commercial pleasures as debased urban forms – neither art nor 'authentic' folk culture – more recently, in post-cultural studies these new commercial forms have been seen as registering previously marginalized or suppressed popular pleasures.

Hansen's account of early American cinema explores some of these issues. She shows how the early American cinema combined an eclectic range of popular pleasures drawn from immigrant 'folk' cultures, cheap urban entertainment and more genteel middle-class forms. Her account is one in which the cinema provided a site, and a series of texts, in which immigrants and new female urban dwellers (relatively uncoupled from traditional forms of family life and gendered roles) could both deal with their dislocation and explore new forms of identity. These were 'unruly' sites and pleasures, escaping the moral tutelage of the middle-class public sphere. However, Hansen charts how the new Hollywood system, both in the spaces and practices of exhibition, and in the visual language it established across its film production – D. W. Griffith is exemplary here – began to codify the immigrant and female urban experience into the more malleable form of a national subject of a 'classless' consumer society. Crucial for us is Hansen's account of Hollywood's ability to shape the 'general horizon of social experience' into a new national-popular configuration around mass consumption.

How might we think the shaping of the 'general horizon of collective experience' in China? Without re-romanticizing 'folk' as authentic-original, a distinction between traditional and commercial popular cultures was crucial for a China where 'traditional' forms were the central cultural experience of the majority of the population. Shanghai exhibited similar qualities to Chicago, Hansen's own New York and the other big American cities, with their uprooted rural immigrants creating lives in an urban squalor which also disrupted traditional social norms and positions. But Chinese traditional cultures, carried from long-settled provincial worlds in mutually incomprehensible dialects, were not, ultimately, as definitively displaced as they were in immigrant America. Their civilizational roots were still very much intact. If W. D. Griffith sought a new visual language to unify the immigrant Babel and create a coherent, unified national language,[64] such a project in China would always confront the persistent, very real power of 'folk' cultural forms even as they sought to interpellate them through the modern technologies of print, film and music.

Shanghai's cultural industries, frequently presented as the *ne plus ultra* of modern living, actually participated in a complex mediation of traditional and commercial popular cultures. This in itself was a challenge to the kinds of literati-professionals that moved into the print – and then film and music – industries. Traditional culture was, in their view, 'feudal'. It was backwards and expressive of a people characterized by Sun Yat-Sen as 'a heap of sand' needing to be integrated within a modern nation state. Yet by the late 1920s, as we have seen, there was a growing sense that the intellectual project of *baihua*, and the renewal of Chinese literature through the importation of literary models from the West (realism, modernism and so on), was at some sort of impasse. This was recognized by the literary theorist and high-ranking CCP official Qu Qiubai, who began to sketch a solution whereby intellectuals might need to address the people in popular forms rather than those taken from the bourgeois culture of foreign nations. In fact, it was through Shanghai's early forms of commercial cultural production that a negotiation of traditional forms and a modern urban public took place.

Mary Farquhar and Chris Berry have shown the ways in which 'shadow opera' (*yingxi*), the early Chinese term for film, was tenaciously linked to popular forms of opera, and how these continued to provide staple 'folk' narratives to an extent unavailable to Western cinema.[65] Lee also shows how the popular melodrama of romantic fiction and of film linked to older popular operatic forms. Haili Ma's study of Yueju opera shows how a folk opera from nearby Zhejiang province entered Shanghai along with migrant workers, where small theatre entrepreneurs, breaking the all-male convention, reframed it as an all-female opera. Intended as a kind of 'girlie show' it became popular with the new female workers in the city, in response to whom this operatic form became more emotionally resonant with their newer concerns.[66] Jones's *Yellow Music* shows, in addition to the almost pathological disgust of May Fourth intellectuals for traditional Chinese music, how the rapid growth of the record industry in China (Shanghai had the biggest industry in Asia by the mid-1920s) was significantly driven by popular opera excepts.[67]

The new mass cultural industries of print, film and music combined the 'folk' and the 'market' popular cultures in complex ways – in terms of both their content (filmed and recorded opera, for example) and their production. In the print industries, the prestige of professional literary writers was strong, even as they engaged in popular literature (Mao Dun at the Commercial Press is a good example).[68] Film and music, on the other hand, as new technologies and industries, combined high levels of capital input with a complex network of semi-professional vernacular production and distribution. As with Hansen's early film publics, *yingxi* intermingled a variety of sites and performance traditions, and its distribution involved myriad agents not yet controlled by any big studios. The recorded music industry was always dominated by foreign capital in its management of studios and printing but at the bottom it involved a disparate input of musicians and intermediaries across China, though with Shanghai at its heart.

These new horizons of collective experience, mediated by new technologies and forms of commerce, were thus marked by a complex set of binaries – feudal and modern, folk and commercial, entertainment and education – which did not quite map onto each other. It had been inconceivable to May Fourth intellectuals that 'feudal' storytelling, performance and music could be compatible with the building of a modern citizenship. Like foot-binding, these things should be eradicated. So too the frivolous entertainment of the popular novels and magazines, as well as the Jazz-influenced dance music of the large urban centres. How then to proceed?

A new role for Shanghai's artist–intellectuals

It was across these tensions that a new cultural project by left-wing intellectuals aligned with the CCP began to emerge. This project was at a distance from the CCP, whose leadership was far away from the urban centres and which was focused on issues deemed more urgent. The CCP itself began to develop a cultural strategy in its base areas, centred on Yan'an, from 1936. In accordance with the 'mass line' approach, the Red Army began work of propaganda in which it tested its ideas in direct contact with the peasantry. Here the pressing question was how to scale up its propaganda activities with little money and very few educated professionals. The Lu Xun academy, established in 1938 at Yan'an, was an attempt to train new cultural professionals, but this took time, especially on a constrained budget. Equally pressing was the question of what forms to use, a consideration that also included participation by the peasants themselves.[69] This could be seen as a response to the situation identified by Qu Qiubai in a series of essays written in the late 1920s and early 30s.[70] He is credited with laying the foundations of a new cultural line by the CCP, in which popular and national forms were now to be used. If traditional arts were feudal, and early reformist modern art (such as Liang Qichao's) 'lacked a common language with the Chinese people', the Communists, under the influence of Qu Qiubai,[71] 'advocated that popular art forms become the common language for revolutionary mobilisation. The popular was to be popularized (*tongsuhua*) and made revolutionary in pursuit of a socialist nation-state'.[72]

This in part laid the basis for post-1949 cultural policy, but already in the 1930s and 1940s it was challenged by the more educated urban professional artist-intellectuals who found their way to Yan'an in increasing numbers after 1937. Their baulking at the rather unsophisticated approach they found in the rural areas, along with their own sense of professional expertise, were a prime target of Mao's famous intervention in the 1942 Yan'an forum (itself linked to a more general 'Rectification

Campaign'). Mao took many elements from Qu Qiubai, and in particular the need to seek out 'the rich deposits of literature and art [that] actually exist in popular life itself'. Foreign traditions had to be used 'in a discriminating way', and 'revolutionary Chinese writers and artists [...] must go amongst the masses'.[73]

> The contrast between these highly educated urban elites and the workers, peasants and soldiers of the Communist Revolution has been a central organising theme of cultural policy in China. A typical account of this situation (and a version of the mythos of Shanghai) was written by a Western observer in 1945: 'The Westernised highly sophisticated art and literature of Shanghai were as far removed from the peasant lore of hinterland China as James Joyce is from Confucius. Under war conditions, away from Shanghai, the literati resembled fish out of water.[74]

However, what we have been sketching out was a very different picture, one in which these literary intellectuals were engaging with the popular not solely as 'peasant lore' but as a complex mix of traditional and commercial popular culture and the 'polyphonic' political, technological, cultural and industrial context in which these were produced and consumed. In the cities, many left-wing intellectuals sought to bring their expertise to developing a new language of the masses that combined elements of the market-popular and the folk-popular to further the party's task of national defence and revolution. They had indeed to fight some bruising intellectual battles to carve out a space for these new cultures against intellectuals who denied them legitimacy[75] and against existing players in this commercial space whose politics were found wanting.[76]

To begin such a process involved infiltrating the new cultural industries of film and music, learning not just the new technologies but the ways in which these forms tried to secure a popular audience. What worked, and what didn't? What did this tell us about the audience? How were these audiences assembled and addressed across multiple forms of media and with what written, visual and aural forms (these converging further after the first Chinese sound film in 1931)? This process of learning also involved working with highly capitalized industries, both Chinese (such as the Lianhua film company)[77] and foreign (such as EMI, RCA-Victor and Pathé).[78] As Liang Luo suggested in relation to the song (which became the national anthem) 'March of the Volunteers':

> Here the technology of songs and the polyphonic cultural scene of the mid-1930s must be emphasised. Print advertisements, gramophone records, radio airwaves, stage and street performances, and film screenings were all important channels through which to market and propagate the song.[79]

105

Lee's own discussion of film culture, drawing on Paul Pickowicz, shows how the political films of the late 1920s and 1930s may have explicitly repudiated 'entertainment' but drew heavily on the forms of popular melodrama to get the message across.[80] Laikwan Pang has done a detailed analysis of the sheer hard work involved in addressing a popular audience in ways that could mobilize a range of emotions and visual pleasures towards a collective end while Ling Luo has done this through a more general frame of 'performance'.[81]

Less explored perhaps has been popular music. Music had always been recognized in China as a 'technology of power', closely related to the Confucian notion of 'rites and music'.[82] The arrival of Western music – its complex polyphony, its highly industrialized (and loud) instruments, its large bands, its tradition of choral (including military) singing – was quickly recognized by reforming intellectuals as a potential 'technology' for the building of a community of new national citizens. Their rejection of a 'feudal' Chinese traditional music went with an absolute embrace of the 'new as Western', an approach which underpinned the emergent elite institutions of Chinese musical education set up from the 1920s onwards.

What was less expected was the power of jazz-inflected music that dominated urban consumption in the 1920s and 30s (by then there were 61 radio stations in Shanghai).[83] As in film, the Communists – especially through the work of Nie Er – developed a new political aesthetic, which Jones calls 'phonographic realism', as a means of 'infiltrating the culture industry with new sonic images of anticolonial resistance, social revolution, and national unity'.[84] In Shanghai, this involved a (highly selective) adaptation both of traditional Chinese forms and instruments and the newer commercial popular forms, much of which the communists had previously rejected as 'yellow music' (though jazz itself remained a taboo).[85] As with the literary innovators of *baihua*, and of film, phonographic realism also had to take cognisance of the commercial demands of the market.[86]

Jones highlights the debts left-wing popular music and film owed to the commercial culture that preceded it, and which it tried to disavow. He suggests – with good reason – that while claiming to speak for the people, they explicitly repudiated the commercialized forms of culture which they had adapted in order to do this speaking. But for Jones, this disavowal comes not only with a charge of irony and hypocrisy – especially in their demonization of those from whom they stole – but also that the left-wing project itself was therefore an act of 'political ventriloquism'.[87]

This accusation is not just about the left's unacknowledged sources but also a questioning of the very project of creating a national revolutionary subject. Rather than showing how the national-popular subject is necessarily interpellated or 'constructed' (as in Ernesto Laclau and Chantel Mouffe's work),[88] the notion of ventriloquism suggests a misappropriated voice. Jones's book constantly implies that the real voice of the people is to be found in the unpoliticized commercial popular cultures that preceded them.[89] We suggest, on the contrary, that the subject of popular consumption is also a (to be) constructed fiction.[90] The 'dreamworld' of mass culture in the United States was about the construction of a certain kind of modern 'classless' consumer society – a dreamworld that shared much with the Soviet modern being constructed at the same time.[91] What we have in Shanghai Modern are competing projects around new popular urban audiences: the one intent on positioning it simply as a consuming audience and the other to create a national popular revolutionary subject. The former is not any less political than the latter.

Hansen's book is important in linking the rise of Hollywood Cinema to a reframing of disparate viewing subjects as part of a wider project to assemble a consumer society in 1920s United States. Many observers see a similar consuming public emerging in a Shanghai that had become the very epitome of *modeng*. Shanghai's emergent modernity, in this reading, was ripe to be enlisted into an international capitalist economy, pulling China with it, only to be thwarted by war and revolution. We have suggested above that Shanghai was an isolated, if powerful, enclave, and there is simply no way a viable Chinese nation state, capitalist or otherwise, could be established on the basis of its entrepreneurial prowess. The current Chinese government often positions Shanghai Modern's historic urban consumer as a precursor to the country's post-1978 modernity but we again must ask, could such an image – the patriotic urban consumer – really generate the kind of affective political identification required to drive a wider national-political project?

Laikwan Pang has described modernity not as a quality defining particular subjects or objects but rather as a system of desire.[92] As such, it is endlessly unsatisfied and also open to organization and mobilization by various forms of representation, including the political. Shanghai Modern as a system of desire was thoroughly traversed by political ideas around anti-colonialism, national defence and revolution. Chinese entrepreneurs often saw themselves as a new 'national bourgeoisie' and frequently donated to political parties. Consumer campaigns against foreign goods and pro-Chinese industries were a common feature of the 1920s and 1930s. As recent work on material culture in Shanghai has shown, those middle classes able to adopt a modern lifestyle also did so as part of a statement about a new strengthened China. However, we would argue that the 'dreamworld' of Shanghai Modern was never a sufficient foundation for a transformed China, as it lacked the ability to mobilize the masses of the countryside. What it did provide was the cultural and technological foundations for a revolutionary project founded on new forms of commercial mass culture.

The project launched by Shanghai artist-intellectuals was perhaps unique in the world of the 1930s, in that it confronted a powerful system of global cultural industries and, largely successfully, sought to redirect it towards a revolutionary end. It did so by combining a political project with a knowledge of its audiences, and techniques for assembling and addressing them, that had been accumulated in the commercial sector. This combination of political purpose and commerce is by no means a contradiction.

> This Chinese left-wing cinema was by and large a commercial one, a successful one indeed, as many of these films set box office records. Its success in ideological terms was necessarily conditioned to the films' popularity amongst the mass [...] It was neither a top-down ideological didacticism in which the filmmakers retained sole power to control this movement nor a pure money-making industry determined merely by the desires and tastes of the spectators.[93]

A similar point can be made about the supposed antagonism between art and commercial culture, and between art and popular culture (these two issues frequently being run together). Chinese intellectuals in the educational sphere sought to reframe their historic task of 'popular enlightenment' through an active engagement with 'print capitalism'. So too, the radical disruption of the traditional scholar-administrator role, by both the new mass political parties and a new commercial culture, resulted in a reframing of the intellectual task to directly engage with the new forms of the popular. As Liang Luo put it:

> [D]espite the seeming divide between commercialised popular culture and mass political movements, the two share a deep-rooted logic of 'popularisation' [...] I thus identify the populist spirit and potential to inspire or instigate political participation in distinctively avant-garde, commercialised and propagandist projects. In the process, the conventional segregation of avant-garde art, commercial popular culture, and political propaganda is renegotiated, and traditional dividing lines are redrawn or erased.[94]

In cultural-political terms, it is this image that we wish to hold onto, a political project vis-à-vis commercial culture and drawing on the professional expertise of artist-intellectuals rooted in a global avant-garde network to create a national-popular subject capable of fundamental political transformation.

A different cosmopolitanism?

In the last chapter we noted the paradigmatic change that had taken place in the decade after 1895, one in which the 'new' becomes associated with the Western and the present (*jin*) becomes opposed to the past (*gu*) – a past whose rejection is a precondition for arriving at the modern.[95] As Chen Duxiu wrote: 'The evolution of human civilisation is replacing old with the new, like a river flowing on, an arrow flying away, constantly continuing and constantly changing'.[96] This association only increases with the existential threat to China. Chen Duxiu's notion of time as an arrow into the future, leaving the past behind, was an embrace of modernization under the threat of extinction, as was the urgent grasping of scientific, philosophical and artistic ideas from the West. The easy image of a cosmopolitan Shanghai, open to the new, fails to register its deeper complicity with China's semi-colonial status, and the cultural dislocation of *erfahrung* – the capacity to reflect, of 'remembering the past and imagining a different future' at the same time as the historical disintegration and transformation of these very capacities'.

It is important then to disrupt the equation of the 'new' with the 'West'. Meng Yue's book, *Shanghai and the Edges of Empire*, attempts to reframe the moment of Shanghai's historical possibility precisely through a refusal of this equation.[97] She builds on Huters's work around the *jindai*, a period between the First Opium War of 1840 and the May Fourth movement of 1919, located 'uneasily between "traditional" (*gudai*, literally "ancient") [...] and "modern" (*xiandai*), at a moment'[98] before the inevitable, unilinear path from one to the other became fixed. Yue excavates those occasions and spaces where an equal exchange or translation takes place between Chinese learning and practice, and those coming in from Japan, from the multiple European streams – Poland, Italy and Ireland ('minor Europe'), not just England, Germany and France – as well as from an 'awakened' Asia. In so doing, she opens up a vista for Duara's small 'c' circulatory culture, including multiple political, cultural and philosophical ideas, along with different practices and imaginaries embodied in the emergent spaces of urban Shanghai. These flows, outside those dominated by states, give a much more diverse image of cosmopolitanism, more imbricated in the political and frequently challenging the discursive domination of Western thought and language, and imagining a different modernity. Yue's account draws on Chakrabarty's postcolonial historical project[99] where a recovery of indigenous 'traditional' forms of thought, belief and practice should be seen as part of the 'history of non-capital'. Such a history of non-capital, he argues, can provide the grounds for a critique not just of capitalist imperialism but also of Western modernity itself.[100] In Yue's semi-colonial Shanghai, we have not only indigenous knowledge but also a proliferation of circulatory ideas from across the globe.

But ultimately, Yue argues, the two key intellectual strands, of national renewal and decolonization, drift apart, with the New Culture and May Fourth intellectuals arguing that Western knowledge and technologies alone were capable of national renewal.[101] She refers to Huters's book, which discusses the conflict between the Beijing-based New Culture movement and journals validating indigenous knowledge, such as *Eastern Miscellany* published by the Commercial Press in Shanghai – a conflict which the former eventually won.[102] Yue quotes Prasenjit Duara's claim that, in China, 'the need to critique the West culturally – to ideologically decolonize in the manner of Franz Fanon or Mahatma Gandhi' – was not felt.[103]

While we can register the impact of the closing down of Huters's *jindai*, along with the heteropolis of Yue's 'imagined community of an anti-imperialist world', the indigenous tradition did not disappear so easily. It persisted and informed thought and practice in the ways we have tried to show in the last two chapters. As such, the history of non-capital represented by Chinese indigenous traditions of practical thought and ethics remained a part of the Chinese revolutionary movement.

This polyphonic circulatory history, and the different imagined communities which drew inspiration from it, might be seen as a form of world history not dependent on Europe even if it is a reaction to it. It is the kind of pan-national world history, running underneath the top-down capital C circulation instigated by the European states.[104] Such a history can be seen in the latter part of the eighteenth century, with the rapid spreading of the discourses of equality and liberty.[105] In our last chapter, we also noted the response of many from the educated colonial elites at the turn of the nineteenth and twentieth centuries, who took up the promise of European modernity only for it to be constantly withheld. This withheld promise was transformed into the 'awakening of Asia', from the 1905 Russian Revolution and Port Arthur defeat, through the Young Turks in 1908, the Chinese Revolution of 1911, the anti-imperialist struggles in India, May Fourth, and the subsequent civil war and revolution in China and so on through the decolonization period.[106]

Lee often portrays Shanghai as a floating island, cushioned by extraterritoriality and commerce, or a 'fortress besieged' by the brutal political world it managed to keep at bay for a few years.[107] It is an image which fatally compromised the manner of its return in the 1990s, where its celebration of the modern lent itself to nostalgia and consumerism. Intellectuals in Shanghai Modern rarely floated free, as their status was challenged by the collapse of traditional sources of income and the exigencies of commercial culture. For many of these, their task was to find the way (*dao*) not of autonomy but the ethical path to create a culture capable of building citizens of a new Chinese nation state. In this project, culture and politics were not separate; their task was to reinvent themselves as intellectuals and find anew the role of culture in the age of the masses, increasingly dominated as it was by new forms of technology and commerce.

Conclusion

In this chapter, we have tried to reframe an image of Shanghai Modern not as a tragic island of proto-modernity – cosmopolitan, consumerist or both – but as a site of struggle around the very definition and direction of the modern. Shanghai's revolutionary modern, as articulated by cosmopolitan left-wing intellectual-artists, sought to articulate its political vision and professional practice in partnership with that of a revolutionary party. The precise terms of that partnership were necessarily indeterminate given the exigencies of the time and distance between Shanghai and Yan'an. Nevertheless, the shared vision was one of a Chinese nation state strong enough to resist Japanese (and other imperialist) aggression through the integration and mobilization of the popular masses. There are three salient points here.

First, Shanghai's role in the revolutionary modern functioned very differently to the images of the urban modern so powerful among the Western avant-garde. Though Shanghai certainly stood for the quintessential Chinese urban modern, this urban image never became a synecdoche for a Chinese 'mass utopia' as it did in the United States, in Weimar Germany and in the USSR. Modern China was to be forged from the peasant masses, under imaginaries drawn not so much from the shock of the new urban publics as from older senses of an extensive and united social body established across centuries. Mao Dun's 'Light, Heat, Power!' may have begun as an urban neon dream, but it ended with a mobilized peasantry. The return of an urban modernity post-1978 or -1992 would thus always be ambiguous.

Second, the Chinese artists-intellectuals saw themselves as avant-garde, but this was constructed very differently than in the West, and in particular the USSR. We have repeatedly made the point that autonomy as a necessary condition of artistic and historical creativity did not play a central role in China; artist-intellectuals found a personal and historical purpose in identifying a path to an ethical-collective polity. We have stressed the geopolitical distance between the CCP base and Shanghai-based artist-intellectuals, but this is not autonomy by another name. The distance allowed the latter to frame a proper professional and ethical relationship to the former. In this sense, we need not see the Chinese avant-garde in the same way as that of the 1920s' Soviet Union. There, the radical reinvention of cultural forms was (for them) equal and parallel to – perhaps more radical than – the political project of the party. The bringing to heel of this avant-garde, sealed by Zhadanov at the Soviet Writers Congress in 1934, is often equated with that of the fate of Chinese intellectuals from Yan'an through to the Thousand Flowers crackdown of the late 1950s. However, we suggest that the conflict in China did not rest on the intellectuals' claim to a parallel and radically distinct project of sociocultural transformation but rather on more established patterns of 'obedient autonomy' where intellectuals sought out a space which recognized their expertise as part of a shared political project.[108] In the end, the increasing conflict between intellectuals and the party was less about their autonomy (or not) from the party but their separation from the masses, their claims to an expertise setting them above and apart from the mass of the people.

Third, the close involvement of an avant-garde with popular and commercial culture gave Shanghai Modern a unique profile. This is not to be seen as a precursor to the salutary effect of 'free markets' on traditional art and popular culture but as a political act in which a new language of the popular might be formed and attached to a revolutionary, anti-imperialist project. As such its parallels might be found more in Indian film in the 1930s, in Brazil with the Bossa Nova movement of the late 1950s, and in pre-revolutionary Cuba.[109] This is part of the historical charge it has for us – a moment of porosity, and of circulatory history, where cultures combine into a new moment of historical possibility. This cosmopolitanism was not opposed to the revolutionary national-popular but informed it, just as it informed a radical rejection of the historical fatalism of Shanghai's literary elites and of the accommodation to imperialism this frequently implied. It was a cosmopolitanism that emerged from, and responded to, that great wave of capitalist-imperialist 'globalization' begun at the end of the nineteenth century.[110]

Like any such moment, that of Shanghai's 'revolutionary modern' was highly provisional and contingent on the historical conjuncture. Equally, like any act of historical creativity it comes with hidden fissures and symbolic violence that needs to be addressed. The accommodation between cosmopolitanism and national-popular often resulted in the easy equation between the sensibility of urban intellectuals and the rural masses[111] – an arrogant assumption vividly highlighted by Mao's political distrust of them. The ambiguous role of women in this project – the friction between new woman as idealized symbol and as subject of real social reform, for example – requires acknowledgement.[112] So too the exclusion of 'superstitious' popular cultural practices, which both intellectuals and party pursued.[113] Other local voices were suppressed too, as 'backwards' non-Han Chinese were forcibly articulated to the body of a national-popular as refracted through the ideals of a modernizing Shanghai intelligentsia.[114]

More fundamentally, we need to address the issue of the national-popular, and indeed the nation state, as an organizing narrative of modernity. We have touched on this in Chapter 2, where we sought to oppose the strict separation between modern and traditional, and the function the nation state plays in securing that distinction. We also need to acknowledge the ways in which, as nation states organized their narratives of progress, they suppressed differences and divergences, often reproducing those structures of internal domination they sought to oppose externally through anti-colonial and/or revolutionary action.[115]

The point is not to erect an exemplary model or assert a correct account of the past 'how it really was'.[116] This period is an 'open field'[117] in which we might find an image of a past that, at the very least, can stand against those images of Shanghai Modern as a proto- or unfinished Chinese capitalist modernity quashed by the Communist Revolution.

The dialectical image we seek is of a unique moment in which a set of new 'cultural industries' are embraced as part of a transformative political project. This was more than simply 'propaganda', though it was also unashamedly that. It was also an attempt to shape a general horizon of social experience in such a way as to create a viable national-popular subject. Lacking capital but somewhat protected from direct foreign competition and being at arms-length from the dominant political parties meant not 'political ventriloquism' but an active engagement with audiences within and across multiple texts, as well as with their lived experiences as urban consumers, as political subjects, as audiences, readers, listeners and the distracted passers-by of urban life.

NOTES

1. For a good overview, see K. Gulliver, 'Shanghai's Modernity in the Western Eye', *East-West Connections* 9, no. 1 (2009).

2. L. O. Lee, *Shanghai Modern: The Flowering of a New Urban Culture in China, 1930–1945* (Cambridge, MA: Harvard University Press, 1999).

3. Ibid., 339.

4. M.-C. Bergere, *The Golden Age of the Chinese Bourgeoisie, 1911–1937* (New York: Cambridge University Press, 1989).

5. Cf. F. Dikotter, *Exotic Objects: Modern Objects and Everyday Life in China* (New York: Columbia University Press, 2006), Ch. 5; Lee, *Shanghai Modern*.

6. Lee, *Shanghai Modern*.

7. For images of this period of transition, see X. Ye, *The Dianshizhai Pictorial: Shanghai Urban Life 1884–1898* (Ann Arbor: University of Michigan Press, 2003).

8. M. -C. Bergere, *Shanghai: China's Gateway to Modernity* (Stanford: Stanford University Press, 2009), 348. 'Harmony' here might be wishful thinking on her part.

9. Ibid., 348.

10. Hong Kong is in many ways the lens through which Lee views the emerging Shanghai and indeed his book comes at the end of a decade in which Shanghai's past had been subject of a concerted effort of remembrance in Hong Kong's academic and popular culture alike. In opening up new directions for the future, the post-1978 reforms necessarily shifted perspectives on the past; they raised questions of 'what if', of paths chosen and paths discarded. Hong Kong (and Taiwan, built on a very different form of exodus) was faced with a re-convergence of paths as 1997 drew close. This was political convergence (with 2046 in the deep background) and also economic, as China's urban commercial-led expansion recalled that of Hong Kong (and Taiwan) since the 1950s. Would Shanghai and Hong Kong represent a cultural convergence, the cosmopolitan culture of the former partially preserved by the latter, and both returning centre stage in a new reformed China?

11. 'The other side of this freedom and openness, however, was a certain isolation – a linkage to the world that went together with a de-linkage from the rest of China. There was always something very fragile about Shanghai cosmopolitanism. After 1949, Chinese Communism, born in Shanghai, quickly made Shanghai's urban culture no more than a memory'. A. Abbas, 'Cosmopolitan Descriptions: Shanghai and Hong Kong', *Public Culture* 12, no. 3 (2000): 772–86, 776.

12. 'It took Mao Zedong's genius to see, against the grain of orthodox Marxism, that even rural spaces, at least in the historical situation of China, had a crucial role to play in modern and national life. This was the insight that allowed Mao to displace cities in general from their role as the sole exclusive site of modernity – and Shanghai in particular from its claim to be China's pre-eminent city. After 1949, the city could no longer enjoy the privilege of being a law unto itself: it was clearly the nation that now held sway over the city' (Abbas, 'Cosmopolitan Descriptions', 775).

13. The small area around Fuzhou Road far outstripped the rest of China in the publication of newspapers, books, textbooks, journals and magazines. Cf. C. Reed, *Gutenberg in Shanghai: Chinese Print Capitalism 1876–1937* (Honolulu: University of Hawai'i Press, 2004).

14. Cf. A. Jones, *Yellow Music: Media, Culture and Colonial Modernity in the Chinese Jazz Age* (Durham, NC: Duke University Press, 2001).

15. Lee, *Shanghai Modern*, 45.

16. Ibid., 46.

17. Ibid.

18. It was one already announced by Li Qichao through his use of the Western dating system in his 1899 travel diaries and made official by the Republic's official adoption of the Gregorian calendar in 1912. A. Greenspan, *Shanghai Future: Modernity Remade* (London: Hurst and Co., 2014).

19. Ibid., 79.

20. Anderson's use of the term is generally adopted, as coterminus with the modern nation and the public sphere. Cf. T. Cheek, *The Intellectual in Modern Chinese History* (Cambridge: Cambridge University Press, 2015), 35–39. We problematize this term in what follows.

21. At least until the rise of 'social media' in the last few years.

22. Reed, *Gutenberg in Shanghai*.

23. Anderson also refers to this book. R. Darnton, *The Business of Enlightenment: A Publishing History of the 'Encylopédie'* (Cambridge, MA: Harvard University Press, 1968).

24. As Christopher Reed suggests, the term 'print culture' concerns intellectual life as carried by print, and 'print commerce' describes the world of publishing outside the formal channels of the Ming and Qing imperial state, in the small-scale artisanal concerns similar to those described by Darnton for eighteenth-century Europe. 'Print capitalism', Reed suggests, is about the extensive mechanization which transformed printing from the point when *The Times* first used steam power in 1807. Print capitalism, Reed suggests quoting Marx, is

when printing is done 'as a form of "industry carried on by machinery"' (Reed, *Gutenberg in Shanghai*, 9).

25. Duara criticizes Anderson (and Ernst Gellner) for their restriction of 'imagined community' to the nation state organized around print capitalism. Cf. P. Duara, *Rescuing History from the Nation: Questioning Narratives of Modern China* (Chicago: University of Chicago Press, 1995), 51–56.

26. Meng Yue, *Shanghai and the Edges of Empires* (Minneapolis: University of Minnesota Press, 2006), Part One. See also Reed, *Gutenberg in Shanghai*, 161–64.

27. Ibid., 27.

28. Reed, *Gutenberg in Shanghai*, 165. New terms such as gentry-merchants (*shenshang*) or gentry-managers (*shendong*) tried to capture these non-Confucian categories.

29. These evolving relations should not be seen in terms of a proto-public sphere set against an authoritarian state(s) but in the light of long-standing traditions of elite service to the Chinese state. The relationship between the imagined community of modern China and its rational disenchanted institutional state form might rather be described as a complex co-creation between intellectuals, party-state and commercial cultural industries. Cf. L. Pang, *Building a New China in Cinema: The Chinese Left-Wing Cinema Movement, 1932–37* (Lanham, MD: Rowman and Littlefield, 2002), Ch. 1.

30. As Reed suggested: 'No other cultural industry was as central to the self-identity of the Chinese elite as the one that produced books, and no other was as close to the heart of the Chinese state' (*Gutenberg in Shanghai*, 11–12).

31. 'For many late-nineteenth century gentry-managers (*shendong*), gentry-merchants (*shenshang*), and elite urban reformers, the public service aspect of education and learning came to be extended beyond imperial administrative service to the printing and publishing of textbooks and reference works' (Reed, *Gutenberg in Shanghai*, 202).

32. G. Davies, *Lu Xun's Revolution: Writing in a Time of Violence* (Cambridge, MA: Harvard University Press, 2013), 254.

33. Reed, *Gutenberg in Shanghai*, 203. Reed adds 'whether for purposes of public service or not'. He then suggests, as we have done above, that from the end of the nineteenth century this 'public service' extended beyond direct service to the state and into a more general project of educational publication.

34. L. Pang, *The Art of Cloning: Creative Production During China's Cultural Revolution* (London: Verso, 2017), 16. See also H. Wang, *China's Twentieth Century* (London: Verso, 2016), 48. According to the first modern Chinese dictionary 《辭源》 first printed in 1915, the term *wenhua* simply means 文治和教化, governance and pedagogy.

35. L. Qichao, 'Foreword to the Publication of Political Novels in Translation', in *Modern Chinese Literary Thought: Writings on Literature 1983–1945*, ed. K. Denton (Stanford: Stanford University Press, 1996), 71–73.

36. L. Qichao, 'On the Relationship between Fiction and the Government of the People', *Modern Chinese Literary*, 74–81, 75.

37. Crucially, *baihua* as a project was also set against the late Qing's attempted new national language of standardized speech and writing *guoyu*. Writers such as Lu Xun saw this dynastic attempt as pedestrian and ineffectual. Davies, *Lu Xun's Revolution*, 10.

38. Ibid., 105.

39. Davies, *Lu Xun's Revolution*, 10: 'By 1920, Beijing's Ministry of Education (in which Lu Xun worked) had formally named *baihua* as the medium of instruction in Chinese schools.'

40. P. E. Link, *Mandarin Ducks and Butterflies: Popular Fiction in Early Twentieth-Century Chinese Cities* (Berkeley: University of California Press, 1981).

41. Davies, *Lu Xun's Revolution*, 101–06.

42. On the global impact of Lenin's party model cf. E. Hobsbawm, *The Age of Extremes: The Short 20th Century, 1914–1991* (London: Abacus, 1994), Ch. 2. Both the KMT and the CCP were avowedly Leninist parties, and indeed, the Soviet Union was the main foreign paymaster for both, until the US entry into the war in 1941. Cf. J. Taylor, *The Generalissimo: Chiang Kai-Shek and the Struggle for Modern China* (Cambridge, MA: Belknap Press, 2009), 41.

43. Cf. Davies, *Lu Xun's Revolution*, 174–77.

44. G. Morou, 'The Echo of the Phonograph', quoted in Jones, *Yellow Music*, 107–09.

45. J. Lovell, 'Introduction', in *The Real Story of Ah-Q and other Takes of China*, ed. L. Xun, trans. J. Lovell (London: Penguin Books, 2009), xxiii.

46. Pang, *Art of Cloning*, 11.

47. '*Baihua* in its formative years from the 1910s to the 30s was a language largely confined to China's urban intellectual elite and inaccessible to the masses [...] [As] Wang Hui puts it [...] the hybridity and cosmopolitanism of *baihua* was, in effect, a sign of its estrangement from the society of the masses for which the language was intended' (Davies, *Lu Xun's Revolution*, 250).

48. Julian Benda's *La Trahison des Clercs* from 1927 has often been interpreted as a betrayal of intellectuals' independence, but its target tended to be intellectuals attaching themselves to political causes at odds with 'enlightenment'.

49. Cf. J. Carey, *The Intellectuals and the Masses: Pride and Prejudice Among the Literary Intelligentsia* (London: Faber, 1992).

50. We use the term 'engagement' in full awareness of the way in which it was used by writers such as Jean-Paul Sartre and Maurice Merleau-Ponty after 1945 to describe the changed historical circumstances of the western intellectual.

51. L. Luo, *The Avant-Garde and the Popular in Modern China: Tian Han and the Intersection of Performance and Politics* (Ann Arbor: University of Michigan Press, 2014), 9.

52. T. Huters, *Bringing the World Home: Appropriating the West in Late Qing and Early Republican China* (Honolulu: University of Hawai'i Press, 2005), 18.

53. Cf. Pang, *Building a New China in Cinema*, 20.

54. For one of the first identifications of the network of modernist cities, see R. Williams, 'Metropolitan Perceptions and the Emergence of Modernism', in *Politics of Modernism*.

Against the New Reformists (London: Verso, 1989), 37–48. For an excellent recent discussion in the Chinese context see Luo, *Avant-Garde and the Popular in Modern China*. On the trans-Asian rejection of Western liberal democracy see Wang, *China's Twentieth Century* and P. Mishra, *From the Ruins of Empire: The Revolt against the West and the Remaking of Asia* (London: Penguin Books, 2012).

55. Pang, *Building a New China in Cinema*.

56. Luo, *Avant-Garde and the Popular in Modern China*, 9. There is no space here to trace further the connections between artist-intellectuals and politics in the European tradition, which have since the 1970s been dominated by notions of autonomy. The deeper relationship between autonomy and the social project of modernity have been incisively traced by S. Olma, *Autonomy and Weltbezug: Towards an Aesthetic of Performative Defiance* (Breda: Avans Hogeschool, 2016).

57. Cf. O. Hatherley *The Chaplin Machine, Slapstick, Fordism and the Communist Avant-Garde* (London: Pluto Press, 2016).

58. O. Negt and Alexander A. Kluge, *Public Sphere and Experience: Towards an Analysis of the Bourgeois and Proletarian Public Sphere* (Minneapolis: University of Minnesota Press, 1993); M. Hansen, *Babel and Babylon: Spectatorship in American Silent Film* (Cambridge, MA: Harvard University Press, 1991).

59. C. Calhoun, *Habermas and the Public Sphere* (Cambridge, MA: MIT Press, 1992).

60. This shift to a wider sphere of experience and how it is organized and negotiated is much more applicable to the Chinese context, as Chris Berry has also argued. He suggests films in China operate in a more affective and informal register, being more about norms than institutions, with the 'persistent presence of the state as referent and central participant in these normative discussions'. This widening of the scope of the public to include norms negotiated informally and through affect, and with the state as a central, often unspoken referent/ participant – rather than an 'over there' to be critiqued – has much more purchase on the Chinese context. Berry was discussing 'post-socialist' film; in the context of *Shanghai Modern*, we might substitute revolution or nation-building as referent for the 'state' in his quote. Chris Berry follows film scholar Ben Xu in rejecting the notion of a public sphere as a frame to understanding the kind of dialogue instigated by the Chen Kaige's 1993 film *Farewell My Concubine*. C. Berry, *Postsocialist Cinema in Post-Mao China* (London: Routledge, 2004), 18. He is referring to B. Xu, 'Farewell My Concubine and Its Nativist Critics', *Quarterly Review of Film and Video* 16, no. 2 (1997): 155–70.

61. Hansen, *Babel and Babylon*.

62. 'One saw with a shock of wonder on the roof of a building a gigantic NEON sign in flaming red and phosphorescent green: LIGHT, HEAT, POWER!' M. Dun, *Midnight* (Amsterdam: Fredonia Books, [1933] 2001), 6

63. As Laikwan Pang suggests, the ability of representation to actively organize a diverse range of experiences around a particular project of modernity needs to be emphasized over against those who would see representation as merely floating ideas overlaying a 'real' embodied

experience. The two are not opposed but strongly connected. L. Pang, *The Distorting Mirror: Visual Modernity in China* (Honolulu: University of Hawai'i Press, 2007), 209–10.

64. Hansen, *Babel and Babylon*, Part II.

65. 'In practice, opera constituted a common Chinese language for conservative, entrepreneurial, and revolutionary filmmakers alike.' M. Farquhar and C. Berry, 'Shadow Opera: Towards a New Archaeology of the Chinese Cinema', in *Chinese Language Film: Historiography, Poetics, Politics*, ed. S. H. Lu and E. Y. Yeh (Honolulu: University of Hawai'i Press, 2005), 29.

66. M. Haili, *Urban Politics and Cultural Capital: The Case of Chinese Opera* (Aldershot: Ashgate, 2015), Ch. 1.

67. Jones, *Yellow Music*.

68. Cf. Reed, *Gutenberg in Shanghai*, 274–79.

69. David Holm has provided a detailed account of the *yangge* movement, in which dance forms originating in the Song Dynasty, were adapted by the Communists to provide a revolutionary message. See: D. Holm, *Art and Ideology in Revolutionary China* (Oxford: Clarendon Press, 1991).

70. Cf. P. Pickowicz, *Marxist Literary Thought in China: The Influence of Ch'u Ch'iu-Pai* (Berkeley: University of California Press, 1981).

71. Ibid.

72. Farquhar and Berry, *Chinese Language Film*, 29.

73. B. McDougall, *Mao Zedong's 'Talks at the Yan'an Conference on Literature and Art: A Translation of the 1943'* (Ann Arbor: University of Michigan Press, 1980), 69–70. See also J. Spence, *The Search for Modern China*, 2nd ed. (New York: Norton, 1999), 447–49. On the similarities and differences between Qu Quibai and Mao, cf. Pickowicz, *Marxist Literary Thought in China*, 222–35.

74. H. Forman, *Report from Red China* (London: H. Holt and Co., 1945), quoted in Pickowicz, *Marxist Literary Thought in China*, 224.

75. On film cf. Pang, *Building a New China in Cinema*, Ch. 2.

76. Jones, *Yellow Music*, organizes much of his book around the rehabilitation of Lin Jinhui, who was subject of much vilification by the left-wing popular music movement, even though, Jones argues, they stole many of his techniques.

77. Pang, *Building a New China in Cinema*.

78. Cf. Jones, *Yellow Music*.

79. Luo, *Avant-Garde and the Popular in Modern China*, 158.

80. Lee, *Shanghai Modern*, 99. Cf. P. Pickowicz, 'Melodramatic Representation and the "May Fourth" Tradition of Chinese Cinema', in *From May Fourth to June Fourth: Fiction and Film in Twentieth Century China*, ed. E. Widmer and D. Der-Wei Wang (Cambridge, MA: Harvard University Press, 1993).

81. Pang, *Building a New China in Cinema*; Luo, *Avant-Garde and the Popular in Modern China*.

82. Jones, *Yellow Music*, Ch. 1; On the Confucian history of music cf. B. Mittler, *Dangerous Tunes: The Politics of Chinese Music in Hong Kong, Taiwan and the People's Republic of China since 1949* (Wiesbaden: Harrassowitz Verlag, 1997).

83. Jones, *Yellow Music*, 22.

84. Ibid., 17.

85. See also Szu-wei Chen, *The Music Industry and Popular Song in 1930s and 1940s Shanghai, a Historical and Stylistic Analysis* (Ph.D. thesis, University of Sterling, 2007), https://pdfs.semanticscholar.org/234e/b1f414d2c062deadbc26ccd11ddc51050b36.pdf?_ga=2.22218363.1121030676.1568173229-16083170.1568173229. Accessed 26 January 2020.

86. As Jones put it: 'Nie Er's music, despite its affiliation with May 4th-derived discourses of realist representation and social engagement, was recorded by the same colonial conglomerate [EMI and others], reflected a similarly sophisticated understanding of the commercial interactivity of the mass media to the same urban audiences as the music of [despised 'yellow' composer-impresario] Li Jinhui' (*Yellow Music*, 18).

87. Jones, *Yellow Music*, 123, see the section heading 'Political Ventriloquism'.

88. E. Laclau and C. Mouffe, *Hegemony and Socialist Strategy: Towards a Radical Democratic Politics* (London: Verso, 1985).

89. Jones' account is deeply marked by 1990s cultural studies which repeatedly sought to counter-pose the popular pleasures of commercial culture to the dour, elitist (usually Marxist) politics with a capital P. Cf. J. McGuigan, *Cultural Populism* (London: Routledge, 1992).

90. See Hansen, *Babel and Babylon* for one notable attempt to uncover this.

91. S. Buck-Morss, *Dreamworld and Catastrophe: The Passing of Mass Utopia in East and West* (Cambridge, MA: MIT Press, 2002).

92. Pang, *Distorting Mirror*, 210.

93. Pang, *Building a New China in Cinema*, 8.

94. Luo, *Avant-Garde and the Popular in Modern China*, 14. Cf. also Pang, *Building a New China in Cinema*, 6–10.

95. Cf. Lee, *Shanghai Modern*, Ch. 2 and Greenspan, *Shanghai Future*, 71.

96. Quoted in M. Jacques, *When China Rules the World: The End of the Western World and the Birth of a New Global Order* (New York: Penguin Books, 2009), 20.

97. Yue, *Shanghai and the Edges of Empires*, Part One.

98. Huters, *Bringing the World Home*. '*Xiandai*', a term ubiquitous in East Asian languages to signify the modern in most of its senses (i.e. '*xiandaihau*' = 'modernization', '*xiandaizhuyi*' = 'modernism').

99. D. Chakrabarty, *Provincializing Europe: Postcolonial Thought and Historical Difference* (Princeton, NJ: Princeton University Press, 2000).

100. This also recalls Wang Hui's notion of 'anti-modern modernity'. Cf. W. Hui 'Depoliticized Politics, From East to West', *New Left Review* 41 (2006): 29–45.

101. 'Non-Western perspectives and non-Western cultures ceased to be considered valuable and useful resources in the critique of imperialism.' Yue, *Shanghai and the Edges of Empires*, 224.

102. Yue writes: 'In Shanghai, as elsewhere, the cultural frontier moved towards Westernization at the price of sacrificing the minor West and the non-West that had once been co-members of an imagined community of an anti-imperialist world' (*Shanghai and the Edges of Empires*, 225).

103. Yue, *Shanghai and the Edges of Empires*, 225. Cf. P. Duara, *Decolonization: Perspectives from Now and Then* (London: Routledge, 2004), 2. We would suggest that Mao's ability to interpellate the 'popular' inevitably drew on many of these older forms and practices, but in an 'authoritative' manner that ultimately gave little space to explore these 'traditions' outside their rigid subjugation to anti-imperialism and anti-capitalism in an autarchic socialism.

104. Cf. P. Duara, *The Crisis of Global Modernity: Asian Traditions and a Sustainable Future* (Cambridge: Cambridge University Press, 2015), Ch. 2, 53–90.

105. Described, for example, by S. Buck-Morss, *Hegel, Haiti and Universal History* (Pittsburgh: University of Pittsburgh Press, 2009) and P. Gilroy, *The Black Atlantic: Modernity and Double Consciousness* (Cambridge, MA: Harvard University Press, 1993). See also C. A. Bayley's survey of the impact of these ideas across the Asian world in the late eighteenth century in C. A. Bayley, *The Birth of the Modern World, 1780-1914* (Oxford: Blackwell Publishing, 2004).

106. Mishra, *From the Ruins of Empire*.

107. Cf. Qian Zhongshu's famous 1947 novel (set in Shanghai 1937) *Fortress Besieged*.

108. E. Evasdottir, *Obedient Autonomy: Chinese Intellectuals and the Achievement of Orderly Life* (Honolulu: University of Hawai'i Press, 2004).

109. Cf. C. Veloso, *Tropical Truth: A Story of Music and Revolution in Brazil* (New York: Da Capo Press, 2002); R. Gordon-Nesbitt, *To Defend the Revolution is to Defend Culture: The Cultural Policy of the Cuban Revolution* (Oakland, CA: PM Press, 2015).

110. We might also think of that prior phase of 'globalization' that took place at the end of the eighteenth century and resulting in the 'age of revolutions'. Cf. Buck-Morss, *Hegel, Haiti and Universal History*.

111. Cf. Pang, *Building a New China in Cinema*, Ch. 7.

112. Cf. Gulliver, 'Shanghai's Modernity in the Western Eye'.

113. Cf. Duara, *Rescuing History from the Nation*.

114. Ibid.

115. Cf. Duara, *Rescuing History from the Nation*; Pang, *Building a New China in Cinema*, 184–87; Buck-Morss, *Hegel, Haiti and Universal History*, 138–48.

116. This is a phrase of Walter Benjamin's 1940 essay *Theses on the Philosophy of History*, VI. Cf. H. Arendt, ed., *Illuminations* (London: Fontana, 1968).

117. Pang, *Building a New China in Cinema*, 2.

4

Post-Reform China and Neo-liberalism

Introduction

At the end of their book on the 'Great Proletarian Cultural Revolution', Roderick Macfarquhar and Michael Schoenhals conclude that the only way open to China was Westernization. The attempt in the late Qing and early Republic 'to modernise whilst preserving their integrity as a people and a culture', a project which had preoccupied China since the Opium War, had floundered with the dissolution of Confucianism as Chinese 'essence'.[1] The CCP had replaced Confucianism with Marxism-Leninism, but, tired of aping foreigners (the USSR), the Cultural Revolution was Mao's 'last best effort to define and perpetuate a distinct Chinese essence in the modern world'. His failures

> led Deng to abandon this vain search for a Chinese version of modernity that had preoccupied the nation's politicians and intellectuals for well over a century. China had to jump on the bandwagon of successful Western-style modernization that had proved so effective in Taiwan and elsewhere in East Asia. The Cultural Revolution became the economic and social watershed of modern Chinese history.[2]

The persistent striving for a different form of modernization, notably that announced by the Communist Revolution of 1949, is set aside as futile. After the willed violence of the Cultural Revolution, neither socialism nor the non-West is viable any longer, with little room even for a distinct East Asian capitalism. In embracing Western modernity, China was to repudiate not just socialism but also the whole anti-imperialist and anti-colonial struggle to carve out a different path from that of the West since the end of the nineteenth century. In fact, the 'watershed' of 1978 represents a foundational break not just with the last century of Chinese aspirations to keep an 'essence', but also with the contemporary relevance of a distinct Chinese history per se.[3]

David Harvey, writing a year earlier in 2005, also presented 1978 as a watershed moment. Now 'Western-style modernization' became 'neo-liberalism', and the implications of the reforms had global significance. The reforms 'would not have assumed the significance we now accord them' without the parallel development of neo-liberalism in the advanced capitalist countries and across world markets. The emerging post-Bretton Woods global order gave China the opportunity to flourish to an extent Deng could barely have imagined. In return, China's entry into that global order, accelerating after the collapse of the USSR, lent it an unprecedented economic dynamism as well as giving this new global system a heightened political legitimacy as the only possible route to modernity. At the same time, the 'market reforms' that Deng sought out in order to drive China's modernization were deeply inflected by the neo-liberalism that was transforming the polities of the United States and Britain, and subsequently to be rolled out globally. In Harvey's account, these market reforms, when combined with 'authoritarian centralised control', were to result in a distinct local configuration, 'neo-liberalism, with Chinese characteristics'.[4] For good or ill, China's course seemed set towards Westernization, though how long it would take to get there, and in what form when it eventually did, remained uncertain.

For many Western observers then, the post-1978 reforms are a direct repudiation of any 'alternative' modernity, or, as in Harvey's formulation, simply gives rise to a distorted, authoritarian version of it. In this chapter, we will take a different view. The reforms initiated by Deng after 1978 cannot be seen as China simply accepting Western capitalism as the only viable form of modernization. Rather, they are an attempt to continue on its own distinct path. Though the adoption of neo-liberal forms of economic policy and governance would have profound effects within China, we argue that neo-liberalism cannot provide an adequate framework though which to understand the path taken by China since 1978.

In what follows, we will try to outline the basic dynamics of neo-liberalism and try to ascertain how this globally dominant political agenda impacted on the Chinese reform process. The intention is not to provide an 'is/is not' answer.[5] As with debates around different routes to the modern, there is much dispute about the globally variegated nature of neo-liberalism, just as there is recognition that neo-liberalism has had different degrees of penetration and success. Indeed, many suggest neo-liberalism is finished, though it might hang around as a form of 'zombie economics' or be entering its 'late' or 'authoritarian' phase.[6] Finished or not, neo-liberalism has transformed the very meaning of 'Western-style modernization' in significant ways. Likewise, China's sheer economic and demographic mass has also bent the geopolitical space-time of the global system, seriously challenging the United States as global hegemon. The global landscape across which China and the West operate is thus profoundly different from that of 1978. We suggest that some account of these transformations is necessary if we are to understand the changing configurations of culture and modernity that are in play around the rapid adoption of a Western-style 'cultural' and then 'creative industries' programme in China. This is even more so if we are to seek in China's distinctive trajectory any sort of perspective or historical opening towards a post-neo-liberal order. How might a different historical trajectory, framed too often as residual or redundant – its socialist past, but also the prior period of reform and civil war, and deeper strands of a Chinese cultural tradition – provide such an opening?

What is neo-liberalism?

Neo-liberalism, as a term used to describe the ways in which the governance of capitalism has been transformed since the late 1970s, has proved capacious.[7] It has been able to accommodate the transformation of the liberal heartlands of the West, inspire a diverse range of reform movements in 'developing' countries as well as the successful state-led economies in East Asia, and, seemingly, to account for new forms of authoritarian governments in post-socialist Russia and Eastern Europe. The entry of the BRIC countries into globalized capitalism from the mid-1990s signalled a transformation on an unprecedented scale, coterminous with neo-liberalism's almost uncontested status as the only viable economic programme. There Is No Alternative.

Debates around neo-liberalism concern its very expansiveness. For some, this opens it up to ridicule, frequently used not to demand a stricter account of capitalism but rather to deflate critique.[8] Others have attempted to disaggregate its different dimensions, the better to pin it down.[9] We would stay with Jamie Peck and Nick Theodore and see it as a unity, albeit highly variegated and context specific. It is not just an abstract set of propositions, derived from the high priests of Mont Pèlerin or Chicago – it is also a highly pragmatic and contingent programme implemented in very different circumstances by a range of actors. It is a process, rather than a thing, and it has no essence or 'core' against which its different manifestations can be assessed as deviations. 'Actually existing neoliberalism' is an 'uneven, frustrated, creatively destructive, adaptive, and open ended process of transformation'.[10] These necessary protocols in place, we need to understand what this principled, pragmatic and variegated policy process might entail for China.

Harvey defines it thus:

> Neoliberalism is in the first instance a theory of economic practices that proposes that human well-being can be best advanced by liberating individual entrepreneurial freedoms and skills within an institutional framework characterized by strong private property rights, free markets, and free trade. The role

of the state is to create and preserve an institutional framework appropriate to such practices.[11]

As a first cut, this definition works well enough, describing the basic orientation behind much of the political and economic transformations of the last 40 years. What is necessarily entailed by such a description is the huge amount of political work (intellectual and institutional) required to establish this as a common-sense truth of the world, thereby rolling back at least a century of anti-capitalist, social-democratic, pro-working (or peasant) class struggles to attenuate the effects of capitalism's core logic. Shifting the Overton window does not begin to describe the depth of this challenge or the consequences of its success.

The emergence of neo-liberal thought from post-First World War Vienna, through the 'Geneva School', the Mont Pèlerin society, post-Second World War ordoliberalism and the Chicago School of the 1950s is now well documented.[12] It was an intellectual labour, financed by various business interests, and also an institutional labour, as members of the various overlapping networks of neo-liberal thinkers gained many positions in leading economic and legal institutions. To carve out a space in which the motivated individual entrepreneur could be seen to act, with unprecedented institutional freedom and support, in her own self-interest, while able to claim an overarching politico-ethical commitment to human well-being, was a huge political task. Neo-liberalism's success within the formal and informal institutions of the public sphere, gradually working its way through the organs of administration, research, education, information, media and culture, resulted in its basic tenets – as outlined by Harvey – being taken as a statement of 'natural' fact. This was not ideology, simply the way it was – Gramscian 'common sense'.[13]

The 'naturalization' of markets has been a fundamental effect of neo-liberalism, but we need to specify various aspects of this ideological common sense that have themselves served to obscure the ways in which this programme has actually operated. First, despite neo-liberalism's emphasis on 'strong private property rights, free markets, and free trade' it is not about the 'spontaneous order of the market'. As Foucault noted, it is specifically about competition, not 'free markets', and this competition has to be established and regulated. In this sense, neo-liberalism is anti-foundational (i.e. not rooted in natural law) and even 'constructivist' in its approach.[14] Second, it is not about the withdrawal of the state from the economy; not only must the state break down obstacles to market competition (trade unions, welfare states, government subsidies, trade barriers and so on) but must actively and continually intervene to secure the workings of this economic system. The neo-liberal state performs both 'roll-back and roll-out', and these are not necessarily sequential but can happen in parallel.[15]

Third, most neo-liberals did not believe in *homo economicus*, and certainly not Hayek. They relied on a certain kind of moral political order, embodied in both custom and law, which allowed *homo economicus* to emerge as a contingent and constructed position, one which would allow the signals of market exchange to move freely.[16] The order of the market relied on the economic being 'insulated' not from the state as a legal-regulative order, but from direct political interference.[17] It is this 'insulation' of the economic from the political – that is, democratic – interference which gives neo-liberalism its reforming energy but also its strongly anti-democratic agenda. While one of its constant tropes has been William H. Hutt's 'consumer sovereignty', democratic-political interference in the economy has been something neo-liberalism expressly set out to limit.[18] Finally, neo-liberalism, following on from its classical predecessor, was to be deployed as a project of the governance of subjects; however, this was to be done 'at a distance'. These subjects did share a subset of customary ethical values, but these were to be embodied in, and reinforced by, a legal-constitutional order. Indeed, in neo-liberalism market *and* morals constitute together the foundations for freedom, 'both being organized spontaneously and transmitted through tradition, rather than political power'.[19] Many neo-liberal thinkers, especially the European ones, very definitely saw the West (and indeed the Christian West) as pre-eminently embodying the values required for a competitive market system.[20] This would always raise questions about the feasibility of neo-liberalism's global roll-out but increasingly its very success posed problems for the underlying order of values that the 'free market' required in order to function.

This neo-liberal success, beyond the wildest dreams of its supporters, including its extension to policy areas never envisaged by its earliest theorists, has created problems for the neo-liberal project. The hollowing out of social support structures and the break up of traditional forms of communal solidarity; the shift towards highly individualized lifeworlds subject to new forms of commodification; and the transformation of the state from the locus of the *demos* to a facilitator for various forms of capital accumulation – especially around finance and debt – have had profound implications for the governance of these new emergent subjects. For in an established neo-liberal society the traditional kinds of conservative values required for social stability, those to which Thatcher and Reagan appealed, have *limited* political traction.[21] Rampant inequality, the individualization of risk, escalating social fragmentation and volatile global flows of capital and labour – dealing with these demanded more than traditions of patriotism, God and family values.[22]

Through the extension of neo-liberal logic to public administration, in the form of 'New Public Management', this agenda sought to introduce private sector efficiency into state bureaucracies via quasi-markets around competitive metrics (the dreaded Key Performance Indicators). This has had enormous impact not just on the organizational ethos of state administrations (at national and local levels) but also on education, health, and social welfare services.[23] Cultural policy has not been exempt, as a range of economic and social indicators have been demanded of it as 'return on investment' from the taxpayer.[24] The public sphere, intimately related to liberal democracy, has been 'emptied', the *demos* undone.[25] The accelerated commercialization of media and culture, the erosion of state broadcasting and other public forms (including the quasi-public newspaper system), has seen 'choice' and 'ability to pay' become central to culture systems. The modern public is being replaced by a series of fragmented, niche customers, organized around the purported sovereignty of the citizen-consumer.[26] The promotion of economic efficiency and growth as the foundational premise of contemporary society is ultimately a form of nihilism, from which, as Wendy Brown has forcefully argued, only monsters can come.[27]

Responding to an earlier phase of this challenge underlay the wave of neo-liberal reforms led by social democratic parties in the 1990s and early 2000s. In very different in contexts, Paul Keating, Bill Clinton, Tony Blair, Lula da Silva, Gerhart Schröder and others saw themselves as economic, social and cultural modernizers of their respective countries and their own parties.[28] They were concerned with providing some form of social protection for their traditional supporters against the harshness of free-market policies, but they adopted many of the key tenets of neo-liberalism (the 'third way', 'workfare' and so on) in order to deliver these. In this sense they acted as a kind of 'soft shell' for the extension of neo-liberalism, preparing the way for subsequent post-2008 'austerity' policies.[29] But 'soft' neo-liberalism did more than simply ease the social impact of market-facing reforms. As Ong and Zhang argued, it was not just about introducing markets but also about creating new subjects – both productive and governable.[30]

The neo-liberal programme sought productive citizens. The collapse of traditional industries and communal identities posed questions for governance and social cohesion but also promised new productive energies. Neo-liberalism's transformative programme could also be experienced as a kind of liberation from many of the oppressive hierarchies, restricted social identities and repressed emotions of the industrial era. Neo-liberalism had what Sam Binkley calls an 'emotional logic' which involved new relations to the self, to the emotions and to forms of sociability.

> Through the minimisation of any plausible collectivist alternative to market autonomy, the subject of neoliberalism is one that is induced to take up a certain instrumental relation to her own capacities and aptitudes, to produce on her own accord those qualities of self that will enable her to compete successfully in a social world reimagined in the image of a market.[31]

Crucial to this, as we have argued above and will discuss more in the next chapters, is the ability of the 'soft' neo-liberal programme to adapt and enlist the counter-cultural movements of the 1960s and 1970s. The kinds of entrepreneurial subjects and institutional frameworks required for the creative economy, for example, demand far more than securing 'strong private property rights, free markets, and free trade'. The neo-liberal programme involved 'not just markets but subjects', and these were thought together as a legal-constitutional order underpinned by shared values or, we might say, a shared culture. As with neo-liberalism more generally, there were a whole range of different forces at play in Australia, the United States, the United Kingdom, Germany and Brazil. From the techno-libertarianism of the 'Californian ideology' to Anglo-European countercultures to deep-rooted Latin American popular cultural radicalism, this new 'imaginary' adapted multiple cultural tropes required for a new kind of economy – networked, knowledge-based, entrepreneurial, 'creative' – along with the appropriate subjects. While 'the sixties' had been considered a major cultural threat to capitalism – eroding family values, spreading anti-authoritarian and anti-capitalist ideas, and promoting hedonistic consumption at the expense of productive work – they became central to a revitalized post-industrial capitalism over the 1980s and 1990s. The 'revenge' of 'bourgeois bohemians', the rise of the 'creative class', the youthful techno-modernism of the 'start-ups', all pointed to a transformative cultural, as well as economic, imaginary.[32]

'Soft' neo-liberalism – 'neo-liberalism 2.0' as we might call it – drew, in part, on a form of utopian promise derived from the 1960s. It was the privileged ability to create new kinds of creative subjects that, as we have seen in Chapter 1, was to give the liberal democratic West its global competitive advantage.

China and neo-liberalism

How does China's post-1978 reform era look from the perspective of the neo-liberal project?

The most salient and problematic aspect would seem to be the presence of a dominant state, which in 1978 controlled all aspects of economic, social and cultural life. The normative liberal-development script positioned the East Asian development state, post-socialist Eastern Europe and post-1978 China, as 'transitional' or 'deformed' forms of the ideal-type modern (Euro-American) state.[33] Here the progress of the Chinese reforms was a zero-sum tussle between the state and the market, which was in turn a struggle between authoritarian control and democracy. However, the neo-liberal programme does not necessarily adhere to this script, neither in the state-market conflict nor in the promotion of democracy.

Neo-liberalism is not simply about the rolling back of the state to allow the spontaneous order of the market. The state has always been essential for the construction, regulation and continued protection of the competitive market system, just as it was in the emergence of capitalism itself.[34] The possibility that an authoritarian state might push through neo-liberal reforms more effectively than liberal democracies has been around since the Chilean coup d'état of 1973. This was not readily admitted in its US and UK heartlands, which framed neo-liberal reforms as 'freedom' from state interference and expanded consumer choice as 'democracy'. A strong state might be required in certain circumstances to push through neo-liberal reforms, a kind of 'primitive accumulation', or 'shock doctrine', but the democratic form was mostly favoured.[35] More recently, the rise of authoritarian states – in the former Eastern Europe, in Russia, in Latin America and the Philippines – has been welcomed as bringing a degree of order necessary for economic opportunity to flourish. The key here is for the state to 'insulate' the economy from direct democratic-political interference – nationalization, protection, excessive taxation and so on – and protect, by force if necessary, the rights of property owners both domestically and globally.

More recent, post-2008, developments have seen a step back from the robust privatization agenda of early neo-liberalism (though it is still on the agenda in Brazil, India and across Africa). In states where there are developed public services, these have been retained as publicly funded but now delivered in partnership with the private sector (including the infamous public-private partnerships) often involving direct rentier relationships.[36] University loans, national health services, public security, prisons, visa processing, education, air traffic control, social services and much of local government is now delivered, underwritten with public money, in partnership with large-scale corporations.[37] The state per se is not necessarily a problem.

The key test for the neo-liberal programme is the extent to which a state guarantees private property and competitive markets, both domestically and globally. The East Asian 'development state', whilst a deviation from the liberal democratic norm, was not necessarily a challenge to neo-liberalism in respect of its authoritarian tendencies. As long as it honoured private property and the legal regulations of the international economic order, then the particular political form of the state was a secondary issue. The 'Washington Consensus' (driven by the World Bank, the IMF, and the WTO) certainly positioned East Asian states as transitional to democracy. The democratic revolutions of the 1990s, along with the salutary effect of the 1997 Asian Financial Crisis, in helping dismantle some of their directive state structures, seemed to confirm this. But the main focus of neo-liberalism at the level of the global economy had primarily been to curtail the political interventions in the economy by governments of the developing world. The challenge posed to a rules-based global economic system by the movement for a new international economic order, driven by political demands emanating from the newly independent countries in the United Nations, was something that was resisted firmly by the United States and United Kingdom in the 1980s. In a sense the neo-liberal victory at this global level was as important as other key 'test sites' such as Chile or Russia.[38] Though the East Asian development state's protection of national champions through tariffs and other preferential treatment presented some issues, these states never threatened the primacy of economic efficiency over issues of social justice (a domestic battle won among the 'tigers' over the course of the 1950s and 1960s). In any event, South Korea, Japan and Taiwan were not fully sovereign states but operated under the tutelage of the United States (Singapore a tolerated city state).

Neo-liberal theorists and practical economists never had a problem with the authoritarian nature of the Chinese state per se, simply its ubiquitous imbrication with the economy. Their concern was how to extricate the state from the economy, allowing full freedom for the price signals of commodities, labour and capital. At the same time, they sought to ensure that China's integration into the global market would also come with a full acceptance of its rules. The problem, then, was less one of how free markets could lead to democracy than how the Chinese state could remain strong enough to ensure order while resisting the claims of social justice and the primacy of the rights of the state over those of capital – both still embedded in its espousal of 'socialist values' and the leading role of the CCP. The rising fear of contemporary China in part relates to its economic, technological and military challenges to US hegemony, but also to a perceived authoritarian shift in the nature of the Chinese state under Xi Jinping. While concerns for democracy, civil society and human rights animate left-liberal opinion in the West, it is the persistent restrictions, even rolling back, of the rights of the private sector that bother neo-liberals. The continued role of the state-owned enterprises (SOEs), and the directive role of the party at multiple levels in the private sector, is seen as highly problematic, and from a global economic system perspective, as some kind of 'cheating' (SOEs benefitting from state investment and blocking domestic access to foreign capital and so on). More than a pragmatic question of occasional rule-breaking, there is a deeper sense of a systemic repudiation of the autonomy and primacy of the economic.[39]

This points to a key difference in attitudes to state power. Neo-liberal authoritarian state action is there to secure the 'free market', its restriction of democracy offset by its contribution to human well-being in the form of an economic efficiency measured in GDP growth and per-capita income. The real democracy was consumer sovereignty, just as the real threat was to the rights of capital in the name of planning and social justice – both futile and destructive. Concerns about the Chinese socialist state and, to some degree, the East Asian development state, relate to a tendency to temper the free run of capital with a commitment to a general social welfare – 'Confucian', socialist, national-patriotic depending – enshrined in ethical-political norms shared (more or less) by both state and society. This shared interest in a common project frequently overrides or tempers the priorities of 'the market' in such states, and they do not readily countenance the handing over of complete social and political power to 'capital'. It is around this fundamental difference in conceptions of the role of the state in securing 'the good life' – which necessarily includes collective cultural-political norms – that seems to form the dividing line between authoritarian neo-liberalism and more socially embedded forms of the developmental state. This latter is simply the *wrong kind* of authoritarian.[40]

Deng and the new era

Deng Xiaoping, and the group of reformers he assembled after taking power between 1976 and 1978, shared with the neo-liberals a concern to extricate the economy from the dominance of the political, the reference here being the chaos of the Cultural Revolution rather than the creeping socialism of planning and the welfare state. How this reform was to be implemented and its (mostly unknown) consequences managed was the central drama of Deng's fourteen-year rule up to his 'Southern Tour' in 1992. After that year, his protégés Jiang Zemin and Zhu Rongji extended Deng's 'socialism with Chinese characteristics' into the fully fledged 'socialist market economy' leading to the accelerated economic development with which we are now familiar. The Chinese economic miracle, we are constantly reminded, stands as testimony to the power of the market, and the country's success in raising the income levels of many millions of people has been foundational to the claims that 'free-market' capitalism is the only viable form of economic development. The influence of (mainly US-based) think-tanks, foundations and (mostly neo-liberal) economists – including leading lights such as Milton Friedman and Ronald Coase – in the early elaboration of the economic reform agenda forms part of an exemplary narrative of a struggle between modernizers and conservatives, in which the realities of the market vanquish the dangerous illusions of the planned economy.[41]

In order to challenge this neo-liberal narrative around China, we need to explore in more detail what the extrication and 'insulation' of the economic meant in the Chinese context. We need to understand the specific role of the Chinese state in this process, the capacities on which it drew and the kinds of legitimation it sought. Finally, we need to look at the configuration of state, social forces, markets and subjects that these reforms brought into being and the challenges they pose.

William Davies's characterization of neo-liberalism as the 'disenchantment of politics by economics' could be applied to Deng's reforms and how he framed them.[42] For Deng, and a whole swath of political cadres, the absolute dominance of politics in Mao's era, especially during the Cultural Revolution, was a source of chaos and weakness. Deng attempted a kind of controlled 'disenchantment', focusing on the practical, the empirical, and tacit common sense. Deng's 1977 article in the *Guangming Ribao* (Sunshine Daily) – 'Practice is the Only Criterion for Truth' – was pivotal for reform. Recalling his earlier pragmatism of 'It does not matter about the colour of the cat, as long as it catches the mouse', Deng outlined a programme of 'learning truth from facts' that was widely welcomed in the wake of twelve years of Cultural Revolution. These calls for clear-eyed realism by Deng and his close collaborators often served to hide the fact that calls for reform – that China had to develop economically, and that some kind of market reforms would be needed – were widespread within the party and across society.[43] As is well known, many of the market reforms were implemented directly at the local level well before Beijing officially sanctioned them. What is often missed, in the characterization of a China frozen by rigid Communist ideology, is that there was extensive debate about what kind of reforms might be required and how they might be shaped, informed by shared concepts and values embedded within high levels of popular political consciousness. It should not be forgotten that in 1978 most of the party cadres had returned from long periods of work in the provinces where they had been in direct contact with the masses. Both peasant and urban workers had been expected to take part in workplace political meetings, where day-to-day questions were couched in politicized form.[44]

There is no reason to suggest that market-based economic reforms were neo-liberal in themselves. Many of the early Chinese reform models came from Eastern Europe, especially Yugoslavia and Hungary, and referenced Lenin's New Economic Policy rather than the Chicago School. Nor can we automatically equate market reforms with the return of capitalism. Commentators on China frequently characterize any sign of market relations or even of the seeking of personal economic gain as 'capitalist'. But markets and extended commodity relations predate capitalism proper by many hundreds of years. Late imperial China was a sophisticated market society, but because the state did not seek to identify itself with the expansion of capital at the expense of other social interests, nor see it as the foundational principle of the policy, it remained a 'Smithian market economy'.[45] We need to avoid framing 'market versus state' as a zero-sum index of capitalism versus socialism, with a strong overlay of freedom versus authoritarianism, and/or individualism versus collectivism. The return of market relations does not necessarily entail the return of capitalism. In this sense, Deng's reforms were precisely as he described them – an efficient economic tool imported from the West that could be used to enhance the strength of Chinese socialism through the development of the 'forces of production'. This classic Marxist terminology obscured the fact that these productive forces would now be equated with the market.

Liberal and neo-liberal narratives position the reforms as an awakening from ideology into practical clear-sightedness. Mao's primacy of the political (founded on class struggle) was an unreal projection of wishful thinking onto a recalcitrant economic reality. Deng's reforms were a practical modernization, focused on real reform rather than pursuing a utopian vision which was now moribund. The counterposition of clear-eyed practical realism to blind ideology, and the wresting of the mantle of modernization from an outdated left, was precisely what Reagan and Thatcher managed to achieve in the same decade. It was this that allowed Deng to engage with the West as somebody with whom one could do business.[46] However, this frequently led to a misinterpretation of what was actually happening in China.

The countryside reforms and the rise of the Town and Village Enterprises (TVAs) from the 1970s are often positioned as prime examples of the acceleration of the market reforms crucial to the neo-liberal project.[47] Coase and Wang adapt the metaphor used by Chen Yun, a senior economic reformer, of the 'bird in the cage', where the bird is the socialist economy and the cage is central planning. The latter is meant to keep the former to socialist principles, though the cage needed to grow as the new market reforms took off. Coase and Wang use the metaphor differently to show that, in reality, it is the market bird struggling to escape the socialist cage. It is this teleological framework, in which all market reforms are in zero-sum relation to socialism, that allows the persistence of very different social principles to those of neo-liberalism to go unnoticed. The TVAs, for example, were as much communal enterprises as they were an unleashing of free market entrepreneurship.[48]

Isabella Weber has convincingly shown how the debates over price reforms were far more complex than 'conservatives' versus 'reformers'. What was at stake was whether China should embark on the kind of 'big bang' all-at-once move from state-determined to market-driven prices that was to occur, with catastrophic results, in Russia and other ex-socialist states. The 'big bang' approach was energetically promoted by the reformers after the 1985 *Bashan* meeting, which came midway through a decade in which Chinese economists had begun to engage in extensive study of economics – both radical (and anti-socialist) reformers in Eastern Europe and neo-liberal economists from the United States and United Kingdom.[49] This approach was narrowly averted not because of 'conservatism' but based, first, on extensive understanding of the realities of life in the countryside by many of the leading cadres, and their realization of the deleterious social impacts such a reform would have. More significantly, from our perspective, the ability to reject such an approach drew on long-standing Communist experience of dealing with price reform after the 1949 Revolution, and before that in Communist controlled areas – in contrast to the rampant inflation bequeathed by the KMT. This in turn, Weber shows, was based on two millennia of imperial statecraft, where judicious intervention into the market emerged from the famous 'discourses on salt and iron' (*Yan Tie Lun*) in 81 BCE. Both these provided the confidence and experiential base to reject radical or neo-liberal market reforms in the name of a wider social and political principle.[50]

Deng's attempt to let prices float freely in 1988 did cause an outcry and was revoked.[51] It was only after the 4 June repression of the Tiananmen protests that the price reforms were finally pushed through. What was clearer in the Chinese context was that the relative (in contrast to the centrally planned socialist economy) 'insulation' of the economy entailed not just a stepping back by the state from direct interference in the market system but a more general depoliticization of society.[52] The 1980s involved a fundamental struggle to remove the economy discursively to a space beyond socialist politics. Hence the constant need to demonize the Cultural Revolution, which represented not just the chaos from which the reforms intended to extricate China but figured to denigrate any form of popular political involvement, especially in the day-to-day running of the economy. It is for this reason that Wang Hui sees the violent repression of the Tiananmen protests as foundational for Chinese neo-liberalism.

For classical liberals, Tiananmen was the moment that economic reform was separated from political reform, something that might be countenanced as pragmatic but could only be transitional. In this account, it was the polystyrene sculpture of the Statue of Liberty erected metres from the portrait of Mao that was unacceptable to the regime, given the widespread protests shaking Poland and other Eastern European Communist countries. For Wang Hui, in contrast, the 1989 protests were a broad and multifaceted social movement, in which calls for democracy were part of a wider set of social concerns about the direction of the reforms and how they were being implemented. The protests were not against reforms per se, nor focused on the removal of the Communist Party and the instigation of liberal democracy. The protesters, the students along with the citizenry who supported them, were concerned not with regime change but with 'the right of citizens to participate in the public life of the country, and the channels that would enable them to do so'.[53]

Though the Tiananmen protests were clearly part of a wider contestation of the reform process, it is debatable if they were an immediate threat to the regime, as the Solidarity trade union was in Poland. Deng saw clearly that the protests threatened his reforms, both in the occasion they might give to conservatives to block them and the encouragement they might give to popular opposition to intervene in their implementation. For Deng, Tiananmen – whose violent repression might

possibly have been averted with a different political will – was a clear demonstration that these reforms would be implemented top-down, by the party, and would
not involve the kinds of popular mobilization that had marked the Cultural Revolution, and indeed the civil war and revolutionary period. As such, Tiananmen
could be seen to represent not some thwarted opening to liberal democracy but
the closing of a 'space [...] for creative imagination and the opportunities it offered
for experiment'.[54]

> What is most striking about [images from the June events] are the expressions
> on people's faces – excitement, anxiety, hope, determination and compassion –
> across all groups and generations [...] [T]hroughout weeks of protest, people
> displayed so much self-discipline. This did not come from a fear of government
> revenge, but from a strong feeling of pride in their ability to take their fate into
> their own hands – visibly a legacy of the Chinese revolution and a socialist past.[55]

A strong authoritarian state would be required to push the reforms through, something that neo-liberalism could countenance with some equanimity. Unfortunate
as it was, tragic even, in the end, they argued, what needed to be done was done.
Coase and Wang describe this tough love, trickle down, approach in ways that
would be familiar to anyone swept up in a neo-liberal reform process:

> Even if everyone was made better off during the reform, the relative position
> in the income ladder would change for many members of society. In this rela-
> tive sense, it was inevitable that some would feel like losers [...] Thus, reform
> without losers in the absolute sense could still give rise to widespread frustra-
> tion and disillusion.[56]

Tiananmen confirmed the depoliticization of the reform process, leaving the
Chinese state to push them through as it saw fit. Thus, the reforms in the countryside which launched the reform period, especially the TVAs, were themselves
depoliticized, the socialized dimension of these enterprises marginalized by the
emphasis on market returns and tax income (often led by local governments) as the
only measure of their worth. More generally, the promise of a newly empowered
Chinese countryside was undermined by the shift in priorities towards urban
development, accelerating in the mid-1980s. Yasheng Huang has made a distinction between these earlier reforms and those that came after 1992, when Deng
gave the green light to Shanghai. The early period involved a 'good capitalism',
made up of small-scale entrepreneurs who retained a large proportion of the value
they produced. After 1992 this was sidelined by the massive developmental forces
unleashed by the coastal cities – the 'great reversal' led by SOEs, large-scale foreign

direct investment, big capital and a squeezing of the countryside for cheap labour.[57] In this process, the peasantry – which had formed the bedrock of the party's support since its founding in 1921 – were dismantled as active political subjects,[58] their economic gains eroded, forcing millions to relocate to coastal cities for work in construction and manufacturing.[59]

'Not just markets but subjects' – how then were the new Chinese subjects to be created after such a massive process of depoliticization?

Depoliticized modernization

The reform period was not, and could not be, a refutation of the Chinese Revolution, whatever liberals and neo-liberals might say. Rather – signalling a commitment to working with previous enemies while preserving, invisibly, the 'cardinal principles' of the Communist Revolution – socialism was to be continued under the sign of a depoliticized modernization.[60] 'Seeking truth from facts' indicated not an abandonment of Communist ideals but a shift 'to the dynamic, open testing of possibilities', a willingness to cooperate with the market unencumbered by Maoist politics. Not only was China hiding its Communist values externally but it was also ensuring these values did not interfere in the workings of the market economy.[61]

Deng's reforms reworked deep-seated tropes of the Chinese political imaginary – wholesale modernization based on imported Western technology and finance, to be used to Chinese, and Socialist, ends.[62] Mao had adopted Khrushchev's 1957 'catch up and surpass' for himself (ganchao), feeding into the 1958 'Great Leap Forward'. In 1975, Zhou Enlai had introduced the 'four modernisations – agriculture, industry, defence, and science and technology' – with Deng and Hua Guofeng, Mao's immediate successor, eagerly promoting a new technology-driven 'Great Leap Forward'.[63]

However, as it became clear, this modernization was to be achieved in direct refutation of the Maoist emphasis on reducing the differences between party and masses, country and city, and manual and intellectual labour.[64] Post-Tiananmen socialism exacerbated the differences on all three registers. The year 1978 had seen the return to power of many of the technocratic cadres sidelined, purged or exiled during the Cultural Revolution.[65] The growing excitement and revived idealism for a new wave of Chinese modernization, as Deng spearheaded the transformation of thinking within the party, is palpable in the accounts of the period. It was the 'red engineers', the technocratic experts – rather than those cadres drawn from the working-class and peasantry – who were to lead this new era of ganchao. The former replaced the latter within the party, just as the party no longer sought to root itself in the concerns of the masses. After 1989, party leaders would lack the kinds of contact with working class and peasant life that marked the previous generations. One key difference was that, over the course of the 1980s, the engineers were joined by the newly founded and prestigious discipline of economics.[66]

We might compare this moment with that of Khrushchev's USSR in the late 1950s and early 1960s, where a similarly modernizing technocratic regime tried to develop the conditions (using cybernetics) for a socialist consumer society.[67] But in 1978 in China, there was no sense that capitalism and socialism were neck and neck, as had been the common perception as the USSR forged ahead in the space race and posted record growth figures. In 1978, the capitalist West far outstripped socialist China (and the USSR) on almost every economic scale, and in seeking material improvement for their population and security for the nation, some form of market-based system was the only place reformers had to look. It was in these circumstances that the CCP began to connect with economic specialists, increasingly from the United States, who had already been converted to the basic tenets of neo-liberalism.[68]

Deng's reforms were less an embrace of the utopia of the free market, and more a process of socialist engineering undertaken via economics. For Deng and the reformers, economics was a tool, to be used to drive a new stage of China's modernization. The survival of socialism demanded 'advanced productive forces', and for Deng this meant the market.[69] Modernization, as we have seen, had deep roots in modern Chinese history, and its reinvention after the 1978 reforms was a return to a central trope of modern Chinese history rather than its final repudiation. Chinese modernization was anti-imperialist. Deng's willingness to radically change tack and adopt Western technology, finance and economic forms was always accompanied by the memory of 'a century of humiliation' which fuelled much of China's nation-building, just as it was the work of a wily old revolutionary whose life had been dedicated to building socialism. But the explicit, 'anti-colonial' mobilization of an indigenous Chinese culture capable of articulating a distinct form of modernity had always been weak in this anti-imperialist 'catch-up'. May Fourth intellectuals had rejected China's 'feudal' past, even though they were steeped in the ethico-political ideals and practices of this very different civilizational entity. We have noted this paradox above: how an explicit rejection of the past, and a wholesale embrace of Western science, technology and social science, could coexist with a deep persistence – a *longue durée* – of statecraft, ethical values and forms of everyday practice rooted in that rejected past.[70]

For Deng and the red engineers, modernization was a practico-scientific project. Western technology, know-how and finance were to be used to provide material abundance and national security. China's modernization was to be secured by Chinese socialism using economics as one would any other technology. It was a return to a heroic modernity of science and engineering – 'Light,

Heat, Power!' – now accompanied by the best modern economics they could muster.[71] Western consumerism was no longer seen as a counter-ideology but as providing for the material abundance that Chinese socialism had promised but never delivered. Now, guided by hard-headed economic realists, the tarnished goods of political idealism would be replaced by the material satisfaction of real consumer durables.

The project facing the Chinese reformers was of a vastly greater order of magnitude than that of the neo-liberal counter-revolution in the United States and United Kingdom. To introduce market relations into a state-directed system required a great deal of practical flexibility and political resolution. It is not enough to frame these actions as 'primitive accumulation', though the dispossession and privatization of socially owned resources went on apace. The state was also an actively constructive agent seeking a Chinese socialist modernization. The problem was that economic reform is not an engineering problem, or rather, in this case it was 'social engineering' using a tool – the market – that was, in the context of global neo-liberalism, increasingly at odds with the substantive values of the party wielding it. The power of market reforms to radically transform the socialist polity was what both liberals and neo-liberals expected; this did not happen, or at least, not in the form they expected.

Performative neo-liberalism

Neo-liberalism broke from both neo-classical and Marxist 'realist' notions of the economy as 'scare resources' or the 'production of needs' and shifted towards the primacy of the 'laws of the market' as the *sine qua non* of practical economic logic. The market was an information processor, the only possible way of eliciting and responding to social needs. States could neither know nor plan for social need, only establish the framework to allow the market to process the price signals and allocate resources and rewards accordingly. In relaunching China's heroic modernization, the progress of these 'laws of the market' through the polity would be the touchstone for the country's transition from a 'backwards' to a 'modern' economy.

It is telling that Coase and Wang see socialism as a tool, one that had become central to the CCP but which had hardened into pure ideology and become useless. The tool of the market was to replace that of socialism, even if the party still needed to pay lip service to the ideology. That socialism might involve a set of values that could shape or override the workings of the market, or even set the ultimate goals for which this market was to be used, is not considered by them.[72] What they point to is the 'organic' logic of the market working in a non-ideological fashion (i.e. not working through the conscious beliefs of individuals) to determine the behaviour patterns of individuals. As Hayek wrote: 'Competition produces [...] a kind of impersonal compulsion which makes it necessary for numerous individuals to adjust their way of life in a manner that no deliberate instructions or commands could bring about.'[73]

The market was a tool, but this tool had an immanent logic which could, and frequently did, cut against the political values it was being used to secure. This would be evermore so as China became integrated into the world capitalist system. 'Reform and opening' was an indissoluble couple, practically and discursively. Opening up to the world was a totem of the new heroic modernization project, making a clear break from the Maoist past. It was also the practical means whereby this project could take place, facilitating Foreign Direct Investment and integrating Chinese manufacturing and agriculture into global supply chains. It meant that any attempt to countermand the laws of the market could be characterized as a return to the political fantasies of the Maoist period and the chaos of the Cultural Revolution. Joining the WTO set the seal on this, as the 'laws of the market' would always be positioned to override any political objectives that threatened to interfere with them. SOEs, for example, were constantly attacked as illegitimate within the rules of global competitiveness, even though they are foundational to the Chinese Communist regime. As Harvey had noted, China's 'reform and opening' came at a time of a reformatting of global trade, and, as has been commonly described, the United States and China worked symbiotically to deliver cheap consumer goods in an era of wage stagnation and budget deficit in the former, and abundant capital (via US bonds) and rapid export-led growth to the latter. The symbiosis that was 'Chimerica' is certainly coming to an end, but while it lasted it allowed a mutual accommodation of a US-dominated global trading system and a socialist developmental state economy. But it was a symbiosis that increasingly challenged the socialist dimension of the Chinese developmental state project, even as it immeasurably strengthened that state.

Economics, we can say, is not just analytic but also performative; it helps bring into being that which it purports to describe. This is so at the level of macro-economic strategy, as 'the economy', identified through a set of metrics and proxies, becomes an entity unto itself to whose laws politics must submit.[74] It is also performative at the mundane level of everyday commerce and consumption.[75] The 'laws of the market' impact on quotidian subject formation. Neo-liberal economics sought a discursive and practical insulation of the economic, dis-embedding actions driven by individual self-interest from any wider social, political and ethical world.[76] Neo-liberalism is a project of governance, seeking to introduce market or market-like relations to everyday life. As Ong and Zhang suggested:

> privatization [is] a set of techniques that optimize economic gains by priming the powers of the private self. Since calculative activities deployed in the

marketplace cannot be easily compartmentalized, they therefore come to shape private thinking and activities in other spheres of social action. In broad terms, we view privatization as a process that both produces free-floating values of self-interest and allows them to proliferate in daily life.[77]

The ethos of profit-seeking entrepreneurial behaviour was discursively promoted in China; Deng's 'to get rich is glorious', widely quoted in the West (echoing Guizot's equally famous *enrichissez-vous*), is apocryphal but telling. The massive entry of overseas (mostly Chinese diasporic) development capital and the expansion of the market for consumer goods and services, along with the enormous legal, regulatory, institutional and infrastructural changes this required, has rightly been described as one of the most impressive feats of the last half century. Equally, the reorganization of labour, infrastructure, finance, logistics and regulation has profoundly transformed social relations in China in ways that have impacted greatly on the forms of intervention and legitimation available to the Chinese state.[78] The insertion into the WTO structures, and the global 'ideoscape' that accompanied this, has constantly demanded more radical restructuring of the Chinese economy, and its logic has increasingly cut into that of the socialist state.[79] Such a radical modernization process could not possibly avoid transforming the sociocultural practices of everyday life, producing new Chinese subjects.

It was commonly assumed by Western observers that the introduction of market relations and the 'consumer society' would entail a modern Western 'lifestyle' in which individualism and related 'Western values' would inevitably take precedence over Asian 'traditional' 'collectivist' values, whether socialist or 'Confucian'.[80] If true, this would certainly drive a wedge between the emergent identities of the new post-socialist Chinese subjects and the ideological legitimacy of the socialist state. However, we cannot simply equate 'market relations' with 'Western modernity' (nor, to repeat, are these relations necessarily in some zero-sum conflict with the socialist state). There is good reason to think, with Ong and Zhang, that the introduction of such market relations would involve a reconfiguration of Chinese society and polity in its own particular terms, derived from its own specific historical trajectory.[81] However, there is no doubt that the dominance of 'market reason' within an ever-expanding zone of contact with globalizing capitalism, coupled with the 'imaginary' of an entrepreneurial and consumer society deeply inflected by Western imagery, has had a crucial impact on Chinese state and society. We would argue that this is as much a cultural impact as it is a material transformation of ways of doing business. The Chinese state launched on a project of modernization aimed at national security and material abundance with very little idea of what the consequences might be. Modernization was being delivered by the CCP but many of its images of success – its cityscapes, ideal-type entrepreneur and consuming citizens – were often Western-inspired. Attempting to assert socialist and collectivist values while promoting 'market reason' and its associated subject positions became increasingly difficult. We shall see in subsequent chapters how this image of a distinctly Chinese modernity was negotiated in Shanghai, as China's modern global city.

'Negotiating modernity' was certainly not a one-way adoption of Western values and lifestyles, as many scholars have shown. At the same time, the ways in which market reforms promoted the construction of new kinds of citizen-consumers imbued with *suzhi*, a new middle-class 'human quality' set up expanding expectations vis-à-vis the state that have been difficult to control.[82] Ideologies of economic efficiency and the primacy of consumer choice have increasingly 'undone the demos'.[83] There is little reason to doubt that much of this has happened in China. Again, this is not simply the market versus the state. At the same time, the ways in which the Chinese middle class has been integrated into a highly financialized system of mortgages, shares, pension schemes and the like has tied both state and citizens into a global finance system which neither of them can afford to treat lightly.[84]

Consumerism, the social relations it sets up and reorders, has ideological as well as material effects. It is not a neutral mechanism for distributing material goods but a highly efficient 'desiring machine', one that reorders social relations in ways that penetrate deep into the lifeworld.[85] The form of this consumerism (and the 'entrepreneurial self' capable of taking advantage of its opportunities) was extensively based on an imagined West (a combination of US popular culture and European luxury goods) that had become the very image of modernity. The post-Tiananmen bargain, of material abundance in exchange for depoliticization, meant that, in the absence of a space for the public articulation of political opinions, consumerism has become the loudest voice. This voice – the famous 'rising middle class' – is not based on the classic 'bourgeoise revolution' model of securing the political conditions for the return on investment but rather on defending a lifestyle against those who would seek to undermine it – a classic 'petty bourgeois' predicament.[86] The concerns of the new urban consumers involve less the desire for democracy (very thin on the ground) than a desire for efficiency coupled with a fear of redistribution.[87] While the (relatively) wealthy urban dwellers can do without democracy, they view socialism as a regression to the past and, more pointedly, a direct threat to their lifestyle.

The reordering of the Chinese lifeworld under the 'impersonal compulsion' of the 'laws of markets' has had real effects on the ability of the Chinese state to create productive and governable subjects. Zhang and Ong suggest that the state has restricted personal expression to 'the commodifiable and the marketable', while retaining control over all other areas, in what Ong and Zhang call 'Socialism from a distance'.[88] These authors suggest China has embraced an economic liberalism uncoupled from any political liberalism. Chinese socialism has instead transformed its structures of governance in a way that links state power and everyday life, 'sovereign power and self-sovereignty', in what they call 'the social', a complex interrelationship between the two.[89] We would agree with this, but should add a caveat: they tend to frame this in the form of individual expression versus authoritarian restraint, and we think the state is more active in its construction of the values that inform everyday life.

We can explain this more by taking the book *Seeing Like a State*, by James C. Scott, an anthropologist, who contrasted abstract, ideological 'epistemic knowledge', usually deployed by states ('sovereignty'), with that gained from practical, everyday experience, or *metis* ('self-sovereignty').[90] The state, for Scott, can see only in standardized, undifferentiated terms and fails to engage with the lived reality of everyday practice.[91] It is a common charge that the ideology of socialism – 'epistemic knowledge' – has been hollowed out by the practical reality, the new 'lifestyle' of consumer capitalism, and that the Chinese state has tried to replace this, in rather clunky fashion perhaps, by a ramped-up nationalism and/or rebooted Confucianism. However, as we have suggested above, one of the charges against neo-liberalism is that it has also hollowed out the practical realities, the embedded *metis* of everyday value and meaning.[92] A glance at Chinese film and literature, fictional and non-fictional, over the last two decades, suggests this pervasive sense of an erosion of social values, in the countryside, in old industrial centres, in the new factories of the South and in the sprawling new cities.[93] As we, and many others, have argued, neo-liberalism is a form of nihilism; its claims to economic efficiency cannot by themselves found the value system, either epistemic or *metis*, required for a society to cohere.[94]

In an important section, Ong and Zhang discuss Foucault's work on governmentality, where self-knowledge and self-expression, care of self and relationship to others, become 'the very stuff of ethics':

> We suggest that modernity as an ethic of 'how one should live' is being proposed again in contemporary China, shaped by an unstable constellation of events: fading collectivist values, the compulsion to self-govern, and the heavy hand of authoritarian socialism. These disparate forces interact to create uncertain situations in which problems of living arise [...] The widespread commodification of things and persons opens up a new horizon of obligation for individuals to plan their lives by developing a reflexive attitude toward confronting a society in flux [...] we identify this individuation as an ongoing process of private responsibility, requiring ordinary Chinese to take their life into their own hands and to face the consequences of their decisions on their own.[95]

This is the Chinese version of Ulrike Beck's 'risk society', Zygmunt Bauman's 'liquid modernity' and Marshall Berman's 'all that is solid melts into air'.[96] Ong and Zhang identify this new form of individuated ethical choice as both exigency – 'the compulsion to self-govern' – and a historical opening – 'taking their life into their own hands'. This unstable combination of compulsion and possibility is crucial to debates around the new creative subject of neo-liberalism discussed above and which will concern us in the next chapters. The state is not just repressive here; it has traditionally played a crucial role in framing these everyday ethics embedded in the *metis* of practical life through the belief and value system it promotes. These include the 'big C' ethical ideals noted by Prasenjit Duara above, the 'epistemic' framings which are associated with national or perhaps civilizational entities.[97] They also involve the transformation of subjects which neo-liberalism sought to effect. Though the meeting of 'sovereignty' and 'self-sovereignty' in the 'social' may only be contingent and fissured as Ong and Zhang suggest, they cannot exist without each other. It is here that the cultural field becomes crucial.

Neo-liberals such as Hayek, and the ordoliberals discussed by Foucault, saw that the market system was underpinned by customary values, a *metis* perhaps, held in place by an ethical-legal and epistemic framework set by the state.[98] What Coase and Wang call the 'organic' growth of a market society within the Chinese polity was far from being the case. It required a state to construct and maintain the conditions in which entrepreneurs and consumers might flourish.[99] Coase and Wang are ideologically blind to the deep disruptions of everyday life and values created by the privatization and commodification of whole swathes of contemporary China. The growing divergence of a market-oriented society and an ideologically socialist state is not a mark of a polity in transition from the traditional socialist to the modern capitalist but one threatening a deepening nihilism. Ong and Zhang suggest an emergent Chinese modernity releasing individual ethical practices from the tutelage of the state; but in this emergent modernity might it be that the traditions of China as a 'civilizational state', and its more recent ones as a socialist state, could be more than the authoritarian deployment of ideological means of regime survival? Might they represent (also) an attempt to provide an epistemic and ethical framing for a new Chinese modernity? Whatever new configuration of 'sovereign power and self-sovereignty' emerges in the new China, the role of that sovereign state power in establishing the ethical and material framework will be crucial. Its attempts might also provide some kind of resource to help move beyond neo-liberalism.[100]

NOTES

1. R. Macfarquhar and M. Schoenhals, *Mao's Last Revolution* (Cambridge, MA: Harvard University Press, 2006), 459.

2. Ibid., 50.

3. Cf. E. F. Vogel, *Deng Xiaoping and the Transformation of China* (Cambridge, MA: Belknap Press, 2011), 693: 'Indeed, the structural changes that took place under Deng's leadership rank amongst the most basic changes since the Chinese empire took shape during the Han dynasty over two millennia ago.'

4. D. Harvey, *A Brief History of Neoliberalism* (Oxford: Oxford University Press, 2005), 120–21.

5. Cf. I. Weber, 'China and Neoliberalism: Moving Beyond China Is/Is Not Neoliberal Dichotomy', in *The Sage Handbook of Neoliberalism*, ed. D. Cahill, M. Cooper, M. Konings and D. Primrose (London: Sage, 2018), 219–33.

6. Cf. H. Wang, 'The Dialectics of Autonomy and Opening', *Critical Asian Studies* 43, no. 2 (2011): 237–60; J. Quiggin, *Zombie Economics: How Dead Ideas Still Walk Among Us* (Princeton, NJ: Princeton University Press, 2011); J. Peck and N. Theodore, 'Still Neoliberalism?', *South Atlantic Quarterly* 118, no. 2 (2019): 245–65.

7. Variants have been tested in countries as far apart as New Zealand and Chile, famously spearheaded by the United States and United Kingdom, spreading to multiple countries at varying speeds and levels of penetration, capturing institutions of global economic governance ('the Washington Consensus') and supra-national entities such as (parts of) the European Union.

8. E.g. T. Flew, 'Six Theories of Neoliberalism', *Thesis Eleven* 122, no. 1 (2014): 49–71.

9. D. Rodgers, 'The Uses and Abuses of "Neoliberalism"', *Dissent* 65, no.1 (2018): 78–87.

10. J. Peck, N. Brenner and N. Theodore, 'Actually Existing Neoliberalism', Cahill et al. *The Sage Handbook of Neoliberalism*, 3–15, 7. Cf. Peck and Theodore, 'Still Neoliberalism?'; N. Brenner, J. Peck and N. Theodore, 'Variegated Neoliberalization: Geographies, Modalities, Pathways', *Global Networks* 10, no. 2 (2010): 182–222. Ong and Zhang call this an 'assemblage'. A. Ong and L. Zhang, 'Introduction', in *Privatising China: Socialism from Afar*, ed. A. Ong and L. Zhang (Ithaca, NY: Cornell University Press, 2008), 1–19, 5.

11. Harvey, *Brief History of Neoliberalism*, 2.

12. For example: P. Mirowski and D. Plehwe, *The Road from Mont Pèlerin: The Making of the Neoliberal Thought Collective* (Cambridge MA: Harvard University Press, 2009); D. Stedman Jones, *Masters of the Universe: Hayek, Freidman and the Birth of Neoliberal Politics* (Princeton, NJ: Princeton University Press, 2012); P. Mirowski, *Never Let Serious Crisis Go to Waste: How Neoliberalism Survived the Financial Meltdown* (London: Verso, 2013); Q. Slobodian, *Globalists: The End of Empire and the Birth of Neoliberalism* (Cambridge, MA: Harvard University Press, 2018); Cahill et al., *The Sage Handbook of Neoliberalism*.

13. 'Common sense is the folklore of philosophy, and is always half-way between folklore properly speaking and the philosophy, science and economics of the specialists. Common sense creates the folklore of the future, that is as a relatively rigid phase of popular knowledge

at a given place and time.' A. Gramsci, *Selections from the Prison Notebooks*, trans. and ed. Q. Hoare and G. N. Smith (New York: International Publishers, 1992), 244.

14. M. Foucault, *The Birth of Biopolitics: Lectures at the College de France, 1978–79*, trans. G. Burchell (New York: Palgrave Macmillan, 2010); M. Feher, 'Self-Appreciation: Or, the Aspirations of Human Capital', *Public Culture* 21, no. 1 (2009): 21–41, 32.

15. J. Peck, *Constructions of Neoliberal Reason* (Oxford: Oxford University Press, 2010).

16. This is what Foucault highlighted as ordoliberalism's 'thinking in orders' and forms a major focus of Hayek's *The Constitution of Liberty*. Cf. Foucault, *Birth of Biopolitics*; F. Hayek, *The Constitution of Liberty* (Chicago: University of Chicago Press, 1960).

17. See discussion in Slobodian, *Globalists*.

18. Slobodian, *Globalists*, 118, 172–73.

19. Cf. W. Brown, *In the Ruins of Neoliberalism* (New York: Columbia University Press, 2019); M. Cooper, *Family Values: Between Neoliberalism and The New Social Conservatism* (New York: Zone Books, 2017). The quote is from D. Zamora and N. Olsen, 'How Decades of Neoliberalism Led to the Era of Right-Wing Populism', *Jacobin Magazine*, 19 September 2019, https://jacobinmag.com/2019/09/in-the-ruins-of-neoliberalism-wendy-brown?fbclid=IwAR1ez8DJch9ladDAjGP1k-j9zWqtZ4Ylq361yr8yYQ_PVQm28-JVGChhL9g. Accessed 21 September 2019.

20. Especially Wilhem Röpke, cf. Slobodian, *Globalists*, 146–81.

21. Cf. C. Lapavitsas, 'The project of Thatcher to promote a return to traditional family values and social mores as part of the neoliberal transformation of Britain has been a complete failure. For a short while in the 1980s and '90s, it seemed as if the advance of neo-liberalism would be accompanied by a backlash against the social freedoms gained in the 1960s and '70s. However, the backlash never became as severe as social conservatives had hoped and the country went in a different direction. On the whole, during the last four decades, British society has been characterized by the advance of social liberalism regarding sexual orientation, gender, race, immigration, and so on, especially among young people.' 'Learning from Brexit: A Socialist Stance Towards the European Union', *Monthly Review* 71 (2019): 5, https://monthlyreview.org/2019/10/01/learning-from-brexit/. Accessed 26 January 2020.

22. Which, of course, is not to suggest that these traditional values of God, Patriotism and the Family have disappeared; they have been reworked in an increasingly authoritarian manner in order to accommodate the kind of social disruption that the market reforms of the 1980s wrought on their traditional constituencies. The current resurgence of the nationalist Right is linked to this. Cf. Cooper, *Family Values*.

23. Cf. C. Pollitt, *Managerialism and the Public Services: The Anglo-American Experience* (Oxford: Basil Blackwell, 1990); C. Pollitt and G. Bouchaert, *Public Management Reform* (Oxford: Oxford University Press, 2011). For an excellent contemporary discussion, see A. Yeatman and B. Costea, eds., *The Triumph of Managerialism? New Technologies of Government and Their Implications for Value* (London: Roman and Littlefield, 2018).

24. J. McGuigan, *Neoliberal Culture* (London: Palgrave Macmillan, 2016); J. Meyrick, R. Phiddian and T. Barnett, *What Matters? Talking Value in Australian Culture* (Melbourne: Monash University Press, 2018).

25. W. Brown, *Undoing the Demos: Neoliberalism's Stealth Revolution* (New York: Zone Books, 2015).

26. The 'insulation' of the economy required the 'disenchantment of politics', in Will Davies's phrase. See: W. Davies, *The Limits of Neoliberalism: Authority, Sovereignty and the Logic of Competition* (London: Sage, 2014), 4.

27. W. Brown, 'Neoliberalism's Frankenstein: Authoritarian Freedom in Twenty-First Century "Democracies"', *Critical Times* 1, no. 1 (2018): 60–79; see also W. Brown, *In the Ruins of Neoliberalism*. Achille Mbembe reads the Western lurch into 'unreason' as recurrent, starting from the early colonial period. A. Mbembe, *Necro-Politics* (Durham, NC: Duke University Press, 2019).

28. Cf. D. Stedman Jones, 'The Neoliberal Origins of the Third Way: How Chicago, Virginia and Bloomington Shaped Clinton and Blair', in Cahill et al., *The Sage Handbook of Neoliberalism*, 167–78. Cf. D. Rodgers, *Age of Fracture* (Cambridge: Belknap Press, 2012); N. Frazer, 'From Progressive Neoliberalism to Trump – and Beyond', *American Affairs* 1, no. 4 (2017): 46–64; O. Nachtwey, *Germany's Hidden Crisis: Social Decline in the Heart of Europe* (London: Verso, 2018); Feher, 'Self-Appreciation'; M. Feher, *Rated Agency: Investee Politics in a Speculative Age* (Boston: MIT Press, 2018); Zamora and Olsen, 'How Decades of Neoliberalism Led to the Era of Right-Wing Populism'.

29. J. Quiggin, 'Neoliberalism: Rise, Decline and Future Prospects', in Cahill et al., *The Sage Handbook of Neoliberalism*, 143–53.

30. Ong and Zhang, *Privatising China*.

31. S. Binkley, 'The Emotional Logic of Neoliberalism: Reflexivity and Instrumentality in Three Theoretical Traditions', in Cahill et al., *The Sage Handbook of Neoliberalism*, 580–95, 581.

32. For a longer account see K. Oakley and J. O'Connor, 'Cultural Industries: An Introduction', in K. Oakley and J. O'Connor, *The Routledge Companion to the Cultural Industries* (London: Routledge, 2015), 1–32.

33. Cf. A. Bolesta, *China and Post-Socialist Development* (Bristol: Policy Press, 2015); H. -F. Hung, *The China Boom: Why China Will Not Rule the World* (New York: Columbia University Press, 2016); H. -J. Chang, *Kicking Away the Ladder: Development Strategy in Historical Perspective* (London: Anthem Press, 2003).

34. T. Skocpol, 'Bring the State Back In: Strategies of Analysis in Current Research', in *Bringing the State Back In*, ed. T. Skocpol, P. Evans and D. Rueschemeyer (New York and Cambridge: Cambridge University Press, 1985), 3–28; M. Lazzarato, *Governing by Debt* (South Pasadena, CA: Semiotext, 2013), Ch. 3 and Ch. 4; M. Mann, *The Sources of Social Power, Vol. 2: The Rise of Classes and Nation-States, 1760–1914* (Cambridge: Cambridge University Press, 2012).

35. Cf. Harvey, *Brief History of Neoliberalism*; N. Kleine, *The Shock Doctrine: The Rise of Disaster Capitalism* (Knopf, Canada: Random House, 2007).

36. For an overview of research on 'rentier capitalism', cf. M. Wolf, 'Why Rigged Capitalism Is Damaging Liberal Democracy', *Financial Times*, 18 September 2019, https://www.ft.com/content/5a8ab27e-d470-11e9-8367-807ebd53ab77. Accessed 22 September 2019.

37. Cf. C. Lapavitsas, *Profiting Without Producing: How Finance Exploits Us All* (London: Verso, 2013); J. Meek, *Private Island: Why Britain Now Belongs to Someone Else* (London: Verso, 2014); L. Adkins, *The Time of Money* (Bloomington, IN: Stanford University Press, 2019).

38. Cf. Slobodian, *Globalists*, Ch. 6 and Ch. 7; C. Sparks and C. Roach, 'Editorial: Farewell to NWICO?', *Media, Culture & Society* 12, no. 3 (1990): 275–81.

39. The current (2019) US administration sees the SOEs as part of China's abuse of global trade rules, as they directly benefit from preferential treatment and are out of bounds to competition from foreign companies. For a detailed documentation of these shifts, see the website *sinocism.com*.

40. As we write Jon Bolton, US National Security Advisor, announced that his country would be supporting the far-right governments of Columbia and Brazil, against the 'troika of tyranny': Cuba, Venezuela and Nicaragua (https://www.theguardian.com/us-news/2018/nov/01/trump-admin-bolsonaro-praise-john-bolton-troika-tyranny-latin-america). Accessed 24 January 2020. Cf. also Q. Slobodian, 'Democracy Doesn't Matter to the Defenders of "Economic Freedom"', *The Guardian*, 11 November 2019, https://www.theguardian.com/commentisfree/2019/nov/11/democracy-defenders-economic-freedom-neoliberalism. Accessed 12 November 2019.

41. For a good overview of the influence of neo-liberal economists in China, cf. C. Connery, 'Ronald Coase in Beijing', *New Left Review* 115 (2019): 29–58. For a detailed account for the period up to 1992, cf. J. B. Gewirtz, *Unlikely Partners: Chinese Reformers, Western Economists, and the Making of Global China* (Cambridge, MA: Harvard University Press, 2017).

42. Davies, *Limits of Neoliberalism*, 4. See also Alan Greenspan, former chair of the Federal Reserve (and Ayn Rand fan): 'we are fortunate that, thanks to globalisation, policy decisions in the US have been largely replaced by global market forces. National security aside, it hardly makes any difference who will be next president'. Quoted in S. Wren-Lewis, 'Bait and Switch', *London Review of Books* 40, no. 20 (2018): 13–14.

43. H. Wang, 'The 1989 Social Movement and the Historical Roots of China's Neoliberalism', in *China's New Order: Society, Politics, and Economy in Transition*, trans. T. Huters (Cambridge, MA: Harvard University Press, 2003), 41–138.

44. Wang, 'The 1989 Social Movement'; C. Pozzana and A. Russo, 'China's New Order and Past Disorders: A Dialogue Starting from Wang Hui's Analysis', *Critical Asian Studies* 38, no. 3 (2006): 329–51; C. Pozzana and A. Russo, 'Continuity/Discontinuity', *Critical Asian Studies* 43, no. 2 (2011): 261–84.

45. Arrighi so characterizes contemporary China, in which extended market relations are present but where capital does not dominate the state. G. Arrighi, *Adam Smith in Beijing: Lineages of the Twenty-First Century* (London: Verso, 2007).

46. Margaret Thatcher's description of Gorbachev: https://www.margaretthatcher.org/document/105592. Accessed 26 January 2020.

47. Cf. R. Coase and N. Wang, *How China Became Capitalist* (London: Palgrave Macmillan, 2012), 46–59.

48. Weber, 'China and Neoliberalism'; Wang, 'The 1989 Social Movement', 48–49; L. T. White, *Unstately Power, Vol. 1: Local Causes of China's Economic Reforms* (New York: East Gate, 1998), 84–164; Coase and Wang, *How China Became Capitalist*, Ch. 4.

49. Cf. Gewirtz, *Unlikely Partners*; Coase and Wang, *How China Became Capitalist*, 72–75.

50. I. Weber, *China's Escape from the 'Big Bang': The 1980s Price Reform Debate in Historical Perspective* (London: Routledge, 2019).

51. Cf. Weber, 'China and Neoliberalism'; Gewirtz, *Unlikely Partners*; Wang, 'The 1989 Social Movement'.

52. Cf. W. Hui, 'Depoliticized Politics, From East to West', *New Left Review* 41 (2006): 29–45.

53. C. Wang, 'Diary', *London Review of Books* 29, no.13 (2007): 38–39.

54. Ibid.

55. Ibid.

56. Coase and Wang, *How China Became Capitalist*, 94.

57. Y. Huang, *Capitalism with Chinese Characteristics: Entrepreneurship and the State* (Cambridge: Cambridge University Press, 2008).

58. Wang, 'Dialectics of Autonomy and Opening'.

59. The political fallout of the 1989 Students Movement was quickly contained. In the long run, the Tiananmen incident did not derail economic reform. In as much as it made the Chinese people more disillusioned with politics, it may have helped to rechannel human talents into private entrepreneurship. See: Coase and Wang, *How China Became Capitalist*, 95.

60. Mihai Craciun calls this 'infrared', the movement of Communism into the 'invisible spectrum of politics', its 'retreat underground' in order to safeguard 'utopia' by compromise and reform. See: M. Craciun, 'Shenzhen', in *Great Leap Forward*, ed. J. Chung, J. Inabu, R. Koolhaas and S. T. Leong (Koln: Taschen, 2001), 44–155, 67.

61. Craciun suggests that it was the separation of 'economic foundation and ideological superstructure' that was at the root of Deng's project. Craciun, 'Shenzhen', 67.

62. Cf. Deng's statements on this in J. Vaide, *Contact Space Shanghai: The Chinese Dream and the Production of a New Society* (doctoral thesis, Lund University, Sweden, 2015), 118–22, https://lup.lub.lu.se/search/publication/10422d86-b14e-408a-a051-f56c89dc4255. Accessed 4 October 2019.

63. F. C. Teiwes and W. Sun, 'China's New Economic Policy under Hua Guofeng: Party Consensus and Party Myths', *The China Journal* 66 (2011): 1–23; J. B. Gewirtz, 'China's Long March to Technological Supremacy: The Roots of Xi Jinping's Ambition to "Catch Up and Surpass"', *Foreign Affairs,* 27 August 2019, https://www.foreignaffairs.com/articles/china/2019-08-27/chinas-long-march-technological-supremacy. Accessed 27 August 2019.

64. Cf. Pozzana and Russo, 'China's New Order and Past Disorders'.

65. As described by Joel Andreas in *The Rise of the Red Engineers: The Cultural Revolution and the Origins of China's New Class* (Stanford, CA: Stanford University Press, 2009). See also R. Karl, *The Magic of Concepts: History and the Economic in Twentieth-Century China* (Durham, NC: Duke University Press, 2017); Coase and Wang, *How China Became Capitalist*; Connery, 'Ronald Coase in Beijing'; Weber, *China's Escape from the 'Big Bang'*; Gewirtz, *Unlikely Partners*.

66. Gewirtz, *Unlikely Partners*

67. Cf. F. Spufford, *Red Plenty: Inside the Fifties Soviet Dream* (London: Faber and Faber, 2010).

68. A process charted in some detail (and with approval) in Julian Gewirtz's *Unlikely Partners*.

69. The internationally successful Chinese science fiction series *Remembrance of Earth's Past* by Liu Cixin perhaps sums up the deep distrust of politics among engineers and scientists, many of them, as in the novel, victims of the Cultural Revolution. In Liu's writings (himself an engineer) politics is ideology, utopianism, chaos and suffering; engineering and science, with which economics can be seen to form a part, provides for utilitarian human happiness through means of expert control. Liu's series includes *The Three-Body Problem* (2014) (translated by Ken Liu, published by Tor Books); *The Dark Forest* (2015) (translated by Joel Martinsen, published by Tor Books); *Death's End* (2016) (translated by Ken Liu and published by Tor Books) and *The Wandering Earth* (2017) (translated by Ken Liu and others), published by Head of Zeus. A review by Nick Richardson brings out the rejection of Communism and the cultural revolution, and the denigration of politics by science: 'the radical political movements are shown to be self-deluding [...] During the stable era brought about by [a fictional leader], human societies enjoy high levels of welfare: no one has to work if they don't want to, and there's no inequality – but this is a consequence of technological progress, rather than political revolution'. N. Richardson, 'Even What Doesn't Happen Is Epic', *London Review of Books* 40, no. 3 (2018): 34–36, 34.

70. The gradual change in this can be traced to Gan Yang's 2005 lecture presented at Tsinghua University on 12 May 2005, '"Unifying the Three Traditions" in the New Era: The Merging of Three Chinese Traditions'. G. Yang, *'Unifying the Three Traditions' in the New Era: The Merging of Three Chinese Traditions*, 2005, intro. and trans. D. Ownby, https://www.readingthechinadream.com/gan-yang-tongsantong-chapter-1.html. Accessed 14 September 2019.

71. Mao Dun's 1933 famous novel *Midnight* starts with the modern Shanghai, 'One saw with a shock of wonder on the roof of a building a gigantic NEON sign in flaming red and

phosphorescent green: LIGHT, HEAT, POWER!'. M. Dun, *Midnight*, trans. Hsu Meng-hsiung, (Beijing: Foreign Languages Press,1957).

72. Coase and Wang, *How China Became Capitalist*, 96–98.

73. F. Hayek, 'Competition as a Discovery Procedure', in *The Market and Other Orders*, ed. B. Caldwell (Chicago: University of Chicago Press, 2014), 304–13, 313.

74. T. Mitchell, 'Fixing the Economy', *Cultural Studies* 12, no. 1 (1998): 82–101.

75. Michel Callon and others have shown the ways in which the world is reordered by the discipline of economics in order to set up the market whose logic it then describes. See: M. Callon, *The Laws of the Markets* (London: John Wiley, 1998); Mirowski, *Never Let Serious Crisis Go to Waste*. For a detailed discussion on 'performativity', see A. Bamford and D. MacKenzie, 'Counterperfomativity', *New Left Review* 113 (2018): 97–124. We should note (with Judith Butler) that performativity does not mean that economic or financial theories 'make things happen just by saying them'. Cf. J. Butler, 'Performative Agency', *Journal of Cultural Economy* 3, no. 2 (2010): 152.

76. Cf. E. M. Wood, *Democracy Against Capitalism: Renewing Historical Materialism* (London: Verso, 1995), Ch. 1.

77. Ong and Zhang, *Privatising China*, 3.

78. For an excellent account of the sheer force of infrastructural integration to remake social, economic and political structures, cf. N. Rossiter, *Software, Infrastructure, Labor: A Media Theory of Logistical Nightmares* (London: Routledge, 2017).

79. Slobodian, *Globalists*; L. Chun, *China and Global Capitalism: Reflections on Marxism, History and Contemporary Politics* (Basingstoke: Palgrave Macmillan, 2013). On the ways in which China (and the BRIC countries) have tried to use the WTO to their own advantage, see K. Hopewell, *Breaking the WTO: How Emerging Powers Disrupted the Neoliberal Project* (California: Stanford University Press, 2016).

80. On consumption in China: E. Croll, *China's New Consumers* (London: Routledge, 2006); D. Davies, ed., *The Consumer Revolution in Urban China* (Berkeley: University of California Press, 2000); Y. Wu, *China's Consumer Revolution* (Cheltenham: Edward Elgar, 1999).

81. See also T. Lewis, F. Martin and W. Sun, *Telemodernities: Television and Transforming Lives in Asia* (Durham, NC: Duke University Press, 2016), 254–72.

82. A. Kipnis, 'Suzhi: A Keyword Approach', *China Quarterly* 186 (2006): 295–313.

83. Wolfgang Streek has shown how the ideal of citizen as consumer, adopted by states under the impact of neo-liberalism and new public management from the 1980s on, undermined many of the public values associated with citizenship as public. See: W. Streek, 'Citizens as Customers: Considerations on the New Politics of Consumption', *New Left Review* 76 (2012): 27–47.

84. Cf. H. Weiss, *We Have Never Been Middle Class: How Social Mobility Misleads Us* (London: Verso, 2019), 84–85.

85. For a good overview see J. Lewis, *Beyond Consumer Capitalism: Media and the Limits to Imagination* (Cambridge: Polity, 2013).

86. Cf. J. -L. Rocca, *The Making of the Chinese Middle Class: Small Comfort and Great Expectations* (Basingstoke and New York: Palgrave Macmillan, 2017). Drawing on the twin traditions of E. P. Thompson and Luc Boltanski, Rocca argues that the middle class 'is less a specific group of people than a way of thinking and foreseeing the structures of Chinese society, a part of the new social imaginary China is elaborating' (11).

87. As David Goodman wrote about the 'intermediate middle classes': '[they] are fundamental supporters of the contemporary Party-state, even if at times some are also the most articulate critics of specific actions and policy settings of the Party-state, particularly wanting it to be more efficient and just'. See: D. Goodman, *Class in Contemporary China* (Cambridge: Polity, 2014).

88. Ong and Zhang, *Privatising China*, 12.

89. Or 'assemblage', in Bruno Latour's terminology. Ong and Zhang, *Privatising China*, 13.

90. J. C. Scott, *Seeing Like a State: How Certain Schemes to Change the Human Condition Have Failed* (New Haven: Yale University Press, 1998).

91. As Zamora and Olsen ('How Decades of Neoliberalism Led to the Era of Right-Wing Populism') argue, Scott was part of a widespread attack on the state as opposed to the diversity opened up by 'consumer sovereignty.

92. One commentary on contemporary nihilism used Scott's work, but argued: 'The 20th century profoundly changed labour, technology and social organisation in the Western world. It's hard to imagine that this didn't change *metis*, or render older forms of *metis* irrelevant.' L. Keep, 'Whence Comes Nihilism, the Uncanniest of All Guests?', *Aeon Magazine*, 2 January 2018, https://aeon.co/ideas/whence-comes-nihilism-the-uncanniest-of-all-guests. Accessed 14 September 2019.

93. Cf. C. Lin, 'The Socialist Market Economy: Step Forward of Backwards for China?', *Science and Society* 73, no. 2 (2009): 228–35. On the dislocation leading to labour protests, see C. -K. Lee, *Against the Law: Labor Protests in China's Rustbelt and Sunbelt* (Berkeley: University of California Press, 2007); E. Friedman, *Insurgency Trap: Labour Politics in Postsocialist China* (Ithaca, NY: Cornell University Press, 2014); H. Ren, *China on Strike: Narratives of Worker's Resistance* (Chicago: Haymarket Books, 2016). The radical dislocation from the past can be seen in Wang Bing's 2003 film *Tie Xi Qu: West of the Tracks*, or the films of Jia Jhangke, discussed below.

94. Davies, *Limits of Neoliberalism*; Brown, 'Neoliberalism's Frankenstein'. See also B. Steigler, *The Decadence of Industrial Democracies* (Cambridge: Polity, 2011).

95. Ong and Zhang, *Privatising China*, 16.

96. U. Beck, *Risk Society: Towards a New Modernity* (London: Sage, 1992); Z. Bauman, *Liquid Modernity* (Cambridge: Polity, 2000); M. Berman, *All That Is Solid Melts into Air: The Experience of Modernity* (London: Verso, 1983).

97. P. Duara, *The Crisis of Global Modernity: Asian Traditions and a Sustainable Future* (Cambridge: Cambridge University Press, 2015).

98. See the discussion on Hayek and the institutional framing of everyday economic activity in Slobodian, *Globalists*, Ch. 6: 'A World of Constitutions', 182–217.

99. Cf. Feher, 'Self-Appreciation', 32: 'Breaking with the idea of liberalism as laissez-faire, Ordoliberals advocated and applied a 'politics of society' (*Gesellschaftspolitik*), which they thought could be as interventionist as a Keynesian or a socialist *dirigiste* policy but which was aimed at arranging and protecting the proper functioning of this fragile thing that is the market, by giving people the means and the desire to behave as competing entrepreneurs. This marked a reversal of liberalism's original core – a first neo-liberalism, in a sense – insofar as market competition was conceived no longer as a gift of nature to be preserved but as a social form to be produced and reproduced, because it is optimal without being given.'

100. Isabelle Weber leaves the question thus: 'China presents a challenge to the prevailing neo-liberal system of global governance. Yet, whether China presents a socialist alternative is an altogether different question'. I. Weber, 'Escaping Shock Therapy', *Progressive Review* 26, no.1 (2019): 99–106, 106.

5

China as a Civilizational State

Introduction

In the last chapter, we looked at China's reforms from the perspective of neo-liberalism. We suggested there were real limits to neo-liberalism, related to the Chinese state's rootedness in a socialist and Confucian past. The Chinese leadership, following Deng Xiaoping, saw the market in terms akin to an imported technology, where the modernization of China's productive forces would secure a strong socialist state. This modernization involved a process of depoliticization – the quashing of any popular political involvement in the reform process – and the attempt to create modern Chinese subjects through new forms of market participation. We noted how the logic of neo-liberal reforms tended to hollow out public or collective values, both at the level of the individual citizen and the state, and the implications of this for Chinese governance. As Ong and Zhang suggested, the Chinese state uncoupled market liberalism from political liberalism, its 'socialism from a distance' occupying a space of sovereignty outside those of the individual 'sovereign consumer'. A complex social space, of 'sovereign power and self-sovereignty', now involved the kinds of individuated subjects associated in the West with Beck's 'risk society' and Bauman's 'liquid modernity', yet these subjects were subject to an authoritarian state form.

However, we suggested that this account, in 'which ordinary Chinese take their life into their own hands and face the consequences of their decisions on their own', underplays two aspects.[1] First, that neo-liberalism constantly undermines not just the large-scale collective or epistemic values commonly associated with the state and big 'C' culture but also the practices of everyday life (what we called *metis*). While individuals are asked to 'take their life into their own hands', the unfettered market constantly disrupts their ability to do this. Second, it underestimates the importance of these foundational values in setting a framework for collective life. For, we have argued, one of the key consequences of neo-liberalism is a creeping nihilism as the logic of markets and capital accumulation undermines even those customary values that Hayek and other neo-liberals saw as crucial for the functioning of an efficient market system.

152

The Chinese state was increasingly faced with this hollowing out of socialist and collectivist values. Hu Jintao's arrival in 2002 was part of a new emphasis on social and environmental concerns, a 'left tilt' in response to the widespread social trauma of the 1990s.[2] Indeed, 'neo-liberalism' itself came under scrutiny within the party, with debates raging as to if and how far it had been imported into China.[3] At the same time, there was a new emphasis on the ideological level, on socialist and 'Confucian' values intended to ensure social cohesion in a country that, as intellectuals and cadres suggested, was rapidly losing these.[4] In this chapter then, we look at these 'civilizational' and socialist resources by which the Chinese state has sought to deal with the disruptions of market-driven modernization, and the newly individuated subjects this has brought in its wake.

A civilizational state?

The rise to dominance of Xi Jinping since 2012 has seen a new emphasis on China's distinctive civilizational past and on its commitment to socialism, including its Marxist-Leninist foundations.[5] The increased assertiveness on both these fronts, along with the very obvious increase in the capacities of the Chinese state, have given rise to a shift in the West's China narrative. No longer now a question of a transition to some kind of democratic policy, whatever kind of capitalism China represents seems, for many, to be built on civilizational values deeply alien to those of the West.[6] Equally, its socialism can no longer be written off as face-saving, with business commentators now routinely seeing a fundamental incompatibility between the presence of a socialist state and a full integration into global capitalism.[7]

We have argued above that China is not just a modern nation state but also a civilizational state. This is not to assert a homogenous 'essential' China, spanning '5,000 years of history', as with many contemporary Chinese claims. For us, China's route to the modern world involved a socio-structural formation very different to that of the West, and its anti-imperialist and socialist history can be seen as a continuation of that history in many respects. This is not to deny the extensive and intensive processes of exchange between China and the West since the late nineteenth century (and before), or with other parts of Asia. China is deeply embedded in those 'circulatory histories' we spoke of above.

This is important, as many versions of the civilizational state frame its radical distinctiveness in a way that is often autarchic. Such a version is presented by Martin Jacques, in which China's distinct historical lineage has resulted in an 'alternative modernity' able to challenge the West.[8] This alternative modernity presents social, political and cultural norms of equal vigour to those of the West and with the potential to recast the international order in its image. China is set to act as a beacon for poorer nations, introducing a new democratic order between nations (based on the imperial 'tribute' system), taking us out of a world organized around US hegemony. Perry Anderson rightly takes Jacques to task in a scathing review, in particular for talking of 'modernity' rather than capitalism.[9] As with David Harvey, Anderson points to the impact of China's integration into the global capitalist system, and the imposition of its logic on the Chinese system. Wanting to dismantle Jacques's 'alternative modernity' based on the premise of a civilizational state, Anderson rejects both of these concepts as misplaced.

> Chinese antiquity stretches back to 1500 BCE or beyond. But this no more makes today's People's Republic a special genus of 'civilisation-state' than comparable claims for *la civilisation française* make one of the Third or Fourth Republic [...] Alternative modernities, so conceived, are cultural, not structural: they differentiate not social systems, but sets of values – typically, a distinctive combination of morality and sensibility, making up a certain national 'style' of life'.[10]

We would disagree with Anderson. In trying to puncture Jacques's overblown claims, he downplays the distinctive historical trajectory of China and its sociopolitical consequences, at the same time counterposing culture and structure, values and social system, in ways that reduce the former to a mere 'style' of life. While not wanting to present an essentialist 'Chinese' meme repeating itself across historical epochs, we have argued for the persistence of the patterns of Chinese thought and historical practice. These are 'cultural' in the sense of *metis*, of practices of everyday life, and *episteme*, the more abstract capital 'C' cultures of organizing and institutional beliefs and values. In highly abstract terms, we might say that the Confucian notion of 'rites' (*li*) is the mechanism for integrating these two levels.[11]

In the last four decades, scholarship on Chinese traditional thought has accumulated evidence for patterns of thought which form a distinct and coherent Chinese tradition stretching back to the Axial Age.[12] François Jullien's work illuminates the very different foundations of Chinese thought, already in stark contrast to those of classical Greece by the time of the era of Plato and Confucius.[13] Jullien's is not an archaeology but an attempt to show how these patterns actively inform current Chinese thinking and might be a corrective to the kinds of thinking associated with Western instrumental-rationalist modernity. Some, following Jullien, see Chinese thought chiming more directly with 'avant-garde' European philosophy, from Deleuze to Latour, in which relationality and immanence play a greater role than enlightenment-humanist (or even ancient Greek) divisions between subject and object, or conception and implementation.[14] Other books, of lesser persua-siveness and scholarly worth, also seek to use Chinese thought for such things as relationships, business and 'self-help',[15] or in managing the very process of organ-izational and wider socio-economic change itself.[16] But there is something more fundamental in play here.

How these patterns of thought and practice – *episteme* and *metis* – might inform practices in contemporary China, at the level of markets and business, labour and law, politics and administration, has been sketched out in works by Michael Keith and others, and explored in great depth by Carsten Herrmann-Pillath.[17] Both take issue with the applicability of *homo economicus* to China, that is, individ-uals rationally maximizing utility and profit, who act as fundamental explanatory particles. This rejection is not new in itself of course, with a whole tradition of political economy thinking, going back through Marx and Hegel to Adam Smith himself, showing how markets for products and labour are embedded in, and in fact assume, wider social relations.[18] Karl Polanyi argued that the fictitious com-modities of land, labour and money were embedded in social systems whose con-ditions of reproduction they systemically denied – to the catastrophic detriment of all.[19] At a more granular level, since the 1980s, economic geographers, institutional economists (including Ronald Coase) and cultural sociologists have argued that economic reality was very different to neo-classical 'atomistic' models. Individuals and firms were embedded in a range of local social, cultural, political and spatial contexts which directly affected how economic decisions were taken. As such, we might say that *homo economicus* does not apply in the West either.

The difference is that, in the West, *homo economicus* has been a historical pro-ject. Adam Smith's bracketing of the act of exchange from any moral consider-ations[20] was a break with older customary ties and obligations long associated with markets. This systemic removal of any obligations beyond the act of exchange and the seeking of advantage in a purely instrumental transaction formed the basis for the expansion of mercantile activities across national markets and globally. Thus, Adam Smith famously declared, self-interest paradoxically founded prosperity and peace for all. These carefully framed market transactions, with anything other than self-interest bracketed out, along with the institutions appropriate to these (such as private property, the rule of law, and a state responsive to 'civil society'), became the hallmark of the modern rational individual and polity. While social and moral philosophers criticized the consequences of the relentless expansion of the 'cash nexus', others, such as Max Weber, saw this as the *sine qua non* of modernity.

Neo-liberalism sought to extract a version of *homo economicus* from the sociopolitical framework in which this had been contained since the post-war social democratic settlement. *Homo economicus* was an ideal type necessary to the free flow of price signals required for the information processing of the market to work. While one might argue that *homo economicus* is, in reality, a constructed fiction (and some neo-liberals would agree), it has been performative in framing social relations of exchange (and all social relations *as* exchange) freed from any other social or cultural obligations other than the (legal) pursuit of utility and profit maximization.

The two books we discuss here directly challenge *homo economicus*. They argue that in China there are multiple social and cultural obligations and they are 'hard-wired', so to speak, into the social, cultural and political fabric. In brief, Chinese traditions of thought and practice emphasize relationality, where the individual is already in a situation surrounded by a web of connections and obligations. These connections, based on family, birthplace, education, work or political association, are often given the catch-all term *guanxi*. In fact, these ties make different claims on the individual, who in turn has different kinds of emotional attachment to them. There is a complex mix of individual self-interest and self-suppression, outlined by anthropologists such as Erika Evasdottir.[21] Essentially, forms of individual subjective belief and action outlined in Western norms of autonomous creativity and authentic choice are less prominent in China, where the individual seeks group norms as a guide to appropriate behaviour. Evasdottir uses the terms orthodoxy (conforming belief) and orthopraxy (conforming behaviour) to highlight the difference. Individuals in China, she suggests, see themselves as already in a web of complex obligations which materially affect how they act (orthopraxy) rather than demanding some interior conforming belief. These obligations are most certainly the object of calculation – some more emotional than others – but they tend to involve longer-term strategies and commitments, and they are based on distinct forms of societal trust and sanctions. Working out what is required of you from a particular group (which can be a restricted or an extended one), and then acting in ways that acknowledge and acquit these obligations at the same time as accumulating obligations towards yourself – these form the context of all social interactions, including economic exchanges.

Keith et al. and Herrmann-Pillath show how the relationality implied by *guanxi* cuts across standard models of Western business practice. Keith et al. show how contract law and the 'theory of the firm' specifically allocates risk and benefits to the parties – who gains and loses what, should an enterprise succeed or fail – whereas in China both are shared or allocated in a more fluid and relational sense as the project unfolds. Herrmann-Pillath details these at length across a range of different economic and business practices. Both books show in a concrete sense how the distinct socio-historical configuration of China has given rise to a set of shared cultural meanings within which 'relational' market relations are embedded. Herrmann-Pillath argues this is more than simply *guanxi* but involves repeated formal patterns of behaviour he calls 'ritual', recalling the Confucian notion of *li* – rites and music – which is foundational for the social order. These repeated patterns of *li*, such as in the historical Confucian case of filial respect, connect the individual family member to the emperor as keystone of the hierarchical society. Herrmann-Pillath relates these not to some archaic Confucian meme but more to patterns of late Qing society in which the elites of commerce and governance had begun to intertwine (as we discussed in Chapter 2, where we called these 'fractal'). In simplified form, what held this society together were obligations expressed in formal ritual patterns of duty and reciprocity, rather than negotiated rights and responsibilities enshrined in legal contract. It has been the commitment to these ritual forms, rather than to the law, that marks a fundamental difference between China and West, and Herrmann-Pillath uses the term 'economic style' to describe the way they work within contemporary China.

This distinct 'economic style' is not confined to *guanxi* but organizes the relationship between markets and state (both local and national, a fundamental distinction in China). Markets, as Herrmann-Pillath defines them, are a combination of networks, technologies (of exchange and payment) and institutions. Embedded as they are in wider meaning structures, markets are inevitably closely intertwined with the local state, which has powerful normative and constitutive power over how these markets operate. The objective of the local state is not to act simply as guarantor but as senior partner in joint enterprises, either directly or indirectly. As in late imperial China, the local state worked closely with local (gentry-)entrepreneurs, often in co-ventures. These 'amphibian institutions' are highly confusing for Western observers, where local government can be co-investors in companies whose ability to trade often depends on the regulatory say-so of the same local state.[22] As we shall see, many 'creative clusters' follow this model. Keith et al. call this 'local state capitalism'; Herrmann-Pillath, the 'market state'. Both echo Ong and Zhang's notion of a complex intermeshing of everyday practice and state action in 'the social'. The (local) market-state is a crucial concept for understanding everyday economic activity. It is, as we also suggest, crucial for understanding wider subject formations in China.

We will discuss this more in a subsequent chapter, where we look at the workings of the cultural industries and 'creative clusters' in Shanghai. It is in these fine-grained interactions between individuals, companies and the local state that cultural labour and creative entrepreneurs must operate in China. Nonetheless, the workings of a neo-liberal market system, closely tied up with China's global competition-collaborations, and acting as exemplar of the economic modernization China has been consistently seeking since 1978, has also worked to change these older configurations. The legal and sociopolitical norms which underpinned both liberal and neo-liberal markets are internalized as ethical and cultural values of 'self-worth' – as with the classic figure of the respectable bourgeois and the contemporary start-up entrepreneur. The high moral worth accorded the figure of the 'business entrepreneur' works to alter social relations in China. The language of the MBA graduate is that of the modernizer, the forward-looking, the winner not the loser, and it cuts deeply into these older social forms. One of the profoundest ideological threats to the Chinese state perhaps does not come from the political works banned from Xinhua bookstores but from the multiple aisles of 'business 101' and entrepreneurial self-help manuals that provide the common-sense view of the world for many aspirational modern urban Chinese.[23] Herrmann-Pillath discusses how the older *guanxi* networks and the practices they underpin are increasingly eroded in big cities like Shanghai. As Akbar Abbas noted two decades ago, Shanghai in particular stages this conflict between Western business practices and ones rooted in older norms as one between the outdated and the future oriented.[24] The days of *mao tai* lunches over fish-head soup at 11:00 a.m. are over in the central business districts of Shanghai, though the wider impact of this new modern persona on ties of relationality and obligation are not yet certain.

These three books show that the binary of market and state, modern efficiency versus the dead weight of authoritarian socialism, is not sustainable in China. Coming from historical sociology, anthropology and institutional economics, they highlight the persistence of forms of everyday practice as a *longue durée* dating from late imperial times and before. *Metis* is cast here as norms of ritual behaviour scalable in ways that mesh the self and the state. This 'social' is organized around a particular internal logic (Herrmann-Pillath's 'style') that allows *metis* and *episteme* to connect, and to actively structure 'the social'. The three accounts focus on the detailed structuration of behaviour at a local and granular level, with two of them very much concerned with the economic dimension. However, in the focus on the everyday and the local it is important not to ignore the national-political level, and how, despite the *longue durée*, there are significant historical political transformations, involving of course the 1949 revolution as well as significant shifts within this, as we have noted.

The national state no longer directly controls the material and ideological context of everyday life as it once did, but 'socialism at a distance' should not be read as a retreat into a repressive ideological-political apparatus that constrains the self-sovereignty of a newly individualized Chinese people. Part of this *longue durée* involves distinctly Chinese forms of governance, which are still being deployed in the context of a changing 'socialist' China. These are being deployed in increasingly sophisticated ways to delineate the differences between Western and Chinese forms of modernity.[25]

Zhang Wei Wei's *The China Horizon*, an orthodox official account of the 'China model', locates the Chinese state's success in avoiding the worst excesses of the United States – inequality, social alienation, the excessive power of capital and so on – in its continuing commitment to China's civilizational project of an ethical polity founded on a notion of the 'people's prosperity', or *Minsheng*. Articulated in the Discourses on Salt and Iron we discussed above, *Minsheng* – with *Minzu* (nation) and *Minquan* (democracy) – was one of Sun Yat-Sen's 'Three Principles of the People' and forms, Zhang claims, an ongoing touchstone for socialist China.[26] Peter Nolan recently traced the idea of the common ownership of property from Confucius' *Book of Rites*, through Kang Youwei's *Da Tong* (Great Harmony) on to Mao's People's Republic.[27] Jae Ho Chung goes so far as to suggest that 'in the long run, the features of a Chinese dynasty may eventually overshadow the features of a Communist regime'.[28] The re-emergence of the old Confucian term *Tianxia,* 'all-under-heaven', since Xi Jinping took office shows that these dynastic concepts have not disappeared.[29] For some Chinese intellectuals, Confucianism – in its stronger 'scriptural' form – still has the potential to provide the legitimation for a contemporary Chinese government.[30]

The reassertion of these concepts is often dismissed as pure ideology, used by a regime whose bankrupted Marxist-Leninist credentials no longer ensure its legitimacy. We suggest this would be far too presumptuous, but before we explore this further we should look at how the regime has drawn on its resources of socialism to help implement the reforms, to mitigate the pervasive effects of 'market logic', and to seek to redirect this logic to its own ends.[31]

Socialist China

Most commentators acknowledge the contribution made by the Communist regime to the post-1978 take-off. In terms of basic social welfare and education, infrastructure and a 'compliant' workforce, there is no doubt that Mao's China provided a level of physical and human capital – in neo-liberal parlance – that allowed the reforms to take-off with the speed and intensity they did.[32] These kinds of instrumental views of the usefulness of the 1949 revolution ignore the historical achievement of a socially integrated nation state with the ability to engage in mass mobilization at multiple scales and modalities, a capacity directly derived from the achievement of the revolution, which in turn built on a century of anti-imperialist struggle. It is simply inconceivable that 'Western-style modernization' could have been achieved without this prior work of the revolutionary regime. We also need to remember the crucial role of American finance and military backing for the other East Asian developmental states; China did this as a sovereign state.

The party-state has been central to this modernization and the question is often posed as to why it succeeded when the USSR failed. Perry Anderson compares the political abilities of the two parties in the crunch years between 1989 and 1991.[33]

He outlines the multiple political failures of Gorbachev, who tried to modernize both economy (*perestroika*) and the political system (*glasnost*) at the same time. More disastrous perhaps was Gorbachev's naivety in assuming that the Soviet intelligentsia, by now deeply influenced by Western liberalism, wanted to follow his programme of saving Communism and the USSR, when they were hell-bent on burying both of them. Deng Xiaoping was not a lifetime bureaucrat like Gorbachev and had actually been involved, along with many others in the leadership, in prolonged revolutionary and military activity. Faced with the threat of the Tiananmen protests, Deng acted without hesitation against what he perceived to be a direct threat to the long-term survival of the Communist regime. The resulting contrast between the two countries in the 1990s does not need to be stressed again here. The post-socialist states of the old Soviet bloc found themselves in a new kind of colonial relationship with the West, not just economically but also in being forced to adapt to a 'normal' state and society, a task to which all their history seemed to suggest they were signally ill-equipped. Not so China. Unlike Russia, China had the capacity to embark on a far-reaching reform process not only with an intact nation state apparatus, but also with a confidence that post-1991 Russia and its former states and allies lacked.

The response to Tiananmen indicated a party leadership that was bold and resolute in a crisis, but they displayed a similar capacity in implementing the subsequent reforms. The journey they embarked on was unprecedented, and there was no road map. To deal with the complexities of a transition to a socialist market economy (without really knowing what that might mean in practice) in a huge country at a time of an expanding globalized economy during a period in which communism, socialism and even social democracy were seen as historical remnants, was a phenomenal achievement.

The capacity to do this was centrally rooted in the previous experiences of the CCP, most of whose cadres rubbed shoulders regularly with the working masses. Flexibility, the ability to improvise, to step back and rethink, to test the waters, to experiment and roll-out – all provided a capacity to engage what had been a historical enemy in a joint process of modernization. This could open up a closed economy to massive levels of foreign investment, opportunities for mass migration and urbanization, and to bring into being a market system in direct contradiction to many of the founding principles of the People's Republic.[34] All this was carried out by a CCP with its revolutionary energies still available. Sebastian Heilmann and Elizabeth Perry suggest this is a 'policy style', a 'guerrilla politics' involving a highly flexible party apparatus able to engage in a transformation which always threatened to dissolve into chaos and fragmentation, but which held.[35] Much of this came from the organizational strength and resilience of the Leninist party that had been transformed by Mao. Its ideology of the mass line, frequently dismissed by Western observers, gave it an ability to seek solutions and respond to concerns in ways its original Soviet model did not possess.

So too its ability to mobilize citizens around issues, to communicate in different registers, and to build a consensus around its activities, all grew out of the mass campaigns of the Maoist years. Looking back from 2011, Heilmann and Perry see not a 'path dependency' in the sense of a planned route formed from determinant historical circumstances, but a more improvisatory and responsive practice which, they suggest, might provide lessons for Western policy-makers. It was not, then, purely in the economic foundations laid by Communism, but also in the political capacity of the CCP, that the secret of China's success could be found; not the dynamism of the market rolling back the socialist state, but the active co-constitution of both by a 'guerrilla state'.

We have already noted how these reforms came out of a highly sophisticated set of debates that, couched as 'practical', were in fact highly conceptual. Coase and Wang themselves – breaking with what we might call vulgar *homo economicus* – recognize that the Chinese reformers were driven by ideas not interests. The reforms were not only about the introduction of 'market reforms' but were a clash of ideas, in which one set of institutions – 'organisers of our interests but also symbols of our identity' – gives way to another.[36] The reforms involved a 'profound cognitive change at the individual and societal level', and it was the openness of the party to the new ideas that testified to its historical energy and relevance. Coase and Wang in turn relate this clear-eyed pragmatism – seeking truth from facts – to an older Confucian philosophy while congratulating Deng for escaping the straight-jacket of socialism.[37] But this misses the deeper sense of purpose and direction that animated the CCP.

Crossing the river stone by stone was not just about pragmatism; it implied a belief that there was another side.[38] Peter Nolan suggests that this is what was lacking in the USSR;

> [O]nce the CPSU leadership's faith in communism evaporated, it lost its way completely. Faced with setting a course forward in new conditions, it had no conception of what the Chinese call 'the other bank of the river' – the concrete situation it wishes to attain. The only resources that Moscow's pre-revolutionary history could offer were idealised visions of western politics and free-market economics.[39]

Much has been written about the CCP's Faustian bargain, of economic growth in return for acknowledgement of sole political leadership, but there are other factors in play. Pre-eminent is the collective ideal of China as a national and civilizational state. Labour conflict, middle-class restlessness and intellectual discontent exist aplenty; but no study has yet shown a widespread opposition to the regime itself.

This strong legitimacy does not rely on GDP growth alone, nor on a repressive state apparatus, as many Western commentators would have it. Legitimacy is also rooted in a sense of collectivity that derives from both socialist and civilizational Chinas.[40] This is not only a resource deployed by the regime to push through its economic reforms but also a counter to their effects, that is, the hollowing out of the collective by market reason.

A 'left tilt'?

In 2002, Deng's protégé Jiang Zemin was (eventually) replaced by Hu Jintao (and Wen Jiabao) who sought to expand the development focus to encompass social and environmental issues. He introduced the idea of 'harmonious socialist society' as a way of framing a response to the social dislocation wrought by rapid development. This, along with China's 'harmonious rise', drew on Confucian tropes (the Confucius Institute was founded in 2004).[41] Xi Jinping has deepened this emphasis on Confucianism but also on China's identity as a socialist state, a 'Chinese Dream' underpinned by 'Core Socialist Values'.[42] He has also promoted the revival of Marxism-Leninism in teaching and research institutes, and within party training programmes. Neo-liberalism, as a term, has come under opprobrium,[43] well-known neo-liberal think-tanks (*Unirule Institute of Economics* foremost) have been shut down and the liberal journal *yanhuang chunqiu* had its editorial board changed.[44] Jude Blanchette suggests a rapprochement between the Central Party and a left which, Deng famously argued in 1992, has been the primary focus of their vigilance.[45] The 'conservative' and Maoist opposition to the reform process, seen as a betrayal of socialism and the Chinese Revolution, had seemed a lost cause at the turn of the millennium.[46] Under Xi it has been given increased exposure, as this Maoist left is used as a way of legitimizing the party's increasing confidence in the 'socialist' capacity of the state to intervene in the workings of the market, not necessarily in the form of public ownership but in a vast and complex range of policy levers. The Maoist left's anti-imperialist rhetoric also provides ideological support – though the party does not need to formally endorse it – to China's increased assertiveness on the global stage.

Zhang Wei Wei's *The China Horizon* gives what we might describe as an 'establishment intellectual' version of this newly assertive 'China model'.[47] Zhang's is a robust, boosterish account of China's success in economic growth, but also in technology, education, social welfare, housing and so on. Zhang is confident enough to contrast this directly with the United States, which comes off worse, especially in the area of welfare and inequality. The China model is justified in terms of efficiency. It delivers results through its meritocratic system of promoting experienced policy-makers, as opposed to the United States' method of choosing those with the money to stand for election.[48] It is a consultative democracy, which allows well-thought out, long-term solutions. It is a mixed economy – a socialist market economy – and one in which the state is able to counterbalance the power of capital and allow for different social voices, not just those with money. This book glosses multiple problems, not least the massive dislocation and suffering experienced by labour, especially the many millions drawn into the cities from the countryside, and the ways in which the consultative process of the party has been accompanied by a strict control over public information and opinion. But what is interesting is the more robust assertion of the socialist nature of the state, along with the recognition of China as a civilizational state and the current regime as in direct lineage with its 'mandate of heaven'. We saw above Zhang's reference to *Minsheng*, the prosperity of the people from the Discourses on Salt and Iron. It is this principle of the state's commitment (lip service or not) to a collective and (relatively) egalitarian material prosperity that marks the difference, for Zhang, between China and a United States dominated by the power of capital. In this account, China has not just caught up but surpassed the West in its efficient delivery of a prosperous and harmonious society, drawing on both its civilizational and socialist resources, as well as acknowledging its deep learning from the West.

Zhang's is a photo-shopped portrait of China but important nonetheless. Since 2008, there have been increasing anxieties about China in the West, in part due to its continuing economic success and assertive foreign policy, but also because it is no longer easy to ignore the fact that it will *not* follow a path determined by the West. This is about more than its rejection of the 'Washington Consensus' and an increased assertion of the developmental state, both of these propositions finding sympathetic ears among mainstream economists, and countries of the Global South. Rather, it is an assertion of the validity of a distinct set of socialist social and political values in the Chinese reform process, values that are now claimed as resources and long-term goals, not deadweights to be thrown off or obstacles to be overcome. Xi Jinping's 'moderately prosperous society' is not just about the levelling-off of China's phenomenal growth but a declaration of a 'New Era' which builds both on Mao and Deng's work. For Jiang Shigong, a law professor at Beijing University and pro-Xi public intellectual, China 'stood up' under Mao Zedong, 'got rich' under Deng Xiaoping and is 'becoming powerful' under Xi Jinping. The post-1978 reforms are thus folded back into China's socialist and, increasingly, civilizational past.[49]

The civilizational and socialist aspects of the Chinese polity have set real limits to neo-liberalism, with the state gaining confidence in asserting its own distinct form of economic development as more equitable and efficient compared to the United States. This has prompted some commentators to suggest that China might lead the way in a world order post-US hegemony. Under Xi Jinping, the party-state has reaffirmed its commitment to the SOEs as central pillars of the socialist market economy, just as it has begun to assert control over planning and development at local state level.[50] Peter Nolan suggests this assertion of state power over the market has roots, prior to Salt and Iron, in the formulations of Guan Zhong (720–645 BC) as to how the market alone should 'not be allowed to decide the abundance or deficiency of commodities'; that the 'right way' involved 'handling the market'.[51] Nolan notes how, 'under this system, China was a world leader in market-driven innovation for two millennia' and is set to continue.[52]

> In the years since 1978, the nature of the 'other bank of the river' has become increasingly clear. It is not the 'common-property-ism' of *'gongchan zhuyi'* [Maoist communism]. Rather, the market plays a central role in stimulating the economy, whilst pragmatic state regulation, with the CPC at its core, aims to ensure that the market serves the needs of the whole population.[53]

China, rather than falling behind the 'mature economies' of liberal democratic capitalism, is, Nolan suggests, pointing the way for a troubled global economy to see 'the other bank'.

This emergent narrative is in sharp contrast to that in the West. David Shambaugh, a prolific 'China watcher', continues to plot China's trajectory against its authoritarianism, which is directly indexed against the ongoing tussle between state and market. Following the standard script, Shambaugh asserts that no country has developed a modern economy without also democratizing, and that 'democratisation is not only a consequence of modernisation but it is also a facilitator of it'.[54] Modernization, we should understand, means capitalism. Outlining the road-map for a future China, Shambaugh suggests four options: neo-totalitarian (a return to the 'conservative' and closed China of 1989–92); hard authoritarian (Xi Jinping); soft-authoritarian (the Hu-Wen years); and semi-democracy (Singapore). This last is China's best hope. For Shambaugh, modernization and liberal democracy are hardwired together, as are socialism and the authoritarian state. There are the modern 'mature' economies with liberal democratic-political forms and various throwbacks or stalled transitions away from authoritarian socialism. Something similar can be seen in the work of another prolific commentator, Kerry Brown, who sees the revival of explicitly socialist opinion in China as a combination of the nostalgic return of Maoist 'religious' certainties (as with similar longings for the old USSR in Russia) and a sophisticated apology for a new authoritarianism. For Brown, the re-emergence of socialist thought in China is a problem to be dealt with by the Chinese government, primarily by holding its nerve and keeping on the transitional track to a form of semi-democratic capitalism.[55]

Others are less sanguine about such a transition, seeing Xi Jinping's 'left tilt' as fundamentality about regime survival. The assertion of state capacity and the renewed commitment to supporting SOEs are framed as a way of shoring up the party's economic resources against a thriving private sector.[56] The regime is not in transition to any kind of liberal democracy as its nature is structurally different. Ian Bremmer is among many who, following a 'varieties of capitalism' tradition, sees in China a version of 'state capitalism': 'a form of bureaucratically engineered capitalism particular to each government that practices it' and one 'in which the state dominates markets primarily for political gain'.[57] Branco Milanovic, in similar vein, calls it 'political capitalism', echoing Yasheng Huang's well-known account of state-directed capitalism. John Lanchester, hedging his bets, calls it 'the system-with-no-name'.[58] The renewed promotion of Marxism is dismissed by Tim Cheek and David Ownby as pure ideology, a 'state Marxism' attempting to 'unify the population behind a national ideology, not to inspire class struggle but to revive the "best" traditions of Chinese governance'.[59] Others identify a concomitant willingness of Chinese intellectuals to legitimate an authoritarian 'statism' via both socialism and Confucianism.[60] This 'Chinese' authoritarianism comes with a robust rejection of 'Western values', as outlined in the (now infamous) leaked 'Communiqué on the Current State of the Ideological Sphere' (Document No. 9).[61]

Rather than read Chinese socialism as the persistent clinging to youthful delusions by a wilful child, we would suggest a more open view, of the kind captured by Arif Dirlik's notion of 'post-socialism'. This term, coined in 1989, was intended to be 'deconstructive', avoiding the 'conceptual prison' of either socialism or capitalism.[62] That is, seeking not to 'name' the system and place it in a fixed taxonomy of forms, but rather explore its open capacities and possibilities. Such an open assessment has been given by Lin Chun, in the updating of her 2006 account of Chinese socialism.[63] In the earlier book, she argued that the new leadership of Hu Jintao and Wen Jiabao was trying to reassert socialist elements, focusing on social inequality and welfare, quality of life and environment. For Lin Chun, in 2016 the Chinese socialist model consists of

> a popularly mandated sovereign state possessing governing and policy making capacities; a substantial public sector (in search of a socialist market) as a secured basis for the nation's prosperity and financial security; an institutional arrangement for taking government and societal responsibility for public welfare and popular well-being (*minsheng*); and the rising social power to fulfil socialism through broad political and socio-economic participation and transformative social movement.[64]

Unlike Zhang Wei Wei, Lin Chun is fully aware of the ways in which labour – especially rural labour – was made to carry the burden of modernization and of the widespread unrest this caused. Similarly, she is clear about the ways in which this model is under mortal threat

> of further political distortion and policy capacity fragmentation of the state; deeper privatisations of SOEs and other public assets and institutions; the persistence of inequalities and deficient public provision; and the destruction and decay of social commitment, power and citizenship.[65]

This is a very different account of the threats facing the Chinese socialist state than the index of open markets and liberal democracy versus closed authoritarianism. Chun is clear about how far China has been absorbed into global capitalism and its impact on the internal structure of state and society. Nonetheless, like Zhang, Chun is trying to assert the tasks facing a socialist China through a set of co-ordinates different from those of Western liberal commentators. Her account is one in which socialist China is a historical gain; not the obstacle to be overcome but the historical stake that needed to be defended. As with Zhang, China is not autochthonic but has learnt from the West; socialism's provenance is Western modernity but at the same time is deeply rooted in China's distinct (but porous) civilizational project.

This more open approach can be seen in the 'New Left' which emerged at the end of the 1990s. This is a complex and multivalent term, as it started as a term of opprobrium – the liberal right used 'left' as an automatic term of condemnation for those seeking a return to the past – and it was also used, by critics and supporters, to describe the revived Maoism of the early millennium.[66]

Barry Naughton takes the open view typical of New Left writers,[67] asking the question in 2017 as to whether China could be considered socialist, a term he sees as having 'evolved and thoroughly changed' in contemporary China.[68] His four tests were the state's 'capacity' and 'intention' to intervene to shape economic outcomes; its success in effecting 'redistribution'; reducing inequality and securing the well-being of the least well-off; and some form of 'responsiveness' to the population. The capacity and intention of the state are clearly established for Naughton, but he highlights the major failings of the Chinese state to effect 'redistribution', reducing inequality (this is as bad as the United States and United Kingdom)[69] and poverty as well as dealing with widespread environmental degradation. This opens up China to much external criticism. Rather than talk abstractly about markets and democracy, Naughton links inequality and poverty with the lack of 'responsiveness'.

> When the predominant objective of policy was economic growth, it was not particularly important to whom policy was responsive, since all groups shared

an interest in growth. Today, as the government tries to redistribute and provide more public goods, policy must reflect the interests and more diverse preferences of a broader population. So far, China has not found a way to do this. China's relatively weak performance in achieving broadly redistributive policies, social fairness, and improved public goods provision appears to reflect the limits of responsiveness and the power of entrenched economic and political interests.[70]

More radical critics on the left dismiss the socialism of the CCP as the moribund ideology of a party 'left over from the peasant wars of the last century', nothing more than regime ideology.[71] Chris Connery suggests Wang Hui's attempts to revive the long tradition of revolution have encountered a neo-liberalism in China with 'deep roots'.[72] More telling is his suggestion that the Chinese left remains state-focused, bound by a deep-seated nationalism to the economic developmentalism. The enhanced capacity of the Chinese state and its confident assertion of its socialist and nationalist objectives is something that can clearly be seen in the accommodation between the resurgent Maoists and Xi Jinping. The New Left too has often been seen as drifting towards that 'statism', though the more likely situation is one of marginalization, in a context where the networks of Chinese intellectuals are 'full of shouting statists, and the New Left's voice is confined increasingly to universities'.[73] Connery sees glimmers of possibility in the growing social movements – feminist, ecological – where new and transformative subjectivities are to be found.[74]

We cannot decide this here. All we can do is highlight the growing disjuncture within that 'assemblage' of 'self-sovereignty' – individuals negotiating the vicissitudes of a market economy – and the sovereignty of a state trying to assert its legitimacy through more symbolic or 'epistemic' discourses of a socialist or civilizational China. The depoliticization of Chinese modernization, via a disenchanted market reason, has made the engagement between these two zones of sovereignty increasingly difficult. The relationship between state and society, Xudong Zhang suggested, was 'frozen' in 1989.[75] The failures of 'responsiveness', of Lin Chun's 'political and socio-economic participation', are clearly evident. Those citizens who are used to expressing themselves in terms of the 'commodifiable and the marketable' take an increasingly transactional view of their relationship to the Chinese state. The consequent increase in the cynicism of the citizens only increases the stridency of the Chinese state's assertion of its epistemic values, a vicious circle within which a general nihilism spreads.[76]

This disjunction of state and society, and the resultant erosion of the ideological capacity of the state, might explain why China has turned to new forms of digital technologies – big data, AI, biometrics, facial recognition and so on – as a form of social control.[77] These do not operate at the level of the symbolic; they are not 'cultural', working with subjects and meanings, but seek to go 'beneath', to grasp the underlying 'real' of everyday behaviour. There is a strong homology with neo-liberal 'behavioural' economics. These new forms of data-based control are highly individualized, concerned with influencing ('nudging') and aggregating micro-behaviours, feeding massive informational regimes that dovetail perfectly with Hayek's market-as-information processor.[78] These technologies are stimulating a very real, often disavowed form of convergence between China and the West – indeed, China is now taking a competitive lead in the export of such technologies.[79]

There are traditional Chinese precedents for such forms of 'total' control. For those who see in traditional Chinese thought a way of thinking that breaks with dominating forms of Western rational-instrumentalist, subject/object binaries, there is François Jullien's demonstration of how Legalism's use of Daoist foundations were employed to justify a totalitarian form of state control.[80] Perry Anderson's quip that Chinese history was about 'Confucian ideals but Legalist practice' reminds us that the revolutions of the twentieth century were *against* Chinese thought and practice, as well as with it.[81] Wang Hui evokes the great experimentation with social and political forms that characterized China's revolutionary century.[82] That is why China's socialist heritage needs to be defended from its burial either by Chinese essence or by capitalist modernity.

Though the Chinese state goes beyond neo-liberalism in its commitment to making the market serve the wider needs of the population, its depoliticization has restricted the energy of its people to personal expression via 'the commodifiable and the marketable'.[83] The party has delivered the 'people's livelihood', but how far has it managed to speak to the new subject positions of an individuated Chinese population, seeking an everyday *metis* or ethics of 'how one should live'? The contradiction between 'the compulsion to self-govern' enforced by market relations, and the glimpse of a historical opening – 'taking their life into their own hands' – is part of the general frustration of neo-liberalism. Only some kind of collective response, a renewed accommodation or 'responsiveness' between society and the state, can address this, but in a depoliticized polity this is made difficult. If growth slows – and an incipient conflict with the United States seems to indicate choppy waters ahead – then these everyday ethical questions may burst into full view. As Ernst Bloch wrote: 'Man does not live by bread alone, especially when he doesn't have any.'[84]

NOTES

1. A. Ong and L. Zhang, 'Introduction', in *Privatising China: Socialism from Afar*, ed. L. Zhang and A. Ong (Ithaca, NY: Cornell University Press, 2008), 1–19, 16.

2. Cf. B. Naughton, 'China's Left Tilt: Pendulum Swing or Mid-Course Correction', in *China's Changing Political Landscape*, ed. C. Li (Washington, DC: Brookings Institution Press, 2008), 144. Cf. J. Blanchette, *China's New Red Guards: The Return of Radicalism and the Rebirth of Mao Zedong* (Oxford: Oxford University Press, 2019), 71–73.

3. Cf. Blanchette, *China's New Red Guards*, 72; Y. Zhao, *Communication in China: Political Economy, Power, and Conflict* (Lanham: Roman and Littlefield, 2008).

4. Cf. Blanchette, *China's New Red Guards*, Ch. 3, 'Unhappy China', for an overview.

5. For a critical overview, cf. W. A. Callahan, 'History, Tradition and the China Dream: Socialist Modernization in the World of Great Harmony', *Journal of Contemporary China* 24, no. 96 (2015): 983–1001; S. Veg, 'The Rise of China's Statist Intellectuals: Law, Sovereignty, and "Repoliticization"', *The China Journal* 82 (2019): 23–45.

6. State Department Director of Policy Planning Kiron Skinner suggested that competition with China is 'a fight with a really different civilization and a different ideology and the U.S. hasn't had that before' and the coming conflict with China is 'the first time that we will have a great power competitor that is not Caucasian'. S. Ward, 'Because China Isn't "Caucasian", the U.S. Is Planning for a "Clash of Civilizations". That Could Be Dangerous', *Washington Post*, 4 May 2019, https: //www.washingtonpost.com/politics/2019/05/04/because-china-isnt-caucasian-us-is-planning-clash-civilizations-that-could-be-dangerous/?utm_term=.c78e53a66f6c. Accessed 12 September 2019.

7. Cf. K. Lee and A. Sullivan, *People's Republic of the United Nations: China's Emerging Revisionism in International Organizations* (Washington, DC: Centre for a New American Security System, 2019), https: //www.cnas.org/publications/reports/peoples-republic-of-the-united-nations. Accessed 14 September 2019.

8. M. Jacques, *When China Rules the World: The End of the Western World and the Birth of a New Global Order* (New York: Penguin Books, 2009).

9. P. Anderson, 'Sinomania', *London Review of Books* 28 (2010): 3–6. Anderson argues that Jacques is merely seeking consolation for the collapse of Communism (Jacques was editor of *Marxism Today*, the Communist Part of Great Britain's magazine) in the global dominance of the country that escaped its post-1989 demise.

10. Ibid., 3.

11. Which is not to say that these is not also a longer standing tradition of Chinese popular culture outside – and mostly tolerated by – these structures of power and value.

12. Cf. D. L. Hall and R. T. Ames, *Anticipating China: Thinking Through the Narratives of Chinese and Western Culture* (Albany: State University of New York Press, 1995).

13. F. Jullien, *The Propensity of Things* (Cambridge MA: Zone Books, 1999); F. Jullien, *A Treatise on Efficacy* (Honolulu: University of Hawai'i Press, 2004). See also Hall and Ames, *Anticipating China*.

14. Cf. S. Lash, 'Chinese Thought, Cultural Theory', in *China Constructing Capitalism: Economic Life and Urban Change*, ed. M. Keith, S. Lash, J. Arnoldi and T. Rooker (London: Routledge, 2014), 32–53.

15. Cf. M. Puett and C. Gross-Loh, *The Path: A New Way to Think About Everything* (London: Random House, 2016).

16. Cf. H. Peyman, *China's Change: The Greatest Show on Earth* (Singapore: World Scientific Publishing, 2018).

17. Keith et al., eds., *China Constructing Capitalism*; C. Herrmann-Pillath, *China's Economic Culture: The Ritual Order of State and Markets* (London: Routledge, 2016).

18. Indeed, it was Smith's *Theory of Moral Sentiments* as much as the *Wealth of Nations* that informed Chinese reform thinking in the 1980s and 1990s.

19. K. Polanyi, *The Great Transformation: The Political and Economic Origins of Our Time* (Boston, MA: Beacon, 1957). These arguments are echoed by writers such as Ellen Meiksins Woods and many others. See, for example, E. M. Wood, *Democracy Against Capitalism: Renewing Historical Materialism* (London: Verso, 1995).

20. Michel Callon refers to this as 'framing'. See: M. Callon, *The Laws of the Markets* (London: John Wiley, 1998).

21. E. Evasdottir, *Obedient Autonomy: Chinese Intellectuals and the Achievement of Orderly Life* (Honolulu: University of Hawai'i Press, 2004).

22. The term is from J. Friedmann, *China's Urban Transition* (Minneapolis: University of Minnesota Press, 2005).

23. See also C. Connery, 'Ronald Coase in Beijing', *New Left Review* 115 (2019): 29–58.

24. A. Abbas, 'Cosmopolitan Descriptions: Shanghai and Hong Kong', *Public Culture* 12, no. 3 (2000): 772–86.

25. Cf. X. Lu and H. W. Simons, 'Transitional Rhetoric of Chinese Communist Party Leaders in the Post-Mao Reform Period: Dilemmas and Strategies', *Quarterly Journal of Speech* 92, no. 3 (2006): 262–86.

26. W. Zhang, *The China Horizon: Glory and Dream of a Civilizational State* (Hackensack, NJ: World Century Publishing Corporation, 2016).

27. P. Nolan, 'The CPC and the Ancien Régime', *New Left Review* 115 (2019): 17–28.

28. J. H. Chung, 'Central-Local Dynamics: Historical Continuities and Institutional Resilience', in *Mao's Invisible Hand: The Political Foundations of Adaptive Governance*, ed. S. Heilmann and E. J. Perry (Cambridge, MA: Harvard University Press, 2001), 297–313, 313.

29. J. -H. Kwak, 'Global Justice Without a Center: Reappraisal of Tianxia with Non-Domination', in *Global Justice in East Asia*, ed. H. El Kholi and J. -H. Kwak (London: Routledge, forthcoming); on Tianxia, cf. T. Zhao, *Redefining A Philosophy for World Governance* (London: Palgrave Macmillan, 2019).

30. Jiang Qing, *A Confucian Constitutional Order*, trans. E. Ryden (Princeton: Princeton University Press, 2013).

31. Evasdottir, as befits an anthropological account of long-term behavioural patterns, is the least interested in moments of historical change. Like her, Keith et al. and Herrmann-Pillath see the Communist regime as both a continuation and an inflection of China's *longue durée*. But focused as these last two are on the post-1978 reforms, they do not specify

these inflections in any detail. As such they do not discuss the 'socialist' in 'socialist market economy' at all.

32. Coase and Wang also point to Mao's decentralization, and even the 'backyard furnaces' of the Great Leap Forward, as providing the space for new practices and ideas to come forward outside the purview of the central state.

33. P. Anderson, 'Two Revolutions', *New Left Review* 61 (2010): 59–98; see also P. Anderson, 'Sino-Americana', *London Review of Books* 34, no. 3 (2012): 20–22.

34. Wang Shaoguang and Hu Angang made a famous 'Report on State Capacity' in 1993. Cf. W. Shaoguang, 'Is the Way of the Humane Authority a Good Thing? An Assessment of Confucian Constitutionalism', in Qing, *Confucian Constitutional Order*, 139–58; S. Anshu, F. Lachapelle and M. Galway, 'The Recasting of Chinese Socialism: The Chinese New Left since 2000', *China Information* 32, no. 1 (2018): 139–59.

35. S. Heilmann and E. J. Perry, 'Embracing Uncertainty: Guerrilla Policy Style and Adaptive Governance in China', in Heilmann and Perry, *Mao's Invisible Hand*, 1–29.

36. R. Coase and N. Wang, *How China Became Capitalist* (London: Palgrave Macmillan, 2012), 97.

37. Ibid., 147.

38. Cf. Connery, 'Ronald Coase in Beijing', 35.

39. Nolan, 'The CPC and the Ancien Régime', 20.

40. Cf. G. Yang, '*Unifying the Three Traditions' in the New Era: The Merging of Three Chinese Traditions*, introduction and trans. D. Ownby, 2005, https://www.readingthechinadream.com/gan-yang-tongsantong-chapter-1.html. Accessed 14 September 2019.

41. Cf. Qing, *Confucian Constitutional Order*.

42. M. Gow, 'The Core Socialist Values of the Chinese Dream: Towards a Chinese Integral State', *Critical Asian Studies* 49 (2017): 192–216.

43. Document Number Nine, the leaked 2013 Party Communiqué suggested: 'Neoliberalism advocates unrestrained economic liberalisation, complete privatisation and total marketisation, and it opposes any kind of interference or regulation by the state. Western countries, led by the United States, carry out their neoliberal agendas under the guise of "globalisation", visiting catastrophic consequences upon Latin America, the Soviet Union and Eastern Europe, and have also dragged themselves into the international financial crisis from which they have yet to recover.' J. Lanchester, 'Document Number Nine', *London Review of Books* 4, no. 19 (2019): 3–10.

44. T. Cheek and D. Ownby, 'Make China Marxist Again', *Dissent Magazine* (Fall 2018): 2–18, https://www.dissentmagazine.org/article/making-china-marxist-again-xi-jinping-thought. Accessed 26 January 2020; J. Golley, L. Jaivin, P. J. Farrelly, with S. Strange, *The China Yearbook 2018: Power Australian Centre on China in the World* (Canberra: ANU Press, 2019); Connery, 'Ronald Coase in Beijing'; Blanchette, *China's New Red Guards*, 127–47.

45. The epigraph to the books is Deng's 1992 Quote: 'China should maintain vigilance against the Right but primarily against the "left"'. Blanchette, *China's New Red Guards*, 1.

46. Richard McGregor helpfully calls this opposition an 'underbelly' of 'dogmatic idealism' on the sleeve endorsements on Blanchette's book.

47. Zhang, *China Horizon*; see also W. Zhang, *The China Wave: Rise of a Civilizational State* (Hackensack, NJ: World Century Publishing Corporation, 2012). On the China Model, see J. Fewsmith, 'Debating the China Model', *China Leadership Monitor* (Summer 2011): 35, https://www.hoover.org/research/debating-china-model. Accessed 15 October 2019; P. Wei, 'Reflections on the "China Model" Discussion', *International Critical Thought* 1, no. 1 (2011): 11–17. On 'establishment intellectuals', see T. Cheek, *The Intellectual in Modern Chinese History* (Cambridge: Cambridge University Press, 2015), 29–32.

48. See also D. A. Bell, *The China Model: Political Meritocracy and the Limits of Democracy* (Princeton: Princeton University Press, 2015).

49. Cheek and Ownby, 'Make China Marxist Again'; D. Ownby and T. Cheek, 'Jiang Shigong on Philosophy and History: Interpreting the "Xi Jinping Era" Through Xi's Report to the Nineteenth National Congress of the CCP', *The China Story*, 11 May 2018, https://www.thechinastory.org/cot/jiang-shigong-on-philosophy-and-history-interpreting-the-xi-jinping-era-through-xis-report-to-the-nineteenth-national-congress-of-the-ccp/. Accessed 19 October 2019. See also Qing, *Confucian Constitutional Order*; G. Davies, 'Talking (Up) Power', in Golley et al., *The China Yearbook 2018*, 37–49; Callahan, 'History, Tradition and the China Dream'.

50. Cf. B. Hillman, 'The State Advances, the Private Sector Retreats', in Golley et al., *The China Yearbook 2018*, 295–307.

51. Nolan, 'The CPC and the Ancien Régime', 23.

52. Ibid., 23.

53. Ibid., 26.

54. D. Shambaugh, *China's Future* (Cambridge: Polity, 2016), xiii.

55. K. Brown and S. Van Nieuwenhuizen, *China and the New Maoists* (London: Zed Books, 2016). Cf. also John Garnaut's recent account of Xi Jinping's 'social engineering': https://nb.sinocism.com/p/engineers-of-the-soul-ideology-in?utm_source=newsletter&utm_medium=email&utm_campaign=newsletter_axioschina&stream=top. Accessed 26 January 2020.

56. Cf. Chuang Collective, 'A State Adequate to the Task: Conversations with Lao Xie', 2017, http://chuangcn.org/journal/two/an-adequate-state/. Accessed 14 October 2019.

57. I. Bremmer, *The End of the Free Market: Who Wins the War between States and Corporations?* (New York: Portfolio Books, 2010), 23; Cf. P. A. Hall and D. Soskice, 'An Introduction to Varieties of Capitalism', in *Varieties of Capitalism: The Institutional Foundations of Comparative Advantage*, ed. P. A. Hall and D. Soskice (Oxford: Oxford University Press, 2001), 1–68.

58. B. Milanovic, *Capitalism Alone: The Future of the System that Rules the World* (Cambridge, MA: Harvard University Press, 2019); Y. Huang, *Capitalism with Chinese Characteristics* (Cambridge: Cambridge University Press, 2008); Lanchester, 'Document Number Nine',

3–10. For a recent discussion of the concept of state capitalism, cf. I. Alami and A. D. Dixon, 'State Capitalism(s) Redux? Theories, Tensions, Controversies', *Competition and Change* (2019), Online First, DOI: 10.1177/1024529419881949.

59. Cheek and Ownby, 'Make China Marxist Again'.

60. Veg, 'Rise of China's Statist Intellectuals'.

61. Cf. http://www.chinafile.com/document-9-chinafile-translation. Accessed 26 January 2020.

62. A. Dirlik, 'Postsocialism? Reflections on "Socialism with Chinese Characteristics"', *Critical Asian Studies* 21, no. 1 (1989): 33–44.

63. L. Chun, *The Transformation of Chinese Socialism* (Durham, NC: Duke University Press, 2006).

64. L. Chun, *China and Global Capitalism: Reflections on Marxism, History and Contemporary Politics* (Basingstoke: Palgrave Macmillan, 2013), 110.

65. Ibid.

66. Blanchette, *China's New Red Guards, 95–96*.

67. The New Left is associated primarily with the writers Wang Shaoguang, Cui Zhiyuan, Gan Yang and Wang Hui, the last by far the best known outside of China, and whose work has informed much of this book. They sought to continue the tradition of Chinese socialism as an open, ongoing project, rejecting its accommodation with capitalism and drawing on older forms of Chinese thought and practice to articulate the possibility of a distinct Chinese modernity. Cf. Anshu et al., 'The Recasting of Chinese Socialism'.

68. B. Naughton, 'Is China Socialist?' *Journal of Economic Perspectives* 31, no. 1 (2017): 3–24, 4.

69. Cf. Lanchester, 'Document Number Nine', 1.

70. Naughton, 'Is China Socialist?', 23.

71. Chuang Collective, 'Editorial: A Thousand Li', 2017, http://chuangcn.org/journal/one/a-thousand-li/. Accessed 14 October 2019.

72. Connery, 'Ronald Coase in Beijing', 56–57.

73. Anshu et al., 'The Recasting of Chinese Socialism', 154.

74. Connery, 'Ronald Coase in Beijing', 57.

75. Cf. X. Zhang, 'Nationalism, Mass Culture, and Intellectual Strategies in Post-Tiananmen China', *Social Text* 55 (1998): 109–40.

76. This situation might be described in terms of Slavoj Žižek's notion of the decline of 'symbolic efficacy', in which representation no longer has social force to designate the real, or to be challenged as true or false. This failure of ideology will be discussed in Chapter 8.

77. K. Strittmatter, *We Have Been Harmonised: Life in China's Surveillance State* (London: Old Street Publishing, 2019); K. Li Xan Wong and A. Shields Dobson, 'We're Just Data: Exploring China's Social Credit System in Relation to Digital Platform Ratings Cultures in Westernised Democracies', *Global Media and China* 4, no. 2 (2019): 220–32.

78. Cf. S. Moyn, 'The Nudgeocrat: Navigating Freedom with Cass Sunstein', *The Nation*, 3 June 2019, https: //www.thenation.com/article/cass-sunstein-on-freedom-book-review/. Accessed 26 January 2020.

79. Cf. N. Thompson and I. Bremmer, 'The AI Cold War That Threatens Us All', *Wired Magazine*, 23 October 2018, https: //www.wired.com/story/ai-cold-war-china-could-doom-us-all/. Accessed 14 September 2019. Lanchester (in his article titled 'Document Number Nine') makes a plea for the West not to follow China, though he does not seem confident.

80. Jullien's (*Treatise on Efficacy*) discussion of Legalism's adoption of Daoism's principle of non-action to justify the total control of the despot could also anticipate forms of neo-liberal governance. '[T]he "legalists" organise power in a completely artificial fashion (it is completely independent of the sentiments of the ruler and rests solely on the norms that are imposed and the control that is exercised). However, they then expect this artificial and technically installed system to operate *on its own*; and by doing so they totally recuperate the non-action of Daoism […] the ruler needs to nothing but allow things to take their course' (102).

81. Anderson, 'Sinomania'. See also Young Pioneers, 'May Fourth Manifesto', *New Left Review* 116 (2019): 69–73, where May Fourth was both anti-imperialist and anti-feudal.

82. H. Wang, *China's Twentieth Century* (London: Verso, 2016).

83. Cf. also P. M. Thornton, 'Retrofitting the Steel Frame: From Mobilising the Masses to Surveying the Public', in Heilmann and Perry, *Mao's Invisible Hand*, 237–68.

84. E. Bloch, *Heritage of Our Times* (Cambridge: Polity, 1991). Translation of *Erbschaft dieser Zeit* (Frankfurt am Main: Suhrkamp Verlag, 1962).

6

Shanghai: Creative City

Introduction

In the last chapters, we looked at the transformations of China through the lens of neo-liberalism, then expanding that viewpoint to China as a civilizational state and as a self-declared socialist state. We suggested that the notion of 'neo-liberalism with Chinese characteristics' had a degree of purchase, and that an authoritarian state is not necessarily antithetical to neo-liberalism. However, we argued that in a state whose legitimacy was founded on a notion of a collective good (as represented by the state) over and above the rights of capital, private property and the market, neo-liberalism had definitive limits. The specific forms of legitimation of the Chinese party-state are derived from a socialist history and ideology, and also from long-standing patterns of China's civilizational past. We remain open as to how this might inflect China's future development, but it is clear that the tensions between the logic of neo-liberal marketization, including the 'imaginary' in which this is set, and the social, political and ideological values of the party-state are becoming exacerbated. The ideological, and more latterly techno-disciplinary, work of the state has become increasingly strident and pervasive, a return, as some see it, to the old 'propaganda state' but in an age of (global) markets and surveillance technologies.[1]

If neo-liberalism needs to construct the framework for markets to function, it also needs productive and governable subjects. China's reforms involved a large-scale transition to a market economy, driven by new forms of market-state entrepreneurialism and the 'proletarianization' of the mass of the population.[2] This might be fine for 'catch-up', but as we saw in Chapter 1, a modern post-Fordist service economy – moving from Deng's 'reform and opening (*gaige kaifang*) to Hu Jintao's 'reform and innovation' (*gaige chuangxin*) – would require different kinds of subjects.[3] In this and the next two chapters, we will look at how these issues play out under the rubric of the 'creative city', 'creative industries' and 'creative class'.

The year 1992 was that of Deng's famous Southern Tour, when, after a post-Tiananmen freezing of the reform process, the ageing leader lit out for the Special Economic Zones (SEZs) he had established in South China. Hailing the burgeoning

175

cities of the Pearl River Delta (PRD) not as an aberration but a beacon for China's future, he also issued a *mea culpa* to the effect that he should have allowed Shanghai to similarly take off in the 1980s. Deng thus gave the 'green light' to Shanghai. This relaunch of 'reform and opening' saw the accelerated extension of the market across all forms of economic, social and cultural life, but the driver for the development of the 'forces of production' was to be an urban one. Though the new market reforms had begun in the countryside, and in the smaller towns, the new focus saw a definitive swing towards the cities, and the coastal cities in particular. Until the reforms, 'the city-as-city never appeared in a serious way as a signifier of revolutionary success or as an indicator of development'.[4]

In 1991, Harriet Sergeant noted that the city of Shanghai had been bypassed by a modernity it once incarnated, its past 'mummified' and its present 'spiritually dead'.[5] Two decades on, the Shanghai skyline had become part of the global image stock. Recognizable only to a few at the turn of the millennium, the skyscrapers of Pudong, clustered around the Oriental Pearl Radio and Television Tower, can be seen floating through the image worlds of Rolex watches, Vogue fashion shoots, Hollywood blockbusters, high-end car ads and all those financial, educational and creative corporations seeking the instant marketing hit of Global Asian Modern. Pudong is a relaxed newcomer to an elite club of global city signifiers, standing for a mix of finance, iconic real estate and 'culture' whose ultimate referent is the presence of the zeitgeist: modernity.

In the Western imaginary, Shanghai represents a path to the modern that China never took, a return to contemporary capitalism, its 'gateway to modernity'.[6] For the post-1978 Chinese government, the city's return to the forefront of Chinese modernization deepened their developmental narrative. Shanghai provides the image of a modernity the Chinese state has been pursuing since 1978, indeed since the radical calls for modernization made by the May Fourth movement in 1919. Shanghai's image is the product of an immense effort and ongoing management, the skyscrapers of Pudong promoted for their sheer image capital and not just as real estate opportunity. But Shanghai's image has depth and complexity compared to many other cities seeking a quick fix from high buildings, iconic architects, luxury shopping, five-star hotels and sleek art galleries. The city is a newcomer, but it has been here before. It is the erstwhile 'New York of the East', with a recovered cultural memory of a Chinese urban modernity, buried and half-forgotten. This historical moment, when the city, as a Western-administered 'concession port', floated free of the Chinese state, we have called Shanghai Modern. Shanghai, though possessed of a difficult heritage, presented an important resource for the government as a memory-image of a cosmopolitan urbanity imbued with the patina of history. Suitably framed, this history could provide the imaginary for a 'creative city', positioning Shanghai as a global commercial and financial centre, the self-conscious, media-savvy driver of a new Chinese cosmopolitan modernity.

In this chapter, we explore the arc between Shanghai as communist living death to a city of life-affirming consumerism, along with the multiple narratives that sustained it. For the return of Shanghai unfolded across a new global mediascape, one in which the 'global city' was to feature prominently. This was the decade in which the city was rediscovered, not just as a 'node' in the 'global space of flows' but as the site for a new kind of modernity, one in which 'culture' was to provide a stage for new kinds of creative subjects. In this chapter, we will explore how this was taken up within Shanghai as a source of global image capital and new forms of urban consumption.

Ground zero: Shenzhen

In the last chapter, we saw how Deng's 'reform and opening' relaunched Communist modernization by the prioritization of the 'forces of production' now identified with the (socialist) market. The triumph of economic realism over political enthusiasm was a repudiation of Mao and the chaotic mass mobilizations of the Cultural Revolution. This new realism, 'seeking truth from facts', went hand-in-hand with a radical rejection of Mao's anti-urban policies. In the urban development that accelerated at a historically unprecedented rate after 1992, the (socialist) market is made visible in the image of the metropolis. The new heroic Chinese modernity was manifested in the buildings shooting skywards and in the crowds of urban consumers thronging the streets and shopping centres. More fundamentally, in the abandonment of socialist urban planning, the very coding of the city form was attuned to flows of capital. The open, undesignated, unplanned, experimental, rapidly mutating spaces of the new Chinese cities were testing ground for, and analogous to, China's own experiment with the market.

In 1980, Deng, looking to the foreign enclaves of Hong Kong and Macau, decided to adapt this long-standing technique of controlled interaction with the West to the new socialist market economy. He established an SEZ near the fishing village of Shenzhen, over the border from Hong Kong, followed by one in Zhuhai, opposite Macau. Deng declared:

> Special Economic Zones are a window to technology, management, knowledge, and foreign policies. Through the zones, we can import technology, acquire knowledge, and learn about management, which is also a form of knowledge. The [SEZs] will become a foundation for the opening to the outside world. We

177

will not only benefit in economics and personnel training, but also extend the positive impact of our country to the world.[7]

The SEZ 'window' was crucial to the accelerating integration of the Chinese economy into global capitalism, allowing in foreign (initially mostly Chinese diaspora) capital and knowledge, building the infrastructure and mobilizing the necessary labour. The SEZs provided the early foundation for the urbanization of China's economy, fuelled by migrant labour from the countryside. What was the quality of the 'urban' being deployed and tested in the SEZs of the PRD? Mihai Craciun suggests the notion of 'window' is not just about opening to the world, but also a way of controlling or framing how the city is viewed:

'[T]he window is an intermediary space that can open or close the possibility of viewing. A figurative space, it frames the metropolitan similitude where the freedom of seeing substitutes for real experience.'[8]

The idea of new Chinese cities as 'fake' or 'artificial' is a recurrent one, often referring to their failure to live up to the exemplary urban models of the West.[9] Here we read 'metropolitan similitude' as the construction of the city as spectacle (for inhabitants and also for a global gaze) and the lack of a 'real' urban experience as a reduced or constrained experience.[10] The urban freedoms announced by the burgeoning metropolis were restricted to the realm of consumption. The SEZ 'provided the stage where new freedoms could be released; controlled access to commodities [...] A new code of the city was addressed to an incipient, virtual "middle class" with the intention of channelling its desires into a new ideology'.[11]

What a 'real' urban experience might entail is moot, and there may be a certain privileging of Western urbanism as exemplary, but the contrast here is explicitly with the erstwhile socialist city. The new cities of the PRD were built according to the logics of capital, mobility and migrant labour, with the image of the city organized around 'middle-class' consumption spaces. It is in this sense that the city operates as 'spectacle' rather than a site to effect collective ownership.[12]

Craciun sees Deng's 'zone' (*qu*) as a constructed *tabula rasa*, a blank where Western influences and the local entrepreneurial spirit could combine to launch a new socialist modernization. Purged of Maoism and leftism, the South's historic position as a 'cultural desert' was ramped up by Deng to create a 'no man's land' of ideology-free experimentation. The dismantling of socialist urban planning gave way to a city of rapidly expanding forms, which self-consciously went beyond any kind of long-term vision. Planners made a virtue of chaos and improvisation:

The Shenzhen SEZ embodied a new state of urbanism where fluctuation of the norm replaced the permanence of law, where the city (if 'making' a city was still possible) assumed its place in a continuum by *variation*: precariousness replaced type. The confrontation between market and planning consistently cancelled any obvious continuities between today's realities and tomorrow's goals: it humiliated vision. The planners of the SEZ confess to: 'guiding urban construction mainly according to short-term targets'; and 'repeatedly readjusting the long-term targets' [...] [T]hese planners see the waning of their competence as evidence of a new science. They make improvisation their method.[13]

We might note that some of this critique reflects the encounter of a certain Western project-oriented mindset, built around the 'model' and the 'goal' to be instantiated, as opposed to the more fluid, improvisational practices (perhaps somewhat turbo-charged) embedded in Chinese culture that we discussed in the last chapter.[14] Nonetheless, the shift from the idea of the socialist city 'produced by and for the masses' to one freed from any form of 'standard' was clear.[15] The market was not an external symbolic referent for the new city – no temples to Mammon – but acted as a '*conceptual* process that makes planning more fluid'.[16]

The Shenzhen SEZ had enormous implications for the wave of urbanization that transformed China in the 1990s. The focus on infrastructure rather than form; the massive scale; the improvisatory proliferation predicated on tracking the flows of capital; the use of multiple single-purpose 'themed blocks' (leisure centres, hi-tech parks, shopping malls, golf, actual theme parks) to direct new flows, often in brutal juxtaposition with the neighbouring blocks; the 'frivolous' architectural replicas evoking an hysterical postmodernism: these are very visible features of the emerging Chinese urban landscape.

But Shenzhen's window framed another encounter with the West, shadowing that of real estate capital and technology-knowledge-management exchange. This concerned how China was perceived, the qualities of its emerging modernization. The careful framing of the new Chinese metropolis for foreign observers – 'to extend the positive impact of our country to the world' – was to be crucial for the development of Shanghai. In Shenzhen's case, the rapid and sprawling expansion of the PRD gave it a 'Wild West' image to foreign observers, leading to the irony of Margaret Thatcher's neo-liberal government adopting the model of the SEZs as pure embodiment of a 'free-market' approach to development.[17]

But its free-market 'chaos' was one ultimately dependent on, and licensed by, the state. The party-state chose a low profile – Craciun's 'infrared'[18] – precisely to give this impression. This was made possible not just by the SEZ form – which Thatcher's ministers interpreted as the withdrawal of the state – but by the new latitude allowed to the local government. This too was pioneered in Shenzhen, and the devolution of responsibility for planning and economic development from Beijing to local government is a central aspect of the post-1978 reforms. This gave rise to a version of the 'entrepreneurial state' in which the local government was a central actor, expected to raise money from the sale or upgrading of land, and to instigate and participate in joint ventures with local and foreign capital. We saw in the last chapter how 'local state capitalism' or the 'market-state' and its 'amphibian institutions' gave rise to a configuration of state-market-society that has become a distinct form in China. These political preconditions were often missed, for the sheer pace of the development not only engulfed observers in a kind of urban sublime, but also wobbled a self-confident Western modernity on its axis.[19]

The PRD's energetic entrepreneurialism was reminiscent of the early industrial 'shock city' of Manchester, seemingly set to transform the landscape of Communist SOEs into a new capitalist 'workshop of the world'. But for close observers, this urban transformation was more than China's return to the capitalist fold. The speed and scale of its urban transformation was somehow shocking, even monstrous. Through books such as Rem Koolhaas's *The Great Leap Forward* – which built on his other Harvard-based projects of the later 1990s such as *S, M, L, XL* – Western readers encountered not just a Chinese rerun of nineteenth-century urban growth but a new kind of 'mega' city-region, on a scale difficult to conceive.[20] Koolhaas, already drawn to an architecture of 'bigness', of juxtaposition, of open programming and of complex interlocking infrastructures, was one of the few to seriously engage with the emerging mega-cities of China (and Asia more generally). His conceptual work was highly critical of Western cities, where since the 1970s a 'plastic urbanism' had emerged, an 'urban condition free of urbanity'. But the explosion of Asian – especially Chinese – cities seemed to be happening without vision. He found (in language also reminiscent of early observers of Manchester, shocked by its radical departure from the city of classical proportion).[21]

> [t]he absence, on the one hand, of plausible, universal doctrines and the pres-
> ence, on the other, of an unprecedented intensity of production have created a
> unique, wrenching condition: the urban seems to be least understood at the very
> moment of its apotheosis [...] There is no conceptual framework to describe,
> interpret and redefine. The field is abandoned to 'events' considered indescrib-
> able or to the creation of a synthetic idyll in memory of the city. There is nothing
> left between chaos and celebration.[22]

Koolhaas ends his introduction to *The Great Leap Forward*, written at the turn of the millennium, with an evocation of these chaotically expanding cities as urban sublime, enhanced by the astonishing range of maps, diagrams and images of a mega-city region few in the West had even heard about at the time.[23]

Through this image of the West encountering a very different urbanism, yet one that somehow evokes its own past, in a China of imitation and improvisation, spectacle and control, we might now look at Shanghai.

Shanghai Modern redux

Deng famously presented his failure to grant a 'green light' to Shanghai earlier in the reform process as a mistake. Of course, it was no such thing. There was little chance that Shanghai could have hosted the kinds of experiment undertaken in Shenzhen SEZ and the PRD. The most salient reason was that Shanghai was politically suspect given its centrality to the Cultural Revolution – the organizational base of the 'Gang of Four', as well as the site of one of Communist China's few workers' communes.[24] It was the deftness whereby the local leadership defused the 1989 protests and emerged as staunch defenders of Deng's Tiananmen intervention and his reform agenda that made possible the green light. More fundamentally, Shanghai was the exact opposite of a *tabula rasa*; its complex history was folded into its sense of identity, its external image and its unique built form. This was the famous *haipai* culture (as opposed *jingpai*, centred on Beijing).[25] Shanghai had a historical and political substance that could not be erased but called for careful handling. It was absolutely not a cultural desert but a densely clustered set of 'affordances' needing to be identified as such through close attention to the contours of the city, real and imagined, hard and soft.[26]

The re-emergence of Shanghai opened up some particularly deep and complex fissures for the new reform narrative. Shanghai had been the site of the foundation of the CCP and of the early workers' struggles against both capitalism and imperialism. But after their suppression in the city by Chiang Kai-shek in 1927, the main Communist forces had moved to the countryside. Their eventual victory was one in which the countryside, in Mao's famous formulation, 'surrounded the cities'. For in the historiography of the People's Republic, Shanghai had not just been China's foremost site of modernization but also of its capitalist and imperialist degradation. The liberation of Shanghai in 1949 was presented by the Communists as a victory not just over a key imperialist foothold but also a definitive rebuttal of a Western capitalist model of modernization and of the urban modernity to which it had given rise. Shanghai represented cosmopolitan decadence and exploitation, a city of workers, prostitutes and beggars lorded over by foreign and Chinese comprador capitalists. The victorious arrival of the ragged, peasant Red Army down Huaihai Road in 1949 was an act of repudiation and cleansing. The high level of contribution required from Shanghai by the national government was as much punitive as it was necessary; the city was to pay for its sins by financing the modernization of the rest of China.

Shanghai was now positioned by the Beijing government to return to its commercial, financial and industrial pre-eminence of the 1920s and 1930s. That is, to mobilize its past as a 'world city' to help attain a new 'global city' status.[27] Shanghai was to be promoted by both national and municipal governments as a strategic intervention into a new global economy, not just as site of exchange, as with Shenzhen. It was to become the dominant city of a Pacific Rim that was replacing the Atlantic as the locus of an emergent global economic boom.[28] The return of Shanghai was not to be a repudiation of the 1949 Revolution. As we saw in the last chapter, 'reform and opening' was not the rejection of Communism, but rather its 'ultra-left' excesses during the Cultural Revolution. Deng was picking up the earlier debates around the role of the market and foreign trade during the 1950s and early 1960s – but now with the examples of the 'Asian Tigers' striding into the distance and in a new, unpredictable context of 'globalization'.

Deng's green light announced more than the resumption of reform and opening. Shanghai's mummified past as the Paris or New York of the East was to be deployed in a new global image landscape, within which Chinese modernity would be presented as urban. At the end of his 1999 book *Shanghai Modern*, Leo Ou-Fan Lee claims the city for the future:

> History has dealt its most ironic coup de grace by making the cities [Hong Kong and Shanghai] important once again as cultural and commercial centers after half a century of rural revolution promoting the triumph of the countryside over the cities. As a century of China's search for modernity comes to an end, the spectres that hang over the not too distant horizon are cities such as Shanghai and Hong Kong.[29]

What is at stake here is not so much – as in development thinking – modernity versus tradition but two different routes to modernity: the (failed, socialist) rural and the (emergent, capitalist) urban. This opening up of a new urban imaginary as part of a restructured national economy was to be a key function of Shanghai in the new China. In Lee's formulation, the rural is a restricted Chinese modernity, in which commerce and culture (the province of the great cities) are sidelined. The rural is now the backwards-looking masses and the urban, the commercial and cosmopolitan future.

This is a highly Western-centric figuration of an urban-led modernization, where historical progress moves from the agrarian to the urban-industrial, from feudalism to modernity, and, as Hegel had it, from Asiatic despotism to

European freedoms.[30] The progressive construction of the modern nation state thus demanded the transformation of the peasantry by the modernizing energies of the metropolis – a view also built into Marxist and Leninist thought (though both had second thoughts).[31] This was replicated in the post-war versions of 'development' launched by the United States.[32] Mao's 'rural revolution' clearly partakes of the transition to the modern, but it was led by, and focused on, the countryside. For that reason, China's peasant revolution provided a powerful alternative image of rural modernization for 40 years. Whatever its specific and serious failings – the Great Leap Forward stands out above all – it looked to a modernization *of the rural*, not the mass removal of the peasantry into the ever-expanding cities.

The reforms in the countryside had given real dynamism to the post-1978 reforms, building on many of Mao's own reforms from the late 1950s, as well as his concern (after breaking with the Soviet model) to decentralize development.[33] As we have seen, many of the reforming cadres were returning from long periods of working and living in the countryside and saw the reform process as primarily about the alleviation of rural poverty and the release of productive energies through the household responsibility system.[34] The shift from rural- to urban-driven development announced by the 'Shanghai model of growth' was to raise profound questions of social justice around the shaping of the reforms and the unequal benefits that accrued from them.[35] Chinese urbanization, Shanghai foremost, was built on the systematic exploitation of the Chinese countryside.[36] It shifted the Chinese reform process away from the small-scale entrepreneurialism of the TVAs and the smaller cities to big capital-intensive development driven by Foreign Direct Investment brokered by the newly empowered Shanghai municipal government. Shanghai was to be the 'dragon head' of a new Yangtze Region.[37] Its growth, like that of the PRD, was based on a huge in-draft of migrant labour from the countryside, workers whose non-Shanghai *Hukou* registration effectively made them the *gastarbeiters* (guest-workers) in the city-region. The dialectical other of Shanghai's *haipai* culture was not just Beijing but the countryside. Shanghai was central to a re-imagination of Chinese modernity which delegitimized the rural as a regressive drag on a necessarily urban modernization. It was no longer to be peasant, or even working-class, income growth that counted in the new narratives of development, rather that of a new 'urban middle class' formed in the interstices of urban consumption and the service industries.

Pudong: The new Manhattan of the East

The 'Shanghai model' marked a significant acceleration in urban development, one driven by the sale of land to generate capital for large-scale infrastructure.[38]

Based on a series of laws and regulations from the late 1980s, local governments were allowed to sell land-use rights. Deng's Southern Tour in effect launched the urban real estate market. Though many of the lessons learnt in the PRD were to be applied in Shanghai, the buildings that represented Shenzhen's historic past had all been levelled; this was not possible with Shanghai's historically rich urban centre. Instead, the agricultural and old residential land in Pudong, on the opposite bank of the Huangpu River to historic Puxi, was designated as the city's development site. The municipal government used the sale of the land-use rights in Pudong to finance the city's infrastructure development. Much of Pudong's development, as well as that of the older villages and agricultural land outside the historic and industrial urban centre, followed that of Shenzhen, with its themed blocks, eclectic architecture and rapid, improvised development.[39] But Pudong also announced a new quality of Chinese urban modernity.

Reactivating Sun Yat-Sen's modernizing vision for the area of the early 1920s, it reconnected with a previous epoch of heroic modernization in which an impoverished China could, back then, only share in its imagination. Mao Dun's neon vision of 'Light, Heat, Power!' could now move back to the city from the countryside. The astonishing development of Pudong begun in the mid-1990s, its cluster of huge skyscrapers in the 'Tomorrow Square' of Lujiazui intended to surpass, not replicate, the colonial buildings on the Bund directly opposite. The new Shanghai would no longer be in the shadow of its imperialist-capitalist past. The earlier phase of modernization, which had built Asia's most modern city, would be dwarfed by new energies propelling the 'dizzying rise of the skyscrapers from the rice paddies of Pudong'.[40] Shanghai, the then mayor Huang Ju declared in 1993, was to be the 'new Manhattan',[41] an ambition made possible only because of its resonance with a prior historical moment of global pre-eminence.[42]

The Pudong skyline has acquired multiple meanings. It proclaims a heroic modernism that had been ironized in the West since the early 1970s. This modernism had already migrated to Asian cities through the work of 'starchitects' such as Norman Foster, Renzo Piano and Richard Rogers.[43] As we have seen, Koolhaas's radical vision of a revived (or 'retroactive') modernism, articulated in *Delirious New York*, now seemed more at home in Asia, and especially China, than in Manhattan.[44] Visitors to China in the 1990s experienced a sort of rerun of an urban future forgotten in the West. Commentators sometimes invoked Ridley Scott's film *Blade Runner* to describe the neon-lit skyline of Shanghai, but Scott's dystopian, futureless urban future, with its synthesized, manipulated individual and collective pasts (visible in the retro-noir form itself) is clearly Los Angeles.[45] In the early 1990s, Francis Fukuyama had proclaimed the end of history, the ultimate triumph of capitalist liberal democracy and a future that could only be more of the same.[46] It coincided with Frederick Jameson's 'postmodern moment', in which the horizon of global capitalism stretched out in all directions, obliterating the idea of a different future and, indeed, historical temporality as such.[47] Yet Chinese cities of the 1990s – Shanghai pre-eminent – seemed to exude an optimistic future of growth, technology and general material improvement.[48] Visitors encountered an urban modernization with a charge of energy and optimism, even libido, which could only provoke a nostalgia for the West's earlier naïve belief in progress; that the future could only get better.[49] If China's growth continued at this rate, then it would not be simply a quirky regional variety of capitalist modernization. Whatever political shape its development was to take, its sheer mass was going to have profound consequences on every imaginable global indicator – from economic to environmental to geopolitical.

In this sense, then, Pudong aspired to capture the very future for China, both for its citizens and a new global audience.

> Shanghai makes magic shows redundant. The city today is an everyday cinematic illusion, capable of conjuring whole skylines into being as if through special effects. Witness the artificial paradise of Pudong, across the Huangpu River. As for religion, foreign or homegrown, it does not hold the city together, but something else, some strong anticipation of what is about to come – the reappearance of Shanghai as China's most important international city.[50]

This local 'buy in' to a home-grown global ambition is certainly widespread, as Aihwa Ong suggests:

> Urban dwellers in Asia's big cities do not read spectacles as a general effect of capitalism, but rather as symbols of their metropolis that invite inevitable comparison with rival cities. Shanghai sees itself as symbolic encapsulation of the world and the potential of globality.[51]

Ong wants to see this moment as opening up a space to create a local distinctiveness, a 'worlding', that is an important part of the creative city imaginary. Others were less convinced, suspecting a rerun, a fake, a Potemkin village. Global city theorists pointed to the gap between aspiration and reality, using various indexes to discount the city's claims. Others suggested this 'mini-Manhattan' was a fake, a late remake of some ersatz global city, like some themed shopping mall.[52] This has rightly led to debates about what is 'authentic', as if this were enshrined in the 'classic' Euro-American city. Akbar Abbas suggested the fake testified to the underground energy of the periphery announcing its arrival onto the global stage of modernity. This 'fake' phase would pass once the city had arrived – and, indeed, today we witness the crackdown on fakes in the city and the rapid proliferation of 'real' global brands.[53] De Kloet and Sheen reject Abbas's account as too linear, as if there is only a singular path to catching up. They prefer to use the idea of *shanzhai*:

> [T]here is the assumption that an Asian city mimics what is labelled as a global city, but whose aesthetics are imagined as western, in particular as New York-ish. A *shanzhai* city may look like a copy, but not quite. With each translation from an assumed original to a copy, meanings slip away while other meanings proliferate.[54]

Shanzhai, derived from a word for 'outlaw', is used to describe local copies of global brands, but with slight modifications of function and at a lower price. De Kloet and Sheen see it as underground, popular innovation, driven by small entrepreneurs providing people with global products on the cheap.[55] As such, they claim, it is crucial to capitalist 'creative destruction' and even perhaps a democratizing force.[56] The *shanzhai* city turns out to be more prosaic:

> When applied to the *shanzhai* global city Pudong, the notion of *shanzhai* enables us to push the alleged archetypical model for the global city further to the background, and instead, to point at how the urban developers of Pudong were able to create a new global city, unique in its own right.[57]

There is no 'true' global city – they are all *shanzhai*, so even Manhattan is *shanzhai* – and Pudong's success comes from the mobilization of Shanghai's particular past. As Ong wrote, 'Asian cities are fertile sites, not for following established pathway or master blueprint, but for a plethora of situated experiments that reinvent what urban norms now count as 'global'.[58] We would concur with much of this, yet at the same time would suggest that Shanghai actively wanted the Western imprimatur of a global city, all the better to excel.

If 'fake' and *shanzhai* imply a copy of a Western 'original', however creative its consequent disruption and proliferation of meanings, the 'Potemkin village' is something else. It is a façade, constructed at break-neck speed, deliberately intended to create an illusion. Non Arkaraprasertkul suggests that 'the tall buildings in Lujiazui were not built to satisfy the need for vertical expansion due to the lack of horizontal space, but for the purpose of generating monumental symbolic value'.[59] Anna Greenspan counters by suggesting that attitudes to the 'façade' are Eurocentric. Screens and facades, surfaces and shadows are, she suggests, part of Chinese culture and philosophy.

> In Shanghai, however, the glittering artifice is not just meant to deceive. Rather it is embraced as a show, a global attraction that [...] need not interfere with the

messy, vibrant entrepreneurial culture that continues to power the everyday life and culture of the street [...] [In China] illusion has long functioned as a crucial currency of power [...] In the case of Shanghai, and, especially Pudong, this is blatantly obvious. Shanghai may be built on hype, but the hype has produced some very real results.[60]

Greenspan specifies these 'very real results' as, essentially, 'PR', a grandiose image-management campaign, in which the identity of Pudong 'was transformed immediately from a former industrial and residential zone into a high-tech city set to rise from Shanghai's shadow'.[61] Facades, screens and shadow-play are, she suggests, part of Chinese culture going back to the *Yijing* (Book of Changes). Criticism of these arrangements by Western observers manifests a 'deep rooted animosity to spectacle', a need to bring the shadows into the light as in Plato's parable of the cave. She prefers to keep the shadows. Nonetheless, Greenspan tells us, there is a 'behind the curtain', where we can catch a glimpse of the 'grand puppeteer', the party, as Richard McGregor has it, intent on 'concealment'.[62] Back to Craciun's infrared.

It is the role of the party-state, the connection between in-front and behind the curtain, that animates Milton Friedman's oft-quoted comment that the skyline of Pudong 'was not a manifestation of the market economy, but a statist monument for a dead pharaoh (the late Deng Xiaoping) on the level of the pyramids'.[63] What is at stake here is less the 'fake' nature of Pudong, or even its function as spectacular PR, but the fact of concealment, the hidden involvement of the party-state. Friedman, as we have seen, was far less tolerant of the role of the state in China's transition to capitalism than his neo-liberal colleague Ronald Coase. For Friedman, if Pudong is the work of the state then it is a problem. In response, Greenspan suggests that though Pudong was the work of the state we should not see it in either/or terms. Pudong was the work of the local, rather than national, state, and she outlines the ways in which the municipal government worked with a complex array of private and public-private entities in its delivery.

Lessons from Shenzhen were applied in Pudong: the zoning, parks and blocks; the improvisation and experimentation allowing the close tracking of the flows of capital; the proliferation of 'amphibian bodies'; and so on. But with land-use sales now established in law, and the process of reform well established and accelerated, there was less need for either a SEZ or for the party to keep a low profile. Indeed, the highly visible presence of the state was crucial – those 'pyramids' established confidence and declared the active and ongoing support of the state (local and national) for the opening up of the city to global capital. The Chinese state was declaring it has the power to secure the interests of global capital in the city in ways that many other developing countries simply were not able to. It was not the state behind the curtain, just the party.

Unlike Shenzhen, Shanghai's historical and political importance required an organizing vision, one that respected the 'grain' of the city. The Shanghai municipal government had more power to direct the general outline of urban change, being politically well connected with the 'Shanghai clique' in power in Beijing across the 1990s. Which is not to say that there was 'a plan' in either the strict urban planning sense or even as a detailed teleological project. In Pudong, and then across the wider city, the municipal government were testing out the new configuration of (local) state-market-society in more complex circumstances. These circumstances involved not merely inserting Shanghai into the circuits of global capital, but doing so at a moment when the competitive success of the global city placed a premium on its long-term cultural capacities. A 'fake' city might present a global image, but if this made no connections with the energies rooted in a local cultural capacity, it would remain a Potemkin village.

Greenspan wants to keep both the façade and the bustling underground in play, as light and shadow, a movement of yin-yang echoed in the opposition of Road (as masterplan) versus Street.[64] The distinctiveness of the Chinese modern, for Greenspan, is that the one does not displace the other. The party-state makes the grandiose infrastructural statements but this 'need not interfere with the messy, vibrant entrepreneurial culture that continues to power the everyday life and culture of the street'. The shadows of bottom-up continue to play beyond the glare of top-down. There is, then, no need to dispel the shadows, as the darkness of the street allows a freedom of action and innovation that would be denied if brought into the glare of the light.

Greenspan extends this opposition regionally. To Yasheng Huang's well-known objection that the small-scale entrepreneurialism of the TVAs has been ousted by the 'dragon's head' of Shanghai's state-dominated, Foreign Direct Investment model, she replies: why not both? Using Fernand Braudel's distinction between markets and capitalism, she argues that the opposition is neither one of period (1980s versus 1990s) nor space (countryside versus city), but 'two different economic orders that operate simultaneously in the city'.[65] High-level capital formations (monopolies, mercantilism, corporations) sit in juxtaposition to the mobile, inventive entrepreneurialism of localized, bottom-up 'markets' (rather like Kloet and Sheen's *shanzhai* culture).[66] Braudel's account of a specific historical moment in the take-off of European capitalism – in which local markets are integrated into a system of mercantilist nation states – is turned into a structural socio-economic opposition of top-down and bottom-up, and made to reflect a Chinese cultural configuration in which both are allowed a place.[67] The key metaphorical image is of the municipal regulatory authorities endlessly chasing – though with a routine blind eye – the street vendors who obligingly disappear, then reappear. The pharaonic skyscrapers tolerate, even shelter, the entrepreneurial innovation occurring in the dark shadows far below. But while the play between state and entrepreneurs accounts for something of the fluidity of the Chinese configuration, the example of Shenzhen suggests it would be wrong to push this into a dualism, yin-yang or otherwise. The transposition of Schumpeter's entrepreneurial 'creative destruction' to the Chinese context does not work, even less so when thus combined with the metaphor of 'the street'.

Leaving aside for the moment the highly problematic linkage of entrepreneurial capitalism to 'bottom-up' emancipation, we have seen that the configuration of (local) state-market is much more complex, with levels of interpenetration and a range of 'amphibian' institutions making the opposition of 'state' and 'street' untenable. In Shenzhen, urban planning was refigured by the local state to provide the maximum flexibility with regard to flows of capital and the demands of the market. Planning 'licensed' the entrepreneurs – as Greenspan's actual account of Pudong illustrates – rather than somehow tolerating them. Equally, the energies of transformation came as much from state actors as they did from entrepreneurs 'on the street'. More literally, the primary economic activities in Pudong are to be found less on the 'street' than in the high-tech parks and factories, linked to government-funded R&D and financed by large-scale foreign and domestic capital.

What is at stake in questions of fakes and facades, state-planning and entrepreneurial invention, certainly concerns the ability of non-Western cities to create their own version of the global modern in conjunction with their own distinct histories and cultures. But behind the scepticism of Western observers – despite their admiration – was also a sense that the copy was out of date. The heroic modernization proclaimed by Pudong had arrived too late. Top-down modernity was redundant. The 'expressway world' – 'shopping centres, over-passes and subways' – would be of limited use in a city lacking Berman's 'modernity of the street'.[68] As the 1990s progressed, an authentic contemporary urban modernity, it seemed, could not emerge in a 'spiritually dead city'; it needed to be manifested in some version of the 'creative city'.

The creative city: Modernism in the streets

If Shanghai was to be a global city, it could not just be a transit hub, or simply a place of spending. Its economic strength demanded 'command and control' functions, but it could not be just an economic power hub, even if the gravitational pull of finance, business services and logistic hubs inevitably creates a mix of global denizens, migrant workers, high-end consumption, lifestyle toleration zones, media services and the art world entrepreneurs common to global city culture. Global image capital requires more than supplying cherry-picked global events, festivals, theme parks and branded 'destination' shopping and entertainment. A city wanting the heft to rival New York, London or Tokyo, one commensurate with its position as China's pre-eminent global city, requires it generate its own culture marked – or branded – with its own identity. That is, it needs the capacity to actually produce images, texts, sounds and (cultural) objects, as well as the technological, regulatory and commercial infrastructures, skills and know-how, agencies and institutions, and those complex real and imagined spaces that form part of the urban ecology. It is from this complex urban cultural ecology that the global city generates its cultural products and into which this cultural production feeds back in turn.

The 'creative city' is usually presented as a policy script written by Charles Landry and, more latterly, Richard Florida, one deeply implicated in gentrification, 'the entrepreneurial city' and neo-liberalism more generally.[69] This script is a combination of 'global city' and 'creative city', in which cultural production – television, films, video games, performing arts, recorded music, publishing, the visual arts, craft and 'design' goods, architecture, graphic design and advertising – feeds directly into real estate, image capital and the new cultural or 'creative' economy of the city. It is predicated on a narrative of culture and economy 'converging', which can mean that economies are increasingly infused by culture or, more plausibly, that culture is increasingly valued for its economic impact. It is cities that stand to benefit from this confluence of culture and economy, and the great metropoles most of all. If cultural consumption – the great art galleries, events, concerts, museums, entertainment zones, boutique shopping and so on – feeds the image capital and real estate development that attracts inward investment, mobile professionals and tourists, then cultural production will provide a new engine of long-term growth.

As Jamie Peck wrote, creative city policies 'might be characterized as the most conspicuously successful innovation in the recent history of urban policy-making'.[70] Peck, a fierce critic, famously called creative cities a symptom of 'fast policy' operating in markets created and sustained by policy-makers in search of a quick fix.[71] In a world of neo-liberalism where cities are set in unending competition with each other, manipulating the 'business climate' has now been replaced by 'manipulating people climates in order to attract mobile talents'. Creative city policies are cheap and easy,

> carriers for fiscally undemanding forms of market complementing interventionism: they are minimally disruptive of extant power structures and established interests, and they 'accessorise' neoliberal urbanism in a manner befitting prevailing cultural tropes of competitive cosmopolitanism.[72]

The thrust of critique has undoubted weight, but we should not ignore the extent to which 'creative city' policy is able to gain affective and imaginative 'buy in'. This 'buy in' can be rather fuzzy, allowing a range of policy agendas to fly the flag of 'creative city', but the appeal is nonetheless real. We would need to understand in what ways the creative urban imaginary manages to link to the specific identities of a city, what it does with this, what it leaves out; to know what kind of future(s) it holds out and how it was differently inflected by policy-makers, intermediaries and by the wider constituency that is 'interpellated' by this promised future.

The creative city agenda taps into and selectively shapes an urban 'imaginary' derived from the complex historical identity of the city.[73] An 'imaginary' is not pure ideology; using actor-network and cultural economy theory, Bob Jessop shows how it actively works to modify a range of discursive practices and affective meanings in order to assemble people and things into a coherent programme around which change can be managed.[74]

The creative urban imaginary, even if 'minimally disruptive of extant power structures', conjures the pressing need for fundamental change rather than routine tinkering, in order for the new urban future to be achieved. Indeed, this creative urban imaginary is usually formulated in terms of the need to radically adapt the resources of this complex historical identity for a new urban future (or risk historical redundancy). The creative city is not just a technical policy matter but has a powerful affective charge in which complex historical and cultural resonances are combined to produce a utopian promise of a new economic future.[75]

The origins of the 'creative city' lie in deep-seated structural changes affecting Western cities from the 1970s onwards. In outline, these changes involved the uncoupling of cities from a 'Keynesian' national space and their insertion into a more global 'space of flows'; meeting the challenges posed by post-industrialism and 'post-Fordism'; a changing 'imaginary' of urban modernity; and a growing focus on the cultural capacities of cities to respond to these global changes. The 'creative city' grew out of a particular moment of transformation in which it seemed a new modernity might be glimpsed, one that embraced all those elements of urban life which the functionalism of Fordist modernity – Berman's 'expressway world' – seemed to have pushed to one side.

Jonathan Raban's 1974 *Soft City* declared:

> The city as we imagine it, the soft city of illusion, myth, aspiration, nightmare, is as real, maybe more real, than the hard city one can locate on maps in statistics, in monographs on urban sociology and demography and architecture.[76]

If this is so, Raban argued, then the language of urban planning needs to change, for if we mould the soft city in our image, then 'it seems to me that living in cities is an art, and we need the vocabulary of art, of style, to describe the peculiar relationship between man and material that exists in the continual creative play of urban living'.[77] Raban's book came at a time when the city was viewed as a subset of a national space, marked by the efficient co-location of production and consumption, rather than any specific sociocultural qualities. A distinct urban sociology, of the sort that flourished in Chicago and Berlin in the 1920s, was almost non-existent by the 1970s.[78] Raban opened a space to rethink the close connections between the city and capitalist modernity made by the great nineteenth-century social theorists Marx, Durkheim and Weber. Similarly, he made space for two relatively unknown German writers, Georg Simmel and Walter Benjamin, who had excavated the city for the specific qualities of a modernity that had since become peripheral to the world of the modern planner. *Soft City* was a recovery of an older urban modern for a post-industrial world.[79]

Marshall Berman's *All That Is Solid Melts into Air* (1983) was seminal, reinvigorating the imaginary of the urban modern at the very moment the Fordist city was slumping into post-industrial decline.[80] In Berman's writing, technological-industrial modernization and the sociocultural forms of modernity to which this gives rise become uneasy bedfellows. Berman's continued commitment to the modern looked back to an older, more rambunctious modernity than that represented by twentieth-century 'high modernism', which either uncritically welcomed or utterly rejected modernization. As with Koolhaas's search for a more unruly modern urbanism than that of the International School, Berman's evocation of 'the street' was part of a wider rejection of the Fordist city, subjected to the sterile dictates of functional planning. Le Corbusier's 'death to the street' had been a call to replace the messiness and serendipity of street level urbanity by a well-managed series of functional zones connected through transportation – the Fordist city-machine. For Berman, on the contrary, it was in the messy, chaotic modernity of 'the street' that the existential historical confrontation between the dangers and possibilities of modernity was located – a modernity in which 'all fixed, fast-frozen relations, with their train of ancient and venerable prejudices and opinions, are swept away; all new-formed ones become antiquated before they can ossify'.[81] But the immense historical possibilities of modernity had been ironed flat by the convergent technocratic modernizations of both capitalism and communism, as had the messy streets by the urban planners and architects who served both of these projects. To retrieve the street was thus to retrieve these open possibilities of modernity.

Berman's rejection of the modernity of the planners and engineers, and embrace of the chaos and conflict of the street, came at the end of a two-decade pushback against top-down planning. In the early 1960s, Jane Jacobs had evoked the communal conviviality of 'mixed use' and the informal serendipity of urban life, challenging the top-down master-planner, Robert Moses.[82] The growing assertion of 'grassroots' community involvement in planning decisions formed part of a wider reclaiming of the 'right to the city'.[83] Berman's intent was to open up the urban culture of modernity and retrieve its possibilities for a contemporary historical moment. The loosening of relations between the sociocultural lived experience of modernity and economic-technocratic modernization was the foundation of his critique of the instrumental rationalism underpinning both capitalist and communist modernization. Berman rejects any reduction of the cultural 'superstructure' to a simple reflection of the 'economic base' and thus introduces a degree of autonomy and agency into this culture. The future is not yet written. In the energies of the street, a new imaginary might be possible. 'Modernity in the streets' then is a political moment, a utopian moment, in which culture – as a way of rethinking our modernity – is to play a pivotal role.

At the same time, the city per se was emerging as a new kind of economic resource. In 1985, Jacobs published *Cities and the Wealth of Nations*, which argued that cities, rather than the nation state, were the real driver of prosperity.[84] Jacobs's evocation of community and mixed use was now tied to a reappraisal of the specific role of cities in economic development. This accorded with a broader shift in economic thinking about the global role of cities, which we will discuss shortly. Jacobs articulated a new positive view of the messy iterations of city life as part of a wider rejection of planning. It intersected with a growing nostalgia for the nineteenth-century city, with its anarchic energies and grotesque excesses, before it was tamed by Le Corbusian high modernism.[85] This retrieval saw a new value placed on the built stock of the historic city, no longer to be demolished as outdated, a *tabula rasa* for new development. Opposition to the levelling of historic buildings was part of the growing assertion of the rights of urban communities – for example Jacobs's defence of Greenwich Village happening at the same time as demonstrations against the 1963 demolition of Penn Street Station in New York. Community anti-development movements, such as historical preservation societies,[86] could be found across Europe, for example the successful defence of Convent Garden in London, which transformed into a small-scale 'arts and craft' shopping area soon to become a key exemplar for a particular kind of urban regeneration.[87]

These previously overlooked or redundant areas of the city were 're-landscaped' in the form of a new urban imaginary in which they recalled an older urbanity, spaces of community and street level enterprise, emergent symbols of a new kind of post-industrial, post-Fordist urbanism.[88] The docks, lofts, factories, market halls, stations, banks and hospitals that had once been key aspects of what Henri Lefebvre called spaces of representation – Raban's 'hard city' of the planners – became representational spaces, in which a new urban imaginary could fold itself around a landscape of the past, catalysing a new future.[89] It is from here that 'culture-led urban regeneration' takes off, part of that 'spatial fix' – where culture works to revalue a built stock otherwise destined to be written-off – that we will discuss more below.[90]

The 'spatial fix' was also a 'global fix'. Cities were increasingly decoupled from a national socio-economic planning space, the effective locus of decision-making moving up to the global and down to the local city level, leaving the nation state weakened. Manuel Castells focused a new attention on cities acting outside the space of the national, reconceived as nodes in the global space of flows, with 'global cities' as supernovas.[91] Cities needed to be 'entrepreneurial' in this new world of urban competitiveness, but this could not be some race-to-the-bottom with tax breaks and compliant labour. Cities had to be more proactive in dealing with the challenges and possibilities of what institutional economists called 'path dependency'. Urban geographers had suggested places were 'sticky'. Land was of course immobile but moving capital and labour around was not 'friction-less' either. They both tended to 'stick' to certain places over time. Cities were possessed of thick layers of skills and know-how, 'tacit' knowledge and dense embedded networks that could not easily be moved or replicated – or easily altered. These embedded capacities would be required if cities were to compete at a global level. Crucially, for Castells these capacities were 'cultural', in that they required high levels of competence in the 'manipulation of symbols': that is, educated, skilled workers.[92]

Castells's co-author Peter Hall's historical survey of urban innovation – based on work done over the 1980s and 1990s – set a seal on the recovery of the city as a distinct social form, making their specific energies available as a potential source of economic transformation.[93] Hall was concerned with reconnecting the themes of innovation and creativity to a much longer history of the city, and indeed cities more generally ('every great burst of human creativity in history is an urban phe-nomenon'[94]). He traced the emergence of particular cities as historical turning points, where their own local history comes to define less a place than a whole epoch. Cities were not an object for planners but complex, cultural entities whose dynamics were unpredictable and even chaotic. Urban creativity, in this account, was as much about bottom-up as it was top-down planning systems.

The roots of the 'creative city' lay in this retrieval and relaunch of the urban as a distinct cultural and economic capacity. Though 'culture-led regeneration' could be reduced to tourism and place-marketing, its broader goal was as contri-bution to the re-articulation of the identity of the city. If cities were to mobilize their distinct histories to compete in this new global space, then this required a cultural capacity – conceived not just in Castells's sense of 'education and skills', but also as part of Raymond Williams's 'whole way of life' or, to use a term from the same author, a local 'structure of feeling'.[95] Williams had suggested 'that the definitive cultural character of any one social formation [...] could best be grasped

194

in the examination of the routine and taken for granted "social practices" that characterised that social formation'.[96] These routine social practices were built up over many years (even centuries) and structured around a complex and collective (if internally differentiated) historical experience. Cities were now encouraged to identify the particular qualities of their historical formation, parlaying their unique identities and embedded cultural capacities into an ability to actively engage the future after Fordism. The 'imaginary' of the creative city, then, was a particular articulation of *erfahrung*, a reframing of Negt and Kluge's 'general horizon of social experience'.[97]

Haipai culture: 'Amnesiac Monument, Nostalgic Fashion'[98]

Shanghai's distinct *haipai* culture was progressively retrieved across the 1980s and 1990s, the work initially of urban historians and literary scholars inside and outside China, but very quickly picked up by the Shanghai government. *Haipai* was an aspect of Shanghai's 'difficult' past, a particular articulation of its 'structure of feeling' made available as a cultural capacity able to enhance the city's ambitions of becoming China's global cosmopolitan city. *Haipai* was derived from Shanghai's historic position as a site of encounter with Western modernity in a semi-autonomous space that allowed, especially in the golden years of the 1920s and 1930s, an outline of a distinctly Chinese modernity to emerge. (We have discussed aspects of this in Chapter 4.)

Haipai was constructed as a particular conjunction of commerce and cosmopolitanism, one which seemed to privilege artists and intellectuals as key intermediaries in its articulation. As in structural linguistics, Shanghai style is that which it is not; neither rural China nor imperial Beijing, it plays within a binary of 'old and new, nostalgia and progress, self-absorption and openness, country and city, indigenous and foreign, disdain for the marketplace and eagerness for profit'.[99] This 'structure of feeling' is manifested as a particular 'style of the metropolis', one 'constituted as much by an attitude, a context, a way of living and behaving as by an aesthetic or a set of definable formal features'.[100] It is formed by the cosmopolitan mix of Shanghai – full of international 'sojourners' and migrant Chinese – and the emergence of commerce:

> Modern Shanghainese have been stereotyped as astute, resourceful, calculating, quick-witted, adaptive and flexible [...] All of these are associated with commerce. Shanghai [...] was the epitome of modern China's commercial culture in which commerce served as the primary motor of society. It seems legitimate to name such a culture after the city [...] *Haipai*.[101]

195

In addition, as Lee suggested: 'If cosmopolitanism means an abiding curiosity in 'looking out' – locating oneself as cultural mediator at the intersection between China and other parts of the world – then Shanghai in the 1930s was the cosmopolitan city par excellence.'[102] Cosmopolitanism and commerce were to be found in the great buildings of the Bund, in the city's distinctive *art deco*, in its vast port and transport infrastructure, its up-to-the-minute gas, water, electricity and lighting. They animated the everyday life of the Shanghainese, as new vernacular housing expanded with the city, bringing in migrants from across China. According to Samuel Liang, this vernacular housing – the *lilongs* with their *shikumen* gates – opened up the 'courtyard to the street', mixing residential and commercial in ways that dissolved old hierarchies and customs, the locals now, as Greenspan puts it, 'liberated to create their own modern rituals of everyday life'.[103] It is little wonder then that

> Shanghai accepted what the twentieth-century world had to offer more readily than other parts of China, be it new technology, ways of thought, cultural forms or artistic styles. Where but in Shanghai would a Chinese so quickly find such modern symbols as escalators, cinemas, dance halls, advertising billboards, popular magazines, gramophone records, motor cars and woman's fashions?[104]

Haipai was a 'structure of feeling' clearly rooted in Shanghai's distinct past – part of its 'path dependency' – but it was one subject to selective editing, reframing, forgetting and foreclosure.[105] In Chapter 4, we suggested that the association of the city with 'commerce and modernity' ignores China's own long history of commercial activity, the city's structural economic and political dependence on global capital flows, and its political isolation from a peasant China where the real process of historical transformation was located. We also suggested that these new cultural forms involved more than simply new forms of 'modern' urban consumption. The quality of an emergent modern experience – *erfahrung* – in pre-war Shanghai was one, in Miriam Hansen's words, of 'remembering the past and imagining a different future' but also of 'the historical disintegration and transformation of these very capacities with the onslaught of industrialisation, urbanisation and a modern culture of consumption'.[106] We might recall Peter Hall's judgement on creative cities in history, which were 'societies troubled about themselves', in a state of tension, of 'transition forward to new and unexplored modes of organisation [...] societies in the throes of a transformation in social relationships, in values and in views about the world'. Creative milieus, he concludes, 'are places of great social and intellectual turbulence: not comfortable places at all'.[107] (It was the response to such a moment of turbulent transition by the city's cosmopolitan and revolutionary left-wing intellectuals that we explored in Chapter 4.)

There were structural homologies between *haipai* and forms of recovered identities in other 'creative cities', where the idea of a return to an older modern was
transformed into a resource for the post-industrial future.[108] Though Shanghai's
unique past was a very powerful resource, the suggestion that the use of such
a past is unique – 'retrofuturism' or 'retromodernity' – we think overstates the
case.[109] In Shanghai, the retrieval was of a world before full-blown socialism.[110]
Its reappearance staged something before communism, 'mummified', 'pickled', in
'suspended animation', 'frozen shock' – now ready to be reactivated.[111] This was
difficult heritage. As 'culture and cosmopolitanism', *haipai* could be deployed as
a refutation of the 1949 revolution per se – Dikotter's 'globalisation not revolution' – or Shanghai as a form of urban futurism in direct contradiction to 'agrarian'
socialism.[112] Either way, the revival of *haipai* neatly stepped over the previous
40 years of socialist Shanghai, Sergeant's 'spiritually dead city'. The return of
Shanghai manifested a tension, as Ong suggested, between 'multiple modernities',
'two competing discursive systems: the modernist imaginary of the nation state
(emphasising essentialism, territoriality, and fixity) in tension with the modernist
imagining of entrepreneurial capitalism (celebrating hybridity, deterritorialisation,
and fluidity)'.[113] We suggest that what was distinctive in Shanghai was that the
past provided important symbolic capital for this globalized modernity, but it also
allowed China to negotiate and defuse the tension between them.[114]

The return of *haipai* after 1992 also held out a particular promise for artists
and intellectuals.[115] The artists of the golden age were quintessential cosmopolitans
able to articulate the desires and aspirations of an emergent Chinese modernity
in ways politicians could not. This ability was facilitated by their insertion within
a local and global cultural commerce that provided the necessary space for such
work away from their traditional dependence on the state. The return of *haipai*
in the new commercial and cosmopolitan space of 'reform and opening' would
reopen debates around artistic and cultural production, its autonomy and proper
functions, which had been disputed over the course of the 1920s and 1930s, and
finally fixed by Mao at Yan'an in 1942.[116] Fixed, that is, as the reduction of culture to ideology and thence to the politics of class struggle as articulated by the
party. Might not a new, global cosmopolitan Shanghai necessarily have to renew
artistic and cultural freedoms as a precondition? In which case, the new Shanghai
would be positioned to pick up the unfinished cultural task of exploring and
shaping the profound challenges of China's encounter with modernity in a post-
Mao era. Yet Shanghai's return was launched by Deng Xiaoping after the events
of Tiananmen, events which had profoundly shaken Chinese intellectuals across
the political spectrum.[117] In what sense, then, would the return of an older urban
modernity allow a new openness, a new place for Chinese artists and intellectuals
in the forging of a Chinese modernity?

Nostalgia as intermediation

The creative city, in Raban's words, demanded the 'vocabulary of art, of style, to describe the peculiar relationship between man and material that exists in the continual creative play of urban living'. Landry and Bianchini, in their 1995 book *The Creative City*, had suggested that the language 'of instrumental, rational and analytic thinking' needed to be supplemented by one that could describe the 'messy' aspects of urban life, those 'which are subjective and not quantifiable: memory, emotions, passions, senses, desires, all of which engender motivations and loyalties'.[118] To bring these dimensions into a new 'holistic' conception of the city saw artists and cultural experts, those at home in the messiness of the soft city, brought into closer contact with policy-makers. We will discuss the concept of 'cultural intermediaries' in the next chapter, but it is clear that the work of turning a 'structure of feeling' into a new 'urban creative imaginary', and transforming an older, redundant urban infrastructure into a representational space where this urban imaginary could be articulated and inserted into the landscape of the city, seemed to require those possessed of this 'special kind of city knowledge'.[119] In Shanghai's case, this work required the retrieval of a particular moment of the past, a memory-image which, as many commentators have noted, appeared in the form of nostalgia.[120] This new imaginary landscape, central as it was to the city's global ambitions, was also directed outwards, to the 'mobile lives' of the cosmopolitan elites.[121] As such, Shanghai, like Shenzhen SEZ, acted as a 'contact space', but one in which nostalgia played a central organizing role.[122]

There was a strong sense, among many diasporic Chinese, of a 'lost world' resurfacing – of their youth, or of their parents' youth, or of that wrapped around buildings, objects, books and music, left pickled on dusty shelves, stumbled upon in bric-a-brac stalls, hunted out along polluted canals and alleyways, in forgotten film stock and chipped shellac. One thinks of the complex nostalgia of Wang Kai Wai's film *In the Mood for Love*, released in 2000 but set in 1962 Hong Kong, where childhood memories of the director's family fleeing Shanghai are recalled via the quasi-fetishistic visual pleasure of Maggie Cheung's *cheongsam* dresses – quintessential *haipai*.[123] Or Wang Anyi's 1995 novel *Song of Everlasting Sorrow*, the heroine living her life in the shadow of her shining moment of glamorous fame, in the dying moments of the 'Hollywood of the East'.[124] The nostalgia brought back memories of a prior artistic and intellectual self, after the devastations of the cultural revolution to be sure, but also pre-1949. Shanghai had been the home of the modern Chinese intellectual, and its glamorous memory-image, infused with commerce and cosmopolitanism, recalled an autonomous cultural-aesthetic space radically separated from politics.[125] Here we might cite Eileen Chung's novels, or those such as Qian Zhongshu's *Fortress Besieged*; or the figure of Zhou Zuoren,

Lu Xun's younger brother, who sought a space to explore a modernity outside politics.[126] Relieving the artist from the burden of the political was certainly a cause for celebration in the 1980s, but what might this mean at the end of the 1990s?[127]

This was also, we might say, a cosmopolitan nostalgia.[128] The return to the city, after exile in Hong Kong or beyond, to revive that which was buried, was something a certain kind of global traveller, and a new kind of sojourner, could share in – an 'imagined nostalgia' generated from their own complex recovered memories.[129] Amanda Lagerkvist has detailed how foreign visitors' memories were intertwined with the city's past and present media representations, along with a local tourism and city promotion industry ready to cater to them.

> These mobile elites constitute, through their own bodily movements, parts of the transformations at hand. The production of 'New Shanghai' as a space of memory and futurity is a process enacted by politicians, urban planners, architects, public relations specialists, general tourism promoters, and media workers, but it also occurs [...] through the movements and performances of visitors.[130]

Visitors could brush against the barely unearthed traces of Shanghai Modern in ways that caught a frisson from an imagined past, which also worked to insert them into the city.[131] The sheer volume of Shanghai Modern buildings that had been preserved from development meant that in the years leading up to the 2010 Expo it was still possible for the casual *flâneur* to gain access to colonial heritage buildings, and even rent some of the older factories and industrial spaces. Shanghai Modern's emergence into the gaze of the present was accompanied by a surge in antiques (real or fake) from Shanghai's 'retromodernity', the kind of outdated objects Raban found in London flea markets of the 1970s – gramophones and radios, old telephones and office furniture, posters for medicines, liquors and cigarettes, with the ubiquitous 'Shanghai beauty' at home with the bright lights and the new technologies. For a certain kind of foreign visitor, this was a glimpse into the past described by J. G. Ballard, though like a lot of this recovered past, he was mostly unknown to the Shanghainese.[132]

The city government rapidly embraced this nostalgia. The difference between the 1985 and 1993 re-edition of the recordings of Zhou Xuan – the famous singer and film star from the 1930s and 1940s – is emblematic. In 1985, a recording was issued as a way of instructing would-be popular music writers on how it could be done, but the decadent sounds of the 1930s 'yellow music' were overlaid by a contemporary 'easy-listening' remix. In 1993, the official edition relished these older sounds, the *haipai* culture she represented now fully rehabilitated in the new Shanghai.[133] Lee evokes the nostalgia fever that gripped the city in the mid-1990s, and the municipal government began to list and preserve the old colonial heritage as key assets. This, it should be noted, went hand-in-hand with the destruction of the old city, 'demolition and preservation at the same time', adding to the patina of nostalgia.[134]

For Lee, the embrace of 'old Shanghai' created an opportunity for a new generation of writers and poets who

> have begun to explore [...] what they call a new 'urban consciousness' (*dushi yishi*) – a subject of which they had previously known practically nothing. A journal called Shanghai Culture (Shanghai *Wenhua*) was launched in 1993 [and] reaffirms the 'deep and solid foundation of the school of Shanghai culture, with its splendid tradition of assimilating outside culture with an open mind'.[135]

Lee welcomed the huge investment by the government in a 'massive research project on Shanghai's history and culture' as a way of realizing this new urban spirit. As Wen-Hsin Yeh described this,

> Shanghai historians rallied to throw their weight behind the city's modernization project and to make the intellectual case in favour of the outlined change [...] [T]he historians, through their descriptions of the city's recent past, embraced Shanghai's modern history as a chronicle of Shanghai's uniqueness, if not China's pride. By doing so they set aside an old-fashioned, revolutionary belief and refashioned the city's urban identity.[136]

Yeh goes on to describe the project in terms perfectly suited to post-1992 China:

> By shifting attention away from colonialism, capitalism, Nationalist betrayal, and Communist martyrdom, new images emerged that described a middle class city of material comfort in everyday life that was making steady progress in the enhancement of wealth and health [...] Instead of dwelling upon the structural injustices in the 'social relations of production' under capitalism, the more innovative historians chronicled the scientific and technological advancement in 'modes of production' as the city underwent modernization [...] Pre-1949 Shanghai was the making [...] neither of the colonialists nor the capitalists. It was, instead the work of the petty urbanites who were the occupants [...] of the shikumen residences. In the words of Zhang Zhongli, president of the Shanghai Academy of Social Sciences, 'The bottom line is: Shanghai was Chinese, Shanghai was Shanghainese. The city developed as a result of the people in Shanghai making innovations on inspirations taken from the West.'[137]

This nicely encapsulates how *haipai*'s difficult baggage – an urban culture seemingly both pre- and post-Communist – helped facilitate the reinsertion of Shanghai into circuits of global capitalism. Colonial extraterritoriality, commerce and cosmopolitanism had allowed Shanghai Modern to act as if it were floating free of the 'feudal' past and of the brutal politics of the present. This aspect was made available for a contemporary China similarly marked by cosmopolitan opening, depoliticization and the return of a market in culture. *Haipai* articulated a structure of feeling as metropolitan style. It did so at the same time that an 'aestheticisation of everyday life'[138] was taking place, *haipai* imbuing the new global citizens of Shanghai with a particularly rich version of *suzhi*, at home in the proliferating flows of texts and highly aestheticized consumer goods.[139]

Rather than nurturing an oppositional, globalizing middle class, the city shaped its practices in multiple ways, through the shopping malls and spectacular cityscape, an all-pervasive urban mediatization, and a proliferation of cultural events and facilities, where the new urban middle class could identify with the spectacle of modern global China.[140] Shanghai, the quintessential urban modern, embodies this middle class, which 'is less a specific group of people than a way of thinking and foreseeing the structures of Chinese society, a part of the new social imaginary China is elaborating'.[141] We can recall Landry's creative city, mobilizing all those aspects of urban living 'which are subjective and not quantifiable: memory, emotions, passions, senses, desires, all of which engender motivations and loyalties'. The interpellation of these subjectivities through a reworking of Shanghai's memory-image as both local identification and global media capital – that 'new code of the city [...] addressed to an incipient, virtual "middle class" with the intention of channelling its desires into a new ideology' we saw in Shenzhen – has been an astonishing success.

Building on this reworked urban identity, Shanghai embarked on a huge programme of cultural infrastructure building. Starting with the Grand Theatre and Museum in People's Square, the Oriental Arts Centre and restored (and relocated) 1930s concert hall, through the 2010 Expo ('Better City, Better Life'), it went on to a proliferation of art galleries (and auction houses), including a massively revamped 'West Bund', housing public, private and overseas galleries (Centre Pompidou x West Bund the latest),[142] along with an art import-export zone (Shanghai has the largest art market in the world).[143] These, along with the festivals, international exhibitions, biennales, touring programmes, theatrical blockbusters and so on contribute to Shanghai's rise up the global creative cities index.[144] Perhaps the 'Pavilion of the Future' at the Shanghai Expo – with massive stacked books with the names of Thomas More, Charles Fourier and Le Corbusier – sums up the city government's attempt to annex the urbanistic future for the city. For us, the ultimate destination of *haipai* can be found in Xintiandi, a redeveloped area of Lilongs, with its offices, shops, bars and restaurants.[145]

Opened in 2004, it marked the arrival of the historical vernacular into Shanghai's commercial urban development scene.[146] It was constructed from recycled elements of an old *lilong* complex, complete with prominent *shikomen* gates, but made fit for modern retail use and provided with open 'piazzas' in trusted *po-mo* fashion. It was telling that the development company was from Hong Kong, and equally so that the architect, Benjamin Wood, was a protégé of Benjamin Thompson, whose 1979 transformation of Faneuil Hall in Boston represents a foundational moment of heritage-led urban regeneration. The Hong Kong developer was asked to incorporate the old Girls' School, which hosted the first meeting of the CCP. Rather than the burden this would represent for most of the Shanghai developers at that time, such historical patina was a godsend. So much so that the developers reconstructed a *Shikomen* house as period museum over and above the brief. Xintiandi has now expanded into the surrounding areas of up-market retail, whose development it catalysed, now complete with its own metro stop. In fact, the original rebuilt *lilong* section is itself almost like a medieval relic inserted into the modern-day array of malls, international hotel chains, soaring offices and luxury apartment blocks which sprang up around it. Whatever commentators might say about Xintiandi being an aspect of the 'temporary loop inherent in Shanghai's futurism', digging out a usable past from under the rubble of Starbucks and Gucci would be like seeking the ethos of *The Great Gatsby* in a Ralph Lauren polo shirt.[147]

Creative city: Endgame?

The 'creative city' progressively excises the illusions and the nightmares from Raban's *Soft City*, just as *haipai* steps over the pain and dislocations of Chinese modernity. Creative cities, *pace* Peter Hall, are now to be places of 'vibrancy' and 'passion', not troubled and uncomfortable. The 1949 Revolution was the answer China gave to the challenge of modernity, and, framed in the ways we have seen, *haipai* was a form of forgetting this. The foregrounding of commerce and cosmopolitanism, which seemed to promise the increased autonomy of the intellectual, was absorbed into Shanghai's global city narrative.

Akbar Abbas had been deeply sceptical of Lee's eulogy to cosmopolitanism. He questioned the assumption that cosmopolitanism is an unproblematic, universal value. Abbas was writing while the brash new Shanghai was springing up in the 1990s,[148] when the world into which Shanghai was 'opening up' was very different from that of the 1930s. It was, he suggested, no longer the age of 'internationalisation' but rather 'globalisation', where global flows bypass the nation state, and the task of translation and intermediation – what Abbas called 'arbitrage' – was no longer the job of the educated cosmopolitan artist-intellectual but undertaken directly by capitalist corporations themselves.[149] It was cosmopolitanism in an era of 'glocalization', that is 'the need to adapt a global outlook to local conditions', a kind of 'micromarketing', where global flows were calibrated to local needs and sensibilities in order to extract profit.[150] The process of intermediating between the local and the global was parcelled out between the (national and local) state and transnational capital. In Shanghai's urban creative imaginary, 'cultural intermediaries' were firmly under the control of the official historians, local media conglomerates, historical preservation committees, architect-developers and so on.

In this way, Shanghai as 'creative city' was an aspect of how China has not only managed Ong's tension between the nation state and entrepreneurial capitalism but also used it to its advantage. The 'creative city', East and West, has increasingly become both 'a commodity and instrument of control', directing capital flows into different areas of the city, using culture to cement the 'spatial fix' under the imperative to *be creative* or lose the future.[151] In this sense, it was not Pudong that was the façade but *haipai* culture itself. The association of artist and entrepreneur, engaged in the ceaseless 'creative destruction' of the street, was part of the framing – Deng's window – of Shanghai as China's most Western city. It was the perfect place to attract a certain kind of Western subject – dreaming of futures past, globally sourced neo-bohemians, from Wicker Park or Whitechapel – into Shanghai's French Concession.[152] This we will explore in the following chapter.

Abbas had insisted that 'cosmopolitanism' was deployed as a key feature of the modern capitalist corporation, and globalization and 'openness' were compatible with new forms of inequality and exploitation, squalor and degradation. 'The cosmopolitan "attitude" in this case consists not in the toleration of difference but in the necessary cultivation of indifference.'[153] Already in 2000, Abbas was pointing to the growing divides and discontents within 'globalisation' and the concerns as to how 'cosmopolitanism' could so easily be annexed to the free movement of global elites and a disengagement from the local 'losers'.

The tensions Ong described between the 'modernist imaginary of the nation state' and the 'modernist imagining of entrepreneurial capitalism' – fixity and essence versus fluidity and hybridity – no longer plays out across the divide of the 'street' versus the 'plan', state versus market. This opposition within modernity has dissipated, as the nation state has increasingly been claimed by the 'losers' as a bulwark against the depredations of 'entrepreneurial capitalism' as manifested in a globalization driven by global elites. That equation of entrepreneurial capitalism with bottom-up emancipation no longer holds, in the way it did in the years after the collapse of the USSR, as the contrast Huang wanted to maintain, between 'good' (small, local) and 'bad' (state-directed, globalized) capitalism has been undermined by financialized neo-liberalism. Since 2008 at least, 'fixity' and 'essence' are increasingly sought out as refuges in face of the kinds of deep social disruptions inflicted by the accelerated liquidity of global capitalism.

In this context, there is a return to questions of the 'ordinary city' – of collective provision, accessible infrastructure, public housing, of cities for the many not the few – that were so often marginalized in the creative city narrative.[154] There has also been a return to the 'threshold moment' at the cusp of the 1970s, when, as Mark Fisher wrote, 'a whole world (social democratic, Fordist, industrial) became obsolete, and the contours of a new world (neo-liberal, consumerist, infomatic) began to show themselves'.[155] The demonization of the planner articulated the deep discontent with Fordism-Keynesianism. In foregrounding the new cultural possibilities excluded by the industrial city, the 'creative city' partook of that wider articulation of the 'artistic critique of capitalism', often by a 'new middle class', associated with the rise of a new kind of networked, 'creative capitalism'.[156]

But the Fordist city had been part of an attempt to respond to the 'social critique of capitalism', its social and economic injustices, historically pursued by the workers' movement. The 'creative city' initially articulated the 'artistic critique', those issues of alienation, of Rimbaud's injunction to 'change life', the aspirations to emancipation articulated by Berman's messy modernism of the streets. It did so in a way that promised new socio-economic as well as cultural possibilities for the city. Yet though its imaginary frequently attracted a widespread 'buy-in', its solutions to the problems of deindustrialization faced by the primary beneficiaries of the Fordist city (notably the working class) were often limited to new forms of urban consumption and precarious employment. The creative city, we might say, is now neither social nor artistic critique.

At the end of his highly critical essay on Shanghai, Abbas looked towards another kind of urban cultural imaginary, one in which different transnational flows involving different actors might be involved.

> [C]ities are the locales or nodal points of this transnational space, which exists not in some abstract dimension but in the very specific sites and problem areas of the city. [...] Whether a cosmopolitanism for the global age will emerge depends on our ability to grasp a space, that of the global city, that is always concrete even in its elusiveness. And this involves not so much imagining a transnational state as reimagining the city.[157]

Such an imaginary would demand a new kind of cosmopolitanism involving

> not only the privileged transnational, at home in different places and cultures [...] [but] will have to include at least some of the less privileged men and women placed or displaced in the transnational space of the city and who are trying to

make sense of its spatial and temporal contradictions: the cosmopolitan not as a universalist arbiter of value, but as an arbitrageur/arbitrageuse.[158]

This is an outline of a transnational cultural intermediary; it is arbitrage not set on 'maximising profits' but on negotiating the 'disequilibria and dislocations that globalism has created'.[159]

This optimistic note points us beyond the 'creative city' as it has become, returning to some of the aspirations that went into its making. Framing *haipai* as an unmediated return of an 'urban cultural sensibility' – objects frozen, pickled, mummified come back to the present as nostalgia – sidestepped the occasion it presented to think through the profound challenges of China's encounter with modernity. The return of Shanghai Modern could have reopened a space of dialogue about the possibilities of modernity in China that had been narrowed by the exigencies of war and revolution, and by the forms in which Communist modernization had been undertaken in parallel to that of Fordist capitalism. This was Shanghai Modern reimagined not as a repudiation of Communism but by a real 'reform and opening', a deepening of its democratic promise.

NOTES

1. T. Cheek, *The Intellectual in Modern Chinese History* (Cambridge: Cambridge University Press, 2015), 125–32.

2. R. Walker and D. Buck, 'The Chinese Road', *New Left Review* 2, no. 46 (2007): 42. 'There are three major routes to proletarianization in China: from the farming countryside, out of collapsing state companies in the cities, and through the dissolution of former village enterprises.'

3. L. Pang, *Creativity and Its Discontents: China's Creative Industries and Intellectual Property Rights Offences* (Durham, NC: Duke University Press, 2012), 8.

4. S. Landsberger, 'The City's (Dis)appearance in Propaganda', in *Spectacle and the City: Chinese Urbanities in Art and Popular Culture*, ed. J. de Kloet and L. Scheen (Amsterdam: Amsterdam University Press, 2013), 121–34, 132.

5. 'When Shanghai fell in 1949 to the Chinese communists a door was shut. During the Cultural Revolution the door was bolted for good. A world had gone [C]ommunism has fallen on the city like a sandstorm, burying and preserving […] Communism has mummified Shanghai's appearance in a manner inconceivable to a Westerner. Shopping centres, overpasses and subways are all missing. So, despite carefully preserved wrappings, is Shanghai's spirit […] To write about a spiritually dead city presents difficulties.' H. Sergeant, *Shanghai* (London: John Murray, 1991), 5–6.

6. M. -C. Bergere, *Shanghai: China's Gateway to Modernity* (Stanford: Stanford University Press, 2009).

7. R. Ming, *Deng Xiaoping: Chronicle of an Empire* (Boulder: Westview Press, 1994), 134.

8. M. Craciun, 'Shenzhen', in *The Great Leap Forward*, ed. C. J. Chung, J. Inabu, R. Koolhaas and S. T. Leong (Koln: Taschen, 2001), 44–155, 89.

9. See the critique in J. Robinson, *Ordinary Cities: Between Modernity and Development* (London: Routledge, 2006).

10. Cf. J. de Kloet and L. Scheen, 'Pudong: The Shanzhai Global City', *European Journal of Cultural Studies* 16, no. 6 (2013): 692–709. The authors tend to focus on the built form of the city as fake, or otherwise, and we discuss this more below. Our concern is with 'experience'. We should say at this point that the actual reality of the new subjects drawn into Shenzhen – from migrant workers to transnational professionals to energetic young designers from Northern China – is a matter we do not discuss in this chapter.

11. Craciun, 'Shenzhen', 89.

12. This shift to urban consumption can be found in Western cities of course, as satirized by John Carpenter in his 1988 film *They Live*, with its neon screens whose revealed message is OBEY, CONSUME and so on. Rem Koolhaas's essay 'The Generic City' has something of this cool satirical intent: 'In the Generic City, people are not only more beautiful than their peers, they are also reputed to be more even-tempered, less anxious about work, less hostile, more pleasant – proof, in other words, that there *is* a connection between architecture and behaviour, that the city can make better people through as yet unidentified methods.' But there is also here, surely, a highly sublimated reworking of the socialist city of the masses. R. Koolhaas, 'The Generic City', in *S, M, L, XL*, ed. R. Koolhaas and B. Mau (New York: The Monacelli Press, 1995), 1248–64, 1262; original emphasis.

13. Craciun, 'Shenzhen', 117; original emphasis.

14. Cf. F. Jullien, *A Treatise on Efficacy* (Honolulu: University of Hawai'i Press, 2004), 16: '[Europeans] set up an ideal form (*eidos*), which we take to be a goal (*telos*), and then we act in such a way as to make it become fact' (2) as opposed to Chinese thought in which 'rather than set up a model to serve as norm for his actions, a Chinese sage is inclined to concentrate his attention on the course of things in which he finds himself involved in order to detect their coherence and profit from the way they evolve'.

15. Craciun, 'Shenzhen', 117.

16. The resulting urban form, Craciun suggests, was a simulated Western city: 'an ersatz metropolis appears, structured on a syntactical set of blueprints controlling combinations of formulaic architectural types. The frivolity of the metropolitan replica is disguised by instrumental reference to the authority of the market, taken over ideologically as a repository of "knowledge".' Craciun, 'Shenzhen', 81; original emphasis. This is meant literally – in the light of de Kloet and Scheen's ('Pudong') – as a direct copy of western architectural forms. We leave more discussion until later.

17. This is to be found also in Rem Koolhaas's more cerebral celebrations of the 'Generic' or 'Asian' city. Cf. E. Durham-Jones: 'Koolhaas focuses on the surreal delight and wild juxtapositions produced by state-run capitalism. However, in his enthusiasm for the surreal

aspects of both Generic Cities and the Pearl River Delta, he often implies a false connection between free trade, free development, and individual freedoms' (31–32). 'Cultural Transformations of the Post-Industrial Landscape', *OASE* 54 (2001): 9–36. (Quoted in de Kloet and Scheen, 'Pudong', 698)

18. See Chapter 6, Note 47.

19. Cf. O. Hatherley, 'The Hyperstationary State: Five Walks in Search of the Future in Shanghai', *Culture Unbound* 4 (2012): 35–80.

20. Koolhaas and Mau, *S, M, L, XL*; R. Koolhaas, B. Chang, M. Craciun, N. Lin, Y. Liu, K. Orff and S. Smith, *The Great Leap Forward*, Harvard Design School Project on the City (New York: Taschen, 2002). Predating this of course was the sci-fi comic *2000 AD*, first published in 1977, especially *Judge Dredd*, which featured a series of post-nuclear 'mega-cities' run on authoritarian lines.

21. See the famous essay on Manchester as 'shock city' in A. Briggs, *Victorian Cities* (London: Odhams, 1963).

22. R. Koolhaas, 'Introduction' in Koolhaas et al., *The Great Leap Forward*, 27. Hence the proliferation of 'copyrighted' terms in the book, a plethora of new concepts followed by ©, intended to set the ground work for a new explanatory frame.

23. We are back with Deng's window, but now obscured, giving onto a landscape difficult to read: 'The emergence of the PRD with the suddenness of a comet, and the present "cloud of unknowing" that creates a kind of stealth envelope around the PRD's existence and performance, are themselves proof of the existence of parallel universes that utterly contradict the assumption that globalisation equals global knowledge'. Koolhaas, 'Introduction', 28.

24. E. J. Perry and L. Xun, *Proletarian Power: Shanghai in the Cultural Revolution* (Boulder, CO: Westview Press, 1997).

25. L. Pan, *Shanghai Style: Art and Design Between the Wars* (San Francisco: Long River Press, 2009).

26. Cf. J. Raban, *Soft City* (London: Hamish Hamilton, 1974), 10: 'The city as we imagine it, the soft city of illusion, myth aspiration, nightmare, is as real, maybe more real, than the hard city one can locate on maps in statistics, in monographs on urban sociology and demography and architecture.'

27. Cf. S. Sassen, 'The Global City Perspective: Theoretical Implications for Shanghai', in *Shanghai Rising: State Power and Local Transformations in a Global Megacity*, ed. X. Chen (Minneapolis: University of Minnesota Press, 2009), 3–30.

28. See the interview with Huang Fuxiang, team leader at the Shanghai Urban Planning and Design Institute, in A. Greenspan, *Shanghai Future: Modernity Remade* (London: Hurst and Co., 2014), 45.

29. L. O. Lee, *Shanghai Modern: The Flowering of a New Urban Culture in China, 1930–1945* (Cambridge, MA: Harvard University Press, 1999), 339.

30. H. Wang, *The Politics of Imagining Asia* (Cambridge, MA: Harvard University Press, 2011), 15–18, 33–34.

31. Ibid., Ch. 1. For Wang Hui cf. W. Hui, *The Rise of Modern Chinese Thought* [现代中国思想的兴起], 4 vols. (Beijing: Sanlian Shudian, 2004). The association of the agrarian with pre-modern backwardness was a part of a refusal to recognize 'empire', and the values that held it together, as a valid historical category for the modern era. The agrarian empire, stultified by tradition and heavy despotism, must give way to the urban industrialism of the modern nation state. Wang Hui's point about the de-legitimization of empire in the modern, was, as we discussed in the last two chapters, concerned the denigration of the Chinese past as a resource for the modern. But the territory of the Chinese Empire did survive into the modern, the civilizational project it represented being the central legitimizing prize for competing political forces. The overwhelming weight of this project lay in rural China, amongst the peasant masses, and it was only by mobilizing these in the name of the Chinese Revolution that the nation state could be founded.

32. In the idea of 'development' launched by Harry Truman and echoed in the United Nations after 1945, urbanization was equated with the break with tradition, as essential to progress.

33. Y. Huang, *Capitalism with Chinese Characteristics* (Cambridge: Cambridge University Press, 2008); R. Coarse and N. Wang, *How China Became Capitalist* (London: Palgrave Macmillan, 2012), Ch. 3; B. Naughton, *The Chinese Economy: Transitions and Growth* (Cambridge, MA: MIT Press, 2007), 240–46.

34. I. Weber, *China's Escape from the 'Big Bang': The 1980s Price Reform Debate in Historical Perspective* (London: Routledge, 2019).

35. Huang, *Capitalism with Chinese Characteristics*.

36. L. Ma and F. Wu, eds., *Restructuring the Chinese City: Changing Society, Economy and Space* (London and New York: Routledge, 2005).

37. Ibid.

38. A. G. Yeh, F. F. Yang and J. Wang, 'Economic Transition and Urban Transformation of China: The Interplay of the State and the Market', *Urban Studies* 52, no. 15 (2015): 2822–48.

39. See Greenspan, *Shanghai Future*, Ch. 7, for a good account.

40. Huang, *Capitalism with Chinese Characteristics*, 231.

41. Cf. N. Arkaraprasertkul, 'Politicisation and the Rhetoric of Shanghai Urbanism', *Footprint* 2 (2008): 43–52; M. Huang, *Walking between Slums and Skyscrapers: Illusions of Open Space in Hong Kong, Tokyo and Shanghai* (Hong Kong: Hong Kong University Press, 2004).

42. As in the famous description by Akbar Abbas: 'Shanghai today is not just a city on the make with the new and brash everywhere – as might be said more aptly of Shenzhen, for example. It is also something more subtle and historically elusive: the city as remake, a shot-by-shot reworking of a classic, with the latest technology, a different cast, and a new audience. Not "Back to the Future" but "Forward to the Past".' A. Abbas, 'Cosmopolitan De-scriptions: Shanghai and Hong Kong', *Public Culture* 12, no. 3 (2000): 769–86, 780.

43. Cf. H. Foster, *The Art-Architecture Complex* (London: Verso, 2010).

44. R. Koolhaas, *Delirious New York: A Retroactive Manifesto for Manhattan* (London: Academy Editions, 1978).

45. See multiple references assembled by A. Lagerkvist, 'The Future Is Here: Media, Memory and Futurity in Shanghai', *Space and Culture* 13 (2010): 3220–38, 227–28.

46. F. Fukuyama, *The End of History and the Last Man* (New York: Free Press, 1992).

47. F. Jameson, *Postmodernism, or, the Cultural Logic of Late Capitalism* (London: Verso, 1991).

48. Hatherley, 'The Hyperstationary State', 35–80.

49. On the death of the future, see D. Graeber, *The Utopia of Rules* (London: Melville House, 2015), Ch. 2, 105–48, 'Of Flying Cars and the Declining Rate of Profit'; cf. D. Murphy, *Last Futures: Nature, Technology and the End of Architecture* (London: Verso, 2016).

50. A. Abbas, 'Play It Again Shanghai: Urban Preservation in the Global Era', in *Shanghai Reflections: Architecture, Urbanism, and the Search for an Alternative Modernity*, ed. M. Gandelsonas (New York: Princeton Architectural Press, 2002), 36–55, 37.

51. A. Ong, 'Hyperbuilding: Spectacle, Speculation and the Hyperspace of Sovereignty', *Worlding Cities: Asian Experiments and the Art of Being Global*, ed. in A. Roy and A. Ong (London: Blackwell, 2011), 205–26, 210.

52. Cf. Huang, *Walking between Slums*.

53. On global city indexes, see the discussion in de Kloet and Sheen, *Spectacle and the City*; A. Abbas, 'Faking Globalization', in *Other Cities, Other Worlds: Urban Imaginaries in a Globalizing Age*, ed. A. Huyssen (Durham, NC: Duke University Press, 2008), 243–64. For a substantial discussion of 'fake' in the Chinese context, see Pang, *Creativity and Its Discontents*.

54. de Kloet and Sheen, 'Pudong', 705–06.

55. Others suggest similar. See, for example: S. Lindtner, 'Hackerspaces and the Internet of Things in China: How Makers are Reinventing Industrial Production, Innovation, and the Self', *China Information* 28, no. 2 (2014): 145–67.

56. de Kloet and Sheen, 'Pudong', 703. 'Furthermore, the broader trend of *shanzhai* culture often is considered to have a democratising power, mostly overlooked by people outside of China. In a recent Chinese survey, for example, 65 percent of the respondents were of the opinion that *shanzhai* culture expresses the "voice of the people", 40 percent agreed that it represented "grass-roots culture", and 30 percent answered yes to the question of whether "individuality" lay at the core of *shanzhai* culture'. *Shanzhai* became a rather modish cultural studies term, designating a kind of Deleuzian hybridity, and became a celebration of 'the streets' with its shadow entrepreneurs, those 'with a special kind of city knowledge' (cf. Raban, *Soft City*, 104). It also echoes Koolhaas's (purported) equation of Asian cities with 'free trade, free development and individual freedoms', but in backstreet workshops and dodgy markets.

57. de Kloet and Sheen, 'Pudong', 703.

58. A. Ong, 'Introduction', in Roy and Ong, *Worlding Cities*, 1–26, 2.

59. Arkaraprasertkul, 'Politicisation and the Rhetoric of Shanghai Urbanism', 47.

60. Greenspan, *Shanghai Future*, 87, 90.

61. Ibid., 61.

62. Ibid., 64. Cf. R. McGregor, *The Party: The Secret World of China's Communist Rulers* (New York: Harper Collins, 2010).

63. Greenspan, *Shanghai Future*, 57.

64. 'Road' is Le Corbusier's grand high-level vision of the city as planned infrastructure, while Robert Moses's 'Cross-Bronx Expressway', the top-down brutality of modernist planning. Discussed by M. Berman, 'Robert Moses: The Expressway World', in *All That is Solid Melts into Air: The Experience of Modernity* (London: Verso, 1983), 290–311. 'Street' is Marshall Berman's vernacular modernity, ever contesting and circumventing the Road, full of energy and invention. This echoes the well-known contemporary opposition of 'tactics' and 'strategy'. Cf. M. de Certeau, *The Practice of Everyday Life*, trans. M. Randell (Berkeley: University of California Press, 1984).

65. Greenspan, *Shanghai Future*, 29. The reference is to F. Braudel, *Civilization and Capitalism: Volume 3: Perspectives of the World* (Berkeley: University of California Press, 1992). However, we suggest this is more Manuel Delanda's than Braudel's – cf. page 59, note 22. Braudel's 'Market/State' also figures in Nick Land's 'Meltdown' (1997) in *Fanged Noumena: Collected Writings 1987–2007* (Falmouth: Urbanomic, 2015).

66. Greenspan, *Shanghai Future*, 59–61.

67. In fact, Braudel's account does provide a route into China's distinctiveness, in that 'capital' never became a project of the state, which kept it at a distance. Cf. G. Arrighi, *Adam Smith in Beijing: Lineages of the Twenty-First Century* (London: Verso, 2007).

68. Greenspan, *Shanghai Future*, 40.

69. R. Florida, *The Rise of the Creative Class* (New York: Basic Books, 2002); R. Florida, *Cities and the Creative Class* (New York: Routledge, 2005); C. Landry, *The Creative City: A Toolkit for Urban Innovation* (London: Earthscan, 2000); C. Landry and F. Bianchini, *The Creative City* (London: Demos, 1995).

70. J. Peck, 'Creative Moments: Working Culture, Through Municipal Socialism and Neoliberal Urbanism', in *Mobile Urbanism: Cities and Policy Making in the Global Age*, ed. K. Ward and E. McCann (Minneapolis: University of Minnesota Press, 2011), 42.

71. J. Peck, 'Struggling with the Creative Class', *International Journal of Urban and Regional Research* 29, no. 4 (2005): 740–70, 767; cf. J. Peck, *Constructions of Neoliberal Reason* (Oxford: Oxford University Press, 2010).

72. Peck, 'Struggling with the Creative Class', 62.

73. The notion of 'imaginary' has been used by Bob Jessop and others to refer to the element of 'semiosis', of meaning production, in 'construing, constructing, and temporarily stabilizing capitalist social formations at least within specific spatio-temporal fixes and their zones of relative stability'. B. Jessop and S. Oosterlynck, 'Cultural Political Economy: On Making

the Cultural Turn without Falling into Soft Economic Sociology', *Geoforum* 39, no. 3 (2008): 1155–169, 1156.

74. B. Jessop, 'Cultural Political Economy, the Knowledge-based Economy, and the State', in *The Technological Economy*, ed. A. Barry and D. Slater (London: Routledge, 2005), 142–64.

75. For more on this cf. J. O'Connor, '"A Special Kind of City Knowledge": Innovative Clusters, Tacit Knowledge and the "Creative City"', *Media International Australia* 112 (2004): 131–49.

76. Raban, *Soft City*, 10.

77. Ibid. This anticipates Landry and Bianchini's *The Creative City* by nearly two decades. 'The dominant intellectual traditions which have shaped urban policies have been profoundly rooted in a belief in the virtues of instrumental, rational and analytic thinking. In respect of planning, sewerage, water, utilities, roads, these approaches helped to transform chaotic, disease-ridden cities into safe and healthy environments. But reasoning grounded in science, governed by logic, has its limits too. It compartmentalises knowledge into separate branches or boxes, imposing order over nature, without letting "messy reality" get too much in the way. Worse, it makes it hard to cope with periods of change' (10). 'Both geography and planning [...] are dominated by the analysis and manipulation of data expressed in a quantifiable form, so that "scientific" decisions can be arrived at. This approach had tended to leave out the other descriptions of reality, which are subjective and not quantifiable: memory, emotions, passions, senses, desires, all of which engender motivations and loyalties. It is likely that a more humanistic and culturally aware approach would have prevented the destruction of many English towns and city centre by insensitive planning in the 1950s and 1960s' (15). These elements have completely disappeared from the contemporary Creative City agenda.

78. Cf. P. Saunders, *Social Theory and the Urban Question* (London: Hutchinson, 1981).

79. Harvey positions Soft City as a key moment in the emergence of postmodernity. D. Harvey, *The Condition of Postmodernity: An Enquiry into the Origin of Cultural Change* (Oxford: Wiley-Blackwell, 1992).

80. Berman, *All That Is Solid Melts into Air*.

81. The well-known quote used throughout the book is from Marx and Engels's pamphlet, *The Communist Manifesto*, published in London in 1848.

82. J. Jacob, *Cities and the Wealth of Nations* (New York: Vintage, 1985).

83. Henri Lefebvre, and later Manuel Castells, saw this exemplified in the events of 1968 in France and elsewhere. H. Lefebvre, *The Production of Space*, trans. D. Nicholson-Smith (Oxford: Blackwell, 1992); M. Castells, *The City and the Grassroots: A Cross-Cultural Theory of Urban Social Movements* (Oakland: University of California Press, 1983).

84. J. Jacobs, *Cities and the Wealth of Nations: Principles of Economic Life* (New York: Vintage Books, 1985).

85. This is the moment of *Blade Runner*, and also the world of 'steampunk', with the key film *Brazil* (Dir. Terry Gilliam) released in 1985.

86. Sharon Zukin pointed to the growing influence of historical preservation societies in the 1970s, and their widened scope to include the kind of nineteenth-century industrial buildings ('lofts') found in SoHo. S. Zukin, *Loft-Living: Culture and Capital in Urban Change* (New York: Rutgers University Press, 1989).

87. The Convent Garden struggle was where Charles Landry started out. Cf. C. Landry, D. Morley, R. Southwood and P. Wright, *What a Way to Run a Railroad: An Analysis of Radical Failure* (London: Comedia, 1985).

88. Cf. S. Zukin, *Landscapes of Power: From Detroit to Disney World* (Berkeley: University of California Press, 1991).

89. Lefebvre, *Production of Space*.

90. Spatial fix is from D. Harvey, *The Limits to Capital* (Oxford: Basil Blackwell, 1982).

91. Manuel Castells's three volumes included in M. Castells, *The Information Age: Economy, Society, and Culture* (Oxford: Wiley-Blackwell, 1996).

92. Cf. M. Castells, 'European Cities, the Informational Society, and the Global Economy', *New Left Review* 204 (1994): 18–32; M. Castells and P. Hall, *Technopoles of the World: The Making of 21st Century Industrial Complexes* (London: Routledge, 1994). On sticky places, etc., cf. O'Connor, 'A Special Kind of City Knowledge'.

93. P. Hall, *Cities in Civilisation* (New York: Pantheon, 1998).

94. Ibid., 3.

95. R. Williams, 'Culture Is Ordinary', in *Studies in Culture: An Introductory Reader*, ed. A. Gray and J. McGuigan (London: Arnold, [1958] 1997), 5–14.

96. I. Taylor, K. Evans and P. Fraser, *A Tale of Two Cities: Global Change, Local Feeling and Everyday Life in the North of England: A Study in Manchester and Sheffield* (London: Routledge, 1996), 5. Cf. also O'Connor, 'A Special Kind of City Knowledge'.

97. O. Negt and A. Kluge, *Public Sphere and Experience: Towards an Analysis of the Bourgeois and Proletarian Public Sphere* (Minneapolis: University of Minnesota Press, 1993).

98. Cf. S. Liang, 'Amnesiac Monument, Nostalgic Fashion: Shanghai's New Heaven and Earth', *Wasafiri* 23, no. 3 (2008): 47–55.

99. Pan, *Shanghai Style*, 10.

100. Ibid., 6.

101. H. Lu, *Beyond the Neon Lights: Everyday Shanghai in the Early Twentieth Century* (Berkeley: University of California Press, 1999), 3123.

102. Lee, *Shanghai Modern*, 315.

103. S. Liang, 'Where the Courtyard Meets the Street: Spatial Culture of Li Neighbourhoods, 1870–1900', *Journal of the Society of Architectural Historians* 67, no. 4 (2008): 483–503; Greenspan, *Shanghai Future*, 122.

104. Pan, *Shanghai Style*, 5.

105. As Abbas suggested, 'preservation is something more complex than just a question of the past remembered: in Shanghai, the past allows the present to pursue the future; hence "memory" itself is select and fissured, sometimes indistinguishable from amnesia'. Abbas, 'Cosmopolitan De-scriptions', 780.

106. M. Hansen, *Babel and Babylon: Spectatorship in American Silent Film* (Cambridge, MA: Harvard University Press, 1991), xvii.

107. P. Hall, 'Creative Cities and Economic Development', *Urban Studies* 37, no. 4 (2000): 639–49, 646.

108. Cf. J. O'Connor and X. Gu, 'Developing a Creative Cluster in a Post-industrial City: CIDS and Manchester', *The Information Society* 26, no. 2 (2010): 124–36

109. 'Retrofuturism', in Lagerkvist, 'The Future Is Here'; 'Retromodernity' in Greenspan, *Shanghai Future*, xiii.

110. Or 'agrarian-oriented national integration' in Nick Land's words, quoted in Greenspan, *Shanghai Future*, xxiii.

111. See account in Greenspan, *Shanghai Future*, xxiii.

112. F. Dikotter, *The Age of Openness: China before Mao* (Berkeley: University of California Press, 2008), 3.

113. A. Ong, 'Chinese Modernities: Narratives of Nation and of Capitalism', in *Ungrounded Empires: The Cultural Politics of Chinese Transnationalism*, ed. A. Ong and D. Nonini (London: Routledge, 1997), 171–202, 172.

114. Abbas, 'Cosmopolitan De-scriptions', 781.

115. Lee had talked about the return of an 'urban cultural sensibility rooted in cosmopolitanism'. Lee, *Shanghai Modern*, 339.

116. Mao Zedong, 'Talks at the Yan'an Forum on Literature and Art', in *Modern Chinese Literary Thought: Writings on Literature, 1983–1945*, ed. K. A. Denton (Stanford: Stanford University Press), 458–84.

117. J. Fewsmith, *China Since Tiananmen: The Politics of Transition: From Deng Xiaoping to Hu Jintao* (New York: Cambridge University Press, 2008).

118. Landry and Bianchini, *The Creative City*, 15.

119. Raban, *Soft City*, 102. Cf. O'Connor, 'A Special Kind of City Knowledge'.

120. An extended discussion of this can be found in L. Scheen, *Shanghai Literary Imaginings: A City in Transformation* (Leiden, NL: IIAS Publications, 2019), 155–200

121. A. Elliott and J. Urry, *Mobile Lives* (London: Routledge, 2010).

122. 'As a conceptual entity, contact space indicates a sociological spatial exploration of how contact can be initiated, enabled and maintained, and thus how the society needs to be configured in order to initiate, enable and maintain contact'. J. Vaide, *Contact Space Shanghai: The Chinese Dream and the Production of a New Society* (doctoral thesis, Lund University, Sweden, 2015), 18, https://lup.lub.lu.se/search/publication/10422d86-b14e-408a-a051-f56c89dc4255. Accessed 4 October 2019. Cf. also M. L. Pratt, 'Arts of

the Contact Zone', in *Ways of Reading: An Anthology of Writers*, ed. D. Bartholomae and A. Petrosky (New York: Bedford Books of St. Martin's Press, 1999), 33–44.

123. Cf. T. Rayns, *In the Mood for Love*, BFI Film Classics (London: British Film Institute, 2015).

124. A. Wang, *The Song of Everlasting Sorrow: A Novel of Shanghai*, trans. M. Berry and S. C. Egan (New York: Columbia University Press, 2008); I. Ho-yin Fong, '(Re-)Reading Shanghai's Futures in Ruins: Through the Legend of an (Extra-)Ordinary Woman in The Song of Everlasting Sorrow: A Novel of Shanghai', *Culture Unbound* 4, no. 1 (2012): 229–48; Scheen, *Shanghai Literary Imaginings*, 174–84.

125. On nostalgia for Shanghai Modernist writers amongst contemporary Chinese citizens, cf. J. Vaide, *Contact Space Shanghai*, 162–69.

126. J. Xiao, 'Belated Reunion? Eileen Chang, Late Style and World Literature', *New Left Review* 111 (2018): 89–110.

127. We should note that both the 'uncanny' return of an unmediated past to the present, and the uncoupling of literature from the exigencies of the political, was something Frederick Jameson had identified in the postmodern moment. *Kiss of the Spider Woman*, a 1985 film, had been used by Jameson to announce a new kind of postmodern cultural politics which was deeply ambivalent about politics as such. Cf. Jameson, *Postmodernism*.

128. Cf. J. Farrer, "New Shanghailanders" or "New Shanghainese": Western Expatriates' Narratives of Emplacement in Shanghai', *Journal of Ethnic and Migration Studies* 36, no. 8 (2010): 1211–28; T. Schilbach, *Shanghai Cosmo-Politics: The Young Middle Class in the Global City* (Ph.D. thesis, University of Sydney, Sydney, 2014), 43, 106–07,111–14, https://www.academia.edu/25586961/Shanghai_cosmo-politics_the_young_middle_class_in_the_global_city. Accessed 4 October 2019.

129. K. Iwabuchi, *Recentering Globalization: Popular Culture and Japanese Transnationalism* (Durham, NC: Duke University Press, 2002); J. Dai, 'Imagined Nostalgia', in *Postmodernism and China*, ed. A. Dirlik and X. Zhang (Durham, NC: Duke University Press, 2000), 205–21.

130. A. Lagerkvist, *Media and Memory in New Shanghai: Western Performances of Futures Past* (London: Palgrave Macmillan, 2013), 20.

131. Cf. J. Farrer, '"New Shanghailanders" or "New Shanghainese"', on the Cosmopolitan Appropriation of "Old Shanghai"'.

132. J. G. Ballard, *Miracles of Life: From Shanghai to Shepperton* (New York: Liveright Publications, 2008). On the indifference of Shanghai dwellers to the pre-socialist city cf. H. Lu, 'Nostalgia for the Future: The Resurgence of an Alienated Culture in China', *Pacific Affairs* 75, no. 2 (2002): 169–86.

133. J. Stock, 'Reconsidering the Past: Zhou Xuan and the Rehabilitation of Early Twentieth-Century Popular Music', *Asian Music* 26, no. 2 (1995): 119–35.

134. Abbas, 'Cosmopolitan De-scriptions', 780. Cf. Schilbach, *Shanghai Cosmo-Politics,* for a discussion of the nostalgia of disappearance.

135. Ibid., 340.

136. W. -H. Yeh, *Shanghai Splendor: Economic Sentiments and the Making of Modern China, 1843–1949* (Berkeley: University of California Press, 2007), 211.

137. Ibid., 211–12.

138. M. Featherstone, *Consumer Culture and Postmodernism* (London: Sage, 1991).

139. In promoting particular modes of consumption as the 'art of living', and in selling the idea that one defines one's identity through consumption, tantalizing, if illusory forms of freedom are promised. Thus propaganda strategies that play into the insecurities about self-image are especially lucrative in Shanghai. Robin Visser, *Cities Surround the Countryside: Urban Aesthetics in Postsocialist China* (Durham, NC: Duke University Press, 2010), 179.

140. On urban mediatization, cf. S. McQuire, *The Media City: Media, Architecture and Urban Space* (London: Sage, 2008).

141. J. -L. Rocca, *The Making of the Chinese Middle Class: Small Comfort and Great Expectations* (Basingstoke and New York: Palgrave Macmillan, 2017), 11. Cf. Y. Guo, 'Class, Stratum and Group: The Politics of Description and Prescription', in *The New Rich in China. Future Rulers, Present Lives*, ed. D. S. G. Goodman (London: Routledge, 2008), 38–52; J. Unger, 'China's Conservative Middle Class', *Far Eastern Economic Review* (April 2006): 27–31.

142. A partnership with Centre Pompidou and directed by Li Zhonghui, Head of the local authority owned development company behind the West Bund, a classic 'amphibian institution', https://www.theartnewspaper.com/news/centre-pompidou-chief-outlines-challenges-of-setting-up-a-satellite-in-shanghai-including-censorship-threats-and-settling-the-project-costs. Accessed 10 November 2019.

143. Cf. N. Dynon, 'Better City, Better Life? The Ethics of Branding the Model City at the 2010 Shanghai World Expo', *Place Branding and Public Diplomacy* 7, no. 3 (2011): 185–96; L. Kong, 'Cultural Icons and Urban Development in Asia: Economic Imperative, National Identity and Global City Status', *Political Geography* 26, no. 4 (2007): 383–404; J. Wasserstrom, *Global Shanghai, 1850–2010: A History in Fragments* (London: Routledge, 2009). Schilbach, *Shanghai Cosmo-Politics*, 37–95.

144. There are many creative city indexes, Cf. Table A in V. Montalto, C. J. T. Moura, S. Langedijk and M. Saisana, 'Culture Counts: An Empirical Approach to Measure the Cultural and Creative Vitality of European Cities', *Cities* 89 (2019): 167–85. On indexes and the creative city cf. D. Ponzini and U. Rosi, 'Becoming a Creative City: The Entrepreneurial Mayor, Network Politics and the Promise of an Urban Renaissance', *Urban Studies* 47, no. 5 (2010): 1037–57.

145. Liang, 'Amnesiac Monument, Nostalgic Fashion'.

146. S. He, 'State-sponsored Gentrification Under Market Transition', *Urban Affairs Review* 43, no. 2 (2007): 171–98; X. Ren, 'Forward to the Past: Historical Preservation in Globalizing Shanghai', *City & Community* 7, no. 1 (2008): 23–43; A. Wing Tai Wai, 'Place

Promotion and Iconography in Shanghai's Xintiandi', *Habitat International* 30 (2006): 245–60.

147. Cf. Greenspan, *Shanghai Future*, 113. On Ralph Lauren, see W. Gibson, *Pattern Recognition* (New York: Putnam, 2003).

148. Abbas, 'Cosmopolitan De-scriptions', 784.

149. Ibid.

150. Ibid.

151. P. Brodie, 'Seeing Ghosts: Crisis, Ruin, and the Creative Industries', *Continuum* (2019): DOI: 10.1080/10304312.2019.1643452.

152. R. Lloyd, *Neo-Bohemia: Art and Commerce in the Postindustrial City* (London: Routledge, 2006).

153. Abbas, 'Cosmopolitan De-scriptions', 765.

154. Cf. two early critiques: A. Amin, D. Massey and N. Thrift, *Cities for the Many Not for the Few* (Cambridge: Polity, 2000); Robinson, *Ordinary Cities*.

155. M. Fisher, *The Ghosts of My Life* (London: Zero Book, 2014), 50.

156. L. Boltanski and E. Chiapello, *The New Spirit of Capitalism* (London: Verso, 2005).

157. Abbas, 'Cosmopolitan De-scriptions', 785.

158. Ibid., 786.

159. Arbitrage 'refers to the larger historical lessons that can be drawn from our experiences of the city [...] Cultural arbitrage may be a way of creating a global culture worthy of the name.' Ibid., 785–86.

7

Reforming the Culture System

Introduction

In Chapter 5, we examined the post-1978 reforms where extension of the market became synonymous with socialist modernization of the 'productive forces', and in which, after 1989, popular debate around the nature of the reforms was restricted. At the same time, we suggested that, alongside markets, the reforms required subjects, both 'productive and governable', citizen-consumers imbued with *suzhi*, a new kind of middle-class 'human quality' or worth.[1] In this chapter, we will look at the transformation of cultural policy since the 1978 reforms, focusing in particular on the idea of the cultural industries, followed, just after the turn of the millennium, by that of the creative industries. We will suggest that the Chinese government, for the historical reasons we explored above, gives a high priority to culture as central to governance. As such, though 'creativity' is a quality to be prized, China was resistant to the full implications of the 'creativity agenda'.

Unlike in many European countries, and among global agencies such as UNESCO and UNCTAD, the term 'cultural industries' was not displaced by 'creative industries'. In fact, this latter term ran into a number of obstacles after it appeared in China in 2005, being adopted in selected areas (Shanghai at the forefront) only. Nonetheless, the 'arrival' of the 'creative industries', at the same moment as China was formalizing its full embrace of culture's economic dimension, was important, as it brought with it a renewed emphasis from the West on the kinds of reforms the country required to fully benefit from the 'creative economy'. In suggesting a new dynamic of socio-economic and cultural transformation, this global discourse of 'creativity' marked a shift from a 'classical' liberal to a neo-liberal critique of China. If the first focused on markets, liberties and the democratic public sphere, the second was more interested in markets, consumer sovereignty and innovation. The replacement of 'culture' by 'creativity' is, as we argued in Chapter 1, emblematic of this shift.

Throughout this book, we have used culture in two senses. On the one hand, the anthropological sense, captured by China as a 'civilizational state' with deep-seated socio-structural patterns and forms of thought. On the other, culture as a system of production of symbolic objects, as in our account of Shanghai Modern. The broad notion of the 'cultural industries' brings these two senses together. They can be found in Raymond Williams's *Keywords* of 1976, where 'culture' describes both 'a general process of intellectual, spiritual and aesthetic develop-ment and (almost indistinguishably) 'the works and practices of intellectual and especially artistic activity'. A third usage of 'culture' 'indicates a particular way of life, whether of a people, a period, a group, or humanity in general'.[2] Opposing 'culture as a way of life' to the 'works and practices' of artistic activity animated much of the radical community arts movement of the 1970s itself linked to older avant-garde tropes of dissolving the barriers between 'art and life'.[3] It became an opposition with which Williams's work was closely associated, as 'culture is ordinary' and 'culture as a whole way of life' became recurrent mottos for 'British Cultural Studies'.[4] Williams's usage was profoundly linked to the wholesale exten-sion of 'cultural citizenship', which had accelerated after 1945, deepening into a more politically contested space in the 1960s, with Williams's arguing for a 'socialist common culture'.[5] The discipline of cultural studies came out of that space in which 'ways of life' were being significantly altered by people's increasing involvement in the consumption and the production of cultural goods, mostly in the form of commercial popular culture.[6] It was this that lay behind the policy interventions around the cultural industries we noted in Chapter 1. What kind of policies should be adopted in a democratic polity where the majority of cultural production and consumption was taking place outside the state subsidized system?

This policy question emerged as the anthropological ('way of life') and the symbolic system ('intellectual-artistic works and practices') were increasingly run together.[7] The situation was addressed academically by both 'political economy' and 'cultural studies', giving rise to an exaggerated cleavage between the two. The former focused on the political economy of the system of cultural produc-tion and distribution, with a strong emphasis on media and communications and their impacts on the public sphere of democratic citizenship. The latter were more focused on the sphere of consumption, and the creative space ('coding/decoding') afforded individuals and groups to expand and transform their subjectivities and ways of belonging, emphasizing the symbolic-aesthetic over the political-informational.[8] The political imaginary of the cultural industries, we could say, involved both a new 'mixed economy' approach to expanding the public sphere and cultural citizenship, and a sense that new forms of symbolic consumption and production were transforming individuals and communities, especially as the structures of Keynesianism-Fordism began to break down.

The grounds were shifted by the 'creative industries'. The symbolic and the anthropological notions of culture were recombined differently. It is not that cul-ture was simply reduced to its economic impact (or at least, not at first). As we

218

tried to show in Chapter 1, the 'creative industries' as a new industrial sector was not just important for 'jobs and growth' but mobilized an economic imaginary around creativity and innovation as socially transformational forces. The creative industries drew on a symbolic system of communication and information, values and tacit understanding, institutions and shared practices, affective and cognitive knowledge (Bourdieu's 'cultural field').[9] But the public policy outcome was no longer to be the articulation and communication of meanings, rather the generation of creative economic subjects and practices. The resultant societal transformation was no longer about extending the expressive symbolic capabilities of individuals and groups but an expanded capacity to 'create' whose ultimate achievement was entrepreneurial monetization and 'innovation'. The common space of symbolization, an expanded (and, for Williams, socialist) public sphere would be privatized, in the sense that only 'expressed preferences' counted, demanding of the public policy system not direct collective provision but the facilitation of market-based, legally regulated consumer choice in culture.[10]

A market in cultural goods has been central to liberalism, where 'print capitalism' was deemed the necessary, if not sufficient, basis for a democratic public sphere. If modernization equates to 'Western-style' capitalism, then the production and consumption of cultural goods and services are set to play a catalytic role in China's transition. Alternatively, if an authoritarian system restricts this, then doubt is cast on China's ability ever to make the transition to liberal democratic capitalism. For as we have seen, the entanglement of markets and freedom, artistic autonomy and innovation, entrepreneurship and creativity in the 'creative economy' has deep roots in Western self-understanding as having privileged access to the dynamic forces of historical creativity.[11] From this perspective, Red Creative is an impossible conjunction.

We have already had an occasion, in Chapter 3, to distinguish 'print commerce' – the artisanal system of market production which underpinned the classical 'bourgeois public sphere' – and 'print capitalism', a high-investment industrialized system that took off in the last third of the nineteenth century. Habermas's account of the public sphere was an attempt (however flawed) to restate its substantive value in the face of an escalating process of commodification introduced by capital's domination of 'the culture industry'.[12] This was also the situation faced by 'political economy' and 'cultural studies' in the 1970s. The plunge towards neo-liberal capitalism hollowed out much of the old social, cultural and political values of liberalism and social democracy within which this commodified cultural system was constrained and opposed.

The 'creative industries' – which we have suggested are closely aligned with neo-liberalism – continue the liberal trope of the market as bottom-up democratic culture versus top-down statist ideology but shifts away from the democratic-symbolic to market efficiency. Justin Lewis and Tony Miller, taking a Foucauldian approach, see cultural policy as 'a site for the production of cultural citizens, with the cultural industries providing not only a realm of representations about oneself and others, but a series of rationales for particular types of conduct'; it is 'a means of governance, of formatting public collective subjectivity'.[13] The 'creativity economy', we suggest, involves the reduction of cultural to economic value, the increased commodification of the lifeworld and the retooling of the self in the new spirit of creative capitalism. At the same time, it organizes subjects not at the collective-symbolic level but in terms of micro-behaviours, shaped and aggregated by markets, and latterly, data technologies. The 'creative industries', as part of a neo-liberal system, is not simply about 'markets' but about new kinds of subjects in a polity that no longer looks to the shared collective-symbolic realm for its effectivity. Closely linked to a version of cultural studies which sees 'nation-building' as both patriarchal and autarchic, where the very possibility of a 'collective horizon of social experience' is in doubt, the neo-liberal subject can be effectively governed by markets and their institutional-legal frameworks, rather than at the national-democratic-symbolic level.[14]

We shall see below how the introduction of a market in culture and communication worked within China's socialist market economy, for a party-state that would insist on its continued control of the ideological and industrial 'commanding heights'. For liberals (ideology/censorship) and neo-liberals (industry/markets), state control marks a limit to China's ability to 'catch-up'. However, both ignore the ways in which cultural or creative industries actually work in neo-liberal capitalism, especially at the global level. These have less and less to do with notions of the public sphere, or some 'bottom-up' entrepreneurial capitalism. They are large-scale, complex, highly capitalized global industrial structures in which finance, telecommunications, logistics, intellectual property, trade treaties and a complex division of labour are combined. This is something China increasingly recognized, and its policies to develop the cultural system often display a better knowledge of how these industries work than do its Western critics. Indeed, China, along with other 'developmental states', still has available industrial policy levers in ways that countries such as the United Kingdom or Australia do not.[15] The transformation of the 'creative economy' by digital technologies, which was to allow the West to outpace its manufacturing-led competitors, has provided the Chinese state with new resources of both industrial development and social control.[16] Indeed, Xi Jinping's 'Internet Plus' policy, introduced in 2015, takes a 'developmental state' approach to the 'sharing economy', promoting 'mass entrepreneurship and innovation' at industrial scale.[17] China's share of world trade in cultural goods and services has continued to rise since the turn of the millennium, with the cultural industries firmly enshrined as one of its 'pillar industries'.[18]

How then to understand, given this overwhelmingly economic policy rationale for the cultural 'sector', China's persistent concern with preserving 'core socialist values' and the central role of ideology in the culture system? A final, increasingly anachronistic bastion of the party-state, blocking the further progress of liberal capitalism in China and its full integration into the global system? Or might we see its concern with 'culture as ideology', upon which it founds its claims to legitimacy, as also keeping open a collective representational space of a 'shared symbolic efficacy', in which contestation around a common future might take place? If a residual 'socialism' and a strong 'civilization' project in China does set some limits to neo-liberal governance in the sphere of the economy, we would also need to assess how far they might also allow a common space of culture and contestation.

We have seen in recent years what we might call, after Polanyi, a 'double movement' of culture, a reactionary countermovement involving an assertion of nativism and cultural essentialism, as part of a desire for a protective nation state in the face of globalization and its associated elites.[19] This has animated much of the recent anti-China shift in the West, as China is blamed for exploiting, to the disadvantage of the populations of the West, the global trading system to which it was admitted.[20] This 'revenge of culture' has been accompanied by a powerful symbolism of cultural belonging, but now mobilized against an open, deliberative public sphere, and any transformative vision for culture.[21] China's retention of an ideological-symbolic mode of governance is portrayed as anachronistic and oppressive (a combination of Communist and Confucian despotism), but might it provide for a residual, even imaginary, space of the social, pointing us beyond the neo-liberal horizon?

Return of the intellectuals

Until the reform period, culture was produced and distributed by state-employed artists and intellectuals. The system that was in place in 1978 had evolved from the Yan'an party base (1935–47) in which culture, and the intellectuals who created it, were brought under the direct control of the party-state. This was extended across the People's Republic after 1949. What some have called the 'propaganda state', concerned with 'social engineering', was by no means a monolithic system.[22] There were complex divisions within the state, the big players being the Ministries of Culture and of Propaganda, the People's Liberation Army (PLA) and the artist associations. These were all in competition, their fortunes waxing and waning with the political tide.[23]

Richard Curt Kraus gives a good account of the real gains for artists and intellectuals brought by the 1949 Revolution. Prior to that, only a handful of artists and writers ever made any money. The era of Shanghai Modern, as we saw, turfed the scholar-administrators onto an underdeveloped market that provided few opportunities to make a living. After 1949, and following the Soviet system, artists and intellectuals received full-time jobs, with time and space to work, along with the broad range of benefits from their allotted work units (*danwei*).[24]

Pang Laikwan makes a Gramscian distinction between 'organic intellectuals' – all kinds of technical-professional experts serving the regime – and 'traditional intellectuals', who perform pedagogical duties 'generation after generation', an unchanging 'moral anchor'. Traditional intellectuals present themselves as autonomous and independent, preserving a historical continuity that can outlast regime change.[25] Pang suggests that 'traditional' intellectuals (artists, writers, historians) in the first seventeen years of the PRC did not want to be technical experts (the *zhuan*, or professional elite), but nor could they be completely identified with the political (*hong*, or red) elite.[26] For Pang, this 'structural tension', between critical and moral distance from power and 'usefulness', would lead to their demise.

We do not fully subscribe to this Gramscian opposition, which is in many ways specific to a European historical trajectory. Gramsci himself saw the workers' movement as generating its own 'organic intellectuals' who would be more than either 'traditional intellectuals' (ultimately defenders of the status quo) or just party functionaries. In Chapters 3 and 4 we suggested the key notion for Chinese intellectual formation was not 'autonomy' in the Western sense of that word. The intellectual was to serve the people, and they sought to do this (there were few other options) through engagement with the party-state. The 'structural tension' between the 'intellectual' professional sphere of competence and the party was certainly real. They might serve the party, but the intellectual-artist was also the guardian of the civilizational project, with a specific expertise in the aesthetic-symbolic field. Yet this occupation of a difficult – and at times fatal – position was not necessarily some categorical confusion between two mutually incompatible functions. It was a tension that had always come with the territory.

In Chapter 3, we suggested that the stark contrast often made between otherworldly, 'traditional' cosmopolitan aesthetes and the uncultured, instrumental party bosses in Yan'an ignored the more sophisticated intellectual revolutionary work going on in Shanghai. Operations directed from Yan'an demanded basic work that could appeal to the peasantry, and that could be easily replicated so as to be performed by hastily trained performance troupes. In these circumstances, Shanghai intellectuals could be an expensive luxury. But post-1949 cultural production involved much more complex negotiations between intellectuals and the party-state, as a national-scale cultural system, including the preservation and conservation of traditional culture and the elaboration of a 'new-democratic' culture, was established. They were 'useful', in two ways. Their adherence to the leadership of the party conferred an important legitimacy (similar to the way the USSR used intellectuals in their 'popular front' organizations), but they were actually needed to elaborate a cultural system in a Maoist regime that, more than in the USSR, believed in the ability of the symbolic to define material existence. Artists and writers, despite the censorship and rectification campaigns, 'came to form a privileged sector that enjoyed a degree of freedom, respect and authority not readily available to most ordinary citizens'.[27]

The 1978 reforms opened against a backdrop in which this contested space of cultural professionalism had been violently attacked in the Cultural Revolution. The intellectuals had been added to an expanded list of nine 'class enemies', occupying the lowest, most 'useless' rung as 'stinking number nine' (*chou laojiu*), demonized as 'cow ghosts and snake gods' (*niugui shesen*), representatives of the dead old order now returned to haunt the living.[28] They were gradually rehabilitated from the early 1970s, as their essential role in modernization was recognized by the party. With the reopening of the universities in 1977 and the subsequent launch of the reform period, both the 'organic' ('Red Engineers') and 'traditional' intellectuals returned to pre-eminence. In both groups, there was a deep-seated desire to blot out the chaos of the Cultural Revolution and to reaffirm the bond with the party in the project of socialist modernization. Deng's reforms too were built on a repudiation of mass participation, which further bound intellectuals to them. The Cultural Revolution had sought to break the division between intellectual and manual labour, undermining the professionalism of the artist-intellectual by the promotion of amateurs and mass participation. The return of artists and writers, in a period of liberalization, was widely seen as a moment in which their professional and ethical role was to be resumed.

The reforms launched a decade of vivid ideas and debates about the past, present and future of China, dubbed 'culture fever'.[29] The Ministry of Culture moved back to a central place within the state, after a decade of marginalization by the PLA and the Ministry of Propaganda, though tellingly the latter asserted control over media and communications sector. There were of course limits to the debate, with two periods of half-hearted counter attacks around 'spiritual pollution' and 'bourgeois liberalism' in 1983 and 1987. Western liberals interpret the 'culture fever' – where debates around Marxist humanism managed to suck in huge undifferentiated drafts of foreign theory and culture – as a transitional moment in which a Marxist 'code' was necessarily used to explore possibilities of reform, which would necessarily leave that Marxism behind.[30] Other observers are less sure. Pang looks to Derrida's argument in *Specters of Marx*, where the collapse of dogmatic Marxism and the regimes that sustained it allowed a new, more open Marxism to emerge, 'understood as possibility not metaphysics'.[31] For Chinese intellectuals, it was probably only when they were displaced from their dominant position to the subdued position – only when they became ghosts – that they could regain the assigned duties of being Marxist intellectuals, to discuss history, rupture and restructuration.[32]

This, Pang says, did not happen. Despite their sufferings, they avoided thinking about 'the relationship between ideology and writing, between the state and the intellectual'.[33] This failure to explore 'the troubled relationship between culture and politics' is a common criticism of the rehabilitated intellectuals who returned to serve the party-state.[34] The failure was only exacerbated when the cultural realm became marketized, which far from bringing liberation brought more subservience to the status quo. Pang suggests that we should 'negate intellectuals as defenders of our polity and humanity', and that in contemporary China 'probably only ordinary people can rekindle the dynamics between culture and politics in their ordinary lives'.[35]

Intellectuals and market reforms

The Cultural Revolution is mostly treated as the ground zero for a modern Chinese culture and polity. Laikwan Pang's work is part of a growing willingness to re-examine these events, taking seriously the powerful emotional and cognitive forces which Mao unleashed in pursuit of his political vision.[36] Though framed in violent, manipulated and ultimately cynical fashion, the popular aspiration for some form of control over their lives, for a real sense of affective unity in an enormous imagined community outside the channels provided by the bureaucratic party-state, was deep-seated. It tapped into Mao's un-Leninist vision of the 'mass line', as well as other forms of popular revolt going back to the Taiping Rebellion. The post-Mao leadership were extremely anxious to exit such chaotic politics, as indeed were an exhausted and cynical population. The fear of the chaotic masses fed into the fatal decision to violently repress the Tiananmen movement. Intellectuals also feared such (literally life-threatening) chaos and in the 1980s were ready to reoccupy a role as partner to the state's modernization project. But if they were not ready to engage in a radical appraisal of culture and politics, nor were they ready to look too closely at the contradictions between their ethical-political aspirations as enlightened humanists in service of socialist modernization, and the social space they occupied as a privileged professional class.[37] The returning traditional intellectuals had little time for the aspirations to popular participation attested, in however distorted form, by the enthusiasms of the Cultural Revolution. In many ways such a popular 'rectification' was to be forced on them by the creation of a market in the cultural system.

Much as liberal intellectuals in China and outside wanted to see a 'civil society', the fact was that both their livelihoods and their universalizing aspirations were linked to the project of the party-state. As the reform of the state cultural system accelerated after 1992, artists and writers, along with market-embracing liberal humanists, who had celebrated the return to their rightful pre-eminent position in the 1980s, experienced a rapid sense of marginalization. Many simply lost their job or suffered a decline in wages, though there were winners among those who 'took the plunge' (*xia hai*) into the market. These commercial opportunities would increase as state- and private-owned enterprises expanded, especially in publishing and media. But the real sting for intellectuals was the decline in their social position.

The post-1992 market acceleration was experienced by many as an ending of the traditional role of the 'Confucian' intellectual in China. Tiananmen profoundly shocked the intellectuals, and the relaunch of the reforms under the sign of depoliticized modernization confirmed that the enlightened humanists were no longer required by the party.[38] There was a growth of professionalization, as intellectuals became experts, academics, members of policy think-tanks, administrative technicians and so on.[39] These were all part of a system with little need for the input of 'public intellectuals'. As Kraus has it, the 'historical domination of the humanist literati has ended, and the new model for artists is the technical expert of science and engineering'.[40] The Red Engineers – which included the burgeoning legion of professional economists – had little time for 'culture workers', at least not until the turn of the millennium when the 'cultural industries' emerged as a clear policy objective and formalized a new set of 'industry' professionals.

Kraus, along with Timothy Cheek, see this as a kind of 'normalisation', the end of Chinese exceptionalism – 'welcome to our world', so to speak.[41] Cheek characterizes the result as a 'managed public sphere', in which there is a certain autonomy but clear limits. His focus is on 'public intellectuals', whereas Kraus's is on artists, or what we might now call 'cultural workers'. Kraus uses Bourdieu's cultural field to explore the emerging tension between art and commerce ('The Price of Beauty') and sees a degree of aesthetic autonomy being opened up as 'literary' or 'artistic' production became somewhat sidelined by the market. Commercial success may elude them, but, as in the West, artists could seek a more exalted status based on their 'restricted production'. Yet 'art for art's sake', he suggests, has limited appeal in China. Artists might be happy to escape the close day-to-day political demands of the Maoist years, but they retained that ethical commitment to a larger political purpose we discussed in Chapters 4 and 5. 'Consecration' by the state thus plays a much more pronounced role in China, and Bourdieu's cultural field acquires a new vector. 'The mission of moral tutelage thus offers a commercial-political polarity parallel to [Bourdieu's] commercial-aesthetic dualism'.[42]

Nonetheless, Kraus suggests that this second polarity is disappearing; renouncing their ethical mission, artists now work as technical experts with a 'focus on skilful manoeuvring for larger budgets for their fine art academies or song-and-dance troupes'.[43] We suggest that this is not so straightforward. First, this parallel state-oriented polarity is still operative in the cultural field, though it is no longer so closely tied to traditional art-form institutions. The burgeoning field of contemporary art, a major motor for urban regeneration and global branding in the big cities, has vastly complicated systems of state consecration. Second, and related to this, Kraus's account restricts the practice of intellectuals to the sphere of 'high culture' rather than locating them in the expanding new world of 'mass' or commercial culture. Though, to be fair, this is also a problem with Bourdieu's own writing, which failed to account for the interconnections established between art and popular culture in the 1960s and 1970s.

Many professional artists and writers certainly did find the 1990s difficult. The accelerated push to a market in culture ignored the absence of that complex field of cultural production that had grown up in the West and which provided an 'ecology' – agents, gallery owners, impresarios, intermediaries, venues, materials and craft support companies, distribution, marketing, and also the critical and communication field (press, gallery openings, literary magazines, art schools) – within which cultural workers could seek a living.[44] Little of this cultural field existed in China before the turn of the millennium outside the state-intellectual structure.[45] However, as the cultural industries began to expand, cultural work did too. In the interstices of the market-state, new forms of corporate, or 'complex', professionals emerged – cultural workers operating within extended, often global, divisions of labour – including the 'independents' or 'creative entrepreneurs', which we will discuss in the next chapter.[46] It is to this space, we will suggest, that many of the ethical-political issues faced by the 'humanist literati' have migrated.

The rise of the cultural market was a kind of revenge of the masses on the intellectuals; certainly not as violently as in the Cultural Revolution, but no less devastating. Many liberal humanists, who had extolled the market in the 1980s, now found it difficult to negotiate making a living, managing a reputation and making their voices heard. They bemoaned the vulgarization of commercial popular culture and 'the culture industry'.[47] After 1992, the commercial cultural sector exploded, with an unprecedented proliferation of cultural goods. TV dramas and soaps, popular magazines and novels, new forms of Western- and East Asian-influenced rock music, video games – all took off while the commodification of everyday life, saturated by the commercial symbols which a new advertising industry were producing, opened a new world of popular culture. It flowed into the new urban centres (of the sort we discussed in the last chapter), but also into rural areas, where television viewing became common for the first time, transforming relations to the city, between generations and to traditional selves.[48]

A younger generation of intellectuals adopted a more 'postmodern' or 'postcolonial' position on the new market culture.[49] For these, the 'grand narratives' of Chinese modernization, as well as the universal values of humanism, had been pushed aside by the commercially oriented desires of the mass market. Xudong Zhang suggests that the theoretical lexicon of 'deconstruction', 'postcolonialism' and other Western imports allowed younger Chinese intellectuals to reject Western civilization as universal. The expansion of mass culture opened up the space to explore a distinct Chinese modernity, one which could also be coupled to a new popular nationalism. Liberal intellectuals clung onto 'universal (i.e. Western) civilization', deeply distrusting a popular nationalism that they saw as threatening China's integration into global capitalism, just as they saw mass culture as destructive of elite culture. Though Tiananmen shocked them, they had moved to a quiet dissent, still invested in the State's modernizing project. But the state increasingly promoted the expansion of mass consumer culture, and were happy to utilize and stimulate popular nationalism, within appropriate bounds.

The expansion of the space of 'popular' or 'mass' culture represents, for the 'postmodern' intellectuals, a liberation of everyday life. Marketization, commodification and consumption delivered, it was said, what so-called enlightenment only promised. Individuality, diversity, pluralism and the expansion of cultural life are being fulfilled in the market, 'the poetic aspiration for a "civilisation" and a "life of abundance" designed by the discourse of modernity have now become a realistic choice in the everyday sphere itself'.[50]

It was this that excited Western observers, who could only see this as a transition to a Western capitalist culture, though perhaps with local quirks. The introduction of the market for culture and communications could only be the first step in a transition to a democratic society, as the new middle classes would demand the kinds of cultural consumer goods enjoyed by their counterparts in the West. It was also to be the space in which new Chinese subjectivities might be explored, as the state withdrew from everyday life, allowing new possibilities to unfold for the self, in the ways suggested by the discipline of cultural studies – now increasingly popular across Asia.[51] However, it needs to be said with Wang Hui that much Chinese 'postmodernism' ignored the role of global capital in the reconfiguration of Chinese consumption, and repeats many of the blind spots of a certain 'cultural populism' in cultural studies and in the creative industries discourse.[52] Chinese postmodernists tend to 'identify the production and reproduction of desire as "demands of the people" in the name of mass culture', interpreting the 'social relations determined by capital in the process of marketisation as constituting a neutral, ideology-free "new state of affairs"'.[53] It also, Zhang Xudong suggests, ignores the role of the state in framing these social desires as popular nationalism, both as an assertion of a new Chinese confidence but also claiming the state as a sovereign site of social protection.

For the state is not just repressive but works to constitute the frame within which self-sovereignty operates, under the sign of depoliticization – what Zhang Xudong calls the post-1989 'freezing' of the relationship between state and society, allowing the former to work more efficiently and the latter to 'get rich'. It has undoubtedly been a successful arrangement for many.[54] The 'frozen' relationship at the level of politics was accompanied by an increasing interpenetration of state and society, as the everyday life of market culture 'invades' the state and becomes intermeshed with the radical commodification and capitalization of state apparatuses and institutions. 'On the one hand, mainstream ideology strengthened its control; on the other, the cultural market and industry increasingly shared the power of the apparatuses of classical ideology and constantly transformed this power into capital.'[55]

Reforming China's culture system

That Deng's market reforms would extend to the system of culture was clear from the start, though how exactly this would be done was less so. 'Crossing the river stone by stone' applied here too. The 'other bank' was to be the 'modernisation' of the cultural system, the expanded provision of cultural goods to a country that was, in 1978, an overwhelmingly peasant and poor country. The modernization of culture goes back to the New Culture and May Fourth era, and Mao's 'new-democratic culture' was foundational for the People's Republic.[56] As we saw in the last chapters, Deng looked to a deep-seated Chinese aspiration for the modernization of the productive forces, to build a 'socialist material civilisation'. It would be necessarily accompanied, as superstructure to base, by a 'high-level socialist spiritual civilisation'.[57] This has remained central to the PRC's cultural policy, with Jiang Zemin continuing to assert (as he welcomed 'entrepreneurs' into the party) that the CCP 'should represent the advanced productive forces in society; should represent advanced modern culture; and should represent the interests of the vast majority of the people'.[58] The modernization of the cultural system was, of course, to be a depoliticized process, serving the needs of national development. As Jiang had it, the goal of 'advanced modern culture' is

> to develop national, scientific and popular socialist culture geared to the needs
> of modernization, of the world and of the future so as to provide the spiritual

and intellectual support for the national economic development and social progress.[59]

This was a move away from the direct coupling of culture and politics that had been the hallmark of Mao's approach in which 'culture' was equated with political consciousness, a merger reaching its pinnacle (or nadir) in the Cultural Revolution. The subsequent post-1978 separation meant a certain 'routinization' of cultural work, intellectuals no longer fatally linked to the ebb and flow of intra-party conflicts. Rather, they were given a degree of professional autonomy as the distance from everyday politics increased – Deng, unlike Mao, was not interested in cultural matters.[60] It opened up everyday life to evermore diverse forms of cultural consumption, removing such activities from the intrusive burden of mass politics. However, as we have seen in regard to new urban China, depoliticization went beyond a relaxation of the link between culture and politics, and towards a wholesale corralling of collective cultural practice into a system of individualized consumption; culture was no exception.

'Advanced modern culture' post-1978 was, like much else, to be measured against a Western model, to which China must 'catch-up and surpass'. Emulating a modern US-style cultural system, in terms of access to television sets and stations, magazine and books, popular music and films for a new prosperous China, became a major goal for the state.[61] Welcome as this new cultural diversity was in many respects, it also aimed at defusing political activity through a new cultural system of commodified entertainment, something bemoaned, in the 1990s at least, by many party officials and intellectuals. At the same time, the party-state was absolutely determined to ensure adherence to 'core socialist values', and it would do so by controlling, in various ways, the most important sectors of the cultural system.[62] That is, it would seek to control media and communications (TV, film, radio, press) and the 'classic' cultural forms of publishing, performance and visual arts. Thus, it retained control over culture as a site of collective consciousness formation – which always threatened to be re-politicized in ways uncomfortable for the party-state.

To keep control over the culture system, the state would follow three broad strategic lines. First, it would seek control over the collective communication system. Content would be controlled negatively, via censorship, and positively, by the promotion of suitable themes and formats, along with the allowing of certain informational flows and the isolating of other, oppositional voices in the system. Second, in promoting the cultural market, the state sector would position itself so as to 'organize' the market and benefit economically from it. Third, it sought to integrate its cultural system into the global market for culture, for reasons both of export earnings and 'soft power'; at the same time, it sought to protect its economic and ideological control over sectors it considered essential, using the notion of 'cultural security'.

In 1978, the 'market' was legally recognized, as was advertising. State-owned and funded Public Service Units (*shiye danwei*), including Cultural Public Service Units (CPSUs), were allowed to engage in commercial activities. From 1987, they could register both as public institutions and commercial enterprises (*qiye*). This 'dual system' expanded across the 1990s and became part of the 'cultural industries' reforms after 2001.[63] The 'dual system' saw a gradual reduction of direct state finance to CPSUs. By 2006, it was estimated that government budget payments covered half their total expenditure. But this was unevenly distributed. Two-thirds of CPSUs under the Ministry of Culture had their budgets covered, only 10 per cent of those under the State Administration of Radio, Film and Television (SARFT). The State Administration of Press and Publications (SAPP) was, on the other hand, a major money earner. CPSUs outside of these big state agencies fared less well, especially in rural areas. In short, CPSUs have been forced into commercial operations or 'paid service' (*shoufei fuwu*) in a process of semi-privatization.[64]

We call it 'semi-privatization' as the 'dual system' was not about state versus market in zero-sum terms, but rather an internal reform process in which state cultural and media entities bifurcated their activities. The paid services they engaged in included private commercial contracts, but they also involved transactions within a whole network of (often local) SOEs in a cultural version of the 'market-state' we discussed above. There was no 'big bang' in the sense of an overnight transformation, as the entangled networks of intellectuals and party elite tussled over the speed of the reforms. But an overarching belief in the ability of the market to organize the efficient allocation of cultural services was uppermost.

The line was not between some state-sponsored intellectual 'high culture' and political communication versus that of a bottom-up, market-driven, entertainment-oriented 'popular culture'. Already by the end of the 1990s, CPSUs could receive state funding and act as commercial enterprises, just as the local and national state either owned or had controlling interests in TV stations and large publication houses, film production and other cultural goods. That is, the 'cultural industries', as they were to be called, were dominated by the state, even as they operated as mass commercial, profit-seeking entities.

Yuezhi Zhao has given us a very detailed picture of the new policies through which 'cultural undertakings' (or CPSUs) were divided into commercial and non-commercial. But the line ran within these state organizations, not between two different sectors. The 2002 reforms were intended to further separate regulatory and operational functions, and editorial and business functions; spinning off market-oriented enterprises, and selling stock market shares; increasing the role of foreign capital; allowing greater latitude in media companies generating capital from the stock market; and focusing on key state-owned or state-dominated cultural enterprises to organize the market.[65]

While pursuing these strategic lines, the state had to negotiate a set of complex, contradictory and fast-moving currents that cut across its modernization project.[66] The opening of the culture system to market-based entrants, and the semi-privatization of many previously state-funded entities, which rapidly accelerated after 1992, involved the possibility of media capital interests coalescing into an oppositional group. That is, while the ideology of market reforms was to remain dominant, the potential of an emergent class of capitalists with powerful media representation was always to be guarded against. This was done by regulating what could and could not be privately owned, and the extent and nature (e.g. cross-media ownership) of that ownership; also, by state-owned media companies becoming 'market-organizers', thus making private capital dependent on state goodwill or more directly integrated into joint ventures. Here, the kinds of 'amphibian' institutions mentioned above, and the (local) market-state configuration came into play. As state media and other cultural industries were required to recoup costs and turn a profit, they became active players in national, and especially local, media markets, creating complex interwoven nets of connections, investments, licensing, franchising and access to markets.[67] Across all this, the state worked hard to dominate the 'commanding heights' – 'let go the small, control the big' – by which it could regulate the markets in which it was itself (local and national) an active player. A similar strategy was used for foreign capital interests, which the state both sought out and strongly regulated. Much of this was *ad hoc* across the 1990s but from the 16th National Congress of the Central Committee of the CCP in 2002, cultural policy became much more central and formalized in China.

The reforms elicited new forms and channels of popular culture, but they also sought to curtail their impact. There was a need to actually develop popular content, the 'use-value' underpinning the market in culture, and to showcase China's advanced modern culture in ways that could stand comparison to Western countries. This would mean providing the kinds of 'quality' culture required by the new urban middle classes, but on the other hand – if it was to represent the 'vast majority of people' – it meant satisfying the needs of all those who lacked purchasing power. However, the PRC's claims to be a socialist culture meant not just popular access to cultural goods and services but also that it performs a collective, ideological function. The party-state's mandate to control the cultural system rests on this claim to be representative of a socialist citizenry; but this was also, therefore, a space of contestation. As the reforms began to result in widespread social dislocation and suffering for large sections of the population at the end of the 1990s, popular discontent and a growing 'leftist' opposition sought out the media and popular culture as a site of protest and challenge. While rightly presented as a process of state repression and isolation of popular opposition, we also need to recognize that this opposition itself made frequent appeals to the socialist claims of the state, and it was a collective space of communication that made this possible.[68] This space, however, may not just be a space of contestation, but also provides the possibility of reimagining a new kind of popular democratic nation.

Cultural industries

If the commercialization of culture was contested in many intellectual and party circles across the 1990s, by the turn of the millennium they both had a clear line on the central role of the market in the development of 'advanced culture':

> Under conditions of a socialist market economy, a market orientation is consistent with the double objectives of serving socialism and serving the people [...] The more our cultural products conquer the market, the more fortified our ideological front will be, the better the social benefits.[69]

The term 'cultural industries' was increasingly used to formalize this new market system for culture. Throughout the 1990s, the term, linked to the classic usage by Adorno and Horkheimer, had mostly negative connotations for party officials and intellectuals. However, by 1998 it was accepted and, in the period from 2001 – when China joined the WTO – to 2006, at the 16th National Congress of the Communist Party, the state used it to frame a wholesale reform and regularization of the cultural system. The cultural industries were adopted in the 11th Five-Year Plan (2005–10) and were a 'pillar industry' in the 12th Five-Year Plan (2011–15). This was backed by an increasing investment in academic research, with academia-based intellectuals rapidly turning around their opposition of the 1990s.[70] An expansion of research centres and industry analysis papers followed, providing a space for a new kind of academic discipline, parallel to similar developments in the West.

Zhao calls the emergence of the cultural industries within the state's policy discourse a 'cultural turn', one seeking to promote the 'cultural productive force' (*wenhua shengchanli*). She quotes two *Xinhua* journalists: 'Development wants to eat off culture; culture wants to eat off the market.'[71] It thus announced a growing emphasis not just on market reforms as providing for the culture of everyday life – *xiaokang*, a 'middle class' or 'moderately prosperous' society – but also on the economic potential of these cultural industries. This was part of an emphasis on the service sector in China in the early twenty-first century, as the country sought to 'move up the value chain', a shift from the 1980s and 1990s *gaige kaifang* (reform and opening) to Hu Jintao's *gaige chuangxin* (reform and innovation).[72] This emphasis on innovation and the need to develop high-value, IP-generating industry sectors accelerated after the WTO accession. During his 2007 keynote speech at the 17th National Congress of the Communist Party of China, President Hu Jintao repeatedly stressed the need for 'autonomous innovation' (*zizhu chuangxin*): 'Culture has become a more and more important source of national cohesion and creativity and a factor of growing significance in the competition in overall national strength'.[73]

> Cultural industries, then, were to be essential to China's post-WTO integration into the global economy, promoting exports, imports, access to foreign capital, stock market floatation (the first cultural industries stock market index was in 2012), and joining the supply chains of a 'new international division of cultural labour'.[74] The economic prowess of the cultural industries would be part of China's 'soft power' (*ruan shili*). Alongside the regulatory control over the cultural industries to 'quarantine' foreign interests, a strong sector would also provide a bulwark against escalating foreign cultural influence in terms of 'cultural security' (*wenhuan anquan*).[75]

The 'cultural turn' came at a moment when China's potential – as viewed by the West – to both move up a value chain now dominated by the 'knowledge economy' and transition to a fully fledged market capitalism came under sharpened scrutiny. The creativity agenda required that China produce newly productive citizens – as consumers, entrepreneurs and innovators – yet the state seemed set on the 'innovation effects' of culture and creativity only without renouncing the 'communication effects', or 'ideology', of the cultural industries. As Laikwan Pang suggested, 'innovation has been hailed not only as the driver of the national economy but as the source of cultural pride, conflating political, aesthetic and economic values'.[76]

Creative citizens

The Chinese word for creative industries (*chuangyi chanye*) – recognized in 2005 via Hong Kong, where the new UK term was first translated – relates specifically to artistic rather than technical innovation (*chuangxin*).[77] It is notable that the two well-established cultural industries powerhouses in Asia – India and Japan – never adopted the term, and that South Korea was also lukewarm. The main appeal of the term was that, in running so close to the new innovation agenda, 'creative industries' spoke to concerns with tech-led innovation that had begun, in the late 1990s, to embrace the business-to-business and consumer-oriented services of 'design' and new media industries, feeding the post-WTO anxiety about intellectual property and in high value-added 'ideas-driven' production. For the Chinese government, worried by the absence of major Chinese brands despite their pre-eminence in manufacture, moving up the value chain – from 'Made in China' to 'Created in China', as the slogan had it – became a key concern.[78]

However, while in the United Kingdom 'creative industries' covered arts, the cultural industries, design and software – causing immense category confusion – most East Asian countries separated 'creative' industries from cultural or 'content' industries, aligning them with high-tech, IP-intensive industries, which included software development, R&D and business consulting. Though the cultural industries were certainly viewed as catalysts of creativity, as goods and services imbued with cultural content they continued to sit alongside more traditional notions of cultural policy as preserving Chinese socialist values ('cultural security') and as the projection of the nation at a global level ('soft power'). More particularly, the state was concerned to retain common public media space through which it would assert its legitimating claims. As such, the 'commanding heights' were the preserve of the party-state.

Writing in 2003, Jing Wang doubted that 'creative industries' as a term would have much practical application. On the one hand, its emphasis on creative SMEs was not applicable to the current wave of big cultural company stock market flotations; on the other, the term failed to pick up on the three subtexts at play in the term 'cultural industries', which were

> a state-owned sector undergoing the rugged process of partial commercialisation; the tenacious hold of state monopoly even while it is pushing the agenda of commodifying public goods; and the thorny issue of mixed ownership and the debate over the hidden process of privatisation.[79]

This did not stop the 'creative industries' challenge being strongly narrativized by Michael Keane and others around the claim that creative consumers and producers would ultimately require the Chinese state to respond to their emerging needs. In Keane's narrative, this sets in motion a kind of cultural rerun of the 1980s, 'conservatives' (top-down, cultural, traditional) fighting it out with 'reformers' (bottom-up, creative, modernizing). Animating the narrative is the real potential of creativity, which China is set to miss out on if it does not adapt. The potential of creativity here is primarily economic, though, as we have noted before, there is an imaginary at work in excess of these economic returns. In this narrative, the key issue is less the absence of a democratic public sphere than the lack of the open markets and entrepreneurial networks conducive to creative consumers and producers. The narrative is founded upon the hope that

> the internationalization of the creative industries would prove transformative in China, encouraging the growth of individual talent, 'content' innovation, and a shift from centrally planned command-and-control industries to a complex dynamic system growing via the self-organized interactions of myriad creative agents.[80]

Creative agency is primarily a driver of economic change, with political change coming, 'though possibly at a slower rate'.[81] Rather than the struggle for democratic rights, it is the 'evolutionary process of the growth of knowledge' that counts.[82] As with neo-liberal thought more generally, markets are at the heart of the social, and the core of its creative freedoms. 'Political economy', both liberal- and social-democratic, has, in this perspective, over-focused on the 'various injustices' of the system – censorship, state control or the power of the big international media – while ignoring the media's contribution to economic growth.[83] 'Political economy' – proxy in this narrative for any form of political critique – is blind to the development of the creative economy in China.[84] It ignores the 'information and coordination services provided by cultural, creative and communications industries', that is, the complex feedback mechanisms between producers and consumers in a service economy in which price information is volatile and uncertain.[85] The creative and communication industries help assemble a knowledge-intensive consumer economy based on identity goods, which is why they are more important than their 'content'.[86] These industries, in helping construct new subject positions, are a *de facto* cultural policy in that, beyond any particular content, they radically reconstruct behaviour within a networked consumer society. Michael Keane suggests that

> The 'old' mass media (television, press) remain under tight control and are barred from foreign investment. On the other hand, periodicals, magazines, animation, video games and mobile content applications are diversifying their market scope, targeting niche markets more than mass consumption, and finding ways to respond to their most valued demographic, the urban youth market.[87]

The ideological content associated with old media and 'citizen formation' is, in this view, increasingly irrelevant; the ostensibly 'safe' creative industries can, under the radar, shape new subjects who can navigate these proliferating niche markets for discerning consumers. As Hartley and Montgomery put it:

consumers armed with information about how to navigate the complex choices offered to them are finding opportunities to consume 'entrepreneurially' – to maximize the status benefits associated with their purchases, to forge and express identities that express the values of 'risk culture', and thereby to explore the ways in which commercial offerings might be applied or adapted to their own needs and circumstances.[88]

Keane links this to new forms of creative production, the gradual shift from 'cultural industries' to 'creative industries' structured around the wider shift from (mass) industrial to (niche) post-industrial and from derivative to original products. It comes with the economic promise of a high-value, knowledge-intensive industry with creative 'spill-overs' into other sectors. Moving from 'Made in China' to 'Created in China' would both require and provoke a general mobilization of creativity.[89]

The creative industries, in this narrative, represent a shift away from the top-down, ideology-heavy cultural industries controlled by the state, towards popular entertainment and new, 'up-market' forms of identity consumption and its attendant marketing. The expansion of the television market, and the consequent need to make an operating profit, saw the import of programmes from Korea, Taiwan and Japan, and of new formats from across the globe. New digital genres such as computer games, the spread of the internet and mobile phones, as well as the proliferation of department stores, public advertising, tourism, urban consumption spaces and so on, represented huge new markets. In order to fully compete in, and take advantage of, these new markets, Keane suggests, the government will need to mobilize creative talent. Such 'autonomous innovation', as Hu Jintao called it, necessarily involves a diminishing of central control over the circulation of knowledge and the sociocultural spaces of innovative practice. Keane writes:

> China's next 'stage of development' may see its cultural producers successfully targeting regional and international markets. In order to achieve this, however, there is a need for Chinese cultural and media industries to break free of institutional and political shackles.[90]

The rhetoric of 'shackles' suggests an older trope of political liberation, but now located in the creative economy. Indeed, the 'creative consumer' is itself a variation on the liberal democratic 'rising middle-class' thesis. Once it was the bourgeoisie as economic producers (holders or agents of capital) that were the driving force; now the 'new Asian middle classes' are positioned as politically transformative consumers. They demand access to the lifestyle consumption rights the developed world takes for granted. Global flows of images, positional goods, people and money – exemplified for Hartley and Montgomery by the Chinese edition of *Vogue* magazine – are taken to undermine the closed world of local authoritarianisms as new subject formations nurtured in these 'mediascapes' begin to kick against local constraints.[91] In a prior Fordist age, the presence of an industrial working class was taken as an index of modernization, now the long-awaited Chinese middle classes – those with education, leisure and disposable income – are the harbingers of creative consumption and thus social progress.[92]

Central to these accounts is that creativity in both consumption and production is seen as inherently 'progressive', necessarily requiring that autonomous, self-organizing creative agents be given full license – something incompatible with authoritarian forms of control. We will say more about cultural producers in the next chapter, but Jing Wang had early on alerted us to the fact that the creative entrepreneurs who are charged with this creative modernization process are very different from the socially responsible bohemians of the Western imaginary: 'the rising "creative class" in Beijing and Guangzhou have deep pockets, networking capital with the state, and a lifestyle characteristic of the nouveau riche'.[93] The BMW-driving denizens of the 'creative clusters' of Beijing and Shanghai do not necessarily have a sense of any wider social responsibilities. In the new 'creative industries', 'breaking the shackles' may involve as much an abandonment of any residual social responsibilities as it does the Trojan horse of political liberalization.

Ultimately, this creative capacity is not dependent on a liberal public sphere but a 'free' market. Key to this is the shift from 'cultural' to 'creative', from the cultural industries controlled by elites and governments to that of a citizen-consumer entrepreneur (or 'prosumer') free to decide what they want to consume and produce. From this perspective, one of the problems of China is that it remains wedded to ideological and paternalist notions of big 'C' Culture, when its citizens want to choose, and make, small 'c' culture for themselves.

The key problem with this narrative is that it freights the sovereign consumer, and the creative entrepreneurs who produce for them, with a transformative power they fundamentally lack. In confining knowledge and creativity to their economic dimensions, and in positioning these as historically transformative and yet outside any political agenda, the narrative severely constrains any emancipatory promise. In short, while new forms of consumption have provided for an expansion of the space of everyday life, outside of any wider political aspirations these choices are ultimately restricted and manipulated.[94]

Aihwa Ong suggested that East Asian states accommodated their middle classes through economic growth, access to new consumer goods and services and the imposition of labour discipline. The *quid pro quo* was an acceptance of a state-centred social hierarchy and cohesion – euphemistically identified with 'Confucian values'.[95] We noted the depoliticized, or 'frozen', relationship between the party-state and society which monopolizes politics, and the marketized sphere of everyday life. Whatever tensions needed to be negotiated in this configuration, it is clear that the clampdown on political radicalism in China at the end of the 1980s was compensated by the rapid economic growth of the 1990s. That is, enhanced consumption was a way of staving off political demands. The emergence of a post-Fordist 'niche' consumption, whether carried by old or new media, does not change this (even if it sets the state new challenges).

The party's dual objectives, Yuezhi Zhao suggests, are 'sustaining economic growth and maintaining its hegemony by securing the "commanding heights" of a reconstructed communication and culture sector, whilst incorporating a consumerist mode of cultural citizenship enfranchisement'.[96] The state 'has rejuvenated its capacity, via the market, to affect the agenda of popular culture':

> The state's rediscovery of culture as a site where new ruling technologies can be deployed and converted simultaneously into economic capital constitutes one of its most innovative strategies of statecraft since the founding of the 'People's Republic'.[97]

The withdrawal of state-owned cultural entities to the 'commanding heights' opened up a space for Ong's 'socialism from afar', through a new synergy of popular culture and socialism.[98] 'What makes possible the contemporary revival of "serving the people" is the equation, contradictory or not, between socialism and democratic consumerism.'[99]

The distinction the Chinese government makes between cultural and creative industries is not to be seen as some conservative finger-in-dyke before the inevitable flood of the creative economy. The separation of 'sensitive' (cultural) and 'safe' (non-cultural) content is part of its active construction of a consumer economy and subjects able to participate in it.[100] Culture remains a key term, and an important site and organizing principle for state action. While by no means frictionless, there is no evidence that 'sovereign consumers' in themselves would pose any form of challenge for the state. The transformation of lifestyles is of major significance to our understanding of the prospects for contemporary China; however, for real political change to occur, 'citizen-consumers' would need to actively challenge the structures of power, symbolically or in practice – that is, be more citizens than consumers. The main sites of public political conflict in China remain in the realm of 'sensitive' information or unacceptable symbolic content. The 'safe zones' of identity consumption remain just that: safe – unless they somehow butt up against these more sensitive areas. When this consumption is disrupted or thwarted – food scandals, sub-standard housing, train crashes, earthquake response, failing schools – that friction increases and moves onto the ground of the political.

Cultural industries and the state

Despite the enthusiasm of the creativity narrative, the Chinese government has not accepted 'creative industries' as a working term. It is used in some of the big cities – Shanghai primarily – and still works for some as a rallying point for market freedoms in the cultural sector. In the main, however, it is restricted to the 'safe' areas of entertainment, R&D, hairdressing, wedding photography and business consulting. Of course, Chinese policy-makers and academics use the term when needed, fading in and out as circumstances dictate. Dealing with the British Council, for example, or international agencies such as UNESCO or UNCTAD, the term will be used, but internally it is not. This is a political-ideological issue, but it also relates to the confused nature of the term itself: to what does it actually apply? How exactly does it guide policy in this area?

In fact, China has followed South Korea in seeing the 'cultural industries' as 'content industries', that is, industries whose primary economic value derives from the production and circulation of symbolic goods.[101] This is the 'political economy' definition, though now set within an overriding objective of economic growth. Using the research capacity of the university system, and the industrial development tools of the state (mostly national, though also the large cities), China has sought to identify and strengthen value chains and market structures in different sub-sectors, to promote access to finance, tax breaks, capitalization, export support, production and investment partnerships, mergers, overseas acquisitions and investment, skills and training, market champions – in short, the whole gamut of industrial development levers available to a 'development state'.[102] As with South Korea, China has the 'legislative, administrative and financial capacity that can "make the policy actually happen"'.[103] In contrast, the kinds of 'creative industry' policies in the West, where they exist, involve various 'supply side' encouragements (training schemes, business advice) to be more creative and entrepreneurial.

Hye-Kyung Lee, speaking of South Korea, makes the telling point that just because the term 'cultural' is used does not mean that these policies are any less instrumental than those badged as 'creative'.[104] Policy documents, speeches and reports on the cultural industries in China are relentlessly econometric, concerned with increases in GDP, market share, 'value-added' and so on. In holding on to 'culture', South Korea and China have taken a more clear-eyed view of how these industries actually work – an instrumental 'political economy' approach – rather than buying in to vague notions of stimulating creativity. They have learnt to ignore what the West says and focus on what it does – how the West has been able to dominate global markets or, indeed, how Japan, Taiwan or India were able to break into global markets in film, computer games, popular music, television and so on. There is no doubt that content development was (and is) a challenge for

China, but they are not blind to the power of ownership and control – of telecoms, media conglomerates, distribution networks and intellectual property regimes – in sustaining the global dominance of the United States, United Kingdom and other European countries.

Xi Jinping has accelerated the promotion of the cultural industries, which, in the context of the 'new normal' in which China's growth rate levels off, are now incorporated into the broader shift to a service economy and the stimulation of domestic consumption. The cultural industries were declared a 'pillar industry' in the 13th Five-Year Plan (2016–20). Since 2014, the reform process has 'deepened', with further attempts to mark the boundaries between the public and commercial sectors, while facilitating the rapid expansion of the latter.[105] The role of the market and the power of corporations to organize that market has been accelerated, with strong encouragement to agglomeration, mergers, acquisitions, joint ventures and so on. The state has promoted links between the cultural industries and the 'creative' sectors of design and digital content.[106] This is of a part with its promotion of 'online culture', for example its 2016 calling for 'letting online culture flourish, strengthening national soft power' by enhancing online culture supply capacities to satisfy the people's diverse needs within modern culture dissemination systems. Also, by encouraging high-value internet and cultural enterprises to jointly foster a batch of novel cultural and media groups with international influence.[107] (The Internet Plus policy grew out of this.) So, too, the government has sought to make links between cultural industries and manufacturing, including 'maker spaces', though of course scaled up into the 'mass entrepreneurship and innovation' campaign.[108] Online cultural services have been the subject of policy concerns, so too support for micro-enterprises, intellectual property protection and various forms of finance, including micro-finance.[109]

Hye-Kyung Lee calls this (referring to South Korea) a 'post-cultural' cultural industries policy.[110] This description is telling, and we shall discuss it more below, but unlike South Korea, which might have moved away from the modernist 'nation-building' phase, China has certainly not. The deployment of the tools of a developmental state for the economic growth of the cultural industries is all set within the 'One Belt, One Road' initiative, which, building on the 'soft power objective', is central to Xi's plan to reverse the flow of global capital and influence from the West that began with The Great Divergence in the late eighteenth century.[111] That is, it is 'post-cultural' only in a limited sense. Nonetheless, what the explosion of the digital sector in China indicates is that the cultural industries 'can no longer be separated from ICT policy in its various forms'.[112] But China's 'mass innovation' is less concerned with unshackling creative subjectivity and more with building the technical and financial infrastructure within which new forms of labour and consumption might be captured and deployed. In this, China is following the evolution of 'platform capitalism' in the West, whose global behemoths now find their counterparts in China – FAANG versus BATX.[113] Both of these evolving digital communications sectors, increasingly intertwined with retail, finance, e-currencies, surveillance and defence, are a long way from the TED Talk imaginary of the democratic entrepreneurialism of Schumpeterian start-ups. We might say, then, that in China, the post-cultural cultural industries are converging with the post-creative creative industries.

Culture: A constricted space?

There are some serious challenges for China in the cultural sector, many of them particular to the configuration of the market-state. A key problem has always been governance by 'policy' – in which government rulings and regulations are expected to set a context for development across such a vast country. Frequent policy pronouncements can be difficult to interpret on the ground, or contradicted by other policies from the same or different state agencies.[114] Eager to please the central bureaucracy, or exploit some new regulatory opening, local governments frequently jump with both feet into the latest policy directive, only to rapidly abandon it when this subsequently changes. Policies have a direct impact on shaping markets – as we shall see with creative clusters in the next chapter – and local governments, with their networks of 'amphibian institutions', chase these new market possibilities, as well as the success they see elsewhere, even if it is entirely inappropriate. Frantic and opportunistic replication across local authorities has marked the cultural industries, from television stations and programmes, publications, to a plethora of failing 'creative clusters' across the nation. We have seen some of the dynamics of this in our discussion of Shenzhen in Chapter 6, in which the local 'entrepreneurial state' has a developed capacity for improvisation and tracking the movement of capital (and policy), resulting in a chaotic proliferation of projects and initiatives.

In part, this also relates to the lack of professional capacity in what we might call 'cultural management', where cultural professionals can assert a specific expertise against the volatile policy oscillations of local governments. Cultural management programmes are springing up in universities across the country, part of an attempt by the central government to enhance and formalize the public administration capacity of the state as a whole. However, such cultural professionals tend in the main to be squeezed by the Bourdieusian polarities we noted above (i.e. between the economic capital of commercial players and the political capital of those with state connections). The cultural capital of cultural producers and managers is easily brushed aside as local states seek those with money to invest or with highly visible track records (commercial cultural capital) in the market. On the other hand, as we shall see, SOEs are frequently required to deliver on social and political outcomes – to 'be creative for the state'.[115]

This reflects the persistent failure of the state to mark out an effective boundary between public service and commercially oriented operations. It is related to the fluid boundaries within state public (*shiye*) and state commercial (*chanye*) entities, and between these and private enterprise per se (*qiye*). This has caused a great confusion of ends, with local governments demanding economic profit from public undertakings (CPSUs above) in order to satisfy their funders. This has had damaging effects on cultural public service provision. As Zhang Xiaoming noted:

> Although public by definition, the majority of CPSUs have moved away from their role as public service providers. Many CPSUs that formerly provided products and services for the good of the public have transformed: some have shrunk in size because of insufficient funds (for instance, public libraries); some have adapted extensive fee-charging practices (workers' clubs and youth cultural and leisure centres); and others have transformed completely owing to their commercial approach (broadcasting and television sectors rely on advertising for survival).[116]

This hollowing out of the public dimension of culture is something frequently overlooked in Western accounts focused on censorship or creativity deficits. This differs from city to city and region to region (as with most things in China), with some cities holding on to a socialist sense of a public provision of culture. Bo Xilai's Chongqing is an extreme, perhaps caricatured version of this; but cities such as Harbin were very reluctant to abandon the public nature of culture in favour of its economic potential.[117] Others, such as Shanghai, have gone full tilt for a commercial creative sector. But even here, as we sketched in Chapter 6, the investment in various cultural institutions, programmes, events, networks and a variety of domestic and international projects has led to a demand for cultural management skills that can establish some professional parameters around policy-driven cultural initiatives.[118] In the last decade, investment (both local and national) in public culture (including heritage preservation and sport) has risen, as has investment in radio, film, TV, press and publication, the core cultural industries sector.[119] This is an attempted reassertion, in the 'complex-professional' era, of the specific competencies of cultural workers and managers to which intellectuals in China have always held. Not only Kraus's fund-seeking manoeuvres, but also a wider commitment to a public good that often sits uncomfortably with Western notions of the artistic, creative persona.

Zhang Xiaoming and Shan Shilian are concerned about the distortion of the public ends of culture by commercial imperatives in the 'market-state'. They point to a more pervasive squeezing of the space of culture, an erosion of that specific competence in culture which we might call 'autonomous' if the term were not so loaded. It is a space that falls within the double polarity of culture vis-à-vis both commercial success and state consecration. For the first axis, we have in mind a space before commercialization or 'entrepreneurship', of self-directed experiment and investigation, of the acquisition of professional expertise, even if neither is paid or institutionalized. The second axis does involve a distance (however coded) from a direct association with some of the more moralistic and propagandistic aspects of state consecration, but it is more than simply the avoidance of 'official art' (as in Bourdieu's recreation of the cultural field of the Second Empire in France). State recognition can also represent a validation of an artist's or cultural worker's wider ethical-aesthetic value. The problem is that state recognition is increasingly about consecrating commercial success – Jing Wang's collusion of 'socialism and demo-cratic consumerism' – rather than the specific conferral of ethical-aesthetic value. In this sense, the space of culture is doubly constricted, by both a highly commer-cialized cultural industries sector and a local state which seeks the symbolic con-firmation (and economic return) of market success.

Yet it is in this constricted space of culture where we still need to look for new forms of culture, and of participation in culture, to emerge. This will be the focus of the final chapter. Zhang's paper ends with a call to enshrine public culture as a constitutional right, framed not as 'creative entrepreneurship' but as active cul-tural participation. Shan's has a similar intent, calling for a properly appointed and regulated system of public – not commercial – culture. This question of a dis-tinct space for culture – for artists, cultural workers and professionals – returns us to Laikwan Pang's distinction between traditional and organic intellectuals. The historical space for traditional intellectuals was closed, in her account, both by the party's shift to the cultural market system, and by intellectuals' self-interested failure to connect with new forms of popular aspiration and participation. All that remained were 'organic' functionaries of either the state or market. In response, we would hold out the possibility of a 'traditional' intellectual committed to social change but not a party functionary, politically committed but retaining the critical distance of a cultural professional. This possibility we evoked in Shanghai Modern. That historical moment suggested an intellectual engagement with commercial, popular culture which we should not abandon in the present, very different, con-juncture. Kraus's restriction of the contemporary cultural intellectual to the ever-diminishing sphere of elite culture and its funding manoeuvres ignores the possi-bilities contained in popular culture. Such popular culture, which in Bourdieu's schema occupies the abject position of both low cultural and low economic capital, is, to us, a space to which any artist or intellectual seeking social change needs to address themselves.[120]

This would be to continue Raymond Williams's quest for a 'socialist common culture', but in very different circumstances. Xudong Zhang puts it thus:

> The challenge of the present is to search for a new way of imagining the nation and formulating its culture under new socioeconomic and cultural circumstances. This discourse would be based on a renewed utopian expectation that these circumstances, unprecedented in human history, bring with them a political message, if not an implicit political form. For all practical purposes, the post-revolutionary secularization is not just tearing down the rituals and taboos of a semi-agrarian society and a semi-Stalinist regime, it is also putting the time-honored institutions and ideologies of 'civil society' to a historical test. It disdains traditional politics and pursues a new, socioeconomically defined selfhood. It also, in its restless and mundane activities of production, consumption, association, experimentation, and imagination, creates a new social-cultural landscape in which to imagine a national community. This imagination [...] may create new possibilities for political participation and democracy within the residual socialist framework.[121]

This is the space in which contemporary artists, cultural professionals and intellectuals must surely operate.[122] At the same time, 'popular culture' is now a primary generator of economic capital, and one that can no longer be the preserve, as Garnham had it, of the 'dominated section of the dominant class'.[123] It is now deeply connected to the projects of states and elites. Xudong Zhang, writing with Arif Dirlik, highlights the 'intricate relationship between the everyday sphere, the state, the (elite) intellectuals, and the omnipresent ideology and culture of global capitalism'.[124] That is, though popular culture articulates a range of new personal expressive possibilities in everyday life, ultimately the stakes which invest it are deeply political.

Conclusion

The emergence of a critical but positive notion of cultural industries in academia and policy circles from the 1960s was part of a wider contestation and renegotiation of the values of autonomy and democracy from within the field of culture.[125] It was also, however incomplete, a critique of a certain form of Fordist-capitalist economy. The creative industries discourse, on the other hand, uncoupled itself from the more radical social, cultural and political values of a previous 'cultural industries' discourse, rooted in urban popular cultures and new social movements, as well as political economy and cultural studies. In the creative industries, the social, cultural and political transformations of the 1960s and 1970s are reduced to the soft skills of the new economy and the individualized, aestheticized consumption practices of post-Fordism. The reduction of this transformative programme to a coordination and information system for a consumer economy can only be regressive. Ultimately, it has little purchase on a Chinese state that attempts to develop a cultural economy and keep a 'frozen' political system intact. Seeing no contradiction between cultural and market value, between the citizen and the consumer, between an economic system and the wider sociocultural values within which it is embedded, the creative industries discourse can offer only technocratic support to a creative economy in the belief that the system will, eventually, evolve.

We have suggested that the ideological sphere required by the party-state for its legitimation also provided a space for contestation, especially in terms of its commitment to 'socialist values'. A 'managed public culture' is still a common space. This was especially so with regards to the popular protests, which proliferated from the end of the 1990s and informed Yuezhi Zhao's work. The party's possession of the 'commanding heights' allowed it to 'control information flows and block popular access to autonomous and effective means of communication, on the one hand, and to monopolise the discourse of socialism as an alternative to capitalism on the other'.[126] The sphere of communication is still controlled by the state, but under Xi Jinping this space has tightened. More pointedly perhaps, since the rapid expansion of the 'digital' under 'Internet Plus', the state has extended its digital surveillance infrastructure significantly, now giving it much greater control over its population down to the granular level of everyday life. As we suggested in Chapter 5, this is by no means unique to China, with 'platform capitalism' and 'surveillance capitalism' established terms in Western critique.[127] How this is developing in China is, as one might imagine, distinctive.

The 'frozen' relationship between state and society, in which the ideological sphere of 'socialism from afar' interacted with an individualized system of 'democratic consumerism', has not thawed. We see the convergence of post-cultural and post-creative industries, intermeshed with the digital communications systems around purchase, payment, data-extraction, and now linked to urban infrastructure ('smart cities') and social welfare or 'citizenship' systems.[128] Artificial intelligence, to whose development the Chinese state is now seriously committed, promises the ability to handle such 'big data' in ways that render the inner workings of the social visible – and thus manipulatable – to all able to access the technology.[129] We can see in this a shift to the 'pre-symbolic' we discussed at the end of Chapter 5. As Marc Andrejevic has suggested,

Of greatest concern is the notion that the proliferation of data means we can leave behind the challenges associated with representational forms of knowledge, narrative, and deliberation rather than working through the impasses they currently confront.[130]

This seems to us a profoundly alluring promise for a party unwilling to 'unfreeze' the state-society dialogue. It represents a far greater threat to the common space of the social than censorship, in that it actually closes down the symbolic space of contestation around democracy, socialism and social change.[131] This, coupled with the doubly constricted space for artists and cultural professionals, outlines a disturbing impasse.

NOTES

1. A. Ong and L. Zhang, 'Introduction: Privatising China: Powers of the Self, Socialism from Afar', in *Privatising China: Powers of the Self*, ed. L. Zhang and A. Ong (Ithaca, NY: Cornell University Press, 2008), 1–19; A. Kipnis, 'Suzhi: A Keyword Approach', *China Quarterly* 186 (2006): 295–313.

2. R. Williams, *Keywords: A Vocabulary of Culture and Society* (London: Fontana, 1976), 76–82.

3. P. Bürger, *Theory of the Avant-Garde*, trans. M. Shaw (Minneapolis: University of Minnesota Press, 1984).

4. For a sympathetic overview, cf. G. Turner, *British Cultural Studies. An Introduction*, 3rd ed. (London: Routledge, 2003).

5. R. Williams, 'Working Class Culture', Review of *The Uses of Literacy* Richard Hoggart, *Universities and Left Review* 1, no. 2 (1957): 29–32. For more context, cf. P. Anderson, 'The Missing Text: Introduction to "The Future of Marxism"', *New Left Review* 114 (2018): 33–51. We recall here T. H. Marshall's definition of cultural citizenship: 'the right to a modicum of economic welfare and security, [...] the right to share to the full in the social heritage and to live the life of a civilized being according to the standards prevailing in the society' ('Citizenship and Social Class', in *Citizenship and Social Class and other Essays* [Cambridge: Cambridge University Press, 1950], 46).

6. The classic text is R. Hoggart, *The Uses of Literacy* (Harmondsworth: Penguin Books, 1958).

7. A convergence recognized early on by Oscar Negt and Alexander Kluge. O. Negt and A. Kluge, *Public Sphere and Experience: Towards an Analysis of the Bourgeois and Proletarian Public Sphere* (Minneapolis: University of Minnesota Press, 1993).

8. S. Hall, 'Encoding, Decoding', in *Culture, Media, Language: Working Papers in Cultural Studies, 1972–1979*, ed. Centre for Contemporary Cultural Studies (London: Routledge, 1980), 128–38. On the cultural studies/political economy divide, cf. D. Hesmondhalgh, *The Cultural Industries*, 4th ed. (London: Sage, 2019).

9. P. Bourdieu, *The Field of Cultural Production* (New York: Columbia University Press, 1993).

10. Perfectly encapsulated by *The Economist*'s Leader Column *Who Will Win the Media Wars. Disney, Netflix and the Battle to Control Eyeballs*, 14 November 2019.

11. As Lucien Pye put it, 'the Chinese authorities know from both their ideology and practical experiences that the dynamism of creativity in all dimensions of life comes from Western societies and their bourgeois cultures'. L. Pye, *The Mandarin and the Cadre: China's Political Cultures* (Ann Arbor: University of Michigan Press, 1988), 168.

12. J. Habermas, *The Structural Transformation of the Public Sphere* (Cambridge, MA: MIT Press, 1989). For a collection of critical essays, cf. C. Calhoun, *Habermas and the Public Sphere* (Cambridge, MA: MIT Press, 1992).

13. J. Lewis and T. Miller, 'Introduction', in *Critical Cultural Policy Studies: A Reader* (Oxford: Blackwell, 2003), 1, 3.

14. In light of Lewis and Miller's critical cultural policy approach, we can refer to Mark Andrejevic's suggestion, that even Foucault's critical method is 'compelled to rely upon a conserved and shared symbolic efficacy. The whole critical apparatus breaks down when this once-removed horizon [...] dissipates.' M. Andrejevic, *Infoglut: How Too Much Information Is Changing the Way We Think and Know* (London: Routledge, 2013), 257.

15. Cf. H. -K. Lee, *Cultural Policy in South Korea: Making a New Patron State* (London: Routledge, 2018). Also: H. -K. Lee, 'The Political Economy of the Creative Industries', *Media, Culture & Society* 39, no. 7 (2017): 1078–88.

16. Cf. K. Strittmatter, *We Have Been Harmonised: Life in China's Surveillance State* (London: Old Street Publishing, 2019).

17. M. Keane and Y. Chen, 'Entrepreneurial Solutionism, Characteristic Cultural Industries and the Chinese Dream', *International Journal of Cultural Policy* 25, no. 6 (2017): 743–55; J. Wang and Y. Tan, 'The Prosaic State Space of Social Factory: Re-Defining Labour in China's Mass Innovation, Mass Entrepreneurship Campaign', *Environment and Planning A: Economy and Space* (forthcoming).

18. According to the *China Statistic Yearbook on Culture and Related Industries* (2018), the percentage of GDP represented by the 'Cultural and Creative Industries' has doubled and its 'value-added' quadrupled between 2004 and 2017.

19. K. Polanyi, *The Great Transformation: The Political and Economic Origins of Our Time* (Boston, MA: Beacon, 1957). Cf. J. Meek, 'Somerdale to Skarbimierz', *London Review of Books* 39, no. 8 (2017): 3–15.

20. J. Delingpole, 'Letting China Join the WTO Was the Worst Decision the West Ever Made', *The Spectator*, 21 September 2019, https: //www.spectator.co.uk/2019/09/letting-china-join-the-wto-was-the-worst-decision-the-west-ever-made/. Accessed 22 September 2019.

21. Cf. W. Brown, 'Neoliberalism's Frankenstein: Authoritarian Freedom in Twenty-First Century "Democracies"', *Critical Times* 1, no.1 (2018): 60–79.

22. Cf. T. Cheek, *The Intellectual in Modern Chinese History* (Cambridge: Cambridge University Press, 2015).

23. R. C. Kraus, *The Party and the Arty in China: The New Politics of Culture* (New York: Rowman and Littlefield, 2004), 47–64.

24. Ibid., 38–42, 153–59.

25. L. Pang, *The Art of Cloning: Creative Production During China's Cultural Revolution* (London: Verso, 2017), 220.

26. Ibid., 220.

27. Ibid., 222.

28. Ibid., 218.

29. J. Wang, *High Culture Fever: Politics, Aesthetics, and Ideology in Deng's China* (Berkeley: University of California Press, 1996).

30. Cf. Cheek, *Intellectual in Modern Chinese History*, 125–32.

31. Ibid., 237. Cf. J. Derrida, *Specters of Marx: The State of the Debt, the Work of Mourning, and the New International*, trans. P. Kamuf (New York: Routledge, 1994).

32. Pang, *Art of Cloning*, 237.

33. Ibid., 238.

34. Cf. Pye, *Mandarin and the Cadre*; X. Zhang, 'Nationalism, Mass Culture, and Intellectual Strategies in Post-Tiananmen China', *Social Text* 55 (1998): 109–40.

35. Pang, *Art of Cloning*, 238

36. Cf. Ibid., 'Introduction' for an overview.

37. Cf. Kraus, *Party and the Arty in China*, 172–74; also J. Andreas, *The Rise of the Red Engineers: The Cultural Revolution and the Origins of China's New Class* (Stanford, CA: Stanford University Press, 2009), 'Conclusion'.

38. Cf. J. Fewsmith, *China Since Tiananmen: The Politics of Transition: From Deng Xiaoping to Hu Jintao* (New York: Cambridge University Press, 2008); Zhang, 'Nationalism, Mass Culture, and Intellectual Strategies in Post-Tiananmen China', 136.

39. Kraus, *Party and the Arty in China*, 163–74; Cheek, *Intellectual in Modern Chinese History*, 273–76; Y. Zhao, *Communication in China: Political Economy, Power, and Conflict* (Lanham: Roman and Littlefield, 2008), 5–7.

40. Kraus, *Party and the Arty in China*, 205.

41. Ibid., 163–74, and 204–05; Cheek, *Intellectual in Modern Chinese History*, 327–28.

42. Kraus, *Party and the Arty in China*, 204. Jian Lin describes it as an 'art-commerce-politics relation', cf. 'Be Creative for the State: Creative Workers in Chinese State-Owned Cultural Enterprises', *International Journal of Cultural Studies* 22, no. 1 (2019): 53–69, 61.

43. Ibid., 206.

44. H. Becker, *Art Worlds* (Berkeley: University of California Press, 1982).

45. Cf. Kraus, *Party and the Arty in China* and X. Zhang, 'From Institution to Industry: Reforms in Cultural Institutions in China', *International Journal of Cultural Studies* 9, no. 3 (2006): 297–306.

46. Hesmondhalgh, *Cultural Industries*, 84–86.

47. W. Su, 'From Culture for the People to Culture for Profit: The PRC's Journey toward a Cultural Industries Approach', *International Journal of Cultural Policy* 21, no. 5 (2015): 513–28; Zhang, 'Nationalism, Mass Culture, and Intellectual Strategies in Post-Tiananmen China'.

48. For a detailed discussion, cf. T. Lewis, F. Martin and W. Sun, *Telemodernities: Television and Transforming Lives in Asia* (Durham, NC: Duke University Press, 2016).

49. Cf. Zhang, 'Nationalism, Mass Culture, and Intellectual Strategies in Post-Tiananmen China'.

50. Ibid., 123.

51. This is the space of 'self-sovereignty' outlined by Ong and Zhang: 'individuation as an ongoing process of private responsibility, requiring ordinary Chinese to take their life into their own hands and to face the consequences of their decisions on their own'. Ong and Zhang, 'Introduction', 16.

52. Cf. J. McGuigan, *Cultural Populism* (London: Routledge, 1992).

53. The quotes are in Zhang, 'Nationalism, Mass Culture, and Intellectual Strategies in Post-Tiananmen China', 133.

54. 'That they are becoming consumers *en masse* does not mean that they have had any choice, although the fact that they have never had any choice does not mean that they would not have wanted to become consumers, either'. Zhang, 'Nationalism, Mass Culture, and Intellectual Strategies in Post-Tiananmen China', 135.

55. Zhang is quoting Feminist and cultural studies academic Dai Jinhua. Zhang, 'Nationalism, Mass Culture, and Intellectual Strategies in Post-Tiananmen China', 133.

56. Q. S. Tong and R. Y. Y. Hung, 'Cultural Policy between the State and the Market: Regulation, Creativity and Contradiction', *International Journal of Cultural Policy* 18, no. 3 (2012): 265–78.

57. Su, 'From Culture for the People to Culture for Profit', 517.

58. Ibid., 518.

59. Ibid.

60. Cf. Kraus, *Party and the Arty in China*, 63–64.

61. Cf. B. Garner, 'The New Cultural Revolution: Chinese Cultural Policy Reform and the UNESCO Convention on Cultural Diversity', *The Political Economy of Communication* 3, no. 1 (2015): 57–82; Y. Zhao, 'The Media Matrix: China's Integration into Global Capitalism', in *The Empire Reloaded: Socialist Register 2005*, ed. L. Panitch and C. Leys (London: The Merlin Press, 2004), 197–217.

62. Cf. M. Gow, 'The Core Socialist Values of the Chinese Dream: Towards a Chinese Integral State', *Critical Asian Studies* 49 (2017): 116–92.

63. Zhang, 'From Institution to Industry', 297–306.

64. Ibid.

65. Zhao, *Communication in China*, 75–136.

66. Ibid.

67. For Shanghai, cf. C.-C. Lee, Z. He and Y. Huang, 'Party-Market Corporatism, Clientelism, and Media in Shanghai', *The Harvard International Journal of Press/Politics* 12, no. 3 (2007): 21–42.

68. Y. Z. Zhao, *Media, Market, and Democracy in China: Between the Party Line and the Bottom Line* (Urbana and Chicago: University of Illinois Press, 1998).

69. Ibid., 1112. Quoting Li Changchun, April 2003.

70. M. Keane, *Created in China: The New Great Leap Forward* (London: Routledge, 2007); M. Keane, *Creative Industries in China: Art, Media, Design* (Cambridge: Polity, 2013); Zhao, *Communication in China*, 109; Su, 'From Culture for the People to Culture for Profit', J. Yang, 'The Chinese Understanding of Cultural Industries', *Santalka: Filosofija, Komunikacija* 19, no. 2 (2011): 90–97; P. Kern, Y. Smits and D. Wang, *Mapping the Cultural and Creative Sectors in the EU and China: A Working Paper in Support to the Development of an EU-China Cultural and Creative Industries' Platform* (Brussels: KEA, 2011).

71. Zhao, *Communication in China*, 110.

72. L. Pang, *Creativity and Its Discontents: China's Creative Industries and Intellectual Property Rights Offences* (Durham, NC: Duke University Press, 2012), 8.

73. Quoted in M. Keane, *Created in China: The New Great Leap Forward* (London: Routledge, 2007), 221.

74. Cf. Garner, 'The New Cultural Revolution', 65; T. Miller, 'The New International Division of Cultural Labor Revisited', *ICONO14: Journal of Communication and Emergent Technologies* 14, no. 2 (2016): 97–121.

75. Cf. Keane, *Creative Industries in China*, 54–65. As Hu Huilin, one of the academics who had enthusiastically embraced cultural industries at the end of the 1990s, wrote in 2007: 'To maintain cultural security in the context of globalization, the state must therefore protect China's cultural resources and cultural ecology, regulate the cultural market and promote online security [...] Domestic cultural industries are encouraged to export cultural products to overseas markets to safeguard cultural security against the cultural imperialist powers.' Quoted in Keane, *Creative Industries in China*, 56. Hu was the director of China's first Cultural Industries Innovation and Development Base at Jiaotong University in 2001, and he has co-edited the annual *Blue Book Report on the Development of China's Cultural Industries*.

76. Pang, *Creativity and Its Discontents*, 9–10.

77. D. Hui, 'From Cultural to Creative Industries: Strategies for Chaoyang District, Beijing', *International Journal of Cultural Studies* 9, no. 3 (2006): 317–31.

78. Keane, *Created in China*; J. Wang, *Brand New China: Advertising, Media and Commercial Culture* (Cambridge, MA: Harvard University Press, 2008).

79. J. Wang, 'The Global Reach of a New Discourse: How Far Can "Creative Industries" Travel?', *International Journal of Cultural Studies* 7, no.1 (2004): 9–19, 16.

80. J. Hartley and L. Montgomery, 'Creative Industries Come to China', *Chinese Journal of Communication* 2 (2009): 1–12, 10.

81. Ibid., 10.

82. Ibid., 10. Though they reject the primacy of the economy over culture as 'a left-over Marxist causality' and allow great agency to autonomous political intervention – such as Deng's decision to launch the 'opening up' process – they seem unconcerned about the ability of the Chinese political structure to stand against the evolutionary tide of the knowledge economy.

83. J. Potts, 'Do Developing Economies Require Creative Industries? Some Old Theory about New China', *Chinese Journal of Communication* 2, no. 1 (2010): 92–108, 98.

84. Hartley and Montgomery, 'Creative Industries Come to China', 3; Keane, *Created in China*, 5.

85. Potts, 'Do Developing Economies Require Creative Industries', 96.

86. 'The film, television, video, publishing sectors serve an important function beyond providing journalistic information and analysis, consumer entertainment, and in delivering an audience for advertisers [...] [I]n a growing economy with increasing social mobility and opportunity, they also play a role in shaping and stabilizing shifting identities and aspirations.' Ibid., 98.

87. Keane, *Created in China*, 5.

88. Hartley and Montgomery, 'Creative Industries Come to China', 10.

89. Keane, *Created in China*; M. Keane, *China's New Creative Clusters: Governance, Human Capital and Regional Investment* (London: Routledge, 2011); Keane, *Creative Industries in China*.

90. Keane, *Created in China*, 5.

91. J. Hartley and L. Montgomery, 'Fashion as Consumer Entrepreneurship: Emergent Risk Culture, Social Network Markets and the Launch of *Vogue* in China', *Chinese Journal of Communication* 2 (2009): 61–76.

92. G. Therborn, 'New Masses? Social Bases of Resistance', *New Left Review* 85 (2014): 7–16

93. Wang, 'Global Reach of a New Discourse', 17

94. It is instructive to note how the 2019 protests in Hong Kong have recently been positioned as a(nother) revolt of the middle class, now driven primarily by political not 'lifestyle' concerns. Cf. H. French, 'Why China Fears Sending Tanks into Hong Kong', *The Guardian*, 16 October 2019, https://www.theguardian.com/commentisfree/2019/oct/16/china-hong-kong-xi-jinping. Accessed 14 November 2019.

95. A. Ong, *Flexible Citizenship: The Cultural Logics of Transnationality* (Durham NC: Duke University Press, 1999).

96. Zhao, *Communication in China*, 121.

97. J. Wang, 'Culture as Leisure, Culture as Capital', *Positions* 9, no. 1 (2001): 71–72, 93.

98. L. Zhang and A. Ong, eds., *Privatising China: Socialism from Afar* (Ithaca, NY: Cornell University Press, 2008).

99. Wang, 'Culture as Leisure, Culture as Capital', 95

100. Potts's claim that the creative industries 'play a role in shaping and stabilizing shifting identities and aspirations' turns out to be correct, though in a way entirely different from his intent, for this is now a project of the Chinese state. Cf. A. Ong, *Neoliberalism as Exception: Mutations in Citizenship and Sovereignty* (Durham, NC: Duke University Press, 2006).

101. Hesmondhalgh, *Cultural Industries*; on Korea, see Lee, 'Political Economy of the Creative Industries'; Lee, *Cultural Policy in South Korea*.

102. See also the Yangtze Delta focused policies outlined in Y. Rong and J. O'Connor, eds., *Cultural Industries in Shanghai: Policy and Planning Inside a Global City* (London: Intellect, 2018).

103. Lee, *Cultural Policy in South Korea*, 115. Also: Kim Taeyoung 'Creative Economy of the Developmental State: A Case Study of South Korea's Creative Economy Initiatives', *The Journal of Arts Management, Law, and Society* 47, no. 5 (2017): 322–32.

104. Lee, *Cultural Policy in South Korea*; Cf. J. O'Connor, 'Cultural Policy in South Korea: Making a New Patron State', *Cultural Trends* (2019), DOI: 10.1080/09548963.2019.1644801.

105. The *Proposal of the General Office of the State Council on the Development of Maker Space, and Promoting Mass Innovation and Entrepreneurship* was issued by the general office of the State Council in March 2015. The aim was to 'accelerate improvement of the system for managing the cultural sector and the mechanism for cultural production and operation, establish and improve a modern public cultural service system, establish the basic framework of a modern cultural market system'.

106. September 2014: *Proposal of the State Council on Promoting the Integration of Cultural and Creative Industries, Design Services and Related Industries*.

107. July 2016: The General Office of the CCP and the State Council jointly released the *Outline of National Informatization Development Strategy*. 国家信息化发展战略纲要 Cf. Yu Hong, 'Reading the 13th Five-Year Plan: Reflections on China's ICT Policy', *International Journal of Communication* 11 (2017): 1755–74.

108. 'Mass entrepreneurship and innovation' not only refers to being innovative in fields of technology, commerce, and culture; its essence lies in the innovation of ideas and systems, which can inject more creative vigour into the public. Since Premier of China Li Keqiang proposed 'mass entrepreneurship and innovation' at the 2014 Summer Davos in Tianjin, it has been viewed as a new engine for China's economic growth. Cf. Keane and Chen, 'Entrepreneurial Solutionism, Characteristic Cultural Industries and the Chinese Dream'; X. Gu and P. Shea, 'Fabbing the Chinese-Maker Identity', in *The Critical Makers Reader: (un) Learning Technology*, ed. L. Bogers and L. Chiappini (Amsterdam: Institute of Network Cultures, 2019).

109. May 2015: General Office of the Ministry of Culture *Plan on Supporting the Growth of Small and Micro Cultural Enterprises*. July 2016: *Outline of the National Informatization Development Strategy*, calling for '*letting online culture flourish, strengthening national*

soft power'. April 2017: Ministry of Finance *Circular on the Application of Cultural Industry Development Special Funds.*

110. Using Polanyi's terminology to describe culture as a 'fictitious commodity', driving economic growth. See: Lee, *Cultural Policy in South Korea*, 115.

111. Cf. Jian Hua, 'The *One Belt, One Road* Initiative and the Masterplan of Shanghai's Cultural Industry', in Rong and O'Connor, *Cultural Industries in Shanghai*, 3–22; W. Su, 'New Strategies of China's Film Industry as Soft Power', *Global Media and Communication* 6, no. 3 (2010): 317–22; W. Sun, 'Slow Boat from China: Public Discourses behind the "Going Global" Media Policy', *International Journal of Cultural Policy* 21, no. 4 (2015): 400–18; A. Vlassis, 'Soft Power, Global Governance of Cultural Industries and Rising Powers: The Case of China', *International Journal of Cultural Policy* 22, no. 4 (2016): 481–96.

112. As Garnham had suggested of the UK 'creative industries' in 2005. N. Garnham, 'From Cultural to Creative Industries: An Analysis of the Implications of the "Creative Industries'" Approach to Arts and Media Policy Making in the United Kingdom', *International Journal of Cultural Policy* 11, no. 1 (2005): 15–29, 2005, 20. Cf. Chapter 2 above.

113. Facebook, Apple, Amazon, Netflix, Google; Baidu, Alibaba, Tencent and Xiaomi; N. Srnicek, *Platform Capitalism* (London: John Wiley, 2016).

114. S. Shan, 'Chinese Cultural Policy and the Cultural Industries', *City, Culture & Society* 5, no. 3 (2014): 115–21.

115. Lin, 'Be Creative for the State'.

116. Zhang, 'From Institution to Industry', 301.

117. On Bo Xilai, cf. J. Blanchette, *China's New Red Guards: The Return of Radicalism and the Rebirth of Mao Zedong* (Oxford: Oxford University Press, 2019), 104–14; On Harbin, cf. K. Wang, 'Creative Industries with Chinese Characteristics: A Comparative Analysis of Public Funding for Culture in Three Chinese Cities', in *Routledge Handbook of Cultural and Creative Industries in Asia*, ed. L. Lim and H. -K. Lee (London: Routledge, 2019), 90–103.

118. Cultural Management is now a growing academic discipline in China, with over 200 such programmes at masters level, and a proliferating number of conferences on this subject (Private Communication with Head of Cultural Management, Shanghai Jiaotong University).

119. Total (local and national) expenditure for *Culture, Sport and Media* increased in the period 2007–17 from 898.64 to 3391.33 million RMB; *Culture* represented over one third of this total, and *Radio, Film, TV, Press and Publication* under a quarter. *China Statistic Yearbook on Culture and Related Industries* (2018).

120. P. Bourdieu, *Distinction: A Social Critique of the Judgement of Taste* (London: Routledge, 1984).

121. Zhang, 'Nationalism, Mass Culture, and Intellectual Strategies in Post-Tiananmen China', 130.

122. Mark Fisher's 'popular modernism' is a way of describing the reformatting of traditional cultural hierarchies after the 1970s. M. Fisher, *Ghosts of My Life: Writings on Depression, Hauntology and Lost Futures* (Winchester: Zero Books, 2014).

123. '[T]he dominant fraction [of the dominant class] cannot safely leave the cultural field to be shaped by the interstatus group competition between subsets of the dominated fraction, since the reproduction of their economic capital now depends directly upon both the costs of production and the size of the markets for symbolic goods.' N. Garnham, 'Bourdieu, the Cultural Arbitrary and Television', in *Bourdieu: Critical Perspectives,* ed. C. Calhoun, E. LiPuma and M. Postone (Cambridge: Polity, 1993), 178–92, 189.

124. A. Dirlik and X. Zhang, 'Introduction: Postmodernism and China', in *Postmodernism and China,* ed. A. Dirlik and X. Zhang (Durham, NC: Duke University Press, 2000), 1–17: 15.

125. cf. Oakley and O'Connor, 'Introduction', 1–31.

126. Zhao, *Communication in China*, 62.

127. Srnicek, *Platform Capitalism*; S. Zuboff, *Surveillance Capitalism: The Fight for a Human Future at the New Frontier of Power* (London: Profile Books, 2019).

128. Strittmatter, *We Have Been Harmonised*; K. Li Xan Wong and A. Shields Dobson, 'We're Just Data: Exploring China's Social Credit System in Relation to Digital Platform Ratings Cultures in Westernised Democracies', *Global Media and China* 4, no. 2 (2019): 220–32; J. Lanchester, 'Document Number Nine', *London Review of Books* 41 (2019): 3–10, 19.

129. For a discussion of investment in AI from a geopolitical viewpoint, cf. J. Johnson, 'The End of Military-Techno Pax Americana? Washington's Strategic Responses to Chinese AI-enabled Military Technology', *The Pacific Review* (2019): DOI: 10.1080/09512748.2019.1676299.

130. Andrejevic, *Infoglut*, 309.

131. 'The innovation under Leninism was democratic centralism, which now seems to be evolving new forms of intensive central surveillance based on automatic systems, which would diminish the party-state's reliance on techniques of political persuasion. The outcome of the present tendencies, in which both state control and individual agency are being enhanced, is unclear.' S. Marginson, 'How Should Universities Respond to the New Cold War?', *University World News*, 16 November 2019, https: //www.universityworldnews.com/post.php?story=20191112103413758. Accessed 16 November 2019.

8

Creative Subjects

Introduction

In the last chapter, we outlined how the reform of the cultural system in China was undertaken, aiming to create a modern market-based socialist culture, addressing the consumption needs of its citizens while maintaining core socialist values. The Chinese party-state sought to ensure these core values, and its determining role in defining them, not through external content control – 'censorship' – but by becoming the prime market organizer of the cultural production system. In so doing, it flew in the face of those who saw the growth of the sovereign creative consumer, and the entrepreneurs who worked to satisfy their needs, as inevitably transformative of China's state-led system. The proliferation of market-based culture after 1978 did have great emancipatory promise, recalling similar cultural transformations in the West from the 1960s – undermining the hierarchical dominance of traditional intellectuals and providing a space in which new subjectivities, individual and collective, could explore the possibilities of China's new sense of modernity.

The ability of the state to structure the market-state system so as to restrict the democratic potential of this new culture system testified both to the organizational capacity of the Chinese state and to the limits of the 'creative consumer' as transformative force. So too the increasing promotion of the cultural industries as a growth sector drew on a developmental state capacity which repudiated a 'creative industries' script reliant on the withdrawal of the state in favour of the private sector animated by 'bottom-up' entrepreneurialism. The state's capacity to control and develop the new cultural system reflects a political economy approach, one which resists the notion of self-organizing markets at the same time as acknowledging the role of the cultural system in the management of social and political subjects. This reflects both the limited adoption of neo-liberalism within China, and, in its concern with the efficacy of the symbolic, its continued commitment to the modern. This, we suggested, provided a space which kept open the possibility of both socialist and democratic contestation within China. However, as the cultural system merged with that of digital information and communications, the desire for automated control 'beneath' the symbolic realm of culture and society has become increasingly strong.

255

This chapter returns to the idea of the 'creative imaginary' that we introduced at the beginning of this book. For Bob Jessop, an 'economic imaginary' is a project of 'semiosis', essential to 'construing, constructing, and temporarily stabilizing capitalist social formations at least within specific spatio-temporal fixes and their zones of relative stability'.[1] Such an imaginary actively works to modify a range of discursive practices and affective meanings in order to assemble people and things into a coherent programme around which change can be managed.[2] For us, the 'creative imaginary' – which underlies the related concepts of creative industries, creative cities and creative class or subjects – worked to manage the contested and emancipatory space of culture at a moment when it was moving from a position relatively peripheral to the economy to one much more central. If the creative imaginary worked to reduce the space of culture to that of the creative industries or creative economy, hollowing out its relationship to democratic citizenship, then at the same time it transformed cultural work into creative labour, similarly reducing its emancipatory promise.

Jessop's use of 'assemblage' suggests that a heterogeneous range of ideas and actors (people, institutions, technologies) is being marshalled under this project, and that any 'solution' is not fully planned in advance but emerges incrementally, through evolutionary patterns of 'variation, selection and retention'.[3] The 'creative imaginary', arriving around 2005, presented a number of challenges to China, as it was meant to; but it was not something that could be ignored, promising as it did a dynamic new wave of economic, social and cultural modernization. However, the Chinese state had a developed capacity to respond to this challenge, and working with 'variation, selection and retention' was an essential aspect of its mode of governance. In Shanghai, it possessed the means to engage with this creative imaginary, to work out a 'spatio-temporal fix' by which its useful elements might be accommodated within the Chinese system. In this chapter, we trace how this creative imaginary – both a new modernizing promise and a detailed 'policy technology' (what we will call the 'creativity bundle') for the mobilization of new creative subjects – was adapted and put to work in China.[4] More specifically, we look at how this happened in Shanghai, and in particular through a closely related policy technology – that of the 'creative cluster'.[5]

The creative imaginary: Setting culture to work

Any 'imaginary' is necessarily a complex and heterogeneous entity. It cannot be reduced to an essential organizing idea open to 'unmasking' by critique, let alone any easy 'falsification'. An 'imaginary' puts into play deep-rooted historical tropes which are as affective-aesthetic as they are rational.[6] There are logics of power at work organizing imaginaries, but they are difficult to challenge as they work to define the very grounds on which any challenge could be intelligible, fixing what Rancière calls the 'distribution of the sensible'.[7] 'Creativity' as an unassailable 'good' worked in this way. The 'creative imaginary' grew out of a moment of transition – schematically, Fordism to post-Fordism – and acquired an emancipatory energy. 'Creative industries' worked to make such energy productive within a neo-liberal political framework, and it produced a codified policy script we call the 'creativity bundle'.

The proliferating critiques of 'creativity' are only possible now because this particular bundle has loosened, with creativity becoming banal and the 'creative imaginary' unravelling around the financialization of the 'creative city' and the everyday reality of labour in the cultural/creative industries. But as 'assemblage' it was always more than the 'C' word; we have already intimated the emancipatory, utopian impulses it articulated, and in its demise these impulses may disarticulate themselves from the 'creativity bundle' to be invested elsewhere. What this future 'something else' is we do not know, but following Walter Benjamin, we suggest that part of it may be found in utopian images of a past now set free from the policy technology that the creative imaginary became.

This 'creativity bundle' sought to promote newly productive creative subjects, working in fluid project teams across networks rather than institutions, entrepreneurs learning how to reinvent themselves in a more dynamic space 'outside the box' of a formal job, picking up new skills, and carving out new opportunities in a transformed creative field. The new creative subject was charged to combine the self-directed autonomy of the avant-garde artist with the 'creative destruction' of the Schumpeterian entrepreneur. This happened in a 'creative milieu', a semiautonomous network embedded in particular urban places and through which new ideas emerge, circulate, mutate and accelerate. This milieu would foster an economy of small business or start-ups, entities operating in a zone between the hierarchical, exclusive firm and looser social networks, between competition and collaboration, between the market and 'civil society'. Milieu operates as a kind of 'ecosystem' neither amenable to top-down state planning nor corporate control. The creative economy thus demanded new kinds of cities (or at least, zones therein) which encouraged creative milieus, new kinds of industrial organization (small business ecosystems) and new kinds of subjects able to autonomously create and innovate.

The creative city discourse positioned cultural industries as quintessentially urban. The new 'cultural industries' had an 'elective affinity' with the city, the 'canary in the cage', a synecdoche of the wider creativity of the city. They were not simply 'replacement industries', but rather the city reimagined. More people were participating in the production and consumption of culture, new 'spatial practices' and a transformation of the urban imaginary in new 'spaces of representation'.[8] These challenged the Fordist city, though they did so when that city's fixed 'representational spaces' were already on the verge of disappearance. Small-scale urban cultural production at the fringes of the 'mainstream' cultural industries was very much part of the claim for greater community involvement in the planning of 'everyday life'. They contested established cultural hierarchies and sought the means to create new spaces of production and consumption, as can be seen in the rise of punk and other forms of 'urban cultural movements' that extended across the cities of Europe and North America from the 1960s. These claims for a wider participation were linked to older avant-garde traditions of bringing art and life together. This had been revived in the community arts movement, but it had also circulated through the spaces of popular culture since the 1960s.[9] The connections between new forms of popular music and radical art traditions in Europe and North America are now widely acknowledged.[10] Increased participation meant an active involvement in the spaces of the production and consumption of culture in new kinds of urban spaces. Punk's 'here are three chords, now go form a band' came out of a long line of such thinking.[11]

There were also crossovers between these new popular cultures and the older spaces of urban bohemia. In film, print, music, photography, fashion as well as the visual and performing arts, new genres and new modes of production were emerging outside or alongside the older cultural industry structures. New aesthetic forms were turning older ones inside out, as they moved between avant-garde and popular currents, and between old and new lefts. This was certainly driven by new technologies of production and distribution; but it was also about new audiences with more knowledge, more money and more time to spend it. Though commonly described as 'new markets', this signally misrepresents the profound cultural transformation set under way, in which these new forms of cultural participation emerged as an extension of T. H. Marshall's 'social citizenship'.[12] By the 1960s and 1970s, cultural participation, and the means necessary for such, was becoming a central part of social citizenship. What was distinctive was that 'cultural citizenship' now extended beyond the subsidized arts to embrace the realities of commercial cultural production and consumption. By the mid-1990s, cultural practitioners and community activists increasingly operated as cultural policy intermediaries both inside and outside the formal policy process, working with and against established policy.[13]

Essential to this new sense of cultural citizenship was the promise of cultural work. Opposed to the rigidly structured, boring, nine-to-five jobs-for-life of Fordism, it promised meaningful, fulfilling ways of making a living – aspirations, among the new educated white-collar workers in France, which were part of a broader contestation of existing life and work structures that exploded in

1968.[14] This contestation drew on the 'artistic critique' of capitalism, concerned with issues of alienation and aspirations to human fulfilment. This contrasted with the 'social critique', which they associated with the claims for social justice led by the workers' movement. We take issue with this hard and fast distinction; though their divergence has become increasingly visible since the 1970s, this was not an inevitable trajectory. Discontent with industrial work per se, not just its remuneration, for example, was famously attributed to the factory workers by the Italian Autonomist school, as well as being attested to by many sociological studies of blue-collar workers in the 1970s.[15] In addition, we would suggest that such a contestation happened not just in the workplace of major corporations and public institutions but across the whole social space of Fordism.

Aspirations to the personal satisfaction and meaning promised by cultural work related to the historical distinction between the drudgery of manual labour and the spiritual fulfilment of artistic work. This in turn related to the wider opposition expressed in aesthetic theory between the disinterested play of art for itself, and the instrumental, disenchanted rationality of economy and administration. The new possibilities of cultural work glimpsed in the interstices of a decaying Fordism contained powerful utopian impulses, the 'artistic critique' finding expression in the contestation of the Fordist city. In many of the abandoned spaces of the city, new communities of cultural producers emerged, new 'representational spaces' in which the city-machine was reconfigured as a space of play, a 'soft city' of mutable subjects and loose social ties.[16] New cultural producers, intermediaries and audiences began to bring back 'junk' spaces of the city into active use, in ways that enhanced their cultural and – it quickly emerged – economic value.[17]

The cultural industries as a local development option emerged at a moment when the 'sense of an ending', of an industrial civilization giving way to something else, was particularly intense across Europe, Australia and North America.[18] By the end of the 1980s, this transition was being framed as a shift from Fordism to post-Fordism. As a repudiation of the Fordist city, and those subjects forced to work in it, the occupation of the abandoned functional spaces by previously marginalized cultural activities was experienced as an emancipation and a vindication. After being told to get a 'proper job', cultural producers now represented the future of work. If Adorno's Culture Industry represented the imposition of Fordist mass production and consumption on a recalcitrant artisanal remnant, these new cultural industries were at the cutting edge of this emergent post-Fordism.[19]

The new 'cultural industries' were not anything like the large corporate entities previously associated with that term. They were small and micro-businesses working often in very un-business-like ways – driven by cultural values rather than (primarily) money, highly fluid in their patterns of organization and distributed across strongly place-based networks, usually in specific zones of the city.

259

Initially outside the ken of most local economic development agencies, they were increasingly addressed over the 1990s via the policy discourse of SME economies.[20] Those promoting the cultural industries looked to the kinds of economic geography of 'embeddedness', a new kind of industrial region, where the Fordist-era opposition of state-directed and corporate-integrated markets made less sense.[21]

Aspirations for the urban cultural economy across the 1990s had a utopian dimension, where the end of Fordism would give rise to a new, more human economy, exemplified in the new centrality of culture.[22] The cultural values produced by the new urban 'independents', 'entrepreneurs', 'neo-bohemians' or 'cultural intermediaries' demanded different ways of organizing work than those of standard business models.[23] Cultural economy was not to be an economy like any other, nor available to standard industrial development strategies. The way in which its work was organized, the complex values and motivations of cultural producers, the dispersed, fragmented yet highly networked nature of the sector, its complex embeddedness in the urban ecology – all these seemed to demand a new kind of economic governance, where cultural industries are seen as inextricably part of a wider set of social and cultural interests and values, not reducible to the economic. The promises of cultural economy could only fully be redeemed when the cultural producers had equity in the values that they produced and full participation in the governance of the cultural ecology. A coherent cultural economy programme, it seemed, must hand over (at least some of) the keys to the city to cultural producers and citizen-consumers alike.

These utopian impulses may not have made the full journey to utopian project, though they persisted within the creative imaginary and the policy bundle which operationalized it.[24] Nonetheless, this policy bundle, now fastened to the new 'creative industries', was ultimately organized around different dynamics. Most directly in relation to the United Kingdom was the shift within New Labour from a European social democracy-focused 'stakeholder capitalism' to the model of a Silicon Valley entrepreneur-driven innovation economy. It also involved the kind of 'soft' neo-liberalism 2.0 we discussed in Chapter 4, where aspirations which cut against the socially conservative agenda of Reagan and Thatcher became the site of a new kind of labour discipline organized around the 'entrepreneurial self'. This also drew on the 'Californian ideology' of Schumpeterian 'creative destruction' undertaken by Randian entrepreneurial heroes, an economic model that was not about expanding and devolving the capacity of the state but of it 'getting out of the way'. The creative industries – at least up to the dot-com bust of 2002 – adopted much of the 'technological imaginary', especially in the field of media and 'new media'.[25] Equally, it picked up elements of the libertarianism associated with the digital and the cybernetic, from the self-organizing subjects of extreme free-markets to the bizarre hyper-modernism of Nick Land's 'Deleuzian

Thatcherism'. The deeply anti-democratic, reactionary nature of this strand is now readily apparent.[26]

Creative clusters

In asserting the need for more 'holistic' 'creative' governance drawing on the non-linear sensibilities of the arts, the 'creative city' thesis connected the agglomeration of cultural industries with an older 'elective affinity' between art, artists and the city. This could be traced back through the metropolitan avant-gardes and modernisms of the pre- and inter-war periods, with their 'villages' and 'quarters', through to *La Vie Bohème* of Baudelaire, and to the early nineteenth century. Of course, the integration of bohemia into the world of work and production was an essential part of the creative imaginary. Though creativity was conceived as a capacity almost coterminous with the history of the city itself, it was not evenly distributed, however, as particular zones of the city stood out, often marginal ex-industrial areas available for cheap, flexible and multiple use.[27] These inner-urban creative milieus became increasingly visible in the later 1990s, and their function for the wider creative 'ecosystem' (a word coming into vogue) noted. Richard Lloyd wrote a good account of one such, Wicker Park in Chicago, seeing it as an example of 'neo-bohemia', training ground for creative labour:

> Being an artist often involves adopting a distinct persona. There is a recognizable lifestyle, including modes of dress and self-presentation. Neo-bohemia, like its modernist forerunners, is a setting in which 'living like an artist' is facilitated, and a habitus amendable to creative pursuits is fostered.[28]

These 'neo-bohemian' zones provided a modicum of employment – a combination of paid (usually low-skilled) and unpaid (usually art-related) – providing a base from which creative careers could take their first steps. While economically marginal activities, they facilitated the building up of 'symbolic' or reputational capital, which allowed (some of) them to eventually move on to more sustainable careers. What these spaces provided was not just economic but also sociocultural; they allowed entry into a creative field and provided a certain emotional security at a vulnerable stage of habitus formation.[29]

The importance of such spaces to nurture artists and cultural workers – to provide entry, learning and protection – was widely acknowledged in the academic and policy literature. This formed part of an informal 'soft' infrastructure of the city that had emerged since the 1970s, as we noted above. They began in low-rent industrial zones of the inner city – Zukin's *SoHo* – where their occupation by

261

artists was barely noticed, though Zukin was quick to show how both niche real estate ('loft living') and new aestheticized forms of urban vernacular consumption ('artistic lifestyles') soon moved in.[30] But such zones could also include public cultural spaces, emerging around museums, concert halls, galleries and educational facilities, along with small-scale informal artist workspaces, or community 'arts and craft' spaces. From the 1980s, new or relocated public, private and non-governmental cultural facilities within refurbished older industrial-era buildings became a way of regenerating rundown parts of the city. From the 1990s, and spurred on by the cultural industries agenda, these urban regeneration interventions began to include space for small-scale arts and cultural industry production – though also with strong leisure (cafes, bars, restaurants) and retail (bookstores, design shops and so on) elements. It was this complex urban infrastructure that was, after Michael Porter's papers of the late 1990s, retrofitted under the term 'cluster'.[31]

Much of the subsequent literature on clusters pointed to the confusion of objectives – urban regeneration, city branding, supporting cultural industries, community outreach – but perhaps this confusion was inevitable, for they sought to be catalytic nodes, spaces which somehow connected to the wider cultural dynamics of the city.[32] Many of these clusters or spaces were envisaged as common spaces, part of the cultural offer of the city, whose benefits could not be solely recouped by cluster management, hence justifying public investment. Though the effects of these clusters ('externalities') were increasingly justified in economic terms (such as 'incubating creative businesses') they were deemed valuable in themselves, part of the public good of city life. Many of these spaces shared an imaginary of new forms of work, of collaboration, of community, a transformative vision of a different kind of city (a 'space of representation' in Lefebvre's sense). Though they could be written up for reporting purposes as creative industry powerhouses, the cultural benefits were mostly more important than their economic impact. They sought to nurture ('curate') common cultural values in their tenants, suppliers and visitors, as part of the 'feel', the shared symbolic capital of the place. Economic relationships within creative clusters are ambiguous, as tenants negotiate values, profit-seeking and business ethics. Indeed, as the 'organic' clusters around them succumbed to real estate speculation, these clusters could see themselves as a counter to such gentrification.[33]

Michael Porter's 'cluster' gradually replaced terms such as 'quarter' or 'village' as descriptive of these urban spaces. Though primarily focused on a larger urban and regional scale, the imprimatur of a Harvard Business School economist was important for city governments, who seized on the word as a way to bring new industries, new spaces and new subjects together in a workable set of operating principles. Whilst Porter referred back to Alfred Marshall's account of nineteenth-century Manchester's industrial agglomeration, its advantage down to it having 'something in the air', his policy script moved rapidly from atmospherics to an abstract 'factors of production' model in which 'traded and untraded' dependencies were the main rational for 'agglomerations'. Porter's neo-classical economic model became the central heuristic in a thousand 'mapping documents'. Richard Florida's famous '3 Ts' – talent, tolerance, technology – paralleled the rise of the 'cluster', allowing the complex embeddedness of urban production to be reduced to statistical proxies amenable to city indexing. In this way, clusters became framed as purely economic concentrations, the connections to a wider transformative agenda reduced to growing the creative economy through encouraging entrepreneurship and start-up incubation. Now the staple of global policy agencies, creative clusters – or 'hubs' as they are often called – have been stripped of their larger urbanistic role, their communal effects replicated by commercial 'co-working' spaces, and their connections to the dynamics of financialized real estate now explicit.

Creative clusters in Shanghai

The 'cluster' was, for a decade after 2005, the primary means whereby Shanghai sought to promote the creative industries.[34] Their success (or otherwise) as active concentrations of creative industries has been subject of much debate, but they are key to understanding how the creative imaginary was accommodated in the city. For a while, in the first decade of the century, these clusters stood for more than agglomerations of creative businesses but became 'spaces of representation' articulating a wider imaginary of creative modernity, both internationally and within Shanghai. This explains the inordinate amount of attention they gained, and the sense of disappointment they generated among observers. But ultimately these clusters were more than policy replication, facilitating a process of learning to take place in Shanghai (and China); that is, how to manage creative labour within the spaces of the post-industrial city.

The Shanghai municipal government enthusiastically embraced the idea of 'creative industries' when it first arrived in 2005. Beijing restricted its general application, but Shanghai was allowed to use the term, testing out its possibilities. The modernizing charge of the creative industries sat well with Shanghai's resurgent narrative as the cosmopolitan city of commerce, China's global gateway to modernity. But it also arrived at a time when Shanghai – like Western cities twenty years before – was faced with a rising glut of redundant industrial built stock. Since the mid-to-late 1990s, Shanghai had pursued a policy of deindustrialization, not only closing down the old 'smoke-stack' industries but also moving large-scale production to the edges of the city (or other cities in the Yangtze region). Shanghai's shiny landscape of the urban modern grew against a backdrop of a cast-off industrial identity, a disavowed past whose local traces yet persisted against the rural origins of the migrant workers and the nostalgias of Shanghai Modern. This is important in understanding why Shanghai, in its adoption of the creative industries over the decade from 2005, prioritized the idea of 'creative cluster'. It was pragmatic, but it also put into play this industrial past as 'structure of feeling' in ways that opened a connection to creative industries as a transformative imaginary.

Creative clusters, as they had emerged in Europe and North America, and extended globally, had become spatially embodied urban scenes, 'cool' zones linked to refurbished ex-industrial spaces.[35] They dotted the informal itinerary of a global epistemic community forming around the 'creative economy'.[36] These 'cool' areas were not the older museum, monument and gallery quarters, nor the traditional or classical cultural cities; they were cities and spaces that had to be sought out by an epistemic community *in the know*. Greg Richards and Julie Wilson also talked of 'creative tourists' (though they resented being called 'tourists') who looked for non-standard destinations and were often cultural practitioners themselves.[37] They headed for sites where 'experiences' involving interaction with locals could be had. The 'clusters' or site-based scenes formed an ideal destination, providing a more authentic experience and the possibility of glimpsing a new, youthful creative culture hidden from mainstream tourists. As global mobility increased, these global flows could bring enhanced visibility of particularly 'cool' urban areas. Indeed, these creative tourists could often seek out longer periods of residence, working remotely and locally, entering deep into the scene.[38]

Their local impact should not be underestimated, as they formed a kind of cosmopolitan micro-site in which global flows of images, sounds, texts, ideas (and people) could be accessed, creating links between similar sites elsewhere. These sites could attract flows of policy-makers, consultants, practitioners and cultural consumers in a way that had real impact on the local and carried this local back to the transnational level (often via PowerPoint slides or guest speaker invites extended to managers or owners of these sites). These milieus had a particular relationship to the global, in which a certain cosmopolitan sensibility was fostered through these flows. They helped structure, and were structured by, a certain cosmopolitan sensibility, a habitus oriented both to the local and to the horizon of the global. We might see it as a form of global modernity that was certainly not a slavish copy of some imagined metropolitan origin but yet looked to these origins as part of an affective identification with the promise of a global creativity. It was more than simply 'culture as resource' in Yudice's sense, where arguments for cultural funding could utilize its various social benefits.[39] It was culture as a resource for a different kind of future, both local and global at once.[40]

In these milieus, or 'micro-sites',[41] unorthodox lifestyles, marginalized and sometimes suppressed, received a certain degree of acceptance. New gender roles, expressions of sexuality, or countercultural views associated with the residents of these areas could now acquire the validity of 'resource'.[42] Such sites could claim to speak for a younger, aspirant 'new middle class', invested in educational and cultural capital, as opposed to the incumbent powers of property and capital. These youthful groups could assemble around 'creative industries' and 'creative cities' in ways that could resonate with the kinds of more radical political interventions of the various 'Twitter' and 'colour revolutions' over the last decade.[43]

For the Shanghai government, the 'creative cluster' was a way of tying the abstractions of the 'creative city' directly to the creative industries, providing a practical policy handle to address Shanghai's strategic shift away from industry into real estate speculation and advanced business services. However, there was more involved. We have already seen how the return of older forms of urbanity mobilized around the creative city could connect with Shanghai's own (selectively) recovered past as Shanghai Modern. Here was another form of this, as the creative cluster would be more than an adapted 'industrial park', a model that had been pioneered in Shenzhen and which had proliferated across China as enclosed spaces for overseas collaboration around research-led technology development. In Shanghai they were to be 'spaces of representation' for a new creative modernity.

Shanghai's cosmopolitan commercialism had positioned the city as a 'contact space' for flows of global capital, know-how and elite workers.[44] Shanghai's *haipai* culture was used to reprogram the urban cultural landscape and rebrand its identity as a global cultural city. The city's heroic urban modernity was focused on producing a Manhattan-style skyline driven by real estate, finance, advanced business services and high-end consumption. The creative industries, which the Shanghai government separated from its more sensitive cultural elements, were seized upon as advanced business services for the new global metropolis – design, advertising, marketing, business consulting and so on. Prime office space slightly outside the CBD – such as that being developed along the old industrial district of Suzhou Creek – seemed the most apt infrastructure. The kind of urbanism we have just evoked – dense interactions, autonomous micro-spaces, affective investment in place, various kinds of artist-bohemian scenes – was as different from this vision as it was from the recycled memorabilia of Shanghai Modern. Creative clusters allowed Shanghai to test out these newer kinds of affective spaces in which a profitable utilization of redundant or undervalued urban stock for new kinds of economic activities could also generate images of the contemporary global modern. At the same time, they provided a manageable context in which the 'creativity bundle' might be managed.

265

Unpicking the bundle

The 'creativity bundle' required some unpicking, as its constituent elements were not immediately assimilable within the Chinese market-state system, nor in its own emergent 'creative imaginary'. The autonomous artist, creating *ex nihilo*; the entrepreneur as free radical within a contract-based market system; the semi-autonomous milieu structured around 'countercultural' values and 'creative destruction' – these were alien to China.[45] This can be seen in the many ambivalences around Richard Florida's 'creative class thesis', which not only concerned the 'gay index' (the connection between this and creative entrepreneurship created intense bemusement in China) but also the 'bohemian index', the sense that loose social ties, non-conformism, individualism and so on were something to be welcomed. This was simply not the case in a Chinese society that sought ways to integrate the individual and the social. Indeed, it had been the association of creative industries with the famous UK government definition as derived from 'individual creativity, skill and talent' that been a stumbling block for Beijing. Yet entrepreneurship, and productive creativity, was something to be valued.

Shanghai, of course, had repositioned its historical DNA as being able to accommodate the image of the entrepreneur. It had welcomed Jiang Zemin's embrace of entrepreneurs into its ranks in 2001, though this had been deeply contested and highly ambiguous in its implementation.[46] The creative industries agenda certainly worked with the global, cosmopolitan, business-oriented image of the city, and the entrepreneurial values associated with the creative industries were much more easily used in its local imaginary as the commercial, money-driven city long open to cosmopolitan influences. Shanghai had been proactive in inscribing a line between cultural and creative industries, basing it on a distinction between 'sensitive' cultural and 'safe' (i.e. ideologically neutral) content. The city's economic committee uncoupled 'design', 'lifestyle' and related business services from those 'cultural' sectors with more ideological baggage. This gave them control of those 'creative' sectors which might have fallen under the purview of the cultural committee.[47] Getting the creative industries designated as 'economic' gave the city much more local autonomy over their development, this based on their conceptualization as advanced business services rather than any loosening of cultural control.[48]

The adoption of the 'creative industry cluster' model (CIC) was key to making the figure of the creative entrepreneur productive within the Chinese system, providing for that process of 'variation, selection and retention' at work at all levels of government in China. CICs allowed the new creative industries agenda to gain traction among local authorities, many of whom were confused by the concept of 'creative industries' as they responded to government signals and the new economic opportunities the new agenda seemed to promise. The CIC model allowed local governments to make a link between 'creative industries' and 'creative city', and to locate the creativity bundle – creative subjects, working in micro-businesses, embedded in a creative milieu – within a manageable spatial format.[49] The CIC model proved to be a useful technology, one that was replicable, scalable and containable, suiting the experimental and pragmatic modularity of the Chinese market-state system.

From 2005 onwards, CICs spread rapidly across China, the big East Coast cities in the forefront. The spurt of CICs was made possible by the rapid adaption of an existing model for promoting high-tech industries through industry and science parks. In turn, these built on the long socialist tradition of 'industry bases' where all elements of the production chain could be integrated and enhanced.[50] As part of a local development state strategy, technology or science parks facilitated the attraction of inward investment and the development of local industrial capacity, capturing the innovation effects of both foreign and smaller companies for the wider industrial sector. At the same time, as major real estate development projects, they opened up great opportunities for the local entrepreneurial state. This 'industry base' model could be scaled up for use in large-scale CIC initiatives if necessary, such as in animation, post-production, film, games software, and indeed mass-produced 'fine art'.[51] As officially designated, geographically bounded (walls, fences and guards) and administratively contained spaces, CICs were separate from the urban spaces in which they were situated.

In the metropolitan cities, pre-eminently Shanghai, pressures of space linked to the ongoing deindustrialization of central areas suggested a different adaption of the industry base model, linked to the reuse of an older, industrial infrastructure. The reforms of the SOEs, which accelerated in the mid-1990s, saw whole industrial histories going the way of the *lilong* cultures, under the bulldozer. The 'creative industries' arrived in China already linked to discourses of urban regeneration and the reuse of industrial space for cultural purposes. In a city with an immense amount of industrial stock, this was a 'spatial fix' welcomed by the municipal government; it sought to couple the industry base model with the transformative imaginary of the 'creative cluster'. This coupling might be seen not just as adoptive 'policy technology' transfer but a form of 'meshwork' – 'connect[ing] unlike things in a distributed structure that could be articulated (and therefore do work in the world) without suppressing their difference'.[52] That is, in a classic 'Global South' fashion, Shanghai's urban CICs could be connected, via a range of improvised couplings, to the flows channelled by a global creative imaginary.[53] Such 'meshwork' required input from 'intermediaries' outside established policy actors. Local governments and developers were brought into contact with newer local actors, some of whom sought to reinvent a Shanghainese 'urban cultural sensibility' through its industrial-era rather than colonial-era past, and others who were aware of the new kinds of transformed industrial spaces that had appeared across the globe in the previous decades.

New urban cultural sensibility

It was Chinese contemporary art which pioneered the reuse of industrial space. The emergence of contemporary art – breaking with both Chinese classical and socialist realist or 'propaganda' traditions – has been well documented, and now of course is a specified genre in the global art world.[54] It is often indexed directly against the fortunes of the post-1978 reforms, rising or falling against the 'liberalisation' or 'regressive authoritarianism' of the regime.[55] However, its position in post-reform China is far more complex, relating as much to the ability of the Chinese state to accommodate the financial flows of the global art market and utilize its cultural capital as it does its inevitable arrival into Western-style modernity. Contemporary art was marginal, though intermittently acknowledged, through the late 1980s into the 1990s. Chinese cities such as Shanghai, seeking to build the cultural infrastructure of a 'modern city', had looked to classical music and the traditional performing arts as a source of international cultural capital. The meteoric rise in the profile of the international art world – from its entanglement with popular culture in the late 1960s to the 'Young British Artists' moment of the late 1990s, central to New Labour's 'Cool Britannia' that helped sell the creative industries – came as a surprise to the Chinese government.

However, in the late 1990s, Beijing, Shanghai and Guangzhou had already witnessed a movement of contemporary artists into old industrial sites, attracted by cheap rent, large spaces and the aesthetic and historical 'feel' of these old factories and warehouses. Beijing's famous 798 Arts District had its Shanghai equivalent in the warehouses along Suzhou Creek, an old industrial district established by the Japanese from the 1930s, where a number of artist workshops and gallery/exhibition spaces had opened.[56] These early spaces were demolished for new developments in the face of opposition from artists and academic conservationists.[57] One space, first occupied in 1998, survived – an old textile factory on Morganshan Road, which came to be known as 'M50'. Though its existence was always precarious, it began to attract attention among international art brokers, conservationists, cultural policy experts and 'creative' tourists; followed in the mid-noughties by local academics concerned with an emergent 'creative industries' agenda.[58]

M50 was a 'micro-site', in which transnational visitors and local art scenes might encounter each other, and in which a different imaginary of the city could emerge. In 2004, one could directly encounter, even interview, artists working in their studios, with two small cafés creating a sense of public space within the building complex. There was minimal architectural intervention in the factory, and even some residual industrial activity to be found in its outer buildings. Yet two international entities – Bizart and the ShanghART gallery – had already moved in, hosting British Council-funded artist-in-residences.[59] The reason for M50's rising international profile was not clear to the authorities (who were suspicious) nor to mainstream developers (who were bemused). It both persisted as a space, and was made understandable to the policy world, by the intermediation of the M50 manager, Jin Wei Dong.[60] He was the factory manager, employed by the huge SOE Shangtex, which owned the factory, and he was charged with finding industrial tenants to replace the older textile workers. A source of revenue was also required to pay the pensions of the redundant workers. The entry of artists into the empty textile factory to become M50 was unplanned; the factory management was looking to light industrial use, which proved to be more problematic and less profitable than envisaged. The artists only paid low industrial rent but it was better than nothing. Surprisingly, income from artists' space began to outstrip light industry tenants, making less noise and less mess. It was through this close and increasingly sympathetic interaction with the artists that Jin Wei Dong felt his way towards the specific challenges of managing a 'creative space' that had challenged many in the West. It was his assertion of the viability of this kind of model for older factories and his committed sense of contributing to the wider cultural and urbanistic capacity of Shanghai that began to register with the policy-makers.

A different trajectory could be seen in Taikang Road, in the former French Concession, a dense industrial district with working-class *shikumen* housing dating from 1926.[61] Since the early 1990s, as Shanghai municipal government began to restructure the inner city away from manufacturing, the local Lu Wan district government sought out new occupants, turning old factories into large food markets for example. In 1998, a Chinese contemporary artist, Chen Yi Fei, moved into an old factory, encouraging others to do similarly. Very quickly, in 1999, the district government set up a committee to deal with the increasing adaptive use of factories by artists. The establishment of the committee allowed more arts and cultural businesses to rent and adapt factories. For example, in 1999, encouraged by the management committee, the Yi Lu Fa cultural development company was able to rent a large factory space as its ceramic exhibition studio, receiving ten years' free rent. In 2001, an old food manufacturing plant was converted into Taikang Road Art Centre by the management committee, further consolidating the cultural identity of the area. By the end of 2002, over 80 arts and cultural businesses were renting factory spaces. Aside from securing the cultural uses of the factory spaces, the management committee had also been involved in organizing cultural events, further raising the profile of Taikang Road. Very quickly, the concentration of cultural businesses, including those producing and dealing in antiques, books, visual arts, photography and ceramics, made Taikang Road one of the four most important 'creative clusters' in Shanghai.

Intersecting with this emergent connectivity of local and global art worlds was a flow of architects and designers. Though architectural firms have long been global players, the 'transnational urbanism' they presented to China was directed towards large-scale projects in association with approved local partners.[62] It was Hong Kong and Taiwanese architects, having the requisite language skills and connections, who began to move more independently into potential development sites. The iconic manufacturing heartland of Suzhou Creek, with its rich industrial heritage, began to attract small-scale architect-led developments at the end of the 1990s, often in association with artist-led spaces. Taiwanese architect Teng Kun Yan began the process in 1998 but others followed.[63] Increasingly these new refurbished spaces – always under threat of demolition for 'real' office development – began to attract not only artists but (increasingly international) also design and media firms. Similarly, design firms had begun to move into and refurbish old warehouses in Taikang Road, increasingly using the adjacent *shikumen* residences themselves as small retail outlets.[64]

These more independent architects and designers sought to retrieve an urban sensibility based on industrial heritage with the 'distressed' aesthetic common in the West, already highly visible (and available) to Hong Kong and Taiwanese architects. It was a different, somewhat vernacular urbanism, and one in which the production of art and design provided a micro-site for a different kind of transnational urbanism. It was of course within these milieus that the 'urban-industrial aesthetic' and its application to creative industries became visible to policy-makers. The potential of historical vernacular for real estate development had been recognized in 2004 with the opening of Xintiandi. It took some time before local authorities and developers recognized the potential of attracting creative businesses that were willing to pay commercial-level rents for low-cost industrial space. The big problem in all these early developments was the ad hoc unofficial nature of these cultural activities, and the kinds of tenancy agreements that went with them. The city authorities' attitude to M50 had alternated between benign tolerance and threatening demolition-redevelopment; they had the power to close down such activities at any time as illegal use of industrial land. It was an uncertain situation. What changed was not initially alternative urbanism or even recognition of urban aesthetic-symbolic value, but real estate regulation policy.

In this process, intermediation took place within the administration, as the option to reuse industrial spaces for creative industries emerged as one clear lesson Chinese official delegations took from their many visits to the United Kingdom after 1998. The new lead body for the sector – the Shanghai Creative Industries Centre (SCIC) – was a hybrid of Chinese-style industry bodies with the sorts of agencies that had developed in London, Manchester and other cities. Headed by an ex-naval administrator who had been charged with developing industrial design strategies, He Zeng Qiang had been an early enthusiast both for creative industries and for the refurbished industrial space in which they seemed to be housed. He Zeng Qiang was a key contributor to the business model that would underpin such a process – the ability to designate what were in fact creative commercial services as 'industry'. That is, using the word industry not to stress their economic dimension as in the West but more literally as able to occupy industrial spaces without their land use being redesignated as 'commercial'.[65]

The deindustrialization of the 1990s had left SOEs with land-use rights over large tracts of land. Being allowed to sell on these land-use rights, the SOEs (in the form of the national *danwei*, with head offices in Beijing) rapidly repositioned themselves as major real estate developers. In 2002, local authorities gained the right to determine land use. Therefore, if an SOE wanted to sell industrial land use for commercial development, they had to go through the local state (giving them enhanced leverage) and pay local tax for such redesignation. However, the model that emerged through initiatives such as M50 was that artistic and cultural – soon to be 'creative' – use of old industrial buildings could be effected without a change of land use designation.

He Zeng Qiang was part of the process of the adoption of the new CIC policy which formalized the occupation of industrial spaces by creative industries.[66] It allowed the owner (of land-use rights) to charge high commercial rent for industrial land without having to seek a formal redesignation or paying the fees associated for such a change and the tax on subsequent commercial land use. More usually, developers (which frequently included the district government's own company) would rent land from the SOEs, invest in minimal refurbishment and charge high commercial rents to the new tenant. At the same time, the resultant high-density clustering of commercial firms generated great tax returns for local government. This was the reason why 90 clusters were setup in Shanghai within five years.

CICs take-off

In the development of CICs, we can see how they were quickly adopted and adapted through 'variation, selection and retention'. M50, emerging within a large SOE, with a long-established manager, was in many ways close to the more public sector developments in Europe. The rental income was certainly important, but large commercial profit was not uppermost as its wider cultural benefits were emphasized. M50's profile within China's globally visible contemporary art scene became evermore important leading up to the Expo in 2010. Increasingly recognized for its contribution to Shanghai's 'creative city' global branding, and an opportunity to achieve the global profile of Beijing's 798, Shangtex recouped far more benefits in terms of political capital than it did commercial rent. M50 gradually gained a more strategic position within Shanghai's contemporary art strategy, and Shangtex itself developed other clusters, more related to fashion and design, which was its core manufacturing business.

As Taikang Road's reputation grew, its artists were integrated more into the organization and branding of the area. Chen Yi Fei was invited to be the head of the Taikang Road Arts Association – a volunteer group to facilitate the visioning of cultural development. Chen's public artwork *The Gate of Art* was placed at one end of Taikang Road. Another famous artist – Er Dong Qiang, whose photography studio was next door to Chen's – hosted many high-profile international cultural events and exhibitions, further extending the cultural significance of Taikang Road. Artist Huang Yong Yu renamed the factories and the adjacent *shikumen* laneways as *Tianzifang* in 1999. So named, and frequently classed as an 'organic' or 'bottom-up' cluster, it rapidly spread into the surrounding *shikumen* laneways.

In November 2004, the first cultural business opened in a private laneway residence; within a year, more than 30 households had rented out their homes to micro 'creative' businesses – graphic design, crafts, photography and advertising companies. They were mostly run by expats and overseas Chinese who valued the nostalgic *shikumen* lifestyle, unimpressed by the modern developments being thrown up in the nearby CBD. By the end of 2006, this had spread to the adjacent laneways. Strictly speaking, the tenancy agreements between the local residents and creative tenants were not legally protected, as existing law prevents residential buildings being used for commercial activities. But the district government tolerated this 'unofficial' adaptive of residential buildings as it provided a cheap way of upgrading old working-class housing – a serious challenge for cash-strapped local authorities with large amounts of such stock. In April 2005, the Shanghai municipal government enthusiastically named it as an official 'Shanghai Creative Industries Cluster', which, with the blessing of the district government, stimulated further activity in the area. However, in a clear illustration of how consumption drives out production, these new 'creative businesses' were relatively expensive bars and restaurants, along with proliferating souvenir shops aimed at tourists. 'Art' gave way to 'culture' as a driver of gentrification – the up-market fashion and design retail, along with the food and drink rapidly becoming part of Shanghai's cosmopolitan consumption offer. Droves of tourists were taken through in search of a *shikumen* heritage, diversifying Shanghai's leisure consumption offer and sparking a thousand imitations across China. *Tianzifang* now is pure tourism, and the surrounding area, which had been earmarked for creative industries, has been given over to the development of a huge shopping mall, with extensive food and drink offers, along with high-rise apartments.

Different again, 1933 (or 'Old Millfun') represented a CIC directly instigated by the city government in the wake of their adoption of a creative industries policy. An old slaughterhouse located in the Hongkou area of the city, previously untouched by the kinds of artist-led occupation found in Suzhou Creek, 1933's combination of Piranesi and Esher made it a particularly striking piece of industrial era architecture. Located next to a very poor district, it had emerged, blinking, right in the centre of a major redevelopment zone. The municipal government, through the Economic Committee which oversaw 'creative' (not 'cultural') industries, took the lead over the local Hongkou district, listing the building as heritage in October 2005. Two months later it commissioned the SCIC to conduct a feasibility study. Six months later it was awarded 'creative cluster' status, and a month after that it established the 'Shanghai Creative Industry Investment Co. Ltd.', between SCIC, Shanghai Automobile Group and 'John Howkins Office'. The new SCCI Co. Ltd. submitted the proposal to the government in preparation for 1933's conversion, obtaining a lease agreement from Shanghai Jinjiang International Development Group, state equity owner of 1933. In November 2007, a refurbished but mostly empty 1933 hosted the Shanghai International Creative Industries Activity Week, the biggest creative industries trade event in China up to that time.

Actually getting tenants was slower and more troubled, as the elite consumption orientation (The Cigar Bar, Ferrari Club) and the close affinities of the SCIC (which had its offices there) with the government, rather than rooted in the creative sector, made it a particularly sterile place. It was a cluster without clustering, engaged in all sorts of strategies to attract activity via offering free space, hosting a regular local design market, setting up a music-cum-fusion food place with an American producer. Here on display were a range of 'amphibian' institutions. SCIC being both strategic policy agency, project developer and cluster certifier, it then sets up a public-private company which leases its premises off a state-owned property development company. 1933 represents a transfer of a Western CIC-led urban regeneration model directly into a real estate project, linked in turn to the city's strategic move towards financial services, urban heritage preservation and lifestyle consumption (especially cultural tourism). 1933 was the inspiration for many other CICs, in less iconic buildings and with less political connections, in which refurbishment of varying quality, linked to a Western-sounding bar or restaurant, would be used to attract creative business tenants. However, by 2014–15 most of these had stretched 'creative' to include more or less any office-based business, and sometimes not even that (delivery companies for example), leading to growing concerns from the Municipal Council about CICs with no creatives in them.

Some CICs were and remain successful. Bridge 8, set up by a well-known media company, managed to assemble a strong tenant list, with a clear media focus. It showed how a CIC set up and run by industry professionals, could evolve into a viable space. It had a limited public space offer, though it did feature in many creative photo shoots, and managed to keep a coherence among its tenants. For tenants, it provided important branding through the Bridge 8 location and access to close networking opportunities. But this was not cheap space and its ethos was relentlessly commercial.

On the other hand, Red Town was a CIC set up in an iconic old steel factory, keeping various industrial artefacts dotted among a refurbished space that had a room comparable to Tate Modern's turbine hall, and a sculpture park.[67] Housing a well-known art gallery and sculpture hall, it nevertheless failed to cover itself commercially. The management was the local district government, and they failed to create any sort of buzz or atmosphere, even though they hosted a well-known music venue. It now stands as a doubled industrial and post-industrial ruin, one of the largest of many such failed speculations around creative clusters. The rapid investment-disinvestment of real and symbolic capital wrapped around a creative future produces what Patrick Brodie has called 'ghost estates'.[68] These creative ruins, which can be found across Shanghai, are often seen as testimony to the failure of the Chinese system to run creative spaces, or the futility of locking creativity up in state-run enclosures. But perhaps it is better to see 'failure' as a learning process. These creative 'ghost estates' were by-products of 'variation, selection and retention': things were tried, things were learnt; those that worked remained, the rest will become something else.

Learning from the West

CICs managed to generate, for a time, some 'high-impact' image capital, the most photogenic CICs rapidly becoming sites for fashion shoots, launches, events and conferences, regularly appearing in the in-flight magazines and ex-pat 'what's on' guides. Just as the 'new Manhattan' of Pudong helped launch the city's global financial status, so too the showcase clusters helped burnish its global creative brand. Shanghai had meshed its industry park model with the reprogramming of old industrial buildings at the very moment these were becoming the very image of the global creative modern.

For a while too they acted as micro contact spaces, in which the flows of foreign visitors, along with resident expats with varying lengths of sojourn, could encounter aspiring locals. An addition to the kind of sites described by James Farrar and others, the night-time landscape of bars, jazz clubs, dance clubs, 'foreigner streets', fusion restaurants and the burgeoning café shops,[69] they were spaces in which some modern personhood might be imagined by aspirant locals, or that could simply provide relief from the grind of the city.[70] We can see them as 'spaces of representation', places to imagine a different kind of modernity, one that, somehow, also existed 'over there', in those other creative hubs in Europe and North America. Yet both the function of image capital and encounter-space were quickly outstripped. With a few exceptions such as M50, these imagined futures no longer uniquely inhabited the Shanghai clusters; as they became ghost estates, the future migrated elsewhere. The rapid expansion of 'up-market' cosmopolitan leisure spaces, and within this, the displacement of the pioneering (often quirky) foreigner business by international brands and new, sophisticated and cashed-up local chains, meant that clusters were no longer privileged zones. Shanghai's bar and restaurant infrastructure is now extensive, with Starbucks Reserves hosting (or perhaps 'curating') their own on-site roasteries, popping up in prime shopping locations. Every respectable mall now has its own locally owned hang-out bars, in which foreigners are neither predominant nor particularly noticed.[71]

CICs allowed the district and municipal governments to test out the viability of quite complex urban projects, in which the 'quality' of the buildings was very different from their normal offer, requiring that they add aesthetic judgement around building and place to the standard measures of rent, office facilities and distance from CBD. So too, they learnt how to attract and retain 'creative' tenants, through architectural aesthetics, alternative 'cool' branding, and rental or other financial inducements. For the most part, this was not the kind of calibration district governments were used to – balancing a need for 'cool' tenants with their ability to pay high rent (or not). Loss leaders, cross-subsidies, getting the tenant mix right – all this required management capacities that were lacking in the early days. As larger investors moved in from 2012 – responding to the prominence of creative industries in the new five-year plan, along with increased restrictions on residential and commercial speculation, thus making investment in 'industrial' clusters more attractive – the requirement for rent yield became more pronounced.[72] If CICs were always part of a planned gentrification – M50, 1933, Tianzifang and Bridge 8 are all now surrounded by major real estate developments – the increased financialization of their planning and operation was notable from 2015 onwards.

Indeed, the central and municipal governments began to demand actual growth in creative industry output, and CICs of small creatives were not producing. The Chinese government's approach to cultural industries involved high capitalization, large-scale supply chain interventions, various forms of foreign partnerships and a strong focus on export. There was an increasing drive for financial 'return on investment' from the interlocking array of amphibian institutions that had moved into the CCI field. District governments, involved in complex ways with the CIC land owners, lease holders, and management companies, came to learn that cultural and creative industries, as in the West, were structured by a small number of very profitable companies surrounded by a large number of small, less profitable ones – both marked by low-paid, precarious employment. Dealing directly with small and independent 'creatives' became less attractive than dealing with large-scale investors or management companies who could attract larger business – especially digital media – able to pay rent and organize the smaller companies who depended on them for business.[73]

This accelerated industrial strategy did not obviate the need for creative, or 'immaterial', labour. In the cultural economy, large-scale production is aimed at elusive and volatile consumer desires; a key ability of creative labour was their ability to attune to consumer desire through accessing and exploiting their own subjectivity and personal networks. The range of skills required, and the habitus able to accommodate these, was traditionally acquired in the West through participation in forms of neo-bohemia and the fluid project-based networks of the cultural industries, embedded in urban life. The urban creative milieu, extended and refashioned through the Internet and social media, is part of how the cultural industries operate. 'Forming the production-communication-consumption circuit requires hard labour to assemble "a heterogeneous arrangement that entails a multiplicity of subjects who are involved in multiple activities both inside and outside the firm (workers, consumers, public)".'[74] As this 'social factory', to use Maurizio Lazzarato's phrase,[75] expanded in the West, the emancipatory image of cultural work has increasingly given way to the routinization and 'precarity' of creative labour.[76] This routinization of cultural work, the reduction of autonomy, the new forms of labour discipline – both at work and through the precarity of the 'gig economy' – have been well documented.[77] At the same time, the data-extraction made possible by social media and its sophisticated use of algorithms and other forms of AI have begun to substitute for the intuitive work done by the 'cool hunters' on the street.[78]

The function of CICs in capturing the energies of the new creative subject within the Chinese system was important but ultimately short lived. The idea that these zones somehow represented enclosed worlds of autonomous creativity was never very convincing, physically, culturally and financially separated as they were from 'hot spots' of cultural activity in the city.[79] CICs were one of the stones government needed to feel their way to the other bank of creative labour discipline. If the government could announce in the mid-1990s that they must 'control the big, let go the small' as part of their market reforms, in the creative industries the small could not be ignored.[80] The cluster model can be understood, in part, as a solution to this challenge, a harnessing of the economic and symbolic energies of the 'creativity bundle' within clearly designated zones. Creative entrepreneurs, if they were to have a role, needed to be integrated into the market-state system, the hierarchically arranged system of connections within which production was to be organized. CICs were not just bounded in the form of being walled compounds, they also allowed a containment of these entrepreneurs within the structured hierarchy of work units (*danwei*). Any employed person needed to be associated with such an entity; that was the condition of *guanxi*. CICs provided a way of containing creatives and integrating them into the market-state.

This integration was not so much about direct censorship – this was achieved in ways that did not require direct scrutiny of creative workers – but linking them to the larger cultural or creative industrial structures in the city. Shanghai is dominated by large-scale cultural industry companies, with hierarchical networks that are hard to penetrate.[81] Increasingly, as the cultural and creative industries took off across Shanghai (and China), with large-scale companies gaining confidence, ambition and profitability, the CIC model was not as useful. Shanghai's 13th Five-Year Plan (2016–20) aimed to position the city as 'China's cultural centre and an international cultural metropolis'. This includes developing Shanghai as a 'global film and TV creation centre'; 'the capital of Asian performing arts'; a 'global comics, animation and gaming creation centre'; playing a 'leading role in China's internet culture'; and 'a creative design centre with international influence'.[82] This imposed a much more demanding regime within which the CICs would need to evolve or die. In fact, as the cultural industries became integrated with China's home-grown digital infrastructure, the need for spatially bounded clusters to organize dispersed 'creatives' was made less pressing, supplanted by social media platforms and other forms of organizational integration that did not require spatial proximity except within the firm itself.

The CIC model had to diversify to provide much more specific functions within this ecosystem. M50 remains as an art cluster, but this is not a place of production, as massive investment in public and private art museums, exhibitions, biennales, auction houses and art 'import/export zones' has made Shanghai the most profitable art market in the world.[83] M50, like *Xintiandi* perhaps, remains as a heritage core of a sprawling global contemporary Chinese art business, with very little access for aspiring visual artists. Bridge 8 sits comfortably in the new media ecology, as it has a strong media industry focus close to some of Shanghai's major companies, especially the Shanghai Media Group. In other areas there has been an expansion of the large-scale industry park model.[84] These parks emerged in the early days of the 'international division of cultural labour', especially around routine animation and post-production. So too in reproduction fine art – in a tradition recalling the porcelain and lacquer-ware factories of pre-modern times.[85] From the 13th Five-Year Plan there was increased research, investment and political will focused on bigger ventures, higher up the value chain. Large-scale parks have been built or are in planning in animation, film and TV, music industry, traditional opera and others. University 'creative clusters' in technology and innovation have become more important as the cultural industries are absorbed into digital media and big data.

Parts of the creativity bundle – those freely associating, milieu-based creative subjects – migrated to smaller 'co-working' spaces which emerged around 2010. A space such as *Xindanwei* ('new work unit'), set up by a Dutch-Chinese woman, tried to articulate the radical creative labour collective ethos that marked such spaces in their early days.[86] These independent initiatives were treated with suspicion by the city authorities, and, as in the West, this 'co-working' was soon reframed as creative office space, becoming the site of new forms of real estate investment. We Work was the most well-known of these, its high-visibility presence in *Xujiahua* rhyming with its other iconic sites across the globe. If the cultural and creative industries increasingly routinized the work of creativity and innovation, the new 'co-working' spaces sought to monetize the sense of community and shared values that had been part of these alternative spaces in the city since the 1970s.[87]

Shanghai's cultural and creative industries are based in a 'social factory', but as one might expect, it is very different from that of the West. The creativity bundle was restructured around the market-state system, which has proved highly resilient in its ability to integrate a large and diverse number of dispersed actors. Mass mobilization is a long-standing state capacity, able to scale up transformation from the micro-level of the immediate work unit or party cell to the large-scale level. As Jun Wang and Yujing Tan have shown, China's 'mass entrepreneurship and mass innovation' policy has mobilized many of the higher education clusters to deliver large-scale training.[88] This does not rely on the heroic individualism of the 'Californian Ideology' but instead a double sense of 'community' (*shequ*): that of the 'maker entrepreneurs' themselves, and the wider community of 'passionate producers' and 'sophisticated consumers'.[89] The mass recreation of a community of passionate producers and sophisticated consumers is the work of a complex array of everyday institutions which forms what Wang and Tan call the 'prosaic state', imbricated in the quotidian life of the social. It is that 'state-society assemblage' noted by Ong and Zhang that has been retooled for the age of creative innovation – one that can now refer approvingly to Mao's capacity to mobilize the masses, rather than repudiate him.[90]

The system of cultural and creative industries – post-cultural and post-creative – faces a challenge in the form of 'lack of talent'.[91] The higher education system has not caught up with the burgeoning of these sectors under the unrelenting promotion by local and national government. This unmet demand for creative talent fuels the massive numbers of Chinese overseas students currently keeping many universities financially afloat in the West.[92] But there are other issues. Ideological conformity is most salient to outside observers: the last-minute cancellation of projects that have been through numerous official checking procedures shows how risk-averse any cultural producer needs to be in the current climate. Less visible, though just as crucial, is the effect of the pressure for immediate financial returns that permeates the commercial system. Here the problem of autonomy is less about ideological control than the lack of space for slow gestation, for the experimentation required in new products. Commercial companies do not provide for such incubation space, nor is its value recognized. In China, as in Japan and South Korea, which have also developed cultural and creative industry sectors, creative labour is heavily disciplined work, with long hours, low pay and a relentless requirement to deliver successful product. In China, this is overlaid by the exhortation to 'be creative for the state'.[93] The habitus of the Chinese creative worker is still under investigation, but what seems clear is an emerging sense of their own route to a middle-class life, underpinned by the (relatively) new validation by the government of their individual and collective role as creatives. This includes both a weak cosmopolitan identification with a modern, global creative subject, and a stronger nationalist sense of beating them at their own game. The idea of a 'creative class' as some kind of force for social and political change is misplaced. It might be that the private sector wants to 'cast off the shackles'; contemporary indications are that many in the sector – especially in Shanghai, where the local government feels it is being held back by Beijing – are unhappy with the tightening under Xi Jinping. But these are large, highly capitalized companies, with global connections, chafing against state restrictions on their own expansion, not an upsurge of neo-Schumpeterian start-ups.

Shanghai's urban culture: Impasse

The rise of new forms of urban culture – contemporary art and performance, live and dance music, prose and poetry reading, stand-up comedy, early games and maker spaces – took place in spaces of the city which barely touched the world of the CICs.[94] The early encounters in M50 and Taikang Road were outliers. The history of the city's 'underground' music and art scenes is one that would lead through cellars and old markets, abandoned office floors, military bunkers, cheap apartments and the back of abandoned shopping malls. Semi-tolerated, it has become hard-pressed in recent years, as the tightening introduced by Xi Jinping has met the relentless commercialization of popular culture. Popular music has always been difficult for the Chinese government, seeing it as a site of mass mobilization (stadium ecstasies and cultic fans) and moral corruption.[95] The success of K-Pop – a combination of state promotion and private sector investment in South

Korea – has encouraged the Chinese government to promote similarly anodyne music, through festivals and stadium events, music industry clusters, export drives and the whole array of value chain interventions. The space for independent publishers, promoters, clubs, live venues and so on has been squeezed.[96] Between these two scissor blades – ideology and commerce – the space for alternative, 'underground' culture in Shanghai has been severely reduced. Indeed, the tightening up has moved into the 'cosmopolitan' landscape of the city's nightlife, with regular clearings of streets involving large numbers of expat-owned or oriented bars, restaurants and clubs.

This urban landscape reflects the wider unavailability of a space in the cultural field in which a certain professional autonomy is possible; a space of experiment, which provides the time to develop as an artist, as a cultural producer. Richard Curt Kraus suggested that such a space *did* exist for the 'art-for-art's sake' artist, who thereby gave up their historical connection to a political role. This might be so for the established art field, connected to state and university departments, but not so for those outside it. If the private sector demands immediate commercial returns, the state sector has its own forms of, and routes to, legitimation. These include artists working in state-sanctioned, often traditional, fields, but much of this consecration too comes from commercial success, especially abroad. Contemporary visual artists with global track records fit within the proliferating art and cultural infrastructure of the city – galleries, museums, festivals, public commissions, media art – much more than local artists. These speak not just for the common preference for artists with global credential over the local; it also reflects the lack of a legitimated social space accorded to artists who have not 'made it'. The habitus of the 'bohemian' artist is barely available in China, even in a city which revels in the romantic nostalgia of Shanghai Modern. China's creative capital is a place for artists to make money – if they can – filling up the bank account from corporate work. It is not, we are repeatedly told, a place to make art.[97]

As we saw, China has heavily invested in 'public culture', and has sought to distinguish it from the commercially oriented sector. The constant blurring of lines between these relates in part to the permeable nature of the enterprises investing in such culture, which often find 'success' hard to qualify in the absence of quantifiable profit. In part, too, it relates to the lack of skills in 'cultural management', which the Chinese government is trying to promote as an overarching concept, one to which cultural, creative and digital industries are supposed to conform.[98] Cultural management here is understood as taking into account the public value of culture, as a service to citizens. But ultimately, the issue is less about 'skills' and more about a shared understanding of what such a public culture might be, and how it might override the overwhelming emphasis on culture-as-economy in the last two decades. Shanghai's enormous infrastructure of cultural and creative industries is more or less uncoupled from those relatively independent spaces of cultural experiment, the not-yet-profitable spaces of 'unpopular culture'. In the West, public sector funding is crucial to sustaining such spaces – a residual legacy of the creative city – but in Shanghai, public funding is unconnected with this social and cultural space. Indeed, there is a sense, currently, that independent artists and cultural producers are not just being left on the outside, but that even this residual space is being shut down as turbo-charged digital commerce combines with heightened ideological restrictions.

There is then a sense of an impasse, though not simply of creative autonomy thwarted, as in the Western imaginary.[99] The ethical commitment of artists and cultural professionals in China is one to a sense of collective responsibility that many in the West see as always-already compromised. In China's 'managed public sphere' – a term which sidesteps the issues of its increasing privatization and monopolization in the West – many artists seek a space in which their professional capacity, autonomous within the specific sphere of its competence, can be recognized. This is what the 'traditional intellectuals' who came back after the Cultural Revolution sought, and failed, to achieve. The dynamic proliferation of popular culture, bubbling up in the interstices of a reconfiguration of state and market across the 1990s, in which many saw the exploration of the multiple new individual and collective possibilities of contemporary China, was recouped in the new system of cultural and creative industries. The *dispositif* of the Chinese 'social factory' finds little space for the kind of 'unpopular culture' which formed part of the ethos of the cultural industries in their transformative, utopian phase.[100] This certainly has implications for the flow of 'creative talent' upon which these industries must rely; the 'quality' the government increasingly seeks in its cultural industries continues to elude it. More importantly, it has implications for China's democracy.

The capacity of the Chinese state to represent the collective interests of its people is built on very different foundations from those of the West. We have argued throughout this book that a deficit model with respect to the forms of liberal democracy is of no use in this account. However, the connections between state and society, between 'sovereign power and self-sovereignty', are currently 'frozen'. The proliferation of new forms of popular – and unpopular – culture was quite rightly heralded as a chance for new explorations and articulations of Chinese modernity. This chance was not taken, and instead was rerouted into the cultural industries. The new forms of digital governance tested out by Xi Jinping are an attempt to govern across this frozen divide. An increasingly strident ideological conformity is accompanied by new forms of digitally enabled behaviour modification and control. It is here perhaps, rather than in shared 'market values', that the convergence of Western and Chinese neo-liberalism occurs. The key difference is that Xin Jinping's digital panopticon is dedicated to making productive citizens within a frame of modernist reason; the West's version is dedicated to the monetization of, and political domination through, the proliferation of unreason.[101]

Platform

Jia Zhangke's 2000 film *Platform* (*Zhàntái*) tells the story of a group of performers over a decade spanning 1979 to 1989. Starting out as members of a state-financed troupe, performing revolutionary songs to factory and mining workers, they are defunded and transformed into an 'enterprise' performing for the new emerging markets of post-reform China. The group gradually fragments, flittering across numerous small-scale, ad hoc stages on which Western-inflected 'rock' and 'pop' is performed to distracted audiences. The film stages an increasing sense of anomie as the coordinates of Mao's China dissolve around them, an anomie heightened by the uncertainty of the market for culture and the kinds of consumer culture following in its wake. The film is set around the depressed mining town of Fenyang, witness (like the film *West of the Tracks*) to a socialist-industrial society in collapse, and counterpoint to the breathy embrace of a Shanghai 'liberated' from the Maoist era.[102] Reflecting the youth of the director – only 30 when he completed the film – this is not a paean to socialist culture troupes or a jeremiad about the vulgarization of Chinese culture, nor a 'postmodern' embrace of a liberated everyday culture.

Platform stages an accelerating dismantling of one kind of socialist state, and the privatization, disruption, exploitation and social fragmentation that was registering across multiple levels of Chinese society by the time the film came out. It tried to show the reality of a new 'civil society' in which the means of production of culture have been privatized and left to the market, leaving the cultural workers in a similar position to many of the other ex-state employees. In the ironic opening scene, after the workers' performance of the revolutionary song *Train to Shaoshan*, miming a locomotive setting off confidently bound for Mao's hometown (and thus Communism), the troupe's tour bus is suddenly plunged into darkness as they wait to depart. In these blank faces peering through the dark to an unknown future we encounter the kind of anomie found in the industrial cities of the West in the 1970s and early 1980s. A space opens up, inviting us to leave one kind of life for another, and yet there seems few means by which one might arrive on that further shore. Somehow the train never leaves the platform.

NOTES

1. B. Jessop and S. Oosterlynck, 'Cultural Political Economy: On Making the Cultural Turn without Falling into Soft Economic Sociology', *Geoforum* 39, no. 3 (2008): 1155–69, 1156.

2. B. Jessop, 'Cultural Political Economy, the Knowledge-based Economy, and the State', in *The Technological Economy*, ed. A. Barry and D. Slater (London: Routledge, 2005), 142–64.

3. Jessop and Oosterlynck, 'Cultural Political Economy', 1155.

4. We use 'bundle' here; others adapt Michel Foucault's *dispositif*. Cf. A. McRobbie, *Be Creative: Making a Living in the New Culture Industries* (London: Polity, 2016); J. Lin, 'Be Creative for the State: Creative Workers in Chinese State-Owned Enterprises', *International Journal of Cultural Studies* 22, no. 1 (2019): 53–69.

5. We have developed our thinking on clusters from various publications over the last fifteen years: J. O'Connor and X. Gu, 'A New Modernity? The Arrival of "Creative Industries" in China', *International Journal of Cultural Studies* 9, no. 3 (2006): 271–83; X. Gu, 'The Art of Re-industrialisation in Shanghai', *Culture Unbound* 4 (2012): 193–211; X. Gu, 'Cultural Industries and Creative Clusters in Shanghai', *City, Culture & Society* 5, no. 3 (2014): 123–30; J. O'Connor and X. Gu, 'Creative Industry Clusters in Shanghai: A Success Story?' *International Journal of Cultural Policy* 20, no. 1 (2014): 1–20; J. O'Connor and X. Gu, 'Making Creative Spaces: China and Australia: An Introduction', *City, Culture & Society* 5, no. 3 (2014): 111–14; X. Gu, 'Creative Industries, Creative Clusters and Cultural Policy in Shanghai', in *Cultural Policies in East Asia: Dynamics between the State, Arts and Creative Industries*, ed. L. Lim and L. Hye-Kyung (Basingstoke: Palgrave Macmillan, 2014); X. Gu, 'Cultural Economy and Urban Development in Shanghai', in *The Companion to the Cultural Economy*, ed. K. Oakley and J. O'Connor (London: Routledge, 2015); J. O'Connor and X. Gu, 'Creative Clusters in Shanghai: Transnational Intermediaries and the Creative Economy', in *Making Cultural Cities in Asia: Mobility, Assemblage and the Politics of Aspirational Urbanism*, ed. J. Wang, T. Oakes and Y. Yang (London: Routledge, 2016), 21–35; J. O'Connor and X. Gu, 'Creative Clusters and the Creative Milieu in China', in *Routledge Handbook on Cultural and Creative Industries in Asia*, ed. L. Lim and H.-K. Lee (London: Routledge, 2018).

6. An imaginary, we could say, is an unstable narrative form, akin to Laclau and Mouffe's 'hegemonic discourse'. See: E. Laclau and C. Mouffe, *Hegemony and Socialist Strategy: Towards a Radical Democratic Politics* (London: Verso, 1985).

7. J. Rancière, *The Distribution of the Sensible* (New York: Continuum Books, 2004).

8. H. Lefebvre, *The Production of Space*, trans. D. Nicholson-Smith (Oxford: Blackwell, 1992).

9. S. Baumann, 'A General Theory of Artistic Legitimation: How Art Worlds Are Like Social Movements', *Poetics* 35 (2007): 47–65; R. Hollands and J. Vail, 'The Art of Social Movement: Cultural Opportunity, Mobilisation, and Framing in the Early Formation of the Amber Collective', *Poetics* 40 (2012): 22–42.

10. Cf. S. Frith and H. Horne, *Art into Pop* (London: Methuen, 1988). And J. O'Connor, *Culture and Creative Industries: A Review of the Literature*, 2nd ed. (London: Creative Partnerships, 2010).

11. J. Savage, *England's Dreaming: Sex Pistols and Punk Rock* (London: Faber and Faber, 1991); M. Worley, *No Future: Punk, Politics and British Youth Culture (1976–1984)* (Cambridge: Cambridge University Press, 2017).

12. T. H. Marshall, 'Citizenship and Social Class', in *Citizenship and Social Class and Other Essays* (Cambridge: Cambridge University Press, 1950).

13. C. Grodach, 'Before and After the Creative City: The Politics of Urban Cultural Policy in Austin, Texas', *Journal of Urban Affairs* 34, no. 1 (2011): 81–97; C. Grodach and D. Silver, eds., *The Politics of Urban Cultural Policy* (London: Routledge, 2012); M. Indergaard, 'What to Make of New York's New Economy? The Politics of the Creative Field', *Urban Studies* 46, no. 5–6 (2009): 1063–93; J. Novy and C. Colomb, 'Struggling for the Right to the (Creative) City in Berlin and Hamburg: New Urban Social Movements, New "Spaces of Hope"?' *International Journal or Urban and Regional Studies*, 37, no. 5 (2013): 1816–38.

14. L. Boltanski and E. Chiapello, *The New Spirit of Capitalism* (London: Verso, 2005).

15. M. Tronti, *Workers and Capital*, trans. D. Broder (London: Verso, [1966] 2019).

16. Cf. the chapter 'City Cultures and Postmodern Lifestyles', in M. Featherstone, *Consumer Culture and Postmodernism* (London: Sage, 1991); M. Featherstone and S. Lash, *Spaces of Culture: City, Nation, World* (London: Sage, 1999).

17. For New York, see S. Zukin, *Landscapes of Power: From Detroit to Disney World* (Berkeley and Los Angeles: University of California Press, 1991); for Manchester, see J. O'Connor and X. Gu, 'Developing a Creative Cluster in a Post-Industrial City: CIDS and Manchester', *The Information Society* 26, no. 2 (2010): 124–36.

18. F. Kermode, *The Sense of an Ending: Studies in the Theory of Fiction* (Oxford: Oxford University Press, 1967).

19. This was systematically argued by two theorists of post-Fordism, or 'disorganised capitalism' as they called it, Scott Lash and John Urry in their 1994 *Economies of Signs and Space*. Identifying, among other tendencies, an intensification of informational and aesthetic/symbolic flows at the level of production, linked in turn to rapid feedback from volatile, niche, symbolic-driven and individualized consumers, they suggested that the cultural industries were a privileged template for a new economy. See: S. Lash and J. Urry, *The End of Organised Capitalism* (London: Polity, 1987); S. Lash and J. Urry, *Economies of Signs and Space* (London: Sage, 1994).

20. Cf. M. Banks, A. Lovatt, C. Raffo and J. O'Connor, 'Risk and Trust in the Cultural Industries', *Geoforum* 31, no. 4 (2000): 453–64; O'Connor and Gu, 'Developing a Creative Cluster in a Post-Industrial City'.

21. M. Piore and C. Sabel, *The Second Industrial Divide: Possibilities for Prosperity* (London: Basic Books, 1986). This was not simply a 'small-business economy', rather these economic activities were rooted in local histories and networks: Catholic church, Communist Party, local community organizations, regional networks, extended families, shared historical cultures and so on. These formed a context for production in which

state capacity and market actors intersected productively. These aspirations accelerated after 1989, as social democratic parties saw a third way between free-market and state-dominated planning. This was not necessarily a 'rolling back of the state' as it was famously framed by Margaret Thatcher; it could also be seen as an attempted devolution or distribution of economic governance to a wider set of participants. As such it formed part of that penumbra of thinking around 'stakeholder capitalism' and 'social markets' that tussled with neo-liberal strands within the EU across the 1990s. It was also present in early versions of the United Kingdom's 'New Times' agenda, which was a key source of ideas for what became New Labour, cf. S. Hall and M. Jacques, eds., *New Times: The Changing Face of Politics in the 1990s* (London: Lawrence and Wishart, 1989).

22. Cf. A. Pratt, 'New Media, the New Economy and New Spaces', *Geoforum* 31, no. 4 (2000): 425–36; A. Pratt, 'Hot Jobs in Cool Places: The Material Cultures of New Media Product Spaces: The Case of South of the Market, San Francisco', *Information, Communication and Society* 5, no. 1 (2002): 27–50; A. Pratt 'Creative Clusters: Towards the Governance of the Creative Industries Production System?', *Media International Australia* 112 (2004): 50–66; A. Pratt, 'The Cultural Economy: A Call for Spatialised "Production of Culture" Perspectives', *International Journal of Cultural Studies* 7 (2004): 117–28; A. Pratt, 'Cultural Industries and Public Policy: An Oxymoron?', *International Journal of Cultural Policy* 11 (2005): 31–44; A. Pratt, 'Creative Cities: The Cultural Industries and the Creative Class', *Geografiska Annaler: Series B, Human Geography* 90, no. 2 (2008): 107–17; A. Pratt, 'Locating the Cultural Economy', in *Cultures and Globalization: The Cultural Economy*, ed. H. Anheier and Y. R. Isar (London: Sage, 2008), 42–51. Cf. A. J. Scott, *The Cultural Economy of Cities* (London: Sage, 2001); A. J. Scott, 'Capitalism, Cities and the Production of Symbolic Forms', *Transactions of the Institute of British Geographers* 26 (2000): 11–23; A. J. Scott, 'Capitalism and Urbanisation in a New Key? The Cognitive-Cultural Dimension', *Social Forces* 85, no. 4 (2007): 1465–82; A. J. Scott, *Social Economy of the Metropolis: Cognitive-Cultural Capitalism and the Global Resurgence of Cities* (Oxford: Oxford University Press, 2008).

23. C. Leadbeater and K. Oakley, *The Independents: Britain's New Cultural Entrepreneur* (London: Demos, 1999); J. O'Connor, 'New Cultural Intermediaries and the Entrepreneurial City', in *The Entrepreneurial City: Geographies of Politics, Regime and Representation*, ed. T. Hall and P. Hubbard (Chichester: John Wiley, 1998), 225–40; J. O'Connor and D. Wynne, 'Left Loafing: Cultural Consumption and Production in the Postmodern City', in *From the Margins to the Centre: Cultural Production and Consumption in the Post-Industrial City*, ed. J. O'Connor and D. Wynne (Aldershot: Ashgate, 1996); J. O'Connor, 'Popular Culture, Reflexivity and Urban Change', in *Creative Cities: Cultural Industries, Urban Development and the Information Society*, ed. J. Verwijnen and P. Lehtovouri (Helsinki: University of Art and Design, 1999).

24. On the Utopian Impulse and the Utopian Moment, see F. Jameson, 'Realism and Utopia in "The Wire"', *Criticism* 52, no. 3/4 (2010): 359–72.

25. On the 'technological imaginary', cf. K. Robins, *Into the Image: Culture and Politics in the Field of Vision* (London: Routledge, 1996); for its re-emergence in 'new media', S. McQuire, *The Media City* (London: Sage, 2008).

26. Cf. 'Deleuzian Thatcherism' coined by Benjamin Noyes, quoted by S. Haider, 'The Darkness at the End of the Tunnel: Artificial Intelligence and Neo-Reaction', *Viewpoint Magazine*, 28 March 2017, https: //www.viewpointmag.com/2017/03/28/the-darkness-at-the-end-of-the-tunnel-artificial-intelligence-and-neoreaction/. Accessed 16 November 2018; cf. B. Noys, 'Cybergothic Remix', in *Malign Velocities: Accelerationism and Capitalism* (Winchester: Zero Books, 2014).

27. T. A. Hutton, *The New Economy of the Inner City: Restructuring Regeneration and Dislocation in the Twenty-First-Century Metropolis* (London: Routledge, 2010); B. Van Heur, *Creative Networks and the City: Towards a Cultural Political Economy of Aesthetic Production* (Brussels: Transcript Verlag, 2010).

28. R. Lloyd, *Neo-Bohemia: Art and Commerce in the Postindustrial City* (London: Routledge, 2006), 364.

29. 'Artists, like entrepreneurs, enter into risky activities with uncertain (though potentially extravagant) rewards. The artistic milieu offers a social structure providing nonmaterial rewards to compensate the would-be artist for his or her relative poverty and life spent waiting tables, "quality of life" compensations revolving around values of aesthetic self-determination and creativity, and involving an internal status system partially unhinged from issues of material compensation.' Lloyd, *Neo-Bohemia*, 366.

30. S. Zukin, *Loft-Living: Culture and Capital in Urban Change* (London: The Johns Hopkins Press, 1982).

31. M. E. Porter, 'Clusters and the New Economics of Competitiveness', *Harvard Business Review* 76 (1998): 77–90; M. E. Porter, 'Location, Competition and Economic Development: Local Clusters in a Global Economy', *Economic Development Quarterly* 14 (2000): 15–34.

32. Cf. H. Mommaas, 'Cultural Clusters and the Post-industrial City: Towards the Remapping of Urban Cultural Policy', *Urban Studies* 41, no. 3 (2004): 507–32; G. Evans and P. Shaw, *The Contribution of Culture to Regeneration in the UK: A Review of Evidence* (London: DCMS, 2004); G. Evans, 'Creative Cities, Creative Spaces and Urban Policy', *Urban Studies* 46, no. 5–6 (2009): 1003–40.

33. The network *Trans Europe Halles*, founded in 1983, is a good example of how grassroots cultural centres have managed to persist throughout from culture-led urban regeneration to post-Creative Industries. Cf. https: //teh.net. For an excellent account of how a radical cultural space struggled with the gentrifying forces of the creative city, see Boukje Cnossen and Seb Olma's account: *The Volkskrant Building: Manufacturing Difference in Amsterdam's Creative City* (Amsterdam: Knowledge, 2014).

34. We have developed our thinking on clusters from various publications over the last 15 years: O'Connor and Gu, 'A New Modernity?'; X. Gu, 'Art of Re-industrialisation in Shanghai', *Culture Unbound* 4 (2012): 193–211; Gu, 'Cultural Industries and Creative

Clusters in Shanghai'; O'Connor and Gu, 'Creative Industry Clusters in Shanghai'; O'Connor and Gu, 'Making Creative Spaces'; Gu, 'Creative Industries, Creative Clusters and Cultural Policy in Shanghai'; Gu, 'Cultural Economy and Urban Development in Shanghai'; O'Connor and Gu, 'Creative Clusters in Shanghai'; O'Connor and Gu, 'Creative Clusters and the Creative Milieu'.

35. W. Straw and J. Marchessault, 'Cities/Scenes', in *Public* 22/23 (Toronto: Public Access/ York University, 2002); A. Bennett and R. A. Peterson, *Music Scenes: Local, Translocal and Virtual* (Nashville: Vanderbilt University Press, 2004); D. Silver, T. Clark and C. Graziul, 'Scenes, Innovation and Urban Development', in *The Handbook of Creative Cities* (Cheltenham: Edward Elgar, 2011), 229–58; D. Silver and T. Clark, *Scenescapes: How Qualities of Place Shape Social Life* (Chicago: The University of Chicago Press, 2016).

36. Cf. P. M. Haas, 'Epistemic Communities and International Policy Coordination', *International Organization* 46, no. 1 (1992): 1–35, 3; O'Connor and Gu, 'Creative Clusters in Shanghai'.

37. G. Richards and J. Wilson, *Tourism, Creativity and Development* (London: Routledge, 2007); G. Richards, 'Creativity and Tourism in the City', *Current Issues in Tourism* 17, no. 2 (2014): 119–44.

38. See also A. Lagerkvist, *Media and Memory in New Shanghai: Western Performances of Futures Past* (London: Palgrave Macmillan, 2013).

39. G. Yúdice, *The Expediency of Culture: Uses of Culture in the Global Era* (Durham, NC: Duke University Press, 2003).

40. This was exemplified in the new global visibility of contemporary art, whose galleries rapidly shouldered out concert halls and opera houses from their emblematic position in the global cultural city. The example of Bilbao and the Guggenheim played a part, its success in attracting tourists and global media attention representing the old industrial city's reinvention of itself. But it is easy to miss the ways in which contemporary art had become articulated to forms of popular culture and lifestyle, becoming an important marker of a contemporary global subject. The ability to interpellate such subject positions became increasingly important for global cultural cities, the latest example being the spate of contemporary art museums in Dubai and Abu Dhabi, not to mention Shanghai and Singapore. The art gallery, increasingly associated with urban gentrification, was also a portal into a cosmopolitan modernity (for practicing artists and visitors alike) as well as providing its local flagship presence.

41. S. Sassen, 'Global Cities and Diasporic Networks: Micro-sites in Global Civil Society', in *Global Civil Society 2002*, ed. M. Glasius, M. Kaldor and H. Anheier (Oxford: Oxford University Press, 2002).

42. Similar things happened with 'gay villages' throughout the Global North, or indeed with the China Towns of previous eras, parlayed into tourism sites.

43. Perhaps here we have Akbar Abbas's modern cosmopolitanism, the cosmopolitan as 'arbitrageur/arbitrageuse', capable of 'creating a global culture worthy of the name'. See: A.

Abbas, 'Cosmopolitan De-scriptions: Shanghai and Hong Kong', *Public Culture* 12, no. 3 (2000): 769–86, 786.

44. J. Vaide, *Contact Space Shanghai: The Chinese Dream and the Production of a New Society* (doctoral thesis, Lund University, Sweden, 2015), 18, https: //lup.lub.lu.se/search/publication/10422d86-b14e-408a-a051-f56c89dc4255. Accessed 4 October 2019.

45. This caused problems around new intellectual property regimes, cf. L. Pang, *Creativity and Its Discontents: China's Creative Industries and Intellectual Property Rights Offences* (Durham, NC: Duke University Press, 2009).

46. For a detailed discussion, cf. H. Holbig, 'The Party and the Entrepreneurs in the PRC', *Copenhagen Journal of Asian Studies* 16 (2002): 30–56.

47. The creative industries were broken down into five categories by the Shanghai Economic Commission and Shanghai Statistical Bureau: (1) research, development and design; (2) architectural and related design; (3) cultural activities, creation and media; (4) consultancy and planning; and (5) fashion, leisure and lifestyle services (SCIC, 2006).

48. This uncoupling can often be misread as liberalization, a reading tacitly promoted by the city with its Westernizing, global branding strategy. Interviews with academic policy analysts in Shanghai have suggested, however, that this was not uncontested, with those promoting the 'cultural industries' concerned to defend core Chinese and socialist values under the guise of 'cultural security'. However, in a city as tightly controlled by the party as Shanghai, it seemed that the economic committee's determination to promote a growing commercial sector won out over these fears. For good background to Shanghai adoption of creative clusters, cf. J. Zheng, 'The "Entrepreneurial State", "Creative Industry Cluster Development in Shanghai", *Journal of Urban Affairs* 32, no. 2 (2010): 143–70; J. Zheng, '"Creative Industry Clusters" and the "Entrepreneurial City" of Shanghai', *Urban Studies* 48, no. 16 (2011): 3561–82; S. Zhong, 'From Fabrics to Fine Arts: Urban Restructuring and the Formation of an Art District in Shanghai', *Critical Planning* 16 (2009): 118–37; S. Zhong, *Industrial Restructuring and the Formation of Creative Industry Clusters: The Case of Shanghai's Inner City* (Ph.D. thesis, University of British Columbia, Canada, 2011). S. Zhong, 'Production, Creative Forms and Urban Spaces in Shanghai', *Culture Unbound* 4 (2012): 169–91; M. Keane, *China's New Creative Clusters: Governance, Human Capital and Regional Investment* (London: Routledge, 2012); Y. Chen, 'Making Shanghai a Creative City: Exploring the Creative Cluster Strategy from a Chinese Perspective', in *Creative Knowledge Cities: Myths, Visions and Realities*, ed. M. Van Geenhuizen and P. Nijkamp (Cheltenham: Edward Elgar, 2012); J. Wang, 'Evolution of Cultural Clusters in China: Comparative Study of Beijing and Shanghai', *Architectoni* 2 (2012): 148–59; J. Zheng and R. Chan, 'The Impact of "Creative Industry Clusters" on Cultural and Creative Industry Development in Shanghai', *City, Culture & Society* 5 (2014): 9–22; S. Zheng and A. Bugatio, *Regeneration and Re-Use in China: Transforming the Existing* (Santarcangelo di Romagna: Maggioli Editore, 2015).

49. Lily Kong called creative clusters a 'technology', a tool transferable from one site to another. L. Kong, 'Transnational Mobilities and the Making of Creative Cities', *Theory, Culture & Society* 31, no. 7/8 (2014): 273–89.

50. A. Ross, *Fast Boat to China: High-Tech Outsourcing and the Consequences of Free Trade: Lessons from Shanghai* (New York: Vintage Press, 2009); Keane, *China's New Creative Clusters*.

51. Keane, *China's New Creative Clusters*; Pang, *Creativity and Its Discontents*.

52. The quote is from Adam Greenfield's private email series *Dispatches* #14, 27 October, 2019. He adapts it from M. De Landa, *A Thousand Years of Non-Linear History* (New York: Zone Books, 2000).

53. On cities in the Global South, cf. J. Robinson, *Ordinary Cities: Between Modernity and Development* (London: Routledge, 2006).

54. See T. Smith, 'Background Story, Global Foreground' in *Art to Come* (Durham, NC: Duke University Press, 2019), 126–55

55. Such an explicit indexing of Contemporary Art to Liberalisation can be found in Madeleine O'Dea's *The Phoenix Years: Art, Resistance and the Making of Modern China* (Sydney: Allen & Unwin, 2016).

56. T. Schilbach, *Shanghai Cosmo-Politics: The Young Middle Class in the Global City* (Ph.D. thesis, University of Sydney, Sydney, 2014), 43, 106–07,111–14, https://www.academia.edu/25586961/Shanghai_cosmo-politics_the_young_middle_class_in_the_global_city. Accessed 4 October 2019.

57. It was a coalition very similar to that which had successfully resisted development in SoHo, in Zukin's Ur-history of culture-led urban regeneration (Zukin, *Loft-Living*).

58. S. He and F. Wu, 'Property-Led Development in Post-Reform China: A Case Study of Xindiandi Redevelopment Project in Shanghai', *Journal of Urban Affairs* 27, no. 1 (2005): 1–23; L. Hee, T. Schroepfer, S. Nanxi and L. Ze, 'From Post-industrial Landscape to Creative Precincts: Emergent Spaces in Chinese Cities', *International Development Planning Review* 30, no. 3 (2008): 249–66; Gu, 'Art of Re-industrialisation in Shanghai', *Culture Unbound* 4 (2012): 193–211; J. Wang, '"Art in Capital": Shaping Distinctiveness in a Culture-Led Urban Regeneration Project in Red Town, Shanghai', *Cities* 26 (2009): 318–30; Zheng, 'The "Entrepreneurial State"'; Zhong, 'From Fabrics to Fine Arts' and *Industrial Restructuring and the Formation of Creative Industry Clusters*.

59. These observations come from personal experience and interviews by the authors. Cf. also Schilbach, *Shanghai Cosmo-Politics*, 63–70. In 2006, the artist-in-residence was the British sound artist Andrew Kötting.

60. Cf. Gu, 'Creative Industries, Creative Clusters and Cultural Policy in Shanghai'.

61. This account is based on interviews and ethnographic work conducted by Xin Gu 2010–15. Cf. also S. W.-H. Wang, 'Commercial Gentrification and Entrepreneurial Governance in Shanghai: A Case Study of Taikang Road Creative Cluster', *Urban Policy and Research* 29, no. 4 (2011): 363–80; A. Greenspan, 'Created in China', in *Shanghai Future: Modernity*

Remade (London: Hurst and Co., 2014), 87–110; Zheng and Chan, 'Impact of "Creative Industry Clusters"'.

62. X. Ren, *Building Globalisation: Transnational Architecture Production in Urban China* (Chicago: University of Chicago Press, 2011).

63. Gu, 'Art of Re-Industrialisation in Shanghai'.

64. Cf. also Zhong, 'Production, Creative Forms and Urban Spaces in Shanghai'.

65. We both met Mr. He in Manchester in 2004. We interviewed him many times subsequently, up to 2016.

66. He Zeng Qiang's role was to certify the CIC and provide consultancy for them.

67. Cf. Wang, 'Art in Capital'; S. He, 'The Creative Spatio-Temporal Fix: Creative and Cultural Industries Development in Shanghai, China', *Geoforum* 106 (2019): 310–19; Gu, 'Art of Re-industrialisation in Shanghai'.

68. P. Brodie, 'Seeing Ghosts: Crisis, Ruin, and the Creative Industries', *Continuum* (2019): DOI: 10.1080/10304312.2019.1643452.

69. Cf. A. Field, 'From D.D.'s to Y.Y. to Park 97 to Muse: Dance Club Spaces and the Construction of Class in Shanghai, 1997–2007', *China: An International Journal* 6, no. 1 (2008): 18–43; J. Farrer, '"New Shanghailanders" or "New Shanghainese": Western Expatriates' Narratives of Emplacement in Shanghai', *Journal of Ethnic and Migration Studies* 36, no. 8 (2010): 1211–28; J. Farrer, 'Shanghai Bars: Patchwork Globalization and Flexible Cosmopolitanism in Reform-Era Urban-Leisure Spaces', *Chinese Sociology and Anthropology* 42, no. 2 (2010): 22–38; J. Farrer, 'Global Nightscapes in Shanghai as Ethnosexual Contact Zones', *The Journal of Ethnic and Migration Studies* 37, no. 5 (2011): 747–64.

70. Schilbach, *Shanghai Cosmo-Politics*, 116–22; Vaide, *Contact Space Shanghai*, 135–47.

71. On the new Chinese café culture, cf. E. Felton, *Filtered: Coffee, the Café and the 21st Century* (London: Routledge, 2019).

72. O'Connor and Gu, 'Creative Industry Clusters in Shanghai'; Zheng and Chan, 'Impact of "Creative Industry Clusters"'; on the post 2014 municipal regulations, cf. Feng Luan, Ying He, Huai Wang, 'Shanghai Cultural and Creative Industry Parks', in *Cultural Industries in Shanghai. Policy and Planning inside a Global City*, ed. Y. Rong and J. O'Connor (United Kingdom: Intellect, 2018), 43–68.

73. Cf. Zheng and Chan, 'The Impact of "Creative Industry Clusters"'.

74. J. Wang and Y. Tan, 'Social Factory as Prosaic State Space: Re-defining Labour in China's Mass Innovation/Entrepreneurialism Campaign' *Environment and Planning A* (2019): DOI: 10.1177/0308518X19889633. Quoted from D. Hesmondhalgh and S. Baker, *Creative Labour: Media Work in Three Cultural Industries* (London and New York: Routledge, 2011).

75. M. Lazzarato, 'Immaterial Labor', in *Radical Thought in Italy: A Potential Politics*, ed. P. Virno, M. Hardt, M. Boscagli et al. (Minnesota: University of Minnesota Press, 1996), 133–48. See also R. Gill and A. Pratt, 'In the Social Factory?: Immaterial Labour, Precariousness and Cultural Work', *Theory, Culture & Society* 25, no. 7-7 (2008): 1–30.

76. For Lash and Urry, writing in 1994, the ability to deal with tacit, highly aestheticized knowledge, linking production to the volatile desires of a future consumer, positioned cultural workers at the cutting edge of the new economy.

77. Cf. Hesmondhalgh and Baker, *Creative Labour*; M. Banks, *The Politics of Cultural Work* (Basingstoke: Palgrave Macmillan, 2007); C. Crouch, *Will the Gig Economy Prevail?* (Cambridge: Polity, 2019).

78. Cf. V. Mangematin, J. Sapsed and E. Schüßler, 'Disassembly and Reassembly: An Introduction to the Special Issue on Digital Technology and Creative Industries', *Technological Forecasting and Social Change* 83 (2014): 1–9. J. Lanchester, 'The Robots Are Coming', *London Review of Books* 37, no. 5 (2015): 1–8; J. Brindle, *New Dark Age: Technology and the End of the Future* (London: Verso, 2018), 130, 214–39.

79. The dashing of these expectations around 2014 can be found amongst most commentators, including us. Cf. Zheng and Chan, 'The Impact of "Creative Industry Clusters"'; Greenspan, 'Created in China'; Schilbach, *Shanghai Cosmo-Politics*. We mapped density of CICs against density of cultural events on the social media site *Douban*, and found the first were well away from the 'hot spots' of the latter, cf. O'Connor and Gu, 'Creative Industry Clusters in Shanghai'; Jinliao He and X. Huang found no evidence to suggest any of the bohemian or gay dimension of the creative milieu stressed by Richard Florida had any bearing on the firms moving into CICs. Xianjin Huang, 'Agglomeration, Differentiation and Creative Milieus: A Socioeconomic Analysis of Location Behaviour of Creative Enterprises in Shanghai', *Urban Policy and Research* 36, no. 1 (2016): 79–96.

80. Y. Huang, *Capitalism with Chinese Characteristics* (Cambridge: Cambridge University Press, 2008); J. Wang, 'The Global Reach of a New Discourse: How Far Can "Creative Industries" Travel?', *International Journal of Cultural Studies* 7, no. 1(2004): 9–19.

81. C. -C. Lee, Z. He and Y. Huang, 'Party-Market Corporatism, Clientelism, and Media in Shanghai', *The Harvard International Journal of Press/Politics* 12, no. 3 (2007): 21–42.

82. Rong and O'Connor, *Cultural Industries in Shanghai*; See also BOP Consulting/Arts and Humanities Research Council (AHRC) (2019), *Creative Industries in China and the UK Scoping and Workshop Report*, https: //ahrc.ukri.org/documents/publications/bop-ahrc-report/. Accessed 14 December 2019.

83. Y. Rong and L. Chen, 'Fine Art and Antiques Sector', in Rong and O'Connor, *Cultural Industries in Shanghai*; BOP Consulting/AHRC, *Creative Industries*.

84. Cf. Rong and O'Connor, *Cultural Industries in Shanghai*, for accounts of the increasing scale and sophistication of parks, their integration with finance, with digital innovation, and with education clusters.

85. T. Miller, 'The New International Division of Cultural Labor Revisited', *ICONO14: Journal of Communication and Emergent Technologies* 14, no. 2 (2016): 97–121.

86. O'Connor and Gu, 'Creative Industry Clusters in Shanghai'; A. Kanngieser, 'Creative Labour in Shanghai: Questions on Politics, Composition and Ambivalence', *Subjectivity* 5 (2012): 54–74.

87. On WeWork, cf. M. Zeitlin, 'Then We Came to the End', *N+1 Online*, 2019, https: // nplusonemag.com/online-only/online-only/then-wecame-to-the-end/. Accessed 14 December 2019; on its use of algorithmic forms as part of gentrification: https: // failedarchitecture.com/the-extractive-growth-of-artificially-intelligent-real-estate/. Accessed 14 December 2019.

88. Wang and Tan, 'Social Factory as Prosaic State Space'.

89. The 'sharing economy' is here parlayed in socialist terms, with Jodie Dean's 'communicative capitalism' reframed as a mass mobilization of innovative entrepreneurs for a collectivist consumer society. See: J. Dean, *Democracy and Other Neoliberal Fantasies: Communicative Capitalism and Left Politics* (Durham, NC: Duke University Press, 2009).

90. A. Ong and L. Zhang, 'Introduction: Privatising China: Powers of the Self, Socialism from Afar', in *Privatising China: Powers of the Self*, ed. L. Zhang and A. Ong (Ithaca, NY: Cornell University Press, 2008), 1–19. Mao is quoted approving by one of Wang and Tan's respondents in the training programme, as being able to mobilize large numbers of people with his collective vision. On Maker Spaces, cf. X. Gu and P. Shea, 'Fabbing the Chinese-Maker Identity', in *The Critical Makers Reader: (un)Learning Technology*, ed. L. Bogers and L. Chiappini (Amsterdam: Institute of Network Cultures, 2019).

91. Cf. BOP Consulting/AHRC, *Creative Industries*, where this lack of talent is presented as an opportunity for UK education and training agencies.

92. Cf. X. Gu and J. O'Connor, 'Teaching "Tacit Knowledge" in Cultural and Creative Industries to International Students', *Arts and Humanities in Higher Education* 18, no. 2–3 (2019): 140–58.

93. See the work of Changwook Kim on South Korea and Japan. 'Labor and the Limits of Seduction in Korea's Creative Economy', *Television & New Media* 15, no. 6 (2014): 562–76; C. Kim, 'The Political Subjectivization of Korean Creative Workers: Working and Living as Urban Precariat in Creative City Seoul', *International Journal of Cultural Policy* 25, no. 6 (2017): 701–13; C. Kim, 'Creative Labor as Moral and Ethical Subjects and Its Limitation: Creative City Yokohama, Japan', *Inter-Asia Cultural Studies* 20, no. 1 (2019): 39–55. On China: Lin, 'Be Creative for the State'.

94. Cf. M. Valjakka and M. Wang, 'Engagement with the Urban: Visual Arts as a Form of Cultural Activism in Contemporary China', in *Visual Arts, Representations and Interventions in Contemporary China: Urbanized Interface*, ed. M. Valjakka and M. Wang (Amsterdam: Amsterdam University Press, 2018), 13–34.

95. On music, cf. N. Baronovitch, *China's New Voices: Popular Music, Ethnicity, Gender and Politics, 1978–1997* (Berkeley: University of California Press, 2003); J. de Kloet, *China with a Cut: Globalisation, Urban Youth and Popular Music* (Amsterdam: Amsterdam University Press, 2010); Jian Xiao, *Punk Culture in Contemporary China* (Singapore: Palgrave Macmillan, 2018); X. Gu, J. O'Connor and J. Ng, 'Worlding and New Music Cultures in Shanghai', *City, Culture & Society* (2019): DOI: 10.1016/j.ccs.2019.05.002.

96. In 2018, the authors conducted a series of interviews with over 20 music industry professionals from Beijing, Wuhan and Shanghai.

97. Many of these observations come from our Australian Research Council Project 'Working the Field'. Some early findings have been written up in the following: X. Gu and J. O'Connor, '(Un)Design, Commerce and Artistic Autonomy: Site-Specific Art in China', in G. Coombs, A. McNamara and G. Sade, *Undesign: Critical Practices at the Intersection of Art and Design* (London: Routledge, 2018); X. Gu and J. Webb, 'The Transformation of the Traditional "Artistic" Position within Tertiary Visual Arts Programs in China', in *Investigating the Visual as a Transformative Pedagogy in the Asia Region*, ed. I. MacArthur et al. (Sydney: Common Ground Publishing, 2018); X. Gu and J. O'Connor, 'Working the Field: Career Pathways Amongst Artists and Writers in Shanghai', in *Hope, Uncertainty and Creative Aspiration: Pathways into and through Contemporary Creative Work*, ed. S. Taylor and S. Luckman (Singapore: Palgrave Macmillan, 2020).

98. Shanghai Jiatong University's School of Cultural Industries Management, a national leader in the field, recently (December 2019) held a large conference on cultural management. There are now 121 University cultural management programmes across China.

99. Such an autonomy – 'banned in China' – carefully managed, can bring returns to Chinese artists working on the global scale, and again, carefully managed, these returns can be made to count back in China.

100. 'Unpopular' here refers to the explorative and the inventive, outside or before the systems of state and commercial ventures.

101. Cf. W. Davies, 'Let's Eat Badly', *London Review of Books* 41, no. 23 (2019): 19–22.

102. *Tie Xi Qu* (West of the Tracks), Dir. Wang Bing, 2003.

Epilogue

That moment, when it was possible to doubt that China's political system could deliver a 'creative economy', has now gone. Of course, a country with 1.1 billion people, with rising incomes, a growing service sector and a push for increased domestic consumption, was always going to have a huge cultural industries sector. The Chinese firewall was not – as Bill Clinton had it – some futile nailing of Jello to the wall but provided the basis for its own distinct digital platform infrastructure. No longer able to present China with a 'transform or lose out' dilemma, the country has been efficiently absorbed into the 'rise and rise' narrative of the creative industries. In this narrative the only politics that matter are those that might impede the development of this 'industrial sector' or restrict trade and transnational collaborative ventures. This is especially important for countries, such as the United Kingdom (especially post-Brexit) and the EU and some of its member states (Germany, France, The Netherlands particularly), who are concerned to keep access to Chinese markets and welcome Chinese investment in their own projects. It is less important to the United States, still the globally pre-eminent cultural industries force, now hyper-charged by its domination of FAANG. For the United States, China is not yet a threat in terms of content – everybody agrees that Chinese soft power is pretty underwhelming even in East Asia. The problem is that China locks the United States out of its markets, especially its digital platforms; moreover, China's digital communications technologies have begun to reach into the infrastructural heartlands of the West itself.

Whilst the idea of 'soft power' kept the focus on content, the US global domination of the cultural industries relied on controlling the infrastructure – business, technological and legal. The United States controlled the cultural industries through the formation of what Timothy Mitchell called (in respect of the oil industry) a 'technological zone' – 'a set of coordinated but widely dispersed regulations, calculative arrangements, infrastructures and technical procedures that render certain objects or flows governable'.[1] To have only restricted access to the world's largest market is one thing; to feel your hold over a key global technological infrastructure weakened is something else entirely. So whilst the

Panglossian accountants of the creative industries are welcoming a new member of their global growth club, the United States have now called time-up.[2] Whatever the disquiet about the specifics of Donald Trump's trade war, it rests on a deeper bipartisan sense that China has been cheating and it no longer can be given a free ride. China has stepped into the role of opposing empire previously played by Germany and Japan in the 1930s, followed by the USSR; of economic rival to be tamed – Japan before the Plaza Accords, the European Union (and Germany) in the 1990s; and of antagonistic civilizations broken – the Middle East after the 1978 oil crisis. As a Communist geo-power, a dynamic economic rival and a radically distinct civilizational entity, China has the all the requisite elements of a super-villain.

In 1792, as his Embassy made its way to China, the teenage son of Earl Macartney's right-hand man, Sir George Staunton, began learning Chinese. The diligent Thomas Staunton acted as informal interpreter, the beginning of a long career studying China and its culture, co-founding the Royal Asiatic Society in 1923. In the famous debate on the Opium War in the House of Commons in 1840, Sir Thomas Staunton argued powerfully in favour of the war, claiming that allowing the Chinese insult of burning the Canton warehouse to stand would irreparably damage the prestige of the British Empire.[3] He can be seen as the first in a long line of Western scholar-sojourners who got to know a country's language, culture and politics close-up and first-hand, only to leave bearing a burning hatred of China and all it seems to stand for.[4] China may not be to everyone's taste; the country's long-standing culture is rarely one in which foreigners can feel completely at home perhaps, and one's *amour-propre* can suffer bruises. However, at times of tension they will be called upon to speak words of alarm. The level of anti-China rhetoric, in the Anglosphere especially, is at its highest since the aftermath of 1989. Back then though, China's economic power, and the West's entanglement with it, was nowhere near what it is today. The dominant rhetorical trope is 'waking up' – to the complacency of the political and business elites, to the dire consequence of slow drift into accommodating tyrants, and to the sleeper cells and silent invasions of the Chinese diaspora.[5] During the golden age of neo-liberalism, after the end of history, capitalism was the only route to growth, to progress, to modernity. China's rapid development could only result in its gradual entry into the global modern under the benign dominance of the United States. We are now urged to 'wake up' to the nativity of this belief; we have been duped, taken for a ride and now we must look beyond our wallets to our fundamental values, which are at stake again. What this does – what it is meant to do – is lock us down into 'our' values which are fundamentally different from 'theirs'. This is not – we are assured – an attack on the Chinese people themselves, just their government. On the seventieth anniversary of the Communist Revolution, *The Guardian* – hardly a Cold War warrior – editorialized about a regime held together by repression, propaganda and an economic prosperity bought at 'horrific cost'. The only hope, it seemed, was a future that did not include the Communist Party.[6]

The West has learnt to talk blithely about 'regime change'. We are not against the people, just the government, they say, as if removing the Communist Party and its system would be like removing Donald Trump, or an electoral victory for a new political party. The West says 'change government' but it means a radical restructuration of the social, cultural and political fabric in the name of 'democracy', made flesh through the divine power of the market. Outside the Westphalian heartlands, it was ever thus. Under 'fundamental values', we have a whole set of economic, administrative, political and technological arrangements which are not to be questioned or touched, only exported, at gun point if necessary. 'Waking up to China' is to accept the leadership of those most willing to stand up firmly against it, and whose articulation of Western values we are to take as self-evident truths. We have been here before. Quite a few times.

In this book we have used the idea of the creative industries to sketch out two distinct narrative arcs of modernity. These two constantly intertwine and separate, in rhyme and dissonance, somehow, like polyphony, headed to what seems like the same modern ends: Progress and Growth. These two animating ideals, at least as they have been understood since the middle of the eighteenth century, are now coming to an end. Neither the West nor China as yet has any idea how to cope with this ending, or what it might mean for them. The most dysfunctional version is that of Western capitalism, its imperial dreams now focused on a new, extractive form of globalization without any of the ideals of multipolarity, diversity, multiplicity or reciprocity with which the golden age of post-history began. We have moved, as Bruno Latour put it, from Globalization Plus to Globalization Minus.[7] China, still believing in Progress and Growth, suspects that modernity can somehow overcome the challenges it has created for itself. Li Cixin has a novella that became a film – *The Wandering Earth* – in which an immanent existential threat to planet Earth from the Sun was solved by using huge propulsion engines to move the Earth out of orbit, heading for another galaxy.[8] Stopping the Earth's rotation produced tsunamis and earthquakes which destroyed half the population of the planet; many of those that remained could not be accommodated in the huge underground living spaces. The Red Engineers had saved the planet and a future humanity (if not all of the living) by the massive exercise of technology, unrestrained by any other considerations than the physical survival of the human biomass. The current government, in less drastic fashion, still looks to the growth of infrastructure, rapid urbanization, massive investment in R&D and the expansion of the economic motor as route to a modernity which is secured by, and in turn will further secure, the leading role of the Communist Party.

The relentless absorption of the sphere of culture into the system of capital accumulation accelerated in the 1990s. At the turn of the millennium, the system of symbolic exchange between producers and audiences became subject to algorithmic governance, resulting in a hyper-accelerated accumulation that could only be facilitated through extensive personal data-extraction, with surveillance its dark matter by-product. What this has done to the idea of the social and its symbolic order, the various public spheres, ideal-speech situations and the possibility of rational dialogue has become a general cause for concern.[9] This dissolution continues apace in both the West and China, but, as we tried to suggest, in different ways. The Big Other is still holding on in China, shouting evermore loudly, whilst in the West there is a deafening cacophony.

The problem with digital platforms and the algorithmic governance they facilitate is more than one of increased and evermore intrusive levels of value extraction. For those concerned about the 'social factory', there is a sense of an ongoing unequal extraction from the lifeworld into capitalist accumulation. As Anna Lowenhaupt Tsing argued, capitalism has always been able to extract value from pre-, non-, or post-capitalist social formations.[10] However, the issue is not just that of unequal extraction and the distortion or disruption of the producers' lifeworlds this might entail. What is surely clear now is that the progressive reduction of the culture system to the logic of the commodity is deeply destructive of the social system itself. It progressively blocks the ability of that cultural activity to become knowledge. This is what Bernard Stiegler calls 'symbolic misery', and he is concerned with our collective inability to articulate our deeper need for meaning, as noetic beings.[11] The progressive dissolution of the culture system under commodification and algorithmic governance results in what he called the 'negation of knowledge itself'.[12] A form of Nihilism.

How we are to overcome the present is the urgent task. No longer can we follow Chen Duxiu's arrow into the future, the linear path of Progress. If we are to avoid the 'dark enlightenment', as articulated by reactionary 'alt-right' philosopher Nick Land in that same city of Shanghai a century later, then the rejection of Progress needs to come not with a total rejection, but a radical re-evaluation of the Enlightenment.[13] We will need to reach again for articulations of an expanded, open sense of Reason before its reduction to a mechanistic and instrumental shell.[14] The articulation of a specific modern task for art at the end of the eighteenth century in Europe, its ability to register and to 'digest' the profound shock of industrial and democratic modernity – this was art's *Weltbezug* or 'world-relevance'.[15] The 'creative industries' not only has nothing to say in the face of this pressing historical task but it has become an active obstacle to our ability to pose the question.

A different modernity will not be articulated from within Europe alone. Prasenjit Duara looked to the Asian religions and cultures arising from the Axial Age as preserving forms of ethical reasoning which will be crucial to articulating a global sense of humanity required if we are to face climate change.[16] China's 'Confucian' heritage, we have argued, structures their society and culture in ways that are still significant, and has resources for us today. Our discussion of non-Western knowledges in early Chinese modernity suggested ways in which these non-Western knowledges attempted to negotiate a different modernity for China. These early modern Chinese negotiations have been revisited in the light of postcolonial, radical feminist and ecological thought and practice, and may still provide useful guidance for a way out of the present. More controversially perhaps, we also think that the resources of Chinese socialism, its revolutionary century, are still in play as a source of transformation. However, if change is to come in China it needs to come on its own terms, a valid member of a global community, not a country that must submit to the existing rules – increasingly centred on *fiat Americana* – or face the consequences.

Real change in China will not come from places where popular unrest rubs up against geopolitical tectonics – in Tibet or Xinjiang, Hong Kong or Taiwan. Conflicts here, at the edges of empire, are quickly taken up into the great game of rival imperialisms. Kipling's original Great Game was one of life itself, and perhaps it is challenges such as the Coronavirus epidemic which speak to this.[17] It is not so much – as in the Western media – that this outbreak 'exposes' the lack of transparency in China, or its heavy-handedness, or (this with delightful *schadenfreude*) its 'incompetence'. Perhaps it is more that in the silent cities, as the endless grind of the economic machine pauses, some space for consideration of the real foundations of 'good living', might enter in. The survival of the 'biomass' is of course a priority and we should recognize the capacity of the Chinese state, once it gets moving, along with the strong sense of social responsibility amongst the citizens who have undergone quarantine. But the silent cities, the rough treatment of many, the inability of citizens to properly communicate with the party leadership – this all brings into focus again the party's bargain to keep Chinese people safe and prosperous in return for their political quiescence. What exactly is this 'good life'?

The particular forms of meaning, knowledge and affective engagement made possible through art and culture will have to be part of such radical change. This surely is the continuing weight of the May Fourth movement on the contemporary Communist Party and the citizens it serves. The moment when an upsurge of popular culture, made possible by the arrival of the market in the space left vacant by marginalized intellectuals (*zhishifenzi*), might have helped expand the field of democracy in China has passed. To reopen a space of responsible autonomy, as a valued social space (and habitus) within everyday Chinese society will be a step forward. This would entail stepping back from the dominating rationale of economic growth as the unique source of prosperity and security for the Chinese people. It would require an acknowledgement of another space in which questions of the good life might be posed and explored, beyond survival, beyond assuaging a century of humiliation, beyond *ganchao* ('catch-up and surpass').

There is no reason why this could not be done by a historic Communist Party, but it would need to reconnect the reality of their practice with the ideological structures through which they frame and justify their actions. The Marxism which it espouses is one that was already moribund in 1989. The CCP has sought its acceptance from the winners of the Cold War – 'look at us, we too are thoroughly modern now!' It has ignored those who sought to renew its ideologies after the collapse of the USSR, looking instead to the Red Engineers in tandem with its market economists, bearing their technologies of Progress and Growth. The CCP could open itself up to new possibilities for radical change that are daily more urgent, connecting with others across the terrestrial community also seeking such change. If it were able to do that, then it really could claim the mantle of Red Creative.

NOTES

1. T. Mitchell, *Carbon Democracy: Political Power in The Age of Oil* (London: Verso, 2011), 40.

2. On the global growth club, cf. S. Cunningham and A. Swift, 'Creative Industries around the World', in *A Research Agenda for the Creative Industries*, ed. S. Cunningham and T. Flew (Cheltenham: Edward Elgar Publishers, 2019), 146–63.

3. H. G. Gelber, *Opium, Soldiers and Evangelicals: Britain's 1840–42 War with China, and Its Aftermath* (New York: Palgrave Macmillan, 2004), 95; S. Platt, *Imperial Twilight: The Opium War and the End of China's Last Golden Age* (London: Atlantic Books, 2018), 382–89.

4. For example, Bill Bishop at the online newsletter *Sinocism* left Beijing in 2015, after various roles in finance and media, and has since become a very influential critic of the Chinese regime, which is given not a millimetre of slack. Kai Strittmatter's long sojourn as a German foreign correspondent in Beijing ended with his 2019 book titled *We Have Been Harmonised: Life in China's Surveillance State*, dripping in sarcasm, vitriol and cynicism from page one.

5. Former Australian Green candidate Clive Hamilton's 2018 book *Silent Invasion* (Hardy Grant Books) is a particularly egregious example of the new cold war paranoia.

6. *The Guardian*, 'The Guardian View on the People's Republic of China at 70: Whose History?', 30 September 2019, https://www.theguardian.com/commentisfree/2019/sep/30/the-guardian-view-on-the-peoples-republic-of-china-at-70-whose-history. Accessed 26 January 2020.

7. B. Latour, *Down to Earth: Politics in the new Climatic Regime* (Cambridge: Polity, 2018).

8. Liu Cixin, *The Wandering Earth*, trans. H. Nahm, Kindle Edition (Beijing: Beijing Qingse Media Co., 2012). Made into a film by Frant Gwo (Dir.) (2019).

9. Cf. William Davies's review of J. E. H. Smith, *Irrationality: A History of the Dark Side of Reason* (Princeton: Princeton University Press, 2019), in 'Let's Eat Badly', *London Review of Books* 41, no. 23 (2019): 19–22.

10. A. Lowenhaupt Tsing, *The Mushroom at the End of the World: On the Possibility of Life in Capitalist Ruins* (Princeton: Princeton University Press, 2015).

11. B. Stiegler, *Symbolic Misery: Volume 1: The Hyperindustrial Epoch* (Cambridge: Polity, 2014).

12. B. Stiegler, *Automatic Society. Volume 1: The Future of Work* (Cambridge: Polity, 2016), 15.

13. https://en.wikipedia.org/wiki/Dark_Enlightenment. Accessed 26 January 2020. Nick Land is based in Shanghai. A version of 'dark enlightenment' makes an appearance as 'Shanghai Gothic' in the chapter of that same name in A. Greenspan, *Shanghai Future: Modernity Remade* (London: Hurst and Co., 2014).

14. The notion of a radical enlightenment can be found in Arran Gare, 'The Arts and Radical Enlightenment. Gaining Liberty to Save the Planet', *The Structurist* 47/48 (2007/08): 20–27. We look forward to its further elaboration in the work of his student, N. Trimarchi, *The Meaning Value of Art: Art as a Science of Meaning and Valuing* (Ph.D. thesis, Swinburne University, forthcoming).

15. Also translated as 'art's appropriate relation to the world'. S. Olma, *Autonomy and Weltbezug: Towards an Aesthetic of Performative Defiance* (Breda: Avans Hogeschool, 2016).

16. P. Duara, *The Crisis of Global Modernity: Asian Traditions and a Sustainable Future* (Cambridge: Cambridge University Press, 2015).

17. Tim Michell (*Carbon Democracy*, 52) makes this point.

Index

301